THE INDICTED SOUTH

NEW DIRECTIONS IN SOUTHERN STUDIES

Editor

Charles Reagan Wilson

Editorial Advisory Board

Robert Brinkmeyer   Thomas Holt   Anne Goodwyn Jones
Alfred J. Lopez   Charles Marsh   Ted Ownby   Tom Rankin
Jon Michael Spencer   Allen Tullos   Patricia Yaeger

THE INDICTED SOUTH

PUBLIC CRITICISM, SOUTHERN INFERIORITY,

AND THE POLITICS OF WHITENESS

ANGIE MAXWELL

THE UNIVERSITY OF NORTH CAROLINA PRESS

Chapel Hill

The paper in this book meets the guidelines for permanence and durability of the
Committee on Production Guidelines for Book Longevity of the Council on Library
Resources. The University of North Carolina Press has been a member of the
Green Press Initiative since 2003.

Library of Congress Cataloging-in-Publication Data
Maxwell, Angie, 1978–
The indicted South : public criticism, southern inferiority, and the politics of
whiteness / Angie Maxwell. — First edition.
pages cm. — (New directions in southern studies)
Includes bibliographical references and index.
ISBN 978-1-4696-1164-8 (paperback : alkaline paper) — ISBN 978-1-4696-1165-5 (e-book)
1. Southern States—Civilization. 2. Southern States—Politics and government. 3. Political
culture—Southern States—History. 4. Southern States—Race relations—History.
5. Southern States—Social conditions. 6. Public opinion—United States—History.
7. National characteristics, American. 8. Regionalism—Southern States—History.
9. Group identity—Southern States—History. 10. Inferiority complex. I. Title.
F209.M29 2014
975—dc23
2013041235

For Sidney Johnson Burris and Elizabeth Maxwell Burris,
always and in all ways

CONTENTS

ACKNOWLEDGMENTS

My list of debts both large and small is as long as one would expect. It takes a village not only to raise a child but also to write a book. And to do both simultaneously requires a troop of mentors, friends, and family. I am lucky that many of you are all three. I am thankful to Steve Hoelscher for his patience, encouragement, and friendship; all are cherished commodities in an often lonely process. I am grateful as well to Julia Mickenberg for pushing me to think big and to write boldly, to Bob Abzug for helping me to connect the dots, to David Oshinsky for advancing my narrative voice, to Charles Reagan Wilson for lending his expertise and his kindness, and to the late Elspeth Rostow for always being the devil's advocate. My colleagues in Old Main—Pearl Ford Dowe, Rafael Jimeno, Ashlie Hilbun, and Margaret Reid—let me grumble as much as I want. My debt to Todd Shields is still more than I can ever hope to pay. He is a true friend in good times and bad. And then there is the wise and generous counsel of those who made time for me when they had little to spare: Joel Dinerstein, Jessica Grogan, Elizabeth Engelhardt, Janet Davis, Stephanie Schulte, Larry Malley, Bob Brinkmeyer, Fred Hobson, Jim Cobb, Wayne Parent, Senator David Pryor and Barbara Pryor, Jeannie Whayne, Roderick Hart, Geshe Thupten Dorjee, and the late Willard Gatewood.

On a practical note, I gratefully acknowledge the support for the publication of this book provided by the J. William Fulbright College of Arts and Sciences at the University of Arkansas.

Over the past several years of writing and editing and rewriting, I have also been blessed by financial support from Jim and Nancy Blair, the Harry S. Truman Foundation, the P. E. O. Women in Education Foundation, and the Homer Lindsey Bruce Fellowship from the University of Texas, Austin. To the archivists at the Tennessee State Library and Archives, the Jean and Alexander Heard Library at Vanderbilt, the Virginia Historical Collection, the Mary and David Harrison Institute for American History, Literature, and Culture at the University of Virginia, the Library of Virginia, and William Jennings Bryan College, thank you for sharing the keys to the kingdom, so to speak. And to the best in the business, David Perry, Caitlin Bell-Butterfield, and Mark Simpson-Vos at the University of North Carolina Press, my sincere gratitude for your patience over the long haul.

{ ix }

On a personal note, I am grateful to my family—Chris and Scotty Maxwell, Catherine and Malloy McDaniel, Marcie Maxwell, and Helen Burris—for championing education and for never asking, "When will this be published?" And to Maxwell, Murphy, Vidrine, Sam, and Elizabeth for injecting the past several years with laughter and delight. Courtney Barton, Jennifer Kestner, Lindsey Garman, Jennifer Condra, Sharon Vraciu, Brittney Henderson, and Mendy Felton always show up, usually with wine, and the Farnets and the Gundermans on Centerwood Road are neighbors in the true sense of the word. During the heavy lifting, I relied on Jessie Swigger for her cheerful smile, unassuming intelligence, fierce loyalty, and limitless empathy. She proves that misery and happiness love company, and that both are best discussed over a breakfast taco.

Finally, I have crossed the country in pursuit of this idea. And in South Louisiana, Austin, Charlottesville, Richmond, Washington, D.C., Durham, Atlanta, Memphis, Nashville, and Dayton, one person rode shotgun. Whether he was trying in vain to watch the Tour de France on his phone in special collections or making hundreds of copies on a quarter machine, my husband, Sidney Burris, never complained. He cranks it up and cruises through it all. There is a heavy toll that comes with writing about rage, prejudice, and fear. Sidney taught me that we are all responsible for paying it. Now here, in the Ozark Mountains, my dedication to him and to our sweet e.m.b. extends far beyond these pages.

THE INDICTED SOUTH

INTRODUCTION

THE ANATOMY OF

INFERIORITY

A constant assault from without, an indictment of every aspect of their civilization, was the burden under which Southerners lived for more than a century
(as if defeat and poverty and failure were not enough), and it is little wonder
that such a legacy created men and women who sought to justify their past and
their tradition.
—Fred Hobson, *Tell about the South: The Southern Rage to Explain*

Despite the crucial roles of prominent southerners in securing America's independence and drafting its fundamental documents of state, with the infant
nation's literary and publishing core already fixed firmly in the Northeast, it
was hardly surprising that, even in its embryonic phase, the dominant vision
of American character emphasized northern sensibilities and perceptions. One
of these perceptions, and a difficult one to dismiss, was that the major impedi-
ment to constructing an inspiring and credible identity for a nation supposedly
committed to the principles of liberty, equality, and democracy was a southern
economy, society, and culture shaped and sustained by human bondage. As the
leaders of the young republic struggled to gain the acceptance and respect of
other nations, northern architects of national identity soon realized that their
vision of America would not only be much simpler to construct but also much
easier to look at and far more emphatic and unequivocal in meaning if they simply focused on what they saw, or sometimes chose to see, in the states above
the recently drawn Mason-Dixon line.
—James C. Cobb, *Away Down South: A History of Southern Identity*

Why do they live there. Why do they live at all.
—Shreve McCanon to Quentin Compson in William Faulkner, *Absalom,
Absalom!*

In February 1950, Eleanor Roosevelt visited the University of North Carolina
at Chapel Hill and made several speeches on campus. When she returned to
New York, her trip served as the subject of her syndicated column, "My Day,"
which she tirelessly produced six days a week from 1935 to 1962, pausing only to
mourn the death of her husband. In the piece devoted to her Carolina sojourn,
Roosevelt discussed her southern roots. Her grandmother had been a member
of the Bulloch family from Georgia, and although she described her southern

relatives with great affection, she also condemned the region for its poverty and provinciality. "One can enjoy oneself superficially," she proclaimed, "but one must shut one's eyes."[1] The criticism stung and unleashed a defensive counter-attack from W. E. B. Debnam, a radio broadcaster in Raleigh, North Carolina, which would spread across the South.

Sponsored by Smith-Douglas Fertilizer, Debnam read the farm news at noon each day.[2] However, on February 8 and 9, 1950, an alarmed Debnam, in a single outburst, invoked two fundamental arguments of white superiority and north-ern hypocrisy that appeared whenever southerners felt compelled to defend themselves, as Debnam now did. Blaming the North for the problems of the South was a popular and deeply familiar strategy at the time, and in Debnam's hands the technique assumed a barbed and personal tone as he replied to Mrs. Roosevelt by name: "There was no Marshall plan for the South 85 years ago, Mrs. Roosevelt. Instead of bearing gifts, our conquerors came in hordes de-manding tribute."[3] Debnam did not deny the hardships and shortages in North Carolina, and throughout the South for that matter, but he insisted that destitu-tion be recognized as a national problem and not simply a regional one: "There are signs of poverty and unhappiness just about everywhere. Mrs. Roosevelt doesn't have to come South to find these things. Almost from the window of her hotel apartment in New York she can look out and see what is possibly the greatest cesspool of heaped-up-and-pressed-down-and-running-over poverty and crime and spiritual and moral and economic unhappiness on the face of the earth."[4] Debnam was pointedly referring to the African American commu-nity in Harlem, deploying a dramatic piece of rhetoric that would have found a receptive audience among many white southerners who had tuned in to hear the latest corn prices. In choosing Harlem as the subject for his aggressive coun-terattack, Debnam was preaching to the choir, of course, and his audience re-sponded approvingly, convincing Debnam to publish in paperback his two-day rant. The sixty-page book, which he titled *Weep No More, My Lady: A Southerner Answers Mrs. Roosevelt's Report on the "Poor and Unhappy South,"* sold close to 140,000 copies between May and December of that year.[5]

Emotions ran high on both sides of the exchange, but one thing remains abundantly clear: nearly a century after the Civil War, the public denunciation of the South triggered a defensive response that transformed a local newscaster into a brash polemicist, compelled to vindicate himself by absolving the region. Debnam's popular manifesto is a tangible example of a ceaseless and signifi-cant pattern that has long occupied white southerners and has been a forma-tive influence on the culture. Fred Hobson, reflecting on W. J. Cash's *The Mind of the South* (1941), William Alexander Percy's *Lanterns on the Levee: Recollections of a Planter's Son* (1941), and Lillian Smith's *Killers of the Dream* (1949), claims that white southerners like Debnam were obsessed with explaining the region to the nation at large. Hobson insisted that this "southern rage to explain stems from a regional inferiority complex, a recognition of failure," and that alongside this anxiety, or perhaps in response to it, there "exists as well a perverse and defiant pride in the Southerner, a sense of distinction, or superiority stemming from this inferior status."[6] I argue that Debnam's indignant response to Roosevelt clearly reads as an expression of defiant pride manifested by a regional inferiority complex triggered by the critical spotlight. And in this book, I point to the sources, power, and repercussions of this heritage of inferiority, which, though evident and relevant, remain unexamined.

The southern lexicon has long been rich in phrases that articulate expressions or manifestations of this behavior. For example, in assessing the emotional and social attitudes that characterized the civil rights movement, historian Fletcher Green proclaimed that "the overwhelming and crushing defeat of the Confederacy in 1865 left the people of the Southern states with a defeatist attitude, an inferiority complex, a tender skin to criticism, and a fear of ridicule. . . . This touchy attitude lingers on after ninety years."[7] And, though indirectly, journalist W. J. Cash's "Savage Ideal," historian Sheldon Hackney's "siege-mentality," and Dr. Martin Luther King Jr.'s "Drum Major Instinct" all describe this same regional spirit, and all attest to its stubborn persistence. Psychologist Alfred Adler coined the term "inferiority complex," and though it is not feasible to apply Adler's individual theories to explain a cultural pattern, his research is useful primarily in that it confirms the significance of a source of disapproval in initiating this complex, and it describes various compensations to this recognition of inferiority. I contend that from a broader perspective, public criticism becomes the cradle of southern consciousness. And such criticism proved particularly debilitating in the South, where preservation of white cultural supremacy and conservative political domination required strict allegiance to regional mythologies such as the Confederate Lost Cause and the post-Reconstruction New South. These self-promotional tales were, after all, inconsistent and impossible to maintain, and they left many white southerners vulnerable to the very scorn these accounts invited.

In fact, journalist Gerald Johnson was not alone when he insisted that by the 1920s it was difficult "to find on the newsstands a serious magazine without an article on some phase of life below the Potomac."[8] Seen by scholars as a turning point in the history of the South and its relationship to the nation, the era of the "Benighted South"—a phrase first used by historian George Tindall[9]— serves as the starting point for this book, for it is this era in which mass media, specifically mass-circulation periodicals and national radio stations and networks, expanded the reach and thus the impact of public criticism. This expansion, I argue, blurred the lines between individual, regional, and national identities. Debnam's individual and personal reaction, for example, to Roosevelt's individual and personal statements about the South entered the public record when it was published, and his ideas, when widely distributed in book form, crystallized a generation's response to northern criticism. Similarly, Roosevelt's own column assumed a collective significance, not least because her unique position as First Lady imbued her statements with a sense of nationalism; she thus embodied for Debnam a northern, elite, Americanism that seemed to be attacking the South yet again. Originally cast as a debate between two individuals, the exchange developed into a regionalist battle waged against what is perceived as an exclusive national image.

Moreover, I maintain that in this climate of battle, the details of the public ridicule have significant ramifications for southern white identity. What began as a racial construct established against a black "other" expanded, as a result of public criticism, into a comprehensive cosmology defined in opposition to a mounting pantheon of enemies old and new. In Debnam's manifesto, for example, poverty and need become fodder for public criticism and thus are defensively incorporated under the white southern label. And for this reason, limiting any assessment of southern whiteness solely to racial issues—as seemingly logical as that may be—belies its real complexity. I assert that over time the structure of southern whiteness became, in effect, an intricate web of inseparable strands, a web that extended beyond a commitment to racial segregation and oppression to rigid stances on religion, education, the role of government, the view of art, an opposition to science, and any other topic that comes under attack. It envelops a community and covers everything. When viewed in this way, what arises is a new sense of just how intimately and productively southern white identity has allied itself with the unifying sense of inferiority.

The power of this awareness of perceived inferiority is visible. Debnam's transformation is not unlike countless examples of equally dramatic collective shifts in southern behavior. In some of the well-known southern narratives, the role of public criticism and the ramifications of such acute attention on the community to which it was directed have all but been ignored. In *The Indicted South*, I reexamine distinct groups of white southerners that were impacted notably—even radically—by the media spotlight via the lens of inferiority. And since the public scrutiny of white southerners was not limited to any particular class or community, these cases span the spectrum of time and place and status. Part I explores the impact of the 1925 Scopes Evolution Trial—arguably the greatest site of national and international media frenzy in American legal history—on the home community of Dayton, Tennessee, a moderately religious, southern town that was converted seemingly overnight into a fundamentalist haven where much of the population ardently continues, even now, to promote creationism. The previously unexamined founding papers of William Jennings Bryan College, a fundamentalist university established in Dayton within three years of the Scopes verdict and named for the three-time presidential candidate and anti-evolution crusader, reveal a community of white southerners in retreat from a public firestorm that rejected them as barbaric and uncivilized.

Part II considers the transformation of an intimate circle of southern writers—including Robert Penn Warren, Allen Tate, Donald Davidson, and John Crowe Ransom—originally known as the Fugitives, from modernist poets to Agrarian defenders of the southern way of life to creators and advocates of a new American school of literary criticism, New Criticism, which ultimately distanced literature from historical context and regional distinctiveness. Written partially in response to the barrage of criticism that accompanied the Scopes Trial, *I'll Take My Stand* (1930), the isolationist southern manifesto of these Fugitives-turned-Agrarians, generated additional public attacks as well as considerable correspondence within this creative community. Eventually, this aesthetic and intellectual metamorphosis, driven by a striving for recognition, resulted in a new American canon that would dominate literary studies for a half century. These southern writers, frustrated by the ridicule they received in their formative years as both artists and social critics, would succeed in establishing a canon that reflected their values and against which the culture wars would be waged.

Finally, Part III examines the initial impetus behind the Virginia campaign for Massive Resistance and Interposition organized in response to *Brown v. Board of Education*. Deemed a moderate voice in southern race relations, Virginia's Gray Commission was expected to offer a reasonable plan for school desegregation that would serve as an example to other southern states. However, the bombardment of public condemnation from the National Association for the Advancement of Colored People (NAACP) and the U.S. State Department (both of which sought United Nations intervention into southern racial practices),[10] to the United Nations Declaration of Human Rights, to nightly national newscasts, all fueled southern resistance, resulting in a complete rebellion against moderation and the eventual closing of public schools in some Virginia counties for up to five years. Attempting to tap into this sense of inferiority, journalist James J. Kilpatrick reminded white southerners of their political ancestry, resurrecting the writings of the founding fathers and resuscitating the Doctrine of Interposition, a legal contention that state decisions were, in some cases, allowed to supersede federal actions. Kilpatrick actively transformed the segregation debate into a question of constitutionality, adding a strand of patriotism to the widening web of southern whiteness.

Though these three well-known narratives from the southern past—which are only a mere sample—may seem disjointed at first glance, they expose a vicious cycle. In each case, the bombardment of public criticism activated a transformative element of cultural anxiety that was either dormant or unexpressed. The political, social, or economic climate was such that the community that perceived itself to be under attack sensed an impending loss of stature or way of life that resulted in a collective about-face, often characterized by retreat or denial. Whether that community included small-town fundamentalists, literary critics and creative writers, or state politicians and journalists, each in its own way demonstrates how public criticism and a common experience of inferiority has contributed to white southern conservatism and homogeneity, which has survived and prospered with dogged perseverance.

THE ROOTS OF INFERIORITY

Perhaps one of the first references to this southern heritage of inferiority appears in sociologist Howard Odum's 1936 book, *Southern Regions of the United States*, in which he offers a sweeping description of what he saw as a homogeneous white southern identity, even pointing to its source:

> There is a like-mindedness of the region in the politics of the "Solid South," in the protestant religion, in matters of racial culture and conflict, and in state and sectional patriotism, much of it tending to take the form of loyalties to the past and to outmoded patterns rather than faith in the future and confidence in achievement. There is therefore an apparent dominance of a general inferiority complex and defense mechanism alongside widely prevailing inner and outer conflict forces of race and manners, of tolerance and conservatism, and of pride and work, which constrains and constricts the whole person. This conflict and constraining from within has been greatly accentuated from without by attitudes, criticisms, and actions of other regions.[11]

Despite Odum's highlighting of its importance, the inferiority complex, as both a phrase and a concept, has become so commonplace that it is necessary to examine its initial formulation in the work of Alfred Adler and assess its usefulness in a more general discussion of southern culture and identity. Born in 1870 in Vienna, Austria, Adler began his career as a medical doctor, though he soon ventured into psychology through his work on organ inferiority. Adler insisted that physical shortcomings had a psychological effect, and in 1907 he published his *Theory of Organ Inferiority*, arguing that "organic defects frequently give rise to heightened feelings of inferiority."[12] In my own expanded sense of the idea, physical culture to a certain degree retains its prominence. A sense of physical change being made to the white southern way of life, whether real, as in the case of integration, or imagined, is often influential. Regardless, Adler's discussions were not limited to physical defects. Adler's biographer, Hertha Orgler, claimed that Adler "opened up new ways of regarding the body-mind problem."[13] For example, Adler maintained that, for some individuals, constant ridicule, neglect, or spoiling could heighten the sense of inferiority—a tendency that, in effect, if aggravated, becomes a complex. While much of the work of the human personality involves conquering feelings of worthlessness and inferiority, Adler felt that some individuals who are subject to extreme ridicule or neglect, or even perceive themselves as subject to such criticism, would not have the stores of psychic energy necessary to contain these damaging and very human feelings of inferiority; hence the complex arises. Moreover, Adler provided for variations among individuals when confronting an inferiority complex. The wide range of compensatory responses includes the drive for superiority, the striving for recognition, and the rejection of society. This pattern of behavior, when considered more generally, is instructive in understanding the evolution of white southern identity.

Despite founding the School of Individual Psychology, Adler, himself, was very much concerned with the relationship between the individual and his or her larger society. Dr. O. H. Woodcock summarized Adler's position: "Modern man is a social animal and can only function usefully as one of a group; he cannot logically be studied apart from his environment or group, hence his [Adler's] teaching may well also be called a Social Psychology."[14] Moreover, Adler himself was concerned with the social dimensions of his ideas; his emphasis on what he called "community feeling" (*Gemeinschaftsgefühl*) represented one of his central disagreements with Freud, from whom he decisively split in 1911. Toward the end of his career, in fact, Adler became a social reformer.[15] Unlike Freud, who maintained that "man is basically narcissistic and driven by the pleasure principle," Adler focused on group dynamics and the influence of culture.[16]

Again, although Adler's individual theories cannot easily be applied to a larger collective, his research provides an important context to the role of inferiority in shaping southern culture. According to historian Loren Grey, Adler "felt that true equality could only be achieved by understanding one's mistaken social perceptions and correcting them."[17] These mistaken perceptions can result from several social factors—three of which Adler often singled out for attention. Just as a child can develop an inferiority complex from factors such as ridicule, neglect, and spoiling, so too can elements of one's environment—education, religion, and poverty—elicit such a response. According to Adler, "Education, finally, is the most important factor in the origin of marked feelings of inferiority. . . . If education does not do its job, it can produce the gravest failures even under the most favorable outward circumstances."[18] Adler added that religion—particularly, authoritarian religion—could prove dangerous as well. Religious beliefs, when imposed on children, could produce derivative feelings of worth and power that mask true feelings of inferiority. And, of course, poverty, like certain aspects of physical inferiority, is often visibly apparent, and so its debilitating legacy in the formation of personality is inescapable. Southerners have long lagged behind the rest of the country in terms of both education and income levels,[19] while maintaining statistically a comparatively high number of churchgoers.[20] Thus, these concerns—education, religion, and poverty—have become staples in southern studies, and their presence as key environmental factors in Adler's work makes a common understanding of his ideas valuable to any interpretation of the region.

Widely read and often quoted, even after his death in 1937, Adler inspired not only students of psychology but also sociologists concerned with the power of social movements. It is not surprising, then, to find his work influencing such key social leaders as Dr. Martin Luther King Jr. King used Adler's theories, for example, as the basis for his famous 1968 sermon, "The Drum Major Instinct," delivered at Ebenezer Baptist Church in Atlanta, Georgia. Beginning with the tenth chapter of the Gospel of Mark, King repeated the story of John and James as they ask Jesus to sit at their side when he rules the kingdom of Israel. The desire for attention exhibited by James and John should not be condemned, argued King, for that desire lies in the hearts of all people. "We all want to be important, to surpass others, to achieve distinction, to lead the parade," King asserted. He further explained that "Alfred Adler, the great psychoanalyst contends that this is the dominant impulse. Sigmund Freud used to contend that sex was the dominant impulse, and Adler came with a new argument saying that this quest for recognition, this desire for attention, this desire for distinction is the basic impulse, the basic drive of human life, this drum major instinct."[21] Though King recognized that this "Drum Major Instinct" exists in all human beings, he also insisted that this instinct could be distorted, and when this occurs violence and racial prejudice often arise in the wake of its distortion. "Do you know that a lot of the race problem grows out of the drum major instinct?"

King asked his congregation. King felt that Adler's theories, of both the inferiority complex and its corollary, the compensating drive for superiority, had a clear application to social development in the South.

Similarly, using Adler's work has informed research on prejudice and bias as well as myth and memory, all ground explored by scholars of the South. Lewis Way, for example, explains that "the prejudiced person does not pit his own personality against the whole world. . . . Instead, he seeks to ally himself with others of a kindred nature. He finds his defense against insecurity by identifying himself with a set of extreme opinions or by taking refuge in a group. While he thus purchases his feeling of security by conformity to the group, he, at the same time, finds an outlet for his aggression by attacking the group's enemies."[22] Here, group consensus becomes, in a sense, a defensive function of the inferiority complex, an idea that offers another way of dealing with the challenge of applying Adler's idea to a larger community. Still other contemporary scholars return to Adler's primary notions in order to deconstruct group attributes such as intolerance. Mary G. Guindon, Alan G. Green, and Fred J. Hanna contend that intolerance is rooted in notions of inferiority and superiority, as defined by Adler. Moreover, these perceptions, though individual, become linked to "historical and societal intolerance of similar people," which in turn creates stereotypes and, in many cases, group efforts to "scapegoat" others.[23]

In addition to resurrecting Adler in order to understand the psychological aspects of prejudice, Robert Powers finds Adler's ideas useful in recognizing the function of mythology and memory in culture.[24] Specifically, Adler addresses the role of myth for neurotics, those who are at odds with their larger society: "We could not understand neither [sic] a healthy nor a sick person, if we had not comprehended, consciously or unconsciously, his habitual, always repeated forms of expression. Any experience and concept formation always occurs under the necessity of exclusion. But the nervous individual formulates his style of life more rigidly, more narrowly; he is nailed to the cross of his narrow, personal, noncooperative fiction."[25] Thus, to Alder, these repeated forms of expression were the source of myths, and the unhealthy individual creates an exclusive and noncooperative counter reality. Moreover, Adler also stressed the notion that "any memory retained by the individual, whether from early childhood or from the more recent past, whether accurate as to the historic facts or mixed with fantasy, could reveal the style of life."[26] For many white southerners in the twentieth century, the memory and mythology associated with the defeat of the Confederacy may have been historically remote, but public criticism resurrected these memories for each new generation and shaped their individual and collective identity—their "style of life," as Adler noted. As this attention became corrosively critical, the responses became correspondingly aggressive and ambitious. And it is in the strength and extremity of these responses that evidence for the underlying stratum of inferiority surfaces.

Still others, such as Oliver Brachfield, have looked to Adler's ideas to examine such expressions as the German inferiority complex, the Jewish inferiority complex, and the Spanish inferiority complex.[27] Though Brachfield admits some reservations in "extending to collectivities the result obtained from analyzing the minds of individuals," he insists that, "all the same, there does seem to be such a thing as a collective inferiority complex."[28] Brachfield cites a 1936 study by Baron de Wesselenyi titled *A Harmadik Birodalom Keletkese* (The Birth of the Third Reich), in which Wesselenyi attempted to "apply the idea of an inferiority feeling to a historic collectivity." Wesselenyi concluded, notes Brachfield, that "the fundamental cause of the German catastrophe was the existence in the German soul of violent inferiority feelings. It was a case of a fixed idea existing, first in the minds of individuals and, since the state or nation consists of individuals, these separate inferiority complexes becoming integrated into one vast national and specifically German inferiority complex."[29]

Wesselenyi further insisted that Germany was not alone in suffering from this collective complex; rather, he found it common in reactionary communities. According to Brachfield, "Wesselenyi claims that many right-wing reactionary political movements were due to the same complexes, especially those that shook various European countries after the First World War."[30] Brachfield compares Wesselenyi's conclusions to those made by Count Keyserling, author of a study of psychoanalysis in the United States. Keyserling, like Wesselenyi, "maintained that an excessive nationalism is the result, not of overflowing national vitality, but, on the contrary, of a feeling of national distress."[31] Adler's theories have also been considered in midcentury analyses of women and in a modern interpretation of masculinity. Orgler's 1963 book-length study of Adler's inferiority complex includes a section titled "The So-called Inferiority of Women," in which she posits a more general model of inferiority and applies it to an entire gender at a specific moment in time. She argues that women's feelings of inferiority are exacerbated by the onslaught of critical input regarding their intellectual abilities, their contributions to society, and their restrictive gender roles, which they experience throughout their lives.[32] More recently, in a study of masculinity and violence, Antony Whitehead cites Adler's premise that inferior feelings of manliness may result in "uninhibited aggression."[33] Clearly, Adler's original ideas have been stretched and bent well beyond their original purpose to cover a host of human behaviors, and here too they are intended only to provide context to the discussion of inferiority.

In each case examined here, the ghosts of inferiority have become quite substantial. And despite the dangers inherent in making such generalizations about the white South, some of the most prominent scholars of the region have laid the foundation for a consideration of inferiority. Lewis Killian's assessment in *White Southerners* pointed to the impact of the legacy of defeat, concluding that "in spite of its changing social structure, the white South could remain solid and could be as defensive as a genuinely persecuted minority."[34] And this was true of the white southern migrant experience as well. Killian's study describes in great detail the discrimination that many white southerners felt when they tried to find jobs in the industrial North. Considered lazy, unreliable, uneducated, and too independent, many white southern migrants were passed over for promotions, if they were hired at all. According to Killian, the discrimination functioned in a way similar to public criticism in that it reinforced a collective identity. "Their group consciousness," he notes, "was defensive in nature."[35] Killian even recounts that white southerners in Chicago joked that there were only two kinds of people—a "hillbilly" and a "son of a bitch"[36]—drawing a hostile line between themselves and those who deemed them inferior.

One particular part of W. J. Cash's *The Mind of the South* (1941) came very close to discussing this idea of the inferiority complex, though in a very general way. His concept of the "Savage Ideal" served as a label for certain behaviors that Cash saw exhibited by many white southerners, behaviors he believed to be continuous since the post–Civil War era. James C. Cobb interprets Cash's theory of the "Savage Ideal" as one that describes "a peculiarly southern strain of conformity and aversion to criticism or innovation forged during Reconstruction and dominant throughout the ensuing decades."[37] Jack Temple Kirby elaborated on the definition, stating that Cash's "Savage Ideal," for the most part, "encompassed the 'darker phrases': militant ignorance and anti-intellectualism; brutal, violent racism; xenophobia; self-righteousness and blind defensiveness."[38] Though savagery has been a pillar of white southern history, there are other equally defensive though less feral responses that result from these feelings of inferiority.

Writing in the 1970s, sociologist John Shelton Reed collected survey and public opinion data that exposed many of the key elements of this complex. "Localism, violence, and a conservative religion," Reed writes, "are all plausible responses for a minority [in this case, white southerners] group, surrounded by a culture which is viewed as powerful, hostile, and unresponsive; all can be seen as adaptive reactions to the situation in which Southerners have, time and again, found themselves." He argues that "these defenses, mobilized in the antebellum sectional crisis, have been sustained by the chronic crisis which has been southern history since."[39] I argue that this long-standing crisis culture was reinforced by this collective sense of inferiority, which relies on a consciousness regarding one's own position and is followed by efforts to overcome or manage these feelings. And further, I contend that it is not the historical crisis, in and of itself, that triggers this cycle of inferiority and compensation, but rather the public criticism—often perceived as abrupt and unwarranted—from nonsoutherners and southerners alike.

THE PROCESS OF PUBLIC CRITICISM

James C. Cobb, in his own analysis of southern identity, stresses "the notion of culture as 'process,' an ongoing cycle of interaction between past and present that sustains the modernizing South's cultural identity as a work in progress rather than fashioning it into a final, finished project."[40] Specifically, the public criticism examined in these cases did not focus solely on the event at hand; rather, as has been noted by southern scholars, criticisms of past southern atrocities are recycled and reapplied. For example, commenting on the racial tension of the 1950s in the South, historian C. Vann Woodward notes that "the flying rumors of plots and counterplot of bands armed with icepick and switchblade knife, of Eleanor Clubs, conspiratorial societies, and subversive northern agitators often recalled the fevered frame of mind that possessed the South in the winter following the Harpers Ferry raid."[41] Moreover, Howard Odum, when discussing the struggles of the twentieth-century South, claims that "many of the same symbols of conflict and tragedy that were manifest in the 1840's were evident again a hundred years later."[42] This overlapping of past and present criticism catalyzed a broader defensive response from white southerners. Critics of the anti-evolution religious fundamentalists of the 1920s never focused their arguments primarily on religious differences; rather, they expanded their target to include a host of southern deficiencies, including poverty, lack of education, racism, and political corruption, to name a few. And the media denunciation of southern Agrarianism in the 1930s revived the sectionalist rhetoric of the 1860s, while the public criticism of the anti-integration politics of the 1950s referenced the violence of the Reconstruction period and came full circle by reiterating the anti-intellectualism of 1920s southern fundamentalism. Thus, public criticism amounted to a full-fledged program of cultural formation, and the undercarriage of that culture was a sense of ostracism and inferiority. Criticism of this sort transcends the present moment and forms a bridge to a collective, regional past. Southern whiteness thus becomes constructed by negative cultural feedback.

Negative identity construction, of course, was not the only way southern whiteness was defined or developed. White southerners promoted their own self-representation, and this vision has attracted much scholarly attention. In the immediate aftermath of the Civil War, for example, many white southerners embraced the Confederacy as more than a political entity. According to Charles Reagan Wilson, the myth of the Lost Cause, the preservation of the Confederate memory, was embraced as religion.[43] The religion of the Lost Cause then became an insistent reassertion of white southern identity, based on the alleged moral superiority of the virtuous white southern Christian. Historians Thomas L. Connelly and Barbara Bellows have argued that "the postwar generation of Southerners fought back with almost grotesque assertions of their moral superiority." They asserted that this sense of superiority "was the absolute heir of the Inner Lost Cause rationale, that whatever had occurred, Southerners were still the better man."[44] If one considers the mythology of the Confederacy and the myths of the Lost Cause to be the fundamental self-promotional elements of white southern identity, then the negative aspects of identity construction must be considered in tandem. Wilson asserts that "the self-image of a chosen people leaves little room for self-criticism."[45] But when this criticism arises, and when it reaches a certain level where it cannot be dismissed or ignored, it is powerful enough to transform its subjects from moderate to reactionary communities. These transformations, marking some of the most dramatic changes in regional identity, offer new insight into the way in which whiteness and "southernness" have developed over time.

The negative or oppositional construction of southern whiteness has its roots in the Civil War period, when white southerners were attempting to defend their racial and economic hierarchies. Writing in 1837, Senator John C. Calhoun of South Carolina revealed precisely how the perception of northern disdain for the South had ultimately reached the white southern consciousness. He argued that "however sound the great body of the non-slaveholding States are at present, in the course of a few years they will be succeeded by those who will have been taught to hate the people and institutions of nearly one-half of this Union." Calhoun's charges were clear and unmitigated, and he insisted that this hatred was "more deadly than one hostile nation ever entertained towards another."[46] Even the bold southern self-critic became part of this northern conspiracy of southern disparagement. On the eve of the Civil War, to name one example, Hinton R. Helper, a journalist from South Carolina, published a scathing critique of slavery, titled *The Impending Crisis of the South: How to Meet It* (1857). The attack focused primarily on the threat that slavery posed to poor whites. Despite being penned by a southerner, the book achieved real prominence when northern Republicans distributed close to 100,000 copies during the election year of 1860. In the South, the book was burned in public ceremonies, and this type of "thought control extended to the suppression and seizure of newspapers."[47] The book added to the "crisis psychology," as Woodward has called it, that "persisted and deepened in the fateful year of 1860 into a pathological condition of mind in which delusions of persecution and impending disaster flourished."[48]

In the decades following the war and Reconstruction, sectional reconciliation seemed possible to many white southerners who wanted to restore their prominence within the larger nation. Advocates for the Lost Cause and critics of the North soon found that their message fell on deaf ears. Confederate defenders were deemed outmoded, and as Woodward has argued, the only "southern spokesmen who commanded national attention in that era were those of the New South school, who swelled the chorus in praise of the new order."[49] Southern historian Dewey W. Grantham has maintained that "the vision of a triumphant New South was based on a number of realistic premises, but it gave rise to an elaborate myth of southern potential and success."[50] This success, of course, was overstated, and the South remained, well into the twentieth century, a "colonial appendage of the North."[51] This vision of renewed economic prosperity and peace was facilitated by a growing northern apathy toward "reconstructing the South." Popular culture began to revise the narrative of the War between the States. For example, Nina Silber argues that theater productions such as *The Blue and the Grey* (1884) and *Shenandoah* (1888) "introduced northern audiences to lush southern settings, opulent plantation mansions, fierce military conflict, and, as always, romantic love threatened by sectional division."[52] Silber also positions the New Orleans World's Fair, held in 1884, as a strategic display of southern progress, one that also made regional reunion seem feasible during this Gilded Age.

This revisionist narrative appealed to white southerners and northerners alike. Jack Temple Kirby surmised that "gradually, the abolitionist tradition that slavery was barbarous, was turned upon its head: slavery became a benign, paternal system that was unfortunately incompatible with other American institutions. Reconstruction—a trauma within the memory of many in 1900—became a foolish, tragic misadventure instead of a noble conclusion to the abolitionist crusade."[53] Despite the North's waning interest in the region, the fundamental characterization of the South did not change. Woodward claims that although many northerners may have lauded the truce between the regions and embraced the plantation mythology, most "continued to think of the South in terms of racial brutality, reactionary politics, poverty, and a backward economy."[54]

However, despite the private thoughts of those outside of the South, the brutal racial policies of the region eventually were ignored, or even accepted, by the region's former critics.

At the turn of the century, as America embarked on its imperial mission abroad, new theories of race surfaced that condoned the actions of white southerners against African Americans. This tolerance of southern racial practices lured many white southerners into a sense of national reunion that would make future criticism all the more destabilizing. In *The Strange Career of Jim Crow*, Woodward cited northern newspapers as sources for this behavioral shift: "The *Boston Evening Transcript* of 14 January 1899, admitted that southern race policy was 'now the policy of the Administration of the very party which carried the country in to and through a civil war to free the slave.' And *The New York Times* of 10 May 1900 reported editorially that 'northern men . . . no longer denounce the suppression of the Negro vote [in the South] as it used to be denounced of the reconstruction days. The necessity of it under the supreme law of self-preservation is candidly recognized.'"[55] Many white southerners saw such changes as evidence of their return to national power. And this would not be the only experience that the region had with delusions of renewed success. The political arena proved particularly promising during this period. For example, to many southerners the Populist movement of the 1890s, with its support of banking reform and agricultural subsidies, offered new hope. However, New South advocates of industrialism, as well as Republicans in the North and the West, considered the movement reactionary in its rejection of capitalism. The national leader of the Democratic Party, William Jennings Bryan, actually ran for president three times—in 1896, 1900, and 1908. Nominated by the Populist contingency of the Democratic Party, Bryan lost all three bids.

For southern Democrats who supported him, Bryan became the embodiment of white southern redemption, a reformer who could correct the abuses of power and the corruption that accompanied the industrial American machine. "White Southerners were drawn to the charismatic Bryan," Grantham argues; they "savored his swelling oratory, and liked his Protestant Christianity, his emphasis on morality in politics, his enunciation of Jeffersonian principles, and his identification with rural progressivism."[56] Moreover, "they also appreciated his endorsement of state rights and his acceptance of the white South's racial settlement at the turn of the century."[57] Bryan's failure to return the South to the nation's seat of power sparked a renewed feeling of failure for the region. Considered anti-intellectual and anticapitalist as well as provincial, Populism for the white southerners who supported it "was largely felt as another alienation from the prevailing spirit in America."[58] Whereas the northern tolerance for

Jim Crow seemed to lessen the impression of southern ostracism, the failure of Populism only strengthened white southern alienation from the nation at large, a cycle that would repeat itself.

Still, Woodrow Wilson's campaign for the presidency in 1912 was seen as yet another vehicle for southern ascension, or so many white southerners believed. Born in Virginia, and having grown up there during the aftermath of the Civil War, Wilson identified himself as a southerner, even though he moved north to attend school. Eventually receiving a Ph.D. from Johns Hopkins University, Wilson also served as governor of New Jersey. But all the while, many white southerners still considered him one of their own. Wilson often encouraged this association; he even went so far as to state publicly in 1896 that there was, indeed, "nothing to apologize for in the past of the South—absolutely nothing to apologize for."[59] Regarding Wilson's successful election, Grantham states:

> The reaction of most Southerners was unmistakable—a feeling of exhilaration and of realizing long-deferred hopes. "Long ago," wrote a North Carolinian, "I had despaired of ever seeing a man of southern birth President." Wilson's election, he declared, "marks an era in our national life. With it we have the ascendancy of men of southern birth and residence to the seats of power and responsibility such as had never been seen in our day." Wilson's national role, the president of the University of Virginia declared, was "a sort of fulfillment of an unspoken prophecy lying close to the heart of nearly every faithful son of the South that out of this life of dignity and suffering, and out of this discipline of fortitude and endurance there would spring a brave, modern national minded man to whom the whole nation, in some hour of peril and difficulty would turn for succor and for helpfulness." The Southerners were at last "back in the house of their fathers."[60]

The election of Wilson inspired an era of optimism among white southerners. The promise of reunion had been fulfilled, or so it seemed, especially when Wilson proclaimed at a Confederate reunion in 1917 that the region was now "part of a nation united, powerful, great in spirit and in purpose . . . an instrument in the hands of God to see that liberty is made secure for mankind."[61] But for good reasons, though perhaps unexpected to white southerners embracing their alleged redemption, this era of optimism gave way to a second wave of public criticism.

Some white southerners claimed to be surprised by the negative attention, but problems with the acclaimed reunion had appeared several years earlier. Many African Americans, who were not included in this white southern vision of a reconciled nation, refused to ignore the continued racial violence in the

South. The NAACP began publishing *Crisis*, under the editorship of W. E. B. Du Bois, in 1910, with the explicit purpose of chronicling the lynchings of African Americans, 3,000 cases of which took place during this reconciliation period.[62] The rise of the second wave of the Ku Klux Klan, organized in Georgia in 1915, also garnered public attention. Once glorified in Thomas Dixon's *The Clansman* (1905) and D. W. Griffith's *The Birth of a Nation* (1915), the Klan became a popular subject for critical journalistic exposés. In fact, for journalists, the Klan provided, according to Tindall, "an almost ridiculously simple formula for fame," and these attacks "on the grotesqueries of the benighted South became for that decade a high road to the Pulitzer Prize."[63]

Politics, race, and economics continued to constitute the barrage of criticism that came in the 1920s. In addition to the extensive newspaper and journal coverage of southern atrocities, internal dissent grew exponentially, making the criticism all the more far reaching. William Skaggs, for example, the former Populist politician from Alabama, published a scathing critique of the region, *The Southern Oligarchy: An Appeal in Behalf of the Silent Masses of Our Country against the Despotic Rule of the Few* (1924). Tindall characterized the work as having "tones of righteous indignation" and as "one of the most thoroughgoing indictments of the region ever published, detailing at length political corruption, landlordism, illiteracy, peonage, lynch law, partisan and racial proscription, and a hundred other delinquencies."[64] However, no matter how biting Skaggs's book was, it proved no match for the sting of H. L. Mencken(a reporter at the *Arkansas Writer* called him the modern Attila.[65] Writing for the *Baltimore Sun* and the *American Mercury*, Mencken began his criticism of the region in 1917 with the publication of "The Sahara of the Bozart" in the *New York Evening Mail*. Rather than cataloging all of the region's deficiencies, as did Skaggs, Mencken (who would later cover the Scopes Trial) offered blanket statements that depicted the entire South as being absolutely devoid of culture, intelligence, or competence of any sort: "If the whole of the late Confederacy were to be engulfed by a tidal wave tomorrow, the effect upon the civilized minority of men in the world would be but little greater than that of a flood on the Yang-tse-kiang. It would be impossible in all history to match so complete a drying-up of a civilization."[66] Mencken's comments—a kind of journalistic carpet bombing—seemed to encapsulate the budding resurgence of public ridicule. And unlike the specific scrutiny of those who came before him, Mencken's general statements could not be dismissed as being inapplicable; if the entire South was devoid of all things good, then communities of white southerners had no alibi.

Even well into the twentieth century, W. E. B. Debnam returned to the post–Civil War period as the source for the future failures of southern white society.

In his counterattack on Eleanor Roosevelt, he insisted that "there was nothing of dignity about Reconstruction. There was only the studied deliberate debasement of a proud and defenseless people."[67] Calling her once again by name, an indignant Debnam proclaimed:

> Through the bitter years of Reconstruction there was no law in the South, Mrs. Roosevelt, except the law of revengeful Radicals who hated the South with a venom that passed all understanding; there was no order save that of rapacious, power-mad, licentious hoodlums out to loot and destroy a stricken people as the Five Horsemen of the Apocalypse and mark us down as just another illiterate Southerner who doesn't have any sense enough to know the Prophet John mentioned only four in his Book of Revelation. True, Mrs. Roosevelt. There was the Conqueror astride a white horse. There was War riding a red horse. There was Famine riding a black horse. There was Death riding a pale horse. The South knew, and intimately, these four . . . but for the South throughout those melancholy years there was a fifth. It was the Horseman whose name is Fear—astride a horse of Federal blue . . . and he, Mrs. Roosevelt, was the most terrible of all.[68]

Just as the criticism of white southerners recycled the accusations and disparagement of the past, so too did the response that came from individuals such as Debnam. I argue that these collective responses—fundamentalism, New Criticism, and Massive Resistance—which are often seen as separate movements, are manifestations of some of the same anxieties and frustrations that characterized Debnam's plea.

THE MUTUALLY CONSTRUCTIVE RELATIONSHIP OF INDIVIDUAL, REGIONAL, AND NATIONAL IDENTITIES

If the intermingling of past and present public criticism maintained this sense of cultural inferiority over time, then its effect on individual white southerners inevitably translated into a shared regional white identity that remained in constant conflict with the American national image. Specifically, the broadly generic nature of the criticism made it impossible for many white southerners to dismiss it as irrelevant or inapplicable to their own lives. For example, in his description of the religious climate at the Scopes Trial, Mencken insisted that "by imposing 'Baptist and Methodist barbarism, . . . the southern clergy had created a cultural vacuum and a fear of ideas."[69] Rather than focusing specifically on what ministers in Rhea County, Tennessee, were preaching to their congregations, Mencken offered an indiscriminate criticism of the entire region. And Roosevelt—though she did, in some ways, compliment the state of North Carolina upon her visit—aimed her criticism at the region at large. "I never go into that part of the country and come away without a certain sense of sadness," she confessed in her column.[70] The often broad accusations of hysterical southern religious practices, the absence of art and high culture in the South, or the widespread racism gave no room for exceptions. Moreover, this criticism often severed the South from the nation, in an attempt to promote the American vision of democracy and liberalism by quarantining southern racial atrocities, poverty, and illiteracy, among other perceived ills, as being uniquely endemic to the region. In her recent book on the relationships among American nationalism, Jim Crow racism, and southern modernism, Leigh Anne Duck argues that "when national discourse has acknowledged the conflict between southern conservatism and national democracy, it has typically done so in ways that localize the conflict—a 'backward South' and a modern or 'enlightened nation.'"[71] This localization proved unifying at a cultural and psychological level, just as the Civil War had unified the region politically and militarily.

The critics, whether northern, southern, or even international, were perceived by many white southerners to be driven by a deep-seated hatred that nearly amounted to a full-scale conspiracy. And after the Civil War, when northern culture became, in a sense, American culture, what began as a war between two regions became for many white southerners a contest between their regional loyalty and their American identity. To Woodward, southern history was, in and of itself, an overwhelming burden: "The South does not share the national myths based on these experiences, not legitimately at least, and only vicariously at best. That is for a good and simple reason that, unlike the nation, the South has known defeat and failure, long periods of frustration and poverty, as well as human slavery and its long aftermath of racial injustice. Some of this heritage lies far enough back to be dimmed by time, but not all—not the poverty, the frustration, nor all of the guilt."[72] Though he coined the phrase, Woodward never explained how this burden operated in the daily lives of specific communities of white southerners, though he did insist that this counternarrative of the southern past and its exclusion from an authentic national past accounted for its continued regional distinctiveness. I assert that the southern perception of exclusion and inferiority resulted from the actual experience of public criticism, which, in turn, compounded individual and regional identity and set it at odds with national identity. This is not a modern development but a mechanism in place in the early days of the Republic. Focusing on the antebellum South, William Taylor, for example, argued that the negative stereotype of the Yankee helped white southerners rationalize their "peculiar institution" as well as fend off criticism from outsiders regarding the Agrarian lifestyle of the South. Moreover, Taylor noted that white southerners "persisted in seeing themselves as different and, increasingly, they tended to reshape this acknowledged difference into a claim of superiority."[73] Cash too has argued that "it was the conflict with the Yankee which really created the concept of the South as something more than a matter of geography."[74]

This growing consciousness of sectional identity proved conflicting to antebellum white southerners. For example, in their defenses of slavery, Edmund Ruffin and George Fitzhugh argued simultaneously for regional commonalities and southern superiority. Mirroring a technique that would be used by southern communities to respond to public criticism in the future, Ruffin and Fitzhugh both highlighted what they saw as northern hypocrisy, an effort to insist that the division between the two cultures was not as different as critics would admit. Moreover, Ruffin appealed to a common source of American morality by citing the biblical justification of slavery. "In a much earlier time," Ruffin wrote, "it was on this institution of domestic slavery that was erected the admirable and beneficent mastership and government of the patriarch Abraham."[75] In an effort to reframe the relationship between the two regions, Fitzhugh prophesied that the North and all of Europe secretly envied the South and that "towards slavery the North and all of Western Europe are unconsciously marching."[76] In the antebellum period, southern whites were already demonstrating early signs of a collective sense of alienation.

These emotions triggered not only individual responses like those made by Fitzhugh and Ruffin but also a concerted collective action—just as occurs in each case examined in this book. Specifically, historian Carl Degler points to this regional dynamic and the accompanying stereotypes it creates as a primary factor in the justification for secession and the Civil War: "As early as the antebellum years North and South had created a myth of difference that went beyond the facts of difference. On the eve of secession many southerners had come to use that sense of difference as justification for breaking out of what they considered the procrustean bed of the Union."[77] Obviously, the perception of distinctiveness, whether resulting from external criticism or from internal motivations, proved powerful in the antebellum period. The continuation of this external criticism, coupled with the internal scrutiny that developed in the twentieth century, often served as a potent and enabling justification for the behavior of various white southerners as they responded to challenges to the cultural, religious, and political establishment.

This collective sense of persecution from northern critics often pervades discussions regarding the cause of the Civil War and also the legacy of the southern defeat, and it is here that the notion of inferiority surfaces yet again. The war seems to permeate the white southern identity at every level and has, at times, been used as a cultural metaphor for a host of anxieties. Seven years before the publication of W. E. B. Debnam's popular piece, for example, John Temple Graves, journalist for the *Birmingham-Post Herald*, argued that "the War Between the States, with its scars and memories and the introspections that came of them, contributed much to the southern attitude. . . . The contribution was psychological. The psychology was one of defense and living dangerously."[78] Robert Penn Warren also highlighted the psychological consequences of defeat in his monograph *The Legacy of the Civil War: Meditations on the Centennial.* Warren introduced the concept of the South's "Great Alibi," a subconscious excuse of sorts that allows white southerners to condone racial violence and to account for various regional failures. "Even now," Warren argued, "any common lyncher becomes a defender of the southern tradition. . . . By the Great Alibi, pellagra, hookworm, and illiteracy are all explained, or explained away . . . [while] resentful misery becomes a high sense of honor, and ignorance becomes divine revelation."[79]

This steadfast vision of persecution has both an observable and a devastating cultural effect. Forty years ago, historian Sheldon Hackney argued that the penchant for violence in the South could be traced back to this very sense of ostracism. He claimed that the South suffered from a "siege mentality"[80] and that this mentality accounts for the proclivity for violence in the region. According to Hackney, this "siege mentality" has resulted from the perception of the "social, political, and physical environment as hostile and casts the white Southerner in the role of the passive victim of malevolent forces."[81] A threatened community is one that will often become acutely aware of its inferiority. Hackney also argued that this siege mentality intensifies when there is a perceived threat to the established order. Therefore, he claimed, southerners are often "likely to be most conscious of being Southerners when they are defending their region against attack from outside forces: abolitionists, the Union Army, carpetbaggers, Wall Street and Pittsburgh, civil rights agitators, the federal government, feminism, socialism, trade-unionism, Darwinism, Communism, atheism, daylight-savings time, and other by-products of modernity. This has produced an extreme sensitivity to criticism from outsiders and a tendency to excuse local faults as the products of forces beyond human or local control."[82] Such a list of outside forces seems radically, even dismayingly, diverse, but inferiority proves to be a refuge for a wide range of causes designed to explain and justify the construction of southern whiteness.

THE OVERDETERMINATION OF SOUTHERN WHITENESS

For many white southerners, the denunciation of southern culture throughout the twentieth century resulted in an intensified clinging to the power and privilege associated with their whiteness. Critical studies of whiteness have focused primarily on the invisibility of this social construct; the acceptance of whiteness as a norm had deemphasized the way in which it was constructed and the power and exclusivity associated with that construction. Thomas K. Nakayama and Judith N. Martin have surmised that "whiteness gains its meaning from its encounters with nonwhiteness."[83] The oppositional nature of the social construction of whiteness thus requires a segregated and oppositional identity. As French poststructuralists such as Michel Foucault and Jacques Derrida contended, whiteness was not an indefinable essence.[84] When whiteness is made visible, the way in which whiteness has maintained its privileges—the extra "wages," as both W. E. B. Du Bois and David Roediger have argued—is suddenly revealed. White identity has most notably targeted African Americans and women as the "other," and many Marxist critics have insisted that the underlying impulse of this dynamic is economics- and class-driven.[85] Roediger, however, argues that the Marxist explanation of racism—often touted by the "political mainstream"—ignores the essential complexity of whiteness.[86]

I agree with Nakayama and Martin that whiteness is "productively understood as a communication phenomenon,"[87] but communication should be extended to include public criticism. Toni Morrison and Frantz Fanon have pointed to the mutually constructive nature of black identity and white identity, which is, of course, the fundamental shaping influence of southern whiteness.[88] However, southern whiteness is unique in the sense that it is constructed by oppressing a black "other," while serving paradoxically as the "other" in the larger construct of American identity in the twentieth century. Over time, as demonstrated in the following chapters, white southernness becomes associated with anti-intellectualism, religiosity, and massive resistance to civil rights, compounding the very nature of whiteness itself. What began and continued to be a nonblack identity became, in effect, a nonnorthern, nonliberal, nonmodern, and nonscientific overdetermined southern whiteness.

Freud first used the term "overdetermination" in *Interpretation of Dreams* to explain the multiple and inextricable sources of dreams. In general, overdetermination, according to Freud, allowed for a broader and nonreductionist vision of the totality of experience that is constituted by multiple causes and effects.[89] The French Marxist Louis Althusser applied Freud's all-encompassing vision of experience to political situations as a means to understand the complex coexistence of conflicting political forces. These contradictions, in constituting the "social formation of the whole," defined a "pattern of dominance and subordination, antagonism and non-antagonism of the contradictions in the structure in dominance at any given historical moment."[90] Overdetermination thus offered a more sophisticated and nuanced way to understand these "contradictory determinants." The theory ultimately influenced mainline literary criticism, when New Critic I. A. Richards, for example, relied on overdetermination to account for multiple meanings in literary texts.[91] Similar to Freud's original contention, overdetermination, which includes visible and invisible determinants, offers a useful way of conceptualizing southern whiteness as it takes on multiple, conflicting, visible, and invisible meanings as demonstrated in the events discussed in this book.

Embedded in the developing construct of southern whiteness lies the equally powerful and complex construct of southern masculinity. Though masculinity is not the primary focus of this book, it is inextricable from southern whiteness, particularly during the early twentieth century, when both constructs were wholly dominant. Until recently, scholars of southern masculinity focused on studies of antebellum southern performances of male honor and chivalry, both of which were cemented in the code of the Confederacy. However, Trent Watts and Craig Thompson Friend have deepened and broadened the definition of southern masculinity. Their anthologies demonstrate the way in which southern masculinity interacted with notions of American and northern masculinity—an important parallel to the argument made in this book.[92] Watts argues that in the antebellum period, as "regional stereotypes quickly hardened and gained broad currency," white southern men envisioned themselves as "superior to their northern countrymen."[93] This superiority and insistence on southern distinction were, according to Watts, "structured around two core values, mastery and independence." The defeat of the Confederacy destroyed both of these premises and destroyed this vision of superiority.

If southern manhood in the twentieth century was, to some degree, constructed in opposition to American manhood, it would reflect the way southern whiteness was constructed in opposition to many aspects of American and northern culture. And the tension inherent in the conflict between American masculinity and southern masculinity and—more important to this work—between southern whiteness and nonsouthern whiteness would result in a heightened sensitivity to criticism. Watts notes that recent work on southern masculinity has recognized the impact of such tension. He points specifically to the work of Glenda Gilmore, Stephen Kantrowitz, and Nancy MacLean, who note that the responses to these perceived threats on southern masculinity have included "public lynching of black men, prickly sensitivity to criticism in southern institutions, and a fierce loyalty to a whites-only Democratic party."[94] In each community examined here, southern white males emerge as the dominant figures, largely because they held the primary positions of authority in politics, academics, and church institutions throughout the South. The fact that southern men in each of these well-known moments in southern history played the leading roles is predictable; but the nature of their masculinity, specifically the connection between male dominance and white supremacy, make them all the more susceptible, perhaps, to developing an inferiority complex.

In recent years, new studies of the South have focused on the role that southern whites played in the civil rights movement and the post–civil rights conservative counterrevolution. Joe Crespino, in his study of white Mississippians in the civil rights era, quotes Charles Payne, cautioning scholars not to ignore the complexity of white southern behavior. "The danger," Crespino has written, "is to reduce white southerners to 'the ignorant, the pot-bellied, and the tobacco-chewing,' images that 'easily supplant more complex and realistic images of racism.'"[95] And Jason Sokol traces his inspiration for his book *There Goes My Everything* to senior southern historian Charles Eagles:

> Eagles pointed out that historians "have tended to emphasize one side of the struggle, the movement side, and to neglect their professional obligation to understand the other side, the segregationist opposition." He urged scholars to take more detached views and seek broader perspectives. When historians analyzed white southerners, in all their diversity, that would "make for a much more complicated story, full of additional conflicts and ambiguities. . . . Told without condescension, the often tragic stories of white southerners' hates, fears, and pride belong in the wider accounts of the civil rights era."[96]

Additionally, Crespino insists that scholars have to understand the "continuity of white racism," which I argue should be considered as a cultural construction arising, at least in part, from thoroughgoing feelings of inferiority. Thus, southern whiteness must be understood as a constructed identity that begins with race but develops well beyond the purview of race. Sokol, focusing primarily on the civil rights movement, has also pointedly argued that "white southerners played decisive roles in determining the depths, and limits, of change."[97] They still do. And although many southern whites eventually abandoned segregationist stances, they adopted equally polarizing positions on education, the role of government, and even literary aesthetics. At the core of this broadened and overdetermined whiteness stands a southern heritage of inferiority that remains significant today.

■ The idea of a white southern inferiority complex has always existed just below the surface of southern studies, popping up here and there, a known quantity rarely analyzed. "It is the nose on the end of the southern face," the late southern historian Willard B. Gatewood Jr. once told me. In the Scopes Trial, theology and religion collide with civil liberties; the New Critics and authors of I'll Take My Stand bring a highly refined sense of aesthetics to bear on an equally refined and defensive sense of regionalism; and Virginia's campaign for Massive Resistance, of course, brings race and education into dramatic relief. Southern whites throughout the twentieth century were often dismissed as ignorant, backward, or just plain "southern," an adjective that implied a long history of weakness and inferiority. And in many cases, the label was well earned. But the alternating periods of reconciliation and rejection, the barrage of public ridicule, often served simply to intensify this reactionary behavior, thereby creating a self-fulfilling prophecy for the South. John Shelton Reed claimed that it was not necessary "that all or even most Southerners feel threatened much of the time, merely that enough feel threatened enough of the time to keep these responses a part of the general regional culture (where they will be shared by threatened and secure alike)."[98] Howard Zinn once argued that rather than being distinctive, "the South represented 'the essence of the nation.'"[99] Thus, denigration of the region was a way of exorcising our national sins. And Christopher Lasch claims that the past is a "psychological treasury from which we draw the reserves we need to cope with the future."[100]

The negative public spotlight created this treasury and draws its subjects together, who then form a strong group association in which the complex becomes an organizing principle. Each group, as Lewis Way described in his social application of Alfred Adler's work, creates a "life lie" that is repeated as a mantra of sorts—the chant of Interposition, for example. Moreover, in these cases, the "life lies" are grounded in what is considered an authoritative text, providing each community that perceives itself to be under attack a concrete and definitive rebuttal to its critics. Christians in Rhea County, Tennessee, embrace biblical literalism, while segregationists in Virginia point to the Constitution as a source of absolute truth. The Agrarians, turned New Critics, elevate all texts to the status of sacred writing and then advocate an objective, context-free interpretation of those texts. The group, the mantra, and the text counter these feelings of inferiority and institutionalize, in each case, a key aspect of white southern identity, the political ramifications of which have been long lasting and are still not fully recognized. Thus, tracing the influence of the southern heritage of inferiority breathes new life into the effort to understand the roots of southern fundamentalism, racism, and anti-intellectualism.

Perhaps the most significant consequence of this ongoing sense of inferiority can be seen in the way in which it has shaped southern and national politics. The region has always proved primarily conservative politically, but the southern association with the modern Republican Party is a late twentieth-century realignment. Based on a states' rights rhetoric inherited from Strom Thurmond's Dixiecrats in 1948, the Republican "Southern Strategy" tapped into this regional sense of ostracism and inferiority, producing a highly successful campaign that convinced many white southerners to break with the Democratic Party by giving them a way to vote their conscience on defensible grounds while retaining the antiquated and indefensible traditions. Inferiority-baiting has replaced race-baiting. And so, in its current incarnation, southern white conservatism is defined primarily by a long list of rallying calls, each of which arises from the cases explored here: fundamentalism, majoritarianism, creationism, anti-elitism, agrarianism, cultural conformity, authoritarianism, states' rights, and a strict constructionist interpretation of the Constitution, to name but a few. All are armor in a regional battle against inferiority that rages on, even now, a cycle of defense and loss, the cost of which is progress.

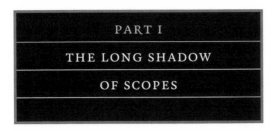

PART I

THE LONG SHADOW

OF SCOPES

An authentic folk movement, beyond a doubt: such was the Klan. And such also, in only comparatively less complete measure was the anti-evolution movement. For it cannot be dismissed as the aberration of a relatively small highly organized pressure group made of ignorant, silly, and fanatical people, as some writers have attempted to do. Having observed it at close range, I have no doubt at all that it had the active support and sympathy of the overwhelming majority of southern people.
—W. J. Cash, *The Mind of the South*

For six days in July 1925, the Scopes Evolution Trial, held in Dayton, Tennessee, captured the attention of the nation, and the world for that matter, and defined the white South for a new generation of Americans. The state of Tennessee had outlawed the teaching of evolution in the Butler Act passed earlier that year. John Scopes, a substitute biology teacher, was arrested and charged with violating the ban. His defense was sponsored by the American Civil Liberties Union, which offered the infamous attorney Clarence Darrow as counsel for the young teacher. William Jennings Bryan, Populist leader and three-time presidential nominee, advocated the creationist viewpoint, and he would be goaded into defending the literal interpretation of the Bible on the witness stand. The city of Dayton and the community at large went to great lengths to get ready for the trial, renovating the courtroom with additional seating to prepare for the large crowds headed to town via the Southern Railway. Extensive media equipment was installed to facilitate the radio broadcast of the event live via a Chicago station. News updates reached both coasts via Western Union, which assigned twenty-two telegraph operators to the event.[1] Despite the technical victory enjoyed by the prosecution—Scopes was found guilty of violating the Butler Act, a decision which the ACLU appealed—the fundamentalist interpretation of the Bible did not fare well under the bright and scrutinizing lights of the defense and the media.

The reporters who descended on the small town expected to focus their stories on the legal events, but many could not resist covering the crowds gathering in the town square: "Before the opening day of the 'monkey trial,' July 13, 1925, the streets of Dayton swarmed with sundry oddments of humanity—and other anthropoids—drawn to the carnival: publicity-hounds, curiosity-seekers, professional evangelists and professional atheists, a blind mountaineer who proclaimed himself the world's greatest authority on the Bible, ballyhoo agents for the Florida boom, hot dog and soda pop hucksters, and a miscellany of reporters and publicists."[2] After witnessing the circuslike atmosphere of Dayton, journalist H. L. Mencken concluded that he had "enough material stored up to last me the rest of my life"[3] and described the local people as "yaps, yokels, morons and anthropoids."[4] Such depictions of the religious environment of this southern town did little to bolster its image to the nation at large. The trial, which many local business leaders had hoped would bring attention and fame to rural Rhea County, had backfired.

Bryan's trial testimony regarding the literal interpretation of the Bible further crystallized the stereotype of provinciality that had been attributed to him two decades earlier. And Clarence Darrow came to represent—at least in the eyes of the churchgoers of Dayton—the liberal, modern, immoral North, persecuting the defenseless South yet again. Religious historian Karen Armstrong claims that the Scopes Trial exemplifies what happens when fundamentalism is attacked:

> Before the Scopes "monkey" trial—when the secular press ridiculed the fundamentalists and said they had no place in the modern agenda—fundamentalist Christians had been literal in their interpretation of scripture but creation science was the preserve of a few eccentrics. After the Scopes trial, they became the flagship of their movement. Before the Scopes trial, fundamentalists had often been on the left of the political spectrum and had been willing to work alongside socialists and liberal Christians in the new slums of the industrializing North American cities. After the Scopes trial, they swung to the far right, where they remained. They felt humiliated by the media attack. It was very nasty. There was a sense of loss of prestige, and, above all, a sense of fear.[5]

Even though fundamentalist groups were active throughout the country, George Marsden argues that the Scopes Trial and its southern, rural backdrop "stamped the entire movement with an indelible image." Public ridicule of Bryan the individual became a collective burden shared by his white southern followers and the region as a whole. Thus, Marsden claims, "fundamentalism, which began amid revivals in northern and West Coast cities, appeared increasingly associated with the rural South."[6] The radicalized community in Dayton combated this aspect of negative identity construction by developing what Edward Larson described as "a separate subculture with independent religious, educational and social institutions."[7]

Compounding this sense of defeat and loss for southern white fundamentalists, Bryan died only days after the trial, even before he could deliver his final speech on what he envisioned to be the legacy of the trial. The community immediately began planning for a memorial to the "Great Commoner." Nestled in the foothills of the Cumberland Mountains, William Jennings Bryan College crowns the most sacred peak in Dayton, Tennessee, and there, mounted atop the memorial space, stands the defining sign, "Christ above All—Bryan College—Founded 1930." Bryan himself had envisioned this "city on a hill" during his weeks in Dayton, claiming that it would make a perfect site for the founding of a religious college where young students would "read the Bible of their fathers."[8] Additionally, Bryan suggested that students attending this fundamentalist institution would wear blue and gray uniforms to symbolize the reconciliation of the North and the South. Bryan's original dual vision for the college attempted to resolve what he perceived as two of the central conflicts that arose during the trial—the old sectional battle and the new war between faith and science.

What was left in Rhea County, once the train with Bryan's body headed east, once Darrow headed home to bask in the glory of his infamous cross-examination, once John Scopes left to pursue his graduate studies on scholarship at the University of Chicago, was a reactionary fundamentalism. It was driven underground, isolated, tucked away from the spotlight that had denigrated it without apology. This public eye had taken a fatal toll on Bryan, and for the newly charged fundamentalists, angered and humiliated by the media ridicule of their faith and their town, Bryan was a martyr. Transforming their frustration and grief into founding a memorial university in Bryan's name, local Dayton citizens quietly recruited contributors nationwide to assist in their cause. At the heart of their campaign to build William Jennings Bryan College figures an intense desire to respond to this acute awareness of inferiority.

Though the actual events of the trial have been thoroughly recorded by historians such as Larson, little analysis has been offered by scholars regarding the long-term implications of this kind of media scrutiny. Moreover, in order to appreciate fully the impact of this negative attention, it is necessary to survey the cultural conditions, including the impressions of the key players, that preceded the trial. Only then can the full weight be measured of national, international, and internal condemnation and of the response of local religious fundamentalists to this barrage of attention, most notably the fundamentalist cultural isolation that characterized much of the Dayton community in the aftermath of the trial.

The Scopes Trial had other far-reaching implications for the white South, and for the country at large. What appears at first glance as a cultural battle between science and religion is revealed as a larger war being fought on multiple fronts. The sectional conflict of the mid-nineteenth century resurfaces repeatedly in both the events of the trial and the media coverage that followed. The clash between the North and the South now incorporated the standoff between those who were designated as the intellectual haves and those who were the have-nots, with southerners, of course, falling into the latter category. Richard Hofstadter, in fact, noted that during the Scopes Trial, "for the first time in history, intellectuals and experts were denounced as enemies by leaders of a large segment of the public."[9] For white southerners, this extended list of oppositional forces—intellectualism, science, modernism, federalism—established a host of inextricable determinants for white identity, including anti-intellectualism, religious fundamentalism, traditionalism, and states' rights.

In 1990, at the age of eighty-two, former Rhea County high school student H. J. Shelton, who was called as a witness for the prosecution and was a lifelong resident of Dayton, corresponded with Jason Blankenship, an Arkansas schoolboy. He wrote: "I don't think the trial put our community in a favorable light and it opened a 'can of worms' so to speak, as the controversy is still very much discussed and debated today."[10] The long shadow of Scopes, including the regional battle with inferiority, still lingers over Dayton, Tennessee. Dedicated to the Great Commoner, the man-who-would-be-president (and almost was three times), Bryan College, a tangible compensation to a benighted community, continues to this day to offer a fundamentalist and evangelical education that, among other disciplines, promotes a literalist, creationist view of biology and the development of mankind. Moreover, this particular brand of evangelism, labeled here as reactionary fundamentalism, became an integral component of modern conservatism in the South. Politically mobilized in the last three decades, this community, driven underground in the late 1920s, now dominates the southern political landscape, a bright shade of crimson beneath the Mason-Dixon Line and beyond.

CHAPTER 1

THE TRIPTYCH OF THE TWENTIES

BRYAN, DARROW, AND MENCKEN AND WHAT

THEY MEANT TO THE WHITE SOUTH

But if Christ is the expression of humanity's struggle up from the beast through the jungle, we have in him a combination and culmination of jungle life in body, soul and spirit, detached from heaven on the same plane with others, with little power to lift or to transfigure. The beast jungle theory of evolution robs a man of his dignity, marriage of its sanctity, government of its authority, and the church of her power and Christ of his glory.
—Rev. Amzi Clarence Dixon, "The Root of Modern Evils" (brother of Thomas Dixon, *The Klansman*)

If Bryan remained as accurate a spokesman for the fears and aspirations of his rural followers as I believe he did, then a sharper understanding of the forces operating upon him and the nature of his response to them should be a step forward in unraveling the enigmas of the rural West and South in the years after 1918.
—Lawrence W. Levine, *Defender of the Faith: William Jennings Bryan, the Last Decade, 1915–1925*

Journalist H. L. Mencken, attorney Clarence Darrow, and politician and activist William Jennings Bryan had known of each other long before the 1925 Scopes Evolution Trial. At times, their opinions, their causes, even their politics were in sync; however, in the aftermath of World War I, they would find themselves on opposite sides of perhaps the greatest domestic cultural crisis of the twentieth century. In order to understand how the interactions of these three individuals contributed to a collective regional identity for white southerners, it is necessary to understand how each was viewed by white southerners in the years before the confrontation in Dayton. For all three men, their reputations preceded them. The trial in Tennessee, however, transformed three individual identities into regional symbols of competing cultural and political values that remain relevant today. Darrow and Mencken (and the larger body of journalists that he represented) would be demonized as liberal skeptics, embracing modernism and the debauchery and chaos that would surely follow. More important, Bryan would come to represent the cause of religious fundamentalism and states' rights. And although this native of Illinois was not a southerner by birth or heritage, he would be cheered by the white southerners who flocked to Dayton, Tennessee, to witness what would be his final public revival. His place within the pantheon of white southern heroes and saints did, indeed, culminate at the Scopes Evolution Trial, but the construction of such a relationship was more than three decades in the making.

From campaigning for the hearts and minds of southern farmers as the Democratic candidate for president to protecting the Ku Klux Klan under the guise of religious freedom, Bryan's political stands were public performances to many white southerners of a man singing their tune. In a time when scientific advances and wide cultural shifts pulsated relentlessly throughout the country, Bryan "embraced the South . . . not because he had changed, but because to his mind it had not."[1] He was, at times, the only voice with a southern "accent," so to speak, on a national stage. All hope of acceptance and reconciliation with the rest of the country, all promise of redemption for the beleaguered South, or at least the perception of a beleaguered South, came to rest in this one man. Only by understanding all that Bryan—the man, the politician, the preacher, and the myth—meant to many white southerners, and by understanding his relationship to figures such as Darrow and Mencken and his fellow critics, can one fully comprehend the impact that ridicule of Bryan and his subsequent demise had on those who crowded the Rhea County courtroom and the town square during those fateful days in the summer of 1925.

BRYAN'S SOUTHERN ACCENT

For many southern whites, William Jennings Bryan's reputation was shaped initially by the divisive presidential election of 1896. Though many white southerners had begun to recover from the physical and economic devastation of the Civil War, anger toward the North, particularly the perception of northern industrial wealth, smoldered among Agrarians and small business owners. The development of modern banking seemed to benefit only the new culture of mass production that boomed in the urban centers of New England and the Midwest. Rural communities in the South and along the western frontier pleaded for relief, specifically supporting the coining of silver in an effort to put more money in circulation throughout the country, which many believed would deflate their debts. The southern economic practice of bartering and trade now proved antiquated, and many white southerners resented the feeling of being left behind with no real way to participate in the new market system. The Populist Party attempted to channel this frustration and to offer an alternative to this new American industrial culture, giving many white southerners their first competitive candidate for national office. At the Democratic Convention in June 1896, support for the Populist cause reached its pinnacle during a debate regarding the future monetary policy of the United States.[2] William Jennings Bryan, already a well-known orator for the cause, delivered his famous "Cross of Gold" speech, securing the presidential nomination for himself and giving the Democratic Party its first solid platform since Reconstruction:

> The farmer who goes forth in the morning and toils all day, who begins in spring and toils all summer, and who by the application of brain and muscle to the natural resources of the country creates wealth, is as much a business man as the man who goes upon the Board of Trade and bets upon the price of grain. . . . Ah, my friends, we say not one word against those who live upon the Atlantic Coast, but the hardy pioneers who have braved all the dangers of the wilderness, who have made the desert to blossom as the rose—the pioneers away out there, who rear their children near to Nature's heart, where they can mingle their voices with the voices of the birds—out there where they have erected schoolhouses for the education of their young, churches where they praise their creator, and cemeteries where rest the ashes of their dead—these people, we say, are as deserving of the consideration of our party as any people in this country. It is for these that we speak. We do not come as aggressors. Our war is not a war of conquest. We are fighting in the defense of our homes, our families, and posterity. We have petitioned, and our petitions have been scorned. We have entreated, and our entreaties have been disregarded. We have begged, and they have mocked when our calamity came. We beg no longer; we entreat no more; we petition no more. We defy them![3]

Though Bryan attempted to be diplomatic at first about the relationship between those he represented and the powers on the East Coast, the hostility and frustration of his fellow Populists was quickly unleashed to the receptive crowd.

South Carolina senator Ben "Pitchfork" Tillman insisted that "we of the South have burned our bridges behind us so far as the Eastern Democrats are concerned. . . . We denounce the Administration of President Cleveland as undemocratic and tyrannical."[4] Tillman's rhetoric excited the most radical factions of the Populist Party, particularly southerners. Though Tillman's more regional vision failed to win him the presidential nomination, Populism began to be associated with radical southern politics. While headlines in the former Confederacy proclaimed Bryan as champion of a "'new battle for freedom,'" northern and eastern periodicals, such as the *Springfield Republican* in Illinois, labeled Bryan's followers as fanatics. The Chicago press described the Democratic convention as "an aggregation of populism, socialism, and idiocy" that foretold of a crisis "greater than the Civil War."[5] The rhetoric of nearly all of the New York press proved even more extreme, declaring that the Populist impulse was merely "the hysterical declaration of a reckless and lawless crusade of sectional animosity and class antagonism. . . . No wild-eyed and rattle-brained horde of the red flag ever proclaimed a fiercer defiance of law, precedent, order, and government."[6] The panicked nature of the public criticism resulted not only from the seemingly radical initiatives promoted by the Populist Party—including the direct election of senators, the president, and the vice president, as well as government ownership and regulation of the railroads[7]—but, more important, from the fact that the mainstream Democratic Party had moved so far to the left by choosing Bryan as its candidate for the presidency. Mass public criticism of the first major political movement in the South since Reconstruction activated a model of negative identity construction that would reoccur throughout the twentieth century.

Southern farmers, organized by the Southern Farmer's Alliance, wanted Tom Watson, Georgia congressman and devoted supporter of the Populist cause, to serve as Bryan's vice presidential running mate. For many white southerners, Watson, as a native southerner, represented the return to power of the southern agrarian way of life, even more so than Bryan. Traditional Democrats, however, nominated their own vice presidential candidate, Arthur Sewall, in an effort to balance the ticket. Eventually, in many states, Bryan appeared as both the presidential nominee for the Populist Party, with Watson listed as his number two man, and as the Democratic nominee followed by Sewall. Despite appealing to both the old Democratic Party and this new radical Populist third party, Bryan still came up short. While Bryan had been traveling by train across the country promoting his vision of America and railing against the corruption and unfair policies of the Republican administrations, his opponent, William H. McKinley, initiated new policies of his own. His campaign manager, Mark Hanna, raised close to $3.5 million to support McKinley's efforts, a figure that eclipsed by tenfold Bryan's war chest and assured McKinley a victory.[8] The election, often cited as a critical realignment,[9] ushered in a new era of political big business, which officially drew a line between the yeoman of the American past and southern present and the industrialists of the American future.

Bryan's loss, along with the defeat of Tom Watson, proved to be a political setback to many white southerners. The success of northern business elites reopened wounds of the sectional crisis that were still part of the collective memory of the region. Bryan thus joined the legions of fallen Confederate heroes, a symbol of a South still suffering under the perception of an oppressive Yankee regime. The political identity of southern whiteness, once determined primarily by the war for slavery, now expanded to include an association with agrarianism and anti-industrialism in direct opposition to the developing northern and eastern culture of big business.

Populism had enjoyed some success, electing a handful of congressmen, and the party continued to support Bryan as its presidential hopeful in both 1900 and 1908. The prize, however, remained elusive, and each loss only intensified this sense of southern failure and inferiority. Bryan did not fade into obscurity after his unprecedented triple defeat; rather, he continued to participate in the political arena, throwing all of his support and influence behind the Georgia-born and Virginia-raised Woodrow Wilson, eventually serving as Wilson's secretary of state from 1913 to 1915. He resigned, to the disappointment of many of his supporters, over a disagreement with Wilson regarding the U.S. response to the sinking of the British ship the *Lusitania* by German U-boats in the early days of World War I. Bryan was committed to a noninterventionist policy, and he feared that Wilson's harsh response to Germany would facilitate American involvement. The president, however, did not want Bryan to step down, but in the end Bryan's rash decision to resign demonstrated what Wilson would characterize as Bryan's "moral blindness,"[10] a charge that would be repeated by critics not only of Bryan but of the entire white South during the Scopes Trial. Bryan's next public, symbolic stand occurred at the Democratic National Convention of 1924, where Bryan would define his position on racial violence and cement his status as a hero to many southern whites.

After leaving the State Department, Bryan moved south to Florida, where the climate benefited the health of his wife. He remained involved with the Presbyterian Church and continued to travel and give speeches on significant national issues such as prohibition and women's suffrage. Additionally, he continued to write for the weekly *Commoner*, a magazine he founded after losing his second presidential bid. Despite the fact that Bryan was never again elected to office after his brief stint in the U.S. House of Representatives from 1890 to 1894, his oratorical skills and his popular writings secured his position as an influential leader in the Democratic Party. Thus, it was no surprise when the party, desperate to appeal to its southern and western constituents, invited Bryan to chair the resolutions committee at the 1924 Democratic National Convention held in Madison Square Garden. Bryan knew he could be called upon to speak in favor of or in opposition to key elements of the proposed party platform. Perhaps, however, he did not know how controversial his opinion would be that summer and how it would isolate him from the Democratic center while further endearing him to his adopted South.

The Democratic platform in 1924 sought to reaffirm the founding freedoms found in the Bill of Rights, which many Americans felt were deteriorating. Freedom of speech, the press, assembly, and religion were all championed by the resolutions committee. Such proclamations resulted from an anxiety that government was encroaching on the choices of citizens regarding what to believe and how to educate their children—issues that would resurface only one year later during the battle over the teaching of evolution in the public school system and would become determinants in the expanding territory of southern whiteness. Many party loyalists, however, wanted to include one additional item in the platform: a denunciation of the Ku Klux Klan and its campaign against Jews, Catholics, and African Americans. The party, in a sense, was attempting to distance itself from the sectional stereotype of bigotry and provincialism associated with the South in the 1920s. But for many white southerners, support for individual freedoms translated into support for the increasingly controversial Jim Crow laws, which had maintained racial segregation since Reconstruction. Most southern Democrats would not have supported a plank that officially condemned the Klan, and Bryan was conscious of the potential repercussions for himself and for his brother, Charles, who was the vice presidential nominee for the party. His support for the condemnation of the reestablished and ever-more-popular white supremacist organization could alienate white southern voters. Charles Bryan and presidential nominee John W. Davis secured only 29 percent of the popular vote in 1924, but they carried Oklahoma and the eleven states of the former Confederacy.[11]

Addressing the convention delegates, Bryan offered the minority opinion. He portrayed the resolutions committee as irresponsible for stubbornly insisting on denouncing the Klan, as opposed to committing to a positive, general platform that would reflect the concerns of the party in its entirety. Attempting to sway the vote, Bryan instructed the electors: "You have listened to the applause when we have had read to you the best Democratic platform that was ever written, the noblest principles that have ever been written into a platform. We have there pleas pathetic for people in distress, but none of our principles, none of our pleas stirred the hearts of these men like the words, 'Ku Klux Klan.'"[12] Interrupted by boos and condemnation from the crowd, Bryan's speech was momentarily suspended by the convention chairman, who called for order and decorum. When Bryan resumed his address, he changed tactics, pitting the crowd against its collective opponent, the Republican Party, and advocating the rights and laws of the land. He insisted that "these three words [Ku Klux Klan], are not necessary. . . . My friends it requires more courage to fight the Republican Party than it does to fight the Ku Klux Klan. Here we have farmers driven into bankruptcy, a million driven from the farms in a single year. We find monopoly spreading. We find nearly every great line of industry in the control of gigantic combinations of capital. . . . Anybody can fight the Ku Klux Klan, but only the Democratic Party can stand between the common people and their oppressors in this land."[13] The crowd changed its response accordingly, offering applause at several points throughout the remainder of Bryan's speech. In the end, the proposed censure of the Klan was rejected by one single vote.

For southern Democrats, once again, Bryan's performance echoed the old defense of the southern way of life: a proclamation of individual rights and choices, a defense of law and order, and, above all, the accusation of northern hypocrisy. Many white southerners questioned why a predominantly southern organization, such as the Klan, had to be singled out for disgrace, when so many others, such as the American Protection Association, founded in Iowa, with national membership had never been subjected to formal party criticism. Bryan did not mention this perceived double standard specifically. Rather, he concluded the speech by contending that groups such as the Klan would eventually self-destruct, noting as well that Catholics and Jews were powerful enough to protect themselves. Influential rabbi Stephen S. Wise described Bryan's silence as a missed opportunity, maintaining that "the Klan could have been stifled at the convention had he been 'true to his mettle and not his metal.'"[14] Perhaps it was not Bryan's courage that was tested but rather his convictions. Bryan had, in fact, spotlighted northern hypocrisy in the past, just as he had consistently depicted the African American race as inferior. In fact, his de facto protection of the Klan that summer was the culmination of a career spent supporting southern injustice—support that slowly and steadily shaped Bryan's image and legacy as a white southern sympathizer. When Bryan died almost exactly one year later, the Ku Klux Klan would burn crosses throughout the South,[15] including one in Dayton, Tennessee, which was inscribed, "In memory of William Jennings Bryan, the greatest klansman of our time."[16]

THE GREAT COMMONER'S RECORD ON RACE

Bryan's speech at the 1924 convention was not his first stand on race relations. In fact, his attitude toward what he identified as "the Negro Question" in America can be traced back to the publication of an editorial by the same name that appeared in a 1901 volume of the *Commoner*. Responding to President Theodore Roosevelt's dinner invitation to Booker T. Washington, Bryan insisted that the presence of an African American at a White House banquet would only "give depth and acrimony to a race feeling already strained to the uttermost."[17] Always the diplomat, Bryan weighed and measured his words carefully; but, regardless of his care, this significant commentary on regional and national race relations exposes a young Bryan as a southern apologist and northern critic, a trait that did not go unnoticed below the Mason-Dixon Line. Throughout the opinion piece, Bryan seems to support constitutional rights and social opportunities for African Americans, at least theoretically.

In an attempt to bolster his support for an imperialist foreign policy (he passionately campaigned for American intervention in Puerto Rico and the West Indies), Bryan compared the treatment of blacks in the South to the treatment of "the brown man." The South, the Great Commoner proclaimed, had never attempted "to take from the negro the guarantees enumerated in our constitution and the bill of rights," whereas the people of the Philippines and the "orient" "suffer the common lot of those who live under arbitrary power."[18] Indeed, Bryan argued, educational prospects for African Americans had increased dramatically since Reconstruction—a fact that Bryan endorsed and credited to southern whites. Northern Republicans were to blame for the heightened racial anxiety that characterized the Old Confederacy, Bryan observed; Republicans "have been inciting the Negro to oppose everything advocated by Southern whites."[19] This prominent orator with a national audience had described in print the hypocrisy of the Radical Republicans of the war years and their descendants. Those who had advocated abolitionism, those who had militarized the defeated South, had, indeed, lost interest in the well-being of the very population they had fought to free, suggested Bryan. Moreover, many northerners held southern whites to standards of racial equality that they themselves could not meet. Bryan's generalizations were opinions, at best. But for his supporters, an increasing number of whom were white southern Protestants, Bryan's finger-pointing and defensive stance against such public criticism seemed heaven sent.

The existence of a racial double standard between the two regions proved to be a powerful idea in the South even before secession, and it remained a prevailing belief well into the twentieth century. When Bryan, as a non-native southerner, echoed this potent sentiment to the nation at large, he gave great credibility to the defensive position held by many white southerners. In 1922, the New York Times commissioned Bryan to write a new assessment of the "Negro problem" in America, hoping to see if Bryan's views had changed since his bold statement in the Commoner from nearly two decades earlier, and to see if Bryan's ten years spent living in the South had, in fact, entrenched his regional sympathies. Bryan agreed and even opted to test his article on a live crowd gathered at a meeting of the New York Southern Society.[20] He offered an expanded commentary on the hypocrisy of not only northern Republicans but of northern whites in general, arguing that the fact that northerners did not elect African Americans to represent them in Congress "is conclusive proof either that the blacks are inferior or that race prejudice keeps them in the background."[21] He further observed that northerners who move south adopt traditional white southern racial attitudes quickly, and he defended the need for segregation.[22] But he saved his highest praise for suffrage restrictions—poll taxes, literacy tests, and the all-white primary—which proved to be one of the most controversial and heated issues of the 1920s. Bryan's stance on suffrage restraints piggybacked on his denunciation of the northern double standard and proved to be critical to his white southern followers.

Bryan's article in the *New York Times* accused Republicans not only of manipulating racial tensions for political advantage but also of being the "prime cause of race antagonism,"[23] in and of itself. "The Republicans of the North," he surmised, "are deceiving the blacks for political purposes when they pretend a greater affection for them than is found in the South."[24] For many white southerners, Bryan's statement captured a regional frustration that had gone unexpressed in the national press. He further countered the northern argument against the voting restrictions passed in the South after the Fifteenth Amendment by vowing that such restrictions were essential rather than cruel or racist. In a community where African American voters would outnumber white voters, white leaders were obligated, according to Bryan, to do what was necessary to maintain white supremacy. He conceded that "where the percentage of blacks is small . . . there will be no restriction of franchise based upon color; neither will there be segregation in school or upon the railroad trains." But there is no state, Bryan proclaimed, north or south, "in which whites would permit black supremacy."[25] Suffrage restrictions, he further claimed, did not breach the Constitution, because all men were guaranteed the right to self-protection; accordingly, argued Bryan, "where two races are forced to live together, the more advanced race, 'will always control as a matter of self-preservation not only for the benefit of the advanced race, but for the benefit of the backward race also.'"[26] The rallying call of self-preservation as justification for Jim Crow laws and the denial of voting rights to African Americans proved particularly effective in courting white southern support, because it echoed the familiar language of secession, self-defense, and self-determination that had permeated white southern political rhetoric for the prior half century. And the tocsin of self-preservation would soon summon white southerners on issues beyond race, with Bryan, once again, leading the charge.

Bryan publically discussed the relationship between what he considered the "greatest of all the races—the Caucasian race"[27] and the African American race, which he insisted benefited from the association that it had with white people. Bryan looked toward the complex and short-lived era of Reconstruction as evidence for his racial cosmology. The memory of what Bryan and many southern whites considered overzealous black legislatures that had committed "legislative robbery"[28]—a term used by Bryan—demonstrated the ultimate necessity of white supremacy. Writing in the third volume of the *Commoner*, Bryan declared that "unless all arguments in favor of civilization are without foundation, the superior race, if dominant, would be more considerate toward the inferior race than the inferior race would, if dominant, be toward the superior race. . . . The white people of the South, if in control, would be more apt to deal justly with the blacks than the blacks would be, if in control, to deal justly with the whites."[29] He further insisted that "slavery among the whites was an improvement over independence in Africa." Moreover, Bryan reasoned, "the very progress that the blacks have made, when—and only when—brought into contact with the whites ought to be a sufficient argument in support of white supremacy—it ought to be sufficient to convince even the blacks themselves."[30] The bold statement, both in the *New York Times* and at the Southern Society dinner, appeared to mixed reviews. While countless southern newspapers and journals chose to republish the article for their readers, African American readers made their opinion of Bryan known through another venue.

Regardless of Bryan's emblematic stands for the common people, African Americans, particularly those suffering under the daily oppression of the Jim Crow system, were not swayed by the theoretically egalitarian and paternalistic rhetoric. Only months after Bryan's article hit newsstands, black Presbyterians voiced their disapproval. Bryan did attempt to run for one last national office, that of the moderator of the National Presbyterian General Assembly, where he could help shape the social and moral fabric of the Protestant faith at one of its greatest moments of controversy. In addition to questions of racial justice, denominations throughout the country were grappling with the growing conflicts between modernism and the traditional church. Scientific advancements demanded new assessments of bedrock convictions, such as the creation of man and the virgin birth. Bryan, unlike the progressive vision of his past, came down on the side of conservatism, and he intended, if elected, to lead the Presbyterian faith as a true believer in the established theology. African American delegates to the convention, however, were not likely to forget Bryan's recent manifesto on race relations. His sympathy for the South and his vision of the great white civilization proved too much for black Protestants to overlook.

Bryan, himself, after losing an extremely close vote, undertook his own investigation of the election, concluding that it was, indeed, the African American vote that had tipped the balance of power, and not in his favor. "Somewhat bitterly," Bryan pronounced "that the 'black vote,' ought to be congratulated and shown 'how it saved the Presbyterian Church from having a conservative Moderator.'"[31] For Bryan, this loss, in particular, heightened the anxiety experienced by many of his followers in the 1920s—a fear of change that "seemed so overpowering, so pervasive, so threatening to familiar values."[32] Moreover, the victor of the election, Charles P. Wishart, served as the president of Wooster College in Ohio, a school that employed an evolutionary biologist, Horace Mateer. The choice humiliated Bryan—especially after Wishart declined to appoint Bryan as vice moderator, as was traditional—and signaled a regional and philosophical split in the Presbyterian community.[33] Whether battling the shifting racial dynamics of the day or fighting to maintain the fundamental tenets of one's faith, many white southerners perceived themselves as an "endangered culture in recoil,"[34] and Bryan, regardless of his intentions, was their relentless and articulate captain.

THE WHITE KNIGHT APPEARS

In 1925, when word spread that William Jennings Bryan would arrive by train in Dayton, Tennessee, a great sense of relief spread among his southern admirers. Bryan was a known quantity, a man of their people, who represented the intersection of populist democracy and religion, and he was willing to make one last stand. Many white southern Christians were well aware of Bryan's views on evolution from at least a decade before the Scopes Trial, for he had traveled throughout the region proclaiming the dangers of Darwinism and encouraging state assemblies to ban the teaching of evolution in public schools. "I am now engaged in the biggest reform of my life," decreed Bryan. "I am trying to save the Christian Church from those who are trying to destroy her faith!"[35] As the conflict gained national attention, Bryan's hostility toward men of science infiltrated his oratory, a hostility, along with the public criticism that accompanied it, that would become yet another determinant of southern whiteness in the aftermath of the Scopes Trial. Speaking to the Georgia General Assembly in July 1923, Bryan insisted that "men who believe in evolution should go to the zoo on Sundays to decide how far they have come, while Christians should attend church to find out how much farther they must go to attain eternal life."[36] His success at influencing southern lawmakers regarding the perils of evolutionary theory elicited numerous invitations to address forums in other southern states, including Kentucky, West Virginia, and Florida.

In Florida, Bryan actually succeeded in passing a resolution that he person-ally authored, wherein he labeled the teaching of Darwinism as "subversive" and as heretical as teaching atheism.[37] Despite the fact that only a handful of states followed Florida's lead, the "Commoner entered the fray with the en-thusiasm of the medieval crusader attempting to wrest the Holy Land from the unholy hands of the infidel Turk."[38] In this case, the "infidel Turk" remained, for many white southerners, the modern North. Bryan's anti-evolution campaign attracted widespread devotees, and he corresponded with key leaders—most notably William Bell Riley, founder of the World's Christian Fundamentals As-sociation, and John Roach Stanton—on a regular basis, offering encourage-ment and providing talking points to use against detractors. Writing to a Ken-tucky advocate, Bryan vowed that "the movement will sweep the country, and we will drive Darwinism from our schools. . . . We have all the Elijahs on our side. Strength to your arms."[39] Just as Bryan had publicly documented his views on race relations, so too did he offer to a national audience a critique of Dar-winism. His two key speeches, "The Menace of Darwinism" and "The Bible and Its Enemies," attacked evolution at its disciplinary roots, labeling it as merely a theory and not a tested scientific conclusion. Though all Americans, including scientists, were free to subscribe to Darwin's theories, he argued that children should not be taught such hypotheses in school because such an endorsement "compelled (rather than convinced) students to accept the doctrine."[40] Both lec-tures were transcribed and disseminated through the burgeoning fundamen-talist organizations, reaching individual Americans of diverse national church denominations, many of which had split as a region from the northern halves of their denominations over just this issue.

Although interest and acceptance of Bryan's anti-evolution message crossed regional divides, white southern audiences embraced his ideas with full faith and, at times, ferocious zeal. The war against Darwinism represented a larger struggle, one cut into an escalating fear of modernism, an anxiety toward change, an anger toward the powerful North, and a growing sense of inferi-ority, which had developed slowly and systematically over time. Scholars such as Kenneth K. Bailey, Willard Gatewood, and Edward Larson have pointed to various explanations regarding the timing of the evolution controversy. Many persuasively argue that World War I gave rise to a new skepticism of science and rationalism, all of which Americans now associated with German power. The materialism that accompanied an adoption of modernism threatened the foundation of Christianity, which, in turn, had opened the door to worldwide hostilities. American culture and identity in general experienced a sense of de-stabilization after participating in the gruesome and bloody conflict. And the position of religious Americans—particularly white southern Protestants—was perceived to be particularly endangered. The advent of biblical exegesis, in the United States and Europe, along with the condemnation of many churches for their support of the war, challenged the pillars of religious belief.[41] Additional sweeping changes threatened to deflate the influence of Victorian morality, including "the popularity of Sunday sports and of automobiling; disgust with the support by some ministers of the Ku Klux Klan; the rising importance of science to the woman in the home as well as to the man at the factory; the spread of scientific information to even the lowest intellectual levels; and the fantastic vogue of the new field of psychology, which according to Freud, Adler, Jung, and Watson, could furnish a scientific explanation for the motivations and actions of men and also cure their psychiatric illnesses and psychoses."[42] Not only was the creation narrative being put to the test, but also human nature, motivation, and behavior—the very core of religious instruction—were now being undermined by science, creating a sense of cultural chaos.

For many white southerners, this sense of destabilization collided with the budding defense of Agrarianism and a well-established distrust of northern industry to produce a collective burden, a desire to protect a racial, religious, economic, and cultural order that seemed destined to self-destruct. Southern journalists such as Thomas Ivey, editor of the *Nashville Christian Advocate*, purveyed the fear of the teaching of evolution, vowing that "the materialistic education of Germany, stripped of Christian ethics and resting on the ethics of the jungle . . . was responsible for the war and its horrible methods."[43] George A. Lofton, a Baptist preacher from Nashville, warned his followers at the Tennessee Baptist Convention that "higher criticism, Evolution, and other forms of infidelity" were infiltrating northern schools and would soon threaten southern students as well. Hence, what began as a critique of an aggressive European power now translated into yet another regional division. Evangelicals in the South thus opted to safeguard and promote a divergent counterculture, removed from the growing modernism. And since part of the southern evangelical mission included "working to extend their beliefs and morals to the larger southern society," argues historian Charles A. Israel, "denominational leaders wanted to preserve the entire South as distinct from the rest of the nation."[44] However, just as the old regional animosity was not the only reason that white southerners flocked to Bryan, so too would it not be the only reason southerners would enlist in the anti-evolution campaign.

Although journalist H. L. Mencken is credited with coining the infamous title "The Monkey Trial," the concept of man descending from the monkey had already come to represent a symbolic generalization of Darwin's complex model.

According to Kary Doyle Smout, Darwin's suggestion about monkeys "threatened not only the difference between humans and animals, but the much more tenuous difference between blacks and whites."[45] In the late nineteenth century, many white scientists espoused Darwin's theory of natural selection as justification for the superiority of the Caucasian race.[46] Consequently, the argument trickled down to lay audiences, and, due to the lack of formal education in many parts of the rural South, a simplistic and somewhat mystic explanation of evolution proliferated. According to southern journalist W. J. Cash, "One of the most stressed notions which went around was that evolution made a Negro as good as a white man."[47] The conflation of the two issues—white supremacy and evolutionary theory—inevitably intensified the debate. According to Jeffrey Moran, African American secular leaders were well aware of the racial undertones of the anti-evolution campaign. "If black and white had a common ancestry, as evolutionary theory suggested," noted Moran, "then the South's elaborate racial barriers might seem arbitrary rather than God-given. Rather than accept that conclusion, black commentators claimed, southern whites attacked evolution."[48] In southern states such as North Carolina, fundamentalists directed their most aggressive and relentless assaults toward progressive sociologists and southern dissenters who were both proponents of Darwinian teachings and racial equality.[49] Bryan himself harped on this particular element of evolutionary theory in his public addresses, perhaps in an effort to simplify the complex concept for a lay audience, or perhaps to exploit the mounting anxiety that resulted from the onset of challenges to segregation, voting restrictions, and lynching laws.

Just as Bryan's speeches and editorials clearly defined his position—and clearly identified him as a southern apologist—his antagonists were equally conspicuous. For Bryan, "On one side were the voices of the people and the truths of the heart; on the other side were the intellectuals, a small arrogant elite given over to false science and mechanical rationalism."[50] Bryan's cultural and intangible foe was a force growing perhaps as rapidly as evangelical Christianity. The perception of the "bigotry and parochialism of rural America in the Twenties had its counterpart in an attitude which might be termed urban fundamentalism,"[51] a term that the Commoner himself helped to define throughout the decade of controversy.

In the late months of 1921, national newspapers began carrying Bryan's Weekly Bible Talks, as they were called, allowing him to reach close to 15 million national and worldwide readers consistently. Without fail, Bryan used his new and powerful soapbox to berate modernists and advocates of evolution, a rhetorical strategy that was uncharacteristic of his political behavior. When it came to affairs of state, Bryan almost always refrained from personal attacks;

but in his later career, he defended his religious beliefs with unbridled emotion. He was "bitter and caustic, cutting and stinging in his taunting, and he used an extremely belligerent tone which, even if it stemmed from a consciousness of righteousness, was certain to provoke controversy and was resented by Modernists as 'bullying.'"[52] His initial column, entitled "A Very Present Help in Trouble," condemned what Bryan labeled the "cultured crowd," who judged religion and faith as crutches for the "superstitious and ignorant."[53] Bryan's numerous biographers have all grappled with explaining this shift from the diplomatic and poised politician to the fire-and-brimstone preacher. Paxton Hibben has suggested that an aging Bryan feared death and so, like many of the elderly faithful, grew progressively more dogmatic. Still others find an unfailing and constant faith to be present throughout Bryan's career, noting that his interest in moral agendas merely resulted from their timeliness.[54]

Regardless of why Bryan embraced anti-evolutionism with such vigor and venom, such passion and rancor, his name quickly became synonymous with the cause. Eminent intellectuals soon lined up against him; men such as John Dewey, for example, believed that Bryan's campaign tested the limits of democratic government. Dewey was concerned that the southern churches to which Bryan was appealing and from whom he received almost universal support prohibited free thinking, a founding principle of American culture, and he expressed equal concern that such a movement could easily sway the masses, even spill outside the boundaries of the South.[55] However, according to Bryan's biographer, Paolo E. Coletta, Bryan "was listened to only in the villages and small towns not far removed from the frontier days which still feared anything that threatened the security and order of the civilization they had achieved."[56] And they did, indeed, listen. As Bryan continued to preach and to circulate his weekly editorials, his stature grew, reaching a point where he was venerated "as both the interpreter and prophet of those who could not articulate their political and religious aspirations."[57] The rural appeal of Bryan's message did not limit its impact; in fact, its regional nature created a clearly defined enemy, which, in turn, allowed Bryan and his colleagues to personify the conflict—to give the enemy a name and a face. With criticism from scientists and intellectuals abounding, countless significant figures were ripe with possibility to assume that role. But one such influential modernist actually extended a written invitation.

ENTER DARROW

On Independence Day 1923, famed attorney Clarence Darrow submitted a list of fifty-five questions, which appeared on the front page of the *Chicago Tribune* (and were printed in their entirety in numerous other major periodicals). All of them were related to the fundamentalist position and, specifically, to the literalist interpretation of the Bible. He requested that the Great Commoner, Bryan, respond, in an effort to clarify the extent of the evangelical and anti-evolutionist position. But Darrow did not solely seek information; the stunt, which Bryan ignored, was intended to highlight the absurdities of a literal acceptance of the Bible. Darrow posed such gems as "Did God curse the serpent for tempting Eve and decree that thereafter he should go on his belly?" and "How did he travel before that time?" He specifically harped on the story of Noah and the flood, asking, "As there were no ships in those days, except the ark, how did Noah gather them [all species] from all the continents and lands of the earth?" and "How could many species that are found nowhere but in Australia or other far off places get there and why did they not stop on the way?" Darrow hinted at the concept of biblical interpretation when he posed one of his last series of questions: "Did Christ drive devils out of two sick men and did the devils request that they should be driven into a large herd of swine and were the devils driven into the swine and did the swine run off a high bank, and were they drowned in the sea? Was this literally true, or does it simply show the attitude of the age toward the cause of sickness and affliction?"[58] Darrow was actually following Bryan's initial lead. Only months earlier, Bryan had submitted his own interrogatory to the president of the University of Wisconsin, Edward Birge, who had ridiculed a lecture given by Bryan as being "more likely to make atheists than believers out of students, essentially concluding that Bryan was crazy."[59] The Great Commoner's queries were intended to push the liberal administrator to grapple with Darwin's theory and its potential social application, and they were soon picked up by the *Chicago Tribune*, where Darrow read them and formulated his own list of questions. Bryan refused even to read Darrow's questions, proclaiming that "I decline to turn aside to enter into controversy with those who reject the Bible as Mr. Darrow does."[60] Despite the fact that Bryan did not respond to Darrow's test, the questions would form the basis of Darrow's cross-examination of Bryan at the Scopes Trial, and the publication served a secondary purpose as well. Darrow's printed confrontations singled him out as the South's symbolic devil to Bryan's salvation.

Clarence Darrow, just like Bryan, wielded a national reputation long before his questionnaire appeared in the Chicago paper, and long before his notorious performance at the Scopes Trial. Darrow was an antagonist by nature, and he claimed that his entire legal career had been spent "fighting the public opinion of the people in the community where I was trying the case."[61] Darrow's legendary status as a defense attorney resulted from his leadership in the American

Civil Liberties Union (ACLU), as well as his success in many high profile cases. He spent his early career working for the railway corporations in Chicago but soon found his rhetorical talent leading him into the political arena. He was nominated for Congress by the Democratic Party in 1896, and he campaigned relentlessly (and with hindsight, somewhat ironically) for the party's presidential hopeful, William Jennings Bryan. Darrow, like Bryan, fell short of victory, in his case by a mere 100 votes.[62] He channeled his liberal spirit into a professional position that would lead him to worldwide distinction—as defense attorney for organized labor. In addition to representing the head of the American Railway Union, Eugene Debs, after the Pullman Strike of 1894, Darrow also defended Bill Haywood, the leader of the Industrial Workers of the World as well as the American Miners Union, who was eventually acquitted for the 1905 murder of Frank Steunenberg, the governor of Idaho.

The clear picture to those who followed the history of such trials was that Darrow was the fierce protector and guardian of the erupting labor movement and its attack on the factory hierarchy, all during a time "when labor was more militant and idealistic and employers more hardened and desperate than ever before."[63] With rare exception, such militant labor unions were nonexistent in the South and were perceived as a negative and perilous result of modernism, materialism, and industrialization. Darrow as an individual would become associated with this burgeoning national culture, which, when pitted against Bryan, made Darrow an enemy of many white southerners. A Baltimore publication, The Manufacturer's Record, actually stoked the sectional fires of the 1920s by describing "Darrow as a close approach to Abraham Lincoln," a comparison intended to reignite the hostilities of the past and to encourage a rejection of all things north of the Mason-Dixon Line.[64] In addition to the distrust of Darrow that resulted from his friendship with labor, his progressive outspoken opposition to capital punishment—a humanitarian streak inherited from his abolitionist father and his liberal, feminist mother—would have also made him disliked in many parts of the white South where vigilantism, or at least home rule, was deemed critical to maintaining racial supremacy.

Perhaps Darrow was never more at odds with white southern Protestant culture than when he defended Nathan Leopold and Richard Loeb, two affluent Jewish teenagers accused of murdering a fellow Chicago classmate. The gruesome crime—the victim was stabbed with a chisel, disfigured with acid, and stuffed in a drainage grate—sparked considerable public outrage. A pair of incriminating eyeglasses dropped at the crime scene would lead to the boys' arrest. Darrow convinced both of his clients to plead guilty, leaving sentencing to a judge rather than a jury, which would inevitably have been drawn from the hostile community. Just as the Scopes Trial, which would follow the next year, would tap into a larger collective anxiety, so too had the prosecution of Leopold and Loeb revealed a far-reaching cultural unease. Both boys were suspected homosexuals and both were characterized as exceptionally intelligent and highly educated. Leopold, nineteen at the time of the murder, had already completed his college degree and was enrolled at the University of Chicago Law School. Loeb, who was one year younger than Leopold, was already enrolled in graduate school at the University of Michigan. And both were obsessed with committing the perfect crime and also the teachings of German philosopher Friedrich Nietzsche, specifically with his concept of the superman.[65]

Rejecting traditional Old Testament constructs of good and evil, Nietzsche envisioned an iconoclastic superman who could break free of the suffocating and oppressive dictates of the church. Able to see beyond the conceptual structures of daily life, the superman tries to rid himself of society's moral and ethical strictures.[66] The complete deconstruction of biblical cosmology posed by Nietzsche easily confused the young teens and was equally distorted by lay audiences. Thus, Nietzsche became a scapegoat of sorts for those outraged by the heinous actions of Leopold and Loeb, and his name and philosophy became emblematic—synonymous with modernism and German rationalism—of the looming threat to American values. Willard Smith has suggested that Bryan's commitment to the anti-evolution crusade deepened when "his attention was called to the connection between German Nietzsche's philosophy of might makes right and Darwin's idea of survival of the fittest."[67] This particular concept posited by Nietzsche argued that with achieving the power of the superman came the ability to shape the moral code of the weak—a general idea that if distorted could be used to condone the actions of Nazi Germany. In this sense, just as Bryan had feared, Nietzsche "carried the Darwinian theory to its logical conclusion."[68] Bryan would even revisit the influence of Nietzsche (he pronounced the name as "Nitchy")[69] at the Scopes Trial, insisting that schools should be responsible for the theories that are presented to their entrusted pupils: "Mr. Darrow thinks the universities are in duty bound to feed out this poisonous stuff to their students, and when the students become stupefied by it and commit murder, neither they nor the universities are to blame. A criminal is not relieved from responsibility merely because he found Nietzsche's philosophy in a library which ought not to contain it. . . . This is a damnable philosophy, and yet it is the flower that blooms on the stalk of evolution."[70] In Dayton, Bryan also proclaimed that the Leopold and Loeb murder was the inescapable and predictable product of the teaching of evolution—a point that elicited passionate objections from Darrow. On the other hand, Darrow had actually used the concept of materialistic determinism—the idea that the future of human behavior is predictable, based on the interaction of outside influences, including the environment, genetics, and nature—to argue that Leopold and Loeb were victims of circumstance rather than premeditated murderers, thus swaying the judge to give them life sentences as opposed to the death penalty. His twelve-hour summation proved successful, and both boys were spared execution, though Loeb was later murdered by a fellow inmate. Although the determinism of which Darrow spoke was not directly related to Darwin's findings, both Darrow and Darwin, in the eyes of fundamentalists such as Bryan, robbed man of his divine connection to his creator and his spiritual quest throughout his earthly life.

Darrow's political opinions and defensive legal tactics aside, evangelical Christians still had logical reason to demonize the renowned attorney. According to historian Edward Larson, "In the courtroom, on the lecture circuit, in public debates, and through dozens of popular books and articles, Darrow spent a lifetime ridiculing traditional Christian beliefs. He called himself an agnostic, but he sounded like an atheist."[71] The kind of religion that angered Darrow had characteristically developed in the backwoods and frontiers of America. The rural landscape, with its lack of structured denominations, encouraged new sects "set up by the personal enterprise of one individual[,] and the teachings that emanated from them were completely at the whim of their founders." Notwithstanding the spirit of freedom of belief, these idiosyncratic flocks often promoted such radical and local rituals as speaking in tongues, snake handling, and the "orgiastic touching of members of the congregation."[72] Darrow's biographer Kevin Tierney claimed that although scientific discoveries and worldly knowledge proliferated at the turn of the century, rural preachers "were incapable of responding intellectually, and so resorted to dogmatic assertion and, when that failed, to a blatant appeal to the emotions through hysterical sermons."[73] These worshippers constituted Bryan's greatest support and, likewise, attracted Darrow's most biting denigration. Moreover, the liberal lawyer, reared in the school of abolitionist doctrine himself, recognized the power of religion to consecrate and permit racism. And southern religion was, of course, the most grotesque offender.

To Darrow, Bryan embodied all the self-righteousness, anti-intellectualism, and hypocrisy that plagued the American soul and kept humanity from evolving. Darrow sensed that "The Prince of Peace" (Bryan)[74] and his disciples felt desperate to convince the jury in Dayton and the worldwide jury at large that the teaching of evolution would demolish Christian faith and the civilization that it upheld. Upon observing Bryan at the trial, Darrow proclaimed that the Great Commoner was "frightened out of his wits[;] after all, the illusions of his life might be only dreams."[75] And to Bryan and his colleagues at the World's Christian Fundamentals Association and his followers throughout the South, Darrow came to embody all that threatened an increasingly unsustainable way of life. He represented, in their minds, an Antichrist of sorts, against which they defined their holy convictions. He was a northern, educated, liberal atheist, who defended murderers and renounced Christianity and ridiculed its adherents. Tierney even notes that "the assumptions of superiority that Darrow and his co-counsel Arthur Garfield Hays brought to Dayton displayed a Northern arrogance worse even than that of the postbellum carpetbaggers,"[76] which is exactly the impression that he gave to those present that summer for the trial. This was a battle between rural and urban America, between the farmers and the suits, between the pious and the academics, between the North and the South. The old conflict thus merged with its contemporary manifestation, and both were made flesh in the figures of two illustrious narrators who arrived in Dayton laden with the weight of their respective symbolisms.

AND THEN THERE WAS MENCKEN

Deciphering exactly what Bryan and Darrow represented to southern whites is necessary in order to comprehend fully the impact of the public criticism that engulfed the small Protestant town and resulted in a regional, cultural inferiority complex. However, just as Bryan and Darrow carried their cultural baggage with them to eastern Tennessee, so too did one journalist—H. L. Mencken—who came to represent the pantheon of international, national, and internal critics of the South. His ridicule of the evangelical, fundamentalist wing of the American Protestant community reached a fever pitch in Dayton at the Scopes Trial, which was actually his first trip to the rural South. Despite his lack of firsthand experience with what he called "Holy Rollers," Mencken published countless articles disparaging their belief system and culture as antiquated and moronic. His writings were abundant and well known, and his view of southern Christianity reached audiences both at home and abroad. As a native of Baltimore, Mencken's "southernness" was fringe at best, although his racial views reflected a social Darwinist perspective, with Anglo-Saxons appearing, at least in his early writings, as the most enlightened and evolved populace. Notwithstanding his archaic racial opinions, Mencken was considered to be and sometimes was called the American Nietzsche—an iconoclast decisively dismantling Victorian values, whether in the political, literary, or spiritual arenas.

Mencken's association with Nietzsche consisted of more than a nickname or a general philosophic similarity. Rather, the "Sage of Baltimore" habitually cited the German thinker as one of his greatest influences. After publishing his first book on the plays of George Bernard Shaw, Mencken edited a comprehensive volume of Nietzsche's philosophy, which he printed in 1907 when the young writer was only twenty-seven years old.[77] He undoubtedly helped popularize the "heretic," as Bryan would have called him, in the United States, a contribution that did not go unnoticed by the religious leaders of the anti-evolution crusade. But perhaps even more than Mencken's association with the Nietzschean perspective, his unrelenting mockery of Protestantism incurred the wrath of Bryan and his brethren. Mencken, because of his libertarian support of free will and democracy, actually feared the increasing power and politicization of fundamentalism, particularly the rural southern brand. For them, Mencken reserved his most vitriolic prose, as demonstrated by biographer Charles Fecher:

> "No more shocking nonsense," he declared, "has been put into words by theoretically civilized men." Its practitioners were "backwoods Wesleys," "sorry bounders of God," "sordid," "swinish," "ignoramuses." They received their knowledge, he [Mencken] charged, from "a faculty of half-idiot pedagogues" in one-building "seminaries" out on some bare pasture lot in that region which he delighted to call the "Bible Belt"—the South and the Midwest—and then went forth to preach not God or love but fear and hatred of every idea that they themselves were incapable of understanding. . . . It was "the implacable enemy of all rational pedagogy and free speech." "The evangelical sects plunge into an abyss of malignant imbecility, and declare a holy war upon every decency that civilized men cherish."[78]

Mencken never shied away from merging what he called his prejudices. Only nine months before the Scopes Trial, he offered an editorial in his successful and popular magazine, the *American Mercury*, that accused both Methodists and Baptists of membership in the Ku Klux Klan. The only way to truly grasp Mencken's disgust and rage toward fundamentalism is to experience it firsthand:

> This connection, when it was first denounced, was violently denied by the Baptists and Methodists ecclesiastics, but now everyone knows that it was real and is real. . . . They are responsible directly and certainly, for all the turmoils and black hatreds that now rage in the bleak regions between the State roads—they are to blame for every witches' pot that now brews in the backwoods of the Union. They have sowed enmities that will last for years. . . . They have opposed every honest effort to compose the natural differences between man and man, and they have opposed every attempt to meet ignorance and prejudice with enlightenment. Alike in the name of

God, they have advocated murder and they have murdered sense. Where they flourish no intelligent and well-disposed man is safe, and no sound and useful idea is safe. They have preached not only the bitter, savage morality of the Old Testament; they have also preached its childish contempt of obvious facts. Hordes of poor creatures have followed those appalling rogues and vagabonds of cloth down their Gadarene hill; the result, in immense areas, is the conversion of Christianity into a machine for making civilized living impossible. It is wholly corrupt, rotten and abominable. It deserves no more respect than a pile of garbage.[79]

He later expanded the piece and reprinted it in the sixth volume of his series of essays, sarcastically entitled *Prejudices*. Mencken's shared disdain for racism and religion made the white South a perfect target for his prose. His conflation of these two "prejudices," as he called them, contributed to the inextricable nature of these two key determinants of twentieth-century southern whiteness and, eventually, modern political conservatism.

■ Just as those who found themselves the butt of Mencken's witty exposé became stereotypes to the nation at large, so too did those who read him religiously. Whether pouring over his work in the *Baltimore Sun* or subscribing to the "arsenic green" volumes of the *American Mercury*, Mencken's readers became the "hallmark of liberal intelligence" in the decade of the great evolution controversy. Where William Jennings Bryan had stood immovable as "a fire-breathing traditionalist," Mencken proved the exact inverse, a "combination of anti-utopian libertarianism and religious skepticism."[80] Where Clarence Darrow had been the embodiment of elitist, industrialist, urban atheism, H. L. Mencken was the American messenger of modernism. And each of these men signified all that was elemental to the culture wars of their time heaped upon a sectional war of the not-so-distant past. This triptych of the 1920s, these incarnations of faith, science, and knowledge, collided—conspired to collide, no less—in Rhea County, Tennessee, in July 1925 to settle once and for all who was right. Their individual identities became the representation of a larger regional drama played out on a national and international stage. For Bryan, it would end in death, but for their audience of white southerners—both those sweating in the Dayton courthouse and those reading and listening at home—respect and acceptance were on the line, as fundamentalism and the white southern way of life waited for judgment day.

CHAPTER 2

TENNESSEE VS. CIVILIZATION

SCOPES TAKES ON

A SOUTHERN ACCENT

The Scopes trial had been an attack on the old South, singling out for scorn its narrow bigotry, although scarcely raising the issue of race, which had been the most bitter source of disagreement between North and South.
—Kevin Tierney, *Darrow: A Biography*

The wrath was so condescending and purposeful that it seemed to have the character of a deliberate attack. It reopened the breach between North and South that everybody had thought long closed, and was so uncompromising that it seemed to confront the valley with the old demand for "unconditional surrender" in a new form.
—Donald Davidson, *The Tennessee: Volume II: The New River: Civil War to TVA*

As the Scopes trial made clear, the Mason-Dixon Line was still very much a real border between the North and the South. The differing demographics of the sections only intensified their mutual disdain, for the South was far more rural, and the North was following the cultural lead of its dynamic cities. At the Scopes trial, the simmering hostility between North and South, city and country, came to a rolling boil.
—Jeffrey Moran, *The Scopes Trial: A Brief History with Documents*

Most scholarly assessments of the Scopes Trial focus primarily on the debate between religion and science, pinpointing this historical moment as the final triumph of modernism. Although the significance of southern evangelical Christianity remains critical in every account, the larger sectional conflict between the North and the South has received limited consideration. The somewhat insatiable and unprecedented media attention (nearly 165,000 words were filed per day on average and approximately 2 million words were transmitted by telegraph)[1] used regionalism to frame the anti-evolution movement in general and the events in Dayton, Tennessee, specifically. The scrutiny triggered a sense of inferiority among white southerners, reviving the sectional conflict and catalyzing a grand battle between science and religion. Allusions to academic freedom, the cause of majoritarianism, and states' rights are also ever present in the actual trial transcripts and in the campaign that preceded it. Thus, the trial and the public criticism that it generated added to the original construction of southern whiteness a new determinant of resistance to an expanding list of what was perceived as northern values.

From the core speeches of the anti-evolution movement, to the jury selection and opening legal formalities, to the local instigators of the case, the North-South divide and the compounded divisions encapsulated within that historical conflict clearly festered just below the surface. And the media was relentless. Though the *New York Times* confined its disparagement to regional stereotypes, characterizing the people of Dayton as "remote mountaineers" who "fear science,"[2] it also carried a special report from London that proclaimed that "Europe is amazed by the Scopes case."[3] Lloyd George, quoted in the article, insisted that "with us the question of teaching Darwinism in the schools has never arisen and it seems incredible to us that it ever could arise, but the belief or non-belief in the Darwinian theory bids fair to become the test of orthodoxy in America."[4] And the master of Christ College at Cambridge University, Sir Arthur Shipley, vowed that the anti-evolution supporters in America were examples of a "naïve mammal."[5] The international criticism associated Dayton with the country at large, thus judging all of America. This, in turn, drove domestic coverage to highlight repeatedly the southern nature of the anti-evolution support. The *New Republic* focused its attack directly on the Volunteer State, christening the trial as "Tennessee vs. Civilization"[6] and pitting this small southern town against all of humanity.

THE WAR BETWEEN THE STATES . . . AGAIN

In the years preceding the Scopes Trial, the anti-evolution message was proclaimed incessantly throughout Tennessee, which appeared prominently on the speaking schedule for Dr. William Bell Riley, president of the World's Christian Fundamentals Association, in 1923. Summoned by several prominent Tennessee attorneys, William Jennings Bryan also delivered a historic address in Nashville, "Is the Bible True?" The sermon proved so stirring that it inspired the sponsors to disseminate thousands of printed copies throughout the state; an additional 500 pamphlets were provided to members of the Tennessee statehouse upon its 1925 opening session. The result was the Butler Bill, House Bill 185, sponsored by John Washington Butler and introduced on January 21, 1925. Initially, the bill was recommended for rejection by the house committee to which it was assigned. But local evangelical ministers held powerful sway in the state of Tennessee.[7] Despite vocal opposition, from university academics to editorials in the *Nashville Banner*, warning about the threat the bill posed to free speech, one particular line of argument proved effective. Rev. A. B. Barrett of the Fayetteville Church of Christ "charged that many college students were returning home atheists and agnostics because of the teachings of Darwinism."[8] The Tennessee preacher, whether knowingly or not, touched on one of the greatest anxieties of God-fearing parents of the 1920s.

The very foundations of the anti-evolutionist argument had long been focused on the fear that children would lose their religious faith if they were exposed to Darwin's theories, and the movement proudly proclaimed that its primary intention was to save American youth from self-destruction. Many of Bryan's early speeches heralding the literalist interpretation of the Bible and denouncing Darwinism were offered as reactions to books such as *The Belief in God and Immortality: A Psychological and Anthropological and Statistical Study* by James Henry Leuba, published in 1916. Leuba's research concluded that during their experience with higher education, particularly throughout the four years of college, many students lost interest in their religious faith.[9] The Butler Act was, in fact, sponsored by a father whose children began questioning the church of their upbringing after their high school science classes presented the theory of evolution. Anti-evolutionists played on this fear of southern Christian parents— the fear that examining the origins of man would lead to a more far-reaching rejection of the Bible and a subsequent embrace of modernity. And, of course, embracing modernity could affect not only one's religious commitment but also the racial contract upon which the Jim Crow system relied.

Walter Lippmann, in his illuminating study of the 1920s, traced this anxiety to a broader cultural shift. Observing a radical change in educational philosophy, Lippmann surmised that the purpose of formal schooling no longer dictated that "the child shall acquire the wisdom of the elders, but that he shall revise and surpass it."[10] Thus, the study of evolution exposed a fear among many fundamentalists, particularly rural southerners, of being left behind and perhaps even rejected by the new modern era exploding all around them. In an effort to respond to the growing sense of inferiority, fundamentalist leaders attempted to alter the perception of the anti-evolutionists. Using the same criticism of close-mindedness and ignorance often heaped on their followers, anti-evolutionists fired back at the scientists and liberal intellectual elite with mirrored accusations. Lowell Harris Coate, in his essay "Evolution Disproved," zealously argued against the infallibility of evolution, insisting that the claims of biologists were based on radical theory rather than on scientific evidence: "It is interesting, indeed, at times even ludicrous, to read in the newspapers and the magazines about the numerous and various conventions and conferences, threatenings and thunderings, discoursings and discussings of one kind or other of a group of men, desiring to be known as scientists, who are just now particularly enraged over the fact that everybody in American is not falling over himself to accept, at full face value, their foolishness about evolution, without their presenting one single fact which can be accepted as proof for their much advertised 'scientific conclusions.'"[11] Moreover, anti-evolution proponents argued that their freedom of religion was being violated by the lack of choices they faced regarding the teaching of this "new" science in public schools. They positioned their community as the inquisitive side of this conflict, insisting they had a right to question Darwin's theories, which they considered to be merely working hypotheses. Still other fundamentalist preachers further polarized the modernists and the biblical literalists by raising the stakes of the argument at hand. In his influential book, *Hell and the High Schools*, T. T. Martin (a fixture at the Scopes Trial) vowed that "if Evolution, which is being taught in our High Schools, is true, the Saviour was not Deity, but only the bastard, illegitimate son of a fallen woman, and the world is left without a real Saviour, a real Redeemer, and only hell is left for responsible human beings."[12] Without the victory of Bryan's crusade against evolution, Christianity would die, and the southern fundamentalists, many of whom were new converts, in Dayton, Tennessee, would stand once again on the wrong side of history.

Many white southerners were particularly concerned with the way history would present their side of the sectional conflict and how it would judge their advocates, such as Bryan. Thus controlling, in some way, what children were taught in schools actually carried a significant sub-agenda. In the decades after the Civil War, white southern veterans groups were adamant that the "true and reliable history" of the Confederacy be an essential element in any school adoption. In Tennessee, the State Teachers' Association actually promoted the use of southern literature that was sympathetic to the Confederacy in the classroom at their 1902 convention.[13] The issue resurfaced at the Scopes Trial when Bryan attempted to conflate the sectional crisis of the nineteenth century with the evolution controversy of the current moment. Bryan promoted the idea that education already was local, and that communities should have jurisdiction over the content of public schooling: "No teacher would be permitted to go from the South and teach in a Northern school that the Northern statesmen and soldiers of the Civil War were traitors; neither would a Northern teacher be permitted to go from the North and teach in a Southern school that the Southern soldiers and statesmen are traitors."[14] Once again, Bryan pointed to the potential hypocrisy of northerners who, he suggested, would fight equally hard to ensure that their own values and story were handed down to their children. The push for local sovereignty or home rule of public education was welcomed by southern white fundamentalists and would continue to characterize much of the campaign against the teaching of evolution and would resurface during the later school integration crisis that followed at midcentury.

Despite the efforts of Bryan and his fellow leaders, evolution continued to be accepted and taught in the public school system. Most southern states attempted at some point to limit this modern encroachment, and the successful passage of the Butler Act garnered national attention. On March 24, 1925, the *New York Times* reported on the new Tennessee law on its front page. As has been well recorded by historians, the ACLU quickly offered to finance and provide representation for any teacher who would challenge the statute. Spearheading the plan to have the trial take place in Dayton, local businessman George Rappelyea hoped for publicity and an economic boom for the fledging community and encouraged John Scopes to take the bait. Rappelyea's relationship with his new hometown (he had moved to Dayton in 1922) exposes, yet again, the local, sectional distrust of northern outsiders. Rappelyea—described as a "sharp-nosed, untidy, intense, argumentative, garrulous man" with "horn-rimmed glasses"[15]—grew up in New York City, starting his career by selling newspapers at subway entrances in Manhattan. His hodgepodge education included some study of geology and civil engineering, leading to an unsatisfying job in the waterway system of New York. A vagabond of sorts, he soon headed south, eventually finding work surveying Tennessee farmland, where he suffered a snakebite that left him unconscious in the hospital. His nurse, Ova Corvin, became his wife, and she encouraged him to take a job in Dayton managing the renamed Cumberland Coal and Iron Company where her brother ran a general store. Despite his best efforts, Rappelyea was considered an outsider in Dayton, "a fringer, hovering on the edge of the drug-store crowd," with "wild ideas."[16] He was ostracized because of his northern upbringing, his education, his wealth, and, eventually, his opposition to the Butler Act. When Rappelyea expressed his opinion, the owner of the main barbershop "became enraged and shouted, 'You can't call my family monkeys.'" He then proceeded to bite Rappelyea.[17] Some insisted that this northern dissenter had "seduced Scopes into sin,"[18] but others were excited by the potential publicity, even hatching a plan to kidnap Rappelyea to generate media buzz. No such stunts, however, were necessary to turn the spotlight their way.

Just as the sectional conflict dominated both the rhetorical campaign tactics of the anti-evolutionists and the vision of the Rhea County people promoted by the media, so too was the old battle between the North and the South resurrected in the Dayton courtroom that summer. The regional divide, which had been the center of southern white identity, now encompassed not only the nineteenth-century war over slavery, but also the twentieth-century war between religion and science, agriculture and industry, and conservatism and modernism. When Bryan, the champion of the southern side of these related conflicts, arrived in Dayton, he received a hero's welcome. On his first night in town, he addressed the Dayton Progressive Club, insisting that "the contest between evolution and Christianity is a duel to the death."[19] The next night, Bryan headed to Morgan Springs, a resort in Walden Ridge about six miles from town, where a crowd of country faithful had gathered on the veranda. There in the twilight, as "a fading summer storm touched the distant hills with flickers of lightning, and a rumble of thunder rolled across the valley,"[20] Bryan conveyed confident pride in the South. His sentiment echoed the words he had once written to Tennessee governor Austin Peay after the passage of the Butler Bill: "The South is now leading the Nation in defense of Bible Christianity. Other states North and South will follow the example."[21]

The regional battle surfaced time and again in the Rhea County courthouse as well. On the first day of the trial, after numerous photographs had been taken for the press mob, Judge John Raulston opened the proceedings with a prayer, eliciting a fiery objection from Darrow. In an effort to appease the northern attorneys, Raulston did offer to have ministers of different denominations pronounce the opening court prayer each day. A northern, modernist pastor, Charles Francis Potter, was even included in the lineup.[22] However, when Potter was invited to speak at the Methodist Episcopal Church, one of the few northern Methodist denominations present in Dayton, the congregation caused such an uproar that their minister, Rev. Howard G. Byrd, was forced to resign.[23] In fact, one church member had warned the pastor that the congregation would fracture the moment that he allowed "a New York infidel"[24] to stand at the pulpit. When questioned about the incident days later, Byrd concluded that the chaos resulted from an inevitable "small town psychology."[25]

Daily prayer was not the only aspect of the trial that angered the northern attorneys. Darrow noted that the prosecution had been seated on the shady side of the courtroom, where even in the sweltering southern July they seemed cool and comfortable, while the defense suffered in the scorching sun. Darrow sarcastically remarked that "as Southern gentlemen, they must have been sorry that there were not enough fans to go around, nor one wee socket left for 'the defense.'"[26] Climate, of course, was not the only provocation that made Darrow sweat; throughout the case his team was constantly reminded of their status as outsiders in Dayton—and the reminders proved highly insulting. At the start of the trial, Judge Raulston welcomed the "foreign lawyers," a phrase that caused the defense lawyers to pause, although they remained silent. Only when former attorney general Ben McKenzie announced that the Butler Act was so clear as to be easily understood by a sixteen-year-old, and asked if "these gentlemen have any laws in the great metropolitan city of New York that conflict or in the great white city of the Northwest," was he rapidly interrupted by the defense, which objected to being singled out geographically.[27] Judge Raulston, perhaps frustrated with the constant interruption, replied somewhat bombastically that "I want you gentlemen from New York or any other foreign state to always remember that you are our guests and that we accord you the same privileges and rights and courtesies that we do any other lawyer."[28]

Of course, the highlight, at least for reporters, came when Darrow, who had been prevented from calling as witnesses the scientific experts that he had spent weeks preparing, summoned the Great Commoner to the stand. If he would not be allowed to demonstrate the facts of evolution—pronounced "EEvolution," "as though the word began with double EE,"[29] teased Darrow, regarding his opposition's southern accent—he must instead discredit Bryan on the stand. Bryan cordially agreed to Darrow's request, insisting that he welcomed any question they could ask. Perhaps the heat or the constant "Amens" finally got to Darrow, and he revealed a flash of anger and condescension in the famous exchange. Bryan's ascension to the stand was greeted with a robust round of applause, eliciting a sarcastic comment from Darrow:

DARROW: Great applause from the bleachers.
BRYAN: From those whom you call "yokels."
DARROW: I have never called them yokels.
BRYAN: That is the ignorance of Tennessee, the bigotry . . . the people whom you insult.
DARROW: You insult every man of science and learning in the world because he does not believe in your fool religion.[30]

Judge Raulston interjected that he would not stand for such acrimony. In his retort, Bryan had goaded Darrow and provoked the audience by appealing to this white southern sense of inferiority, and Darrow played directly into his hands, angering the audience with his hostile depiction of their collective faith.

But Darrow's skillful interrogation and Bryan's botched and flustered justification of biblical literalism, exaggerated and made famous in the fictional film *Inherit the Wind* (1960), exposed the fundamentalist movement as exactly what modernists like Darrow had deemed it to be—devoid of reason, hypocritical, and violently defiant of any alien ideas from outsiders and infidels. According to Darrow, Bryan's performance at the trial "had reached a stage of hallucination that would impel him to commit any cruelty that he believed would help his cause."[31] In his memoir, Darrow further attempted to grasp the larger historical context of his days in Rhea County; he surmised that "Tennessee is a Southern State and, like all the South was almost destroyed by the Civil War and reconstruction, and like the rest of the South, has never recovered from the scourge."[32] But for the white southern fundamentalists who gathered in Dayton, and for those who followed the trial via print or listened on the radio, Darrow was not the greatest offender. Rather, the condemnation that came from the media—from both northern media and dissenting southern media—shaped the sense of inferiority that plagued them long after the circus had left town.

DAYTON AS THE BLACK EYE OF AMERICA

The historical image of Dayton as an overzealous religious community prior to the trial was exaggerated by media outlets. Paul Conkin has argued that despite official membership, many of Dayton's faithful did not attend church regularly; the community was moderately religious at best.[33] Conkin described the inconsistency in detail:

> At least half of the young people attended weekly dances at a resort up on Walden Ridge. Scopes attended different churches on Sunday, but was not a member of any one and not personally devout. This seemed true of many of the men who gathered at Robinson's Drugstore, and who conspired to have the trial in Dayton. Yet reporters, looking for that strange breed of people called "fundamentalists," did locate a congregation up on Walden Ridge that matched their image—with an illiterate minister who, if the reporters were correct, believed the earth was flat. Not one ever bothered to identify the denomination. Likewise in Dayton, some reporters visited a black Pentecostal congregation and confronted a type of near ecstatic worship that about scared them out of their wits.[34]

It was only when Bryan and the other anti-evolution crusaders arrived that their influence energized and solidified the local belief in the fundamentalist doctrine of biblical literalism, particularly because it was under attack. Thus, even though prior to the trial Rhea County was not atypical as compared to the rest of the Old Confederacy, the overwhelming impression, an impression that would thrive in the wire reports and the political caricatures, remained that of "images of ignorant and intolerant representatives of an Appalachian subculture who had suppressed people like Scopes."[35] The image was not one for which the citizens of Dayton were prepared. This local culture "suffered an invasion from the outside,"[36] which found the town to be an "undesirable place," for "it lay in the South, which least conformed to the accepted traits of national character."[37] Some of the educated northern elites, such as Darrow, came across as superior and condescending. The disdain only energized the fundamentalist position for Dayton citizens, who "read the same fashion magazines, purchased the same radio sets, bought the production of the same trade outlets as Cleveland, Ohio, or Denver, Colorado." Dayton "naturally resented for itself, and on behalf of all the small towns of America, the unwarranted condescension of its visitors."[38] But the local businessmen, determined to profit from the spotlight, actually encouraged the journalistic gawking by selling everything from stuffed monkey toys to "watch fobs shaped like monkeys, and umbrellas imported from Germany with handles shaped like monkey heads. Pressure on the monkey's throat made him roll his eyes and stick out his tongue. The monkey notion was exploited to the breaking point."[39] In the end, the besieged community got more than it bargained for and could only watch as the eccentric tourists they had solicited clashed with northern reporters, deepening the imprint of southern backwardness that would stamp Dayton with a permanent and self-fulfilling ink.

The Los Angeles Daily Times ridiculed the Dayton debate over evolution in a feature section entitled "Man vs. Monkey Tilt Has Aspect of Circus," complete with cartoon drawings of monkeys hanging from the headline banner. It opened by announcing that "this week Dayton, Tenn., an obscure little village of less than 2000 normal population becomes the center of the concentrated interest of most of the civilized world."[40] Indeed, the condemnation that accompanied the passage of the Butler Act paled in comparison to the scathing denunciation that the Christian fundamentalists of Dayton received during the days of the trial. The international and national media ridicule abounded that July. Even African American critics and southern agitators, as they were called, voiced their denunciation of the anti-evolution spectacle, though for very different reasons. Specifically, the international scrutiny tended to describe the controversy as an all-encompassing American problem, one that resulted from the fact that the young country, according to Dr. Heinrich Hermelink, professor of church history at the University of Marburg in Germany, had not experienced a social or intellectual renaissance: "To say the least," he proclaimed, "we have attained a stage of popular enlightenment that make such a sensational episode as the Tennessee monkey trial inconceivable in our country."[41] And André Siegfried, a French journalist, condemned all Tennessee evangelicals, who he insisted had "preserved their Protestant faith on ice," as well as their pastors, who "preached medieval dogma with the fervor of the Inquisition."[42] Likewise, English writer S. K. Ratcliffe extended his criticism to the country at large, arguing that "it falls to the generation now reaching maturity to realize that the material progress of America has been made without a corresponding advance in mental enlightenment and spiritual experience."[43]

Bryan's involvement in the matter obviously prompted considerable international attention; and northern audiences feared that his prior experience in national politics would taint the European image of the United States as a whole. And, in fact, it did. The *Living Age*, a New York journal that collected and republished a selection of articles from European periodicals, noted in its August 15, 1925, issue that "Europe, and especially England, was amused and delighted by the Scopes evolution trial while it lasted; and the further progress of the case is being watched with an interest which is quite as lively as it is malicious. To behold the shrewd Yankee—in foreign eyes there is no difference between one part of the United States and another—fighting the battle of belief that was over and done with decades ago causes the average British journalist acute pleasure; and the Continental papers, so far as they have command on the case at all, followed the British lead."[44] D. W. Brogan, a British commentator, clearly revealed the Old World's fascination with the American monkey trial and noted the influence of the sectional conflict as well: "Here was the most powerful, richest, most complacent society in the world making a fool of itself over Jonah and the Whale, over the literal accuracy of Genesis. To a continent weakened and, in its heart of hearts, thinking itself disgraced by its recent civil war, the spectacle of William Jennings Bryan, former Secretary of State, thrice candidate for President, floundering over primitive cosmology was funny and comforting."[45]

The *Weekly Dispatch* in London sponsored a limerick contest for amateur poets to comment on the Scopes Trial. Amid thousands of entries, E. J. Rackham of Southampton took first prize:

If we take the Daytonian mind,
As an average of men's I'm inclined
    To ask, not if man
    With a monkey began,
But did monkeys descend from mankind.[46]

The *London Times*, which offered daily coverage of the trial during the entire two-week affair, used colorful language to paint a bold, dramatic vision of American fundamentalists, while the *London Spectator* published a biting commentary. Bryan and his flock were simply trying to avoid "sending the children of America into everlasting torment," the paper insisted, and then followed with the cynical tagline: "There is some evidence too, that the inhabitants of Dayton are attempting to think; and this is very difficult for them."[47] The rest of the United

Kingdom seemed equally appalled, though a variety of critics did single out the southern state. Irish playwright George Bernard Shaw claimed that as a result of the "Monkey Law," Tennessee was "a mere reservation of morons."[48] At the first meeting of the World Federation of Education Associations, held in Scotland in July 1925, the moderator elicited peals of laughter when he noted that "we still believe that the law of evolution operates here, notwithstanding the decision of Tennessee."[49]

Even as far away as India, journalists, academics, and cultural critics could not resist excoriating the United States for what many considered an embarrassing historical moment. Dr. S. L. Joshi, a Hindu professor from the University of Bombay, announced that in his homeland, "they laugh at William J. Bryan's ideas on the evolution of man and hold his criticism of Darwin's famous theory to be but a hodge-podge of unscientific thinking." The great minds of the period, however, were not only concerned with whether Bryan's interpretation was scientific; rather, many, such as Albert Einstein, recognized the danger inherent in the fundamentalist position. While in Berlin, he warned, "any restriction of academic liberty heaps coals of fire upon the community which tolerates such suppression."[50] His words rang true, for Dayton indeed was permanently burned by the firestorm of criticism aimed its way. Perhaps of all of the international detractors, Sir Arthur Keith, a British anthropologist and protégé of Charles Darwin, summed up the "foreign" mockery most succinctly. He jived, "Father, forgive them, for they know not what they do."[51]

Though international criticism abounded, few African American voices received attention during the evolution controversy, particularly since both sides of the debate actively employed racial stereotypes to further their causes. Some advocates of Darwin's teachings pointed to the diversity among the races to deny the creationist conception of all mankind descending from the biblical Adam. But other scientists actively promoted, as evidence for evolution, a racial hierarchy, "with white Anglo-Saxons at the top and Africans and their descendants at the bottom."[52] Southern evangelical Christians, on the other hand, balked at the idea that whites and blacks—and monkeys, for that matter—shared a common ancestry. The very concept threatened the tenuous and vulnerable racial pecking order in the Old Confederacy. African American Christians, particularly the large denominations in the South, were conflicted. Though secondary school attendance increased exponentially in the early decades of the twentieth century, segregation continued to prevent many black youth and their parents from participating in evolution debates directly.[53]

Still, the greater war between religious belief and liberal modernism forced many African American congregations to support the fundamentalist crusade.

Rev. John W. Norris, head of the African Methodist Episcopal Church of Baltimore, concluded as such in the *A.M.E. Church Review*. However, in an effort to avoid succumbing to the racist implications of the southern anti-evolution crusade, Norris invoked the memory of slavery as a direct contradiction to Darwin's theories. He reasoned that if Darwin's work was accepted as true, some subscribers could potentially imply that slavery (or the contemporary eugenics initiative) was merely a step along the evolutionary ladder—an idea he vehemently rejected.[54] But not all African American communities were willing to stand by Bryan, overlooking his history of acquiescing to the white supremacists of his contingency. An editorial published by the *Chicago Defender*, one of the most ferocious and relentless critics of the South, defined clearly the black opposition to Bryan without pulling any punches:

> Anything which conflicts with the South's idea of her own importance, anything which tends to break down her doctrine of white supremacy, she fights. If truths are introduced and these truths do not conform to what southern grandfathers believed, then it must be suppressed. The Tennessee legislators who passed the law making it a crime to teach Darwinism in that state probably have never read the text themselves and all they know about the subject is that the entire human race is supposed to have started from a common origin. Therein lies their difficulty. Admit that premise and they will have to admit that there is no fundamental difference between themselves and the race they pretend to despise. Such admission would, of course, play havoc with the existing standards of living in the South. And so, encouraged by America's champion long distance presidential "white hope," William Jennings Bryan, Tennessee blazes the trail that makes ignorance compulsory. . . . It is too bad the monkeys cannot speak and show the South just how ridiculous she is becoming in her efforts to convince the world that she is "superior."[55]

Perhaps the most well-known black intellectual of his time, W. E. B. Du Bois, advanced the most threatening argument of all, actually echoing the jesting rebukes of Europe in the signature magazine of the NAACP. He exposed the true intentions of the northern media—they must persuade the rest of the world that Dayton, Tennessee, "is a huge joke and very, very exceptional." But Du Bois was not fooled by the words of H. L. Mencken and Joseph Wood Krutch, to name a few such reporters. Ironically, it was Du Bois who would expose, just as Bryan had proclaimed in his speeches across the South, the hypocrisy of the journalistic finger-pointing: "The truth is and we know it: Dayton, Tennessee, is America." He continued, "Who is to blame? They that know; they that teach;

they that have; they that sit silent and enjoy; great universities that close their doors to the mob; great scientists who prostitute truth to prejudice." There was a reason why the great showdown between modernism and fundamentalism of 1925 reared its ugly head in America. "The folk who leave white Tennessee in blank and ridiculous ignorance of what science has taught the world since 1859," Du Bois insisted, "are the same ones who would leave black Tennessee and black America with just as little education as is consistent with fairly efficient labor and reasonable contentment; who rave over the 18th Amendment and are dumb over the 15th; who permit lynching and make bastardy legal in order to render the race 'pure.' It is such folk who, when in sudden darkness they decry the awful faces of the Fanatic, the Fury and the Fool, try to hide the vision with gales of laughter."[56] Du Bois saw the conflict as yet another example of southern suppression and northern compliance. And for the Bible Belt Christians of the Old Confederacy, the battle against the teaching of evolution was but one more effort to reject Yankee values.

The reporters who descended on Rhea County that summer, whether intentionally or not, told a story that the rest of the nation—excluding the South—wanted to hear. Dayton must be the exception, not the rule. All bigotry, all ignorance, all provincialism and anti-intellectualism, must live and breathe within the boundaries of Rhea County and the larger South from which it sprung. American progressive leader Jane Addams was traveling in England during the trial, where she faced a virtual inquisition from her colleagues there who promoted a British exceptionalism[57] of sorts—that such an event could never happen in England. Addams attempted to defend America by quickly pointing out the regional distinctions that accounted for the circus in Dayton. She carefully explained that "in states of small isolated communities steeped in the tradition of Christian fundamentalism, such conflicts . . . were, indeed, evidence of the vitality of American democracy, whereby simple, poorly educated people refused to be overawed by intellectuals and 'experts.'"[58] Some progressive academics did not offer such a rosy spin. The New York Times reported that a dean at Columbia University—in an effort to distinguish the principles of northern higher education—advised that any secondary school diploma from the state of Tennessee be deemed null and void since the school curricula was not based necessarily on facts.

American journalists and critics were equally quick to enlighten their international counterparts. Life magazine, in addition to carrying numerous political cartoons mocking Bryan, actually awarded the "fundamentalist pope"—as Mencken called him—their "Brass Medal of the Fourth Class," a tongue-in-cheek honor bestowed on the old Democrat for having "successfully demonstrated that by the alchemy of ignorance hot air may be transmuted into gold, and that the Bible is infallibly inspired except where it differs with him on the question of wine, women, and wealth."[59] *Time* magazine called the great standoff in Dayton "the fantastic cross between a circus and a holy war," and WGN, the Chicago radio station that carried the trial live to the masses, mirrored *Time*'s fascination with the whirlwind. The station managers had originally hoped to broadcast the Leopold and Loeb trial, but the public rejected the proposal due to the morbidity and gore that characterized the case. Somewhat disappointed, station executives were thrilled to have a new story to air. Announcer Quin Ryan revealed the network's anticipation: "Then here comes this big, clawing thing down in Tennessee, and everybody is making fun of it, so that's for us. . . . Good entertainment."[60] Even Clarence Darrow commented on the response he received from fundamentalists in the days after the trial: "The number of people on the borderline of insanity in a big country is simply appalling," Darrow claimed, and "it takes only a slight stimulus to throw them entirely off their balance."[61] The *New York Times* even characterized many members of the crowds that flocked to Dayton as "Cranks and Freaks."[62]

The *Nation* published some of the most piercing condemnation of the anti-evolution crusade and labeled the case "the State of Tennessee vs. Truth." At times, the *Nation* usurped evangelical rhetoric, offering the Great Commoner and his supporters a taste of their own medicine. "Then on the fourth day Darrow arose," proclaimed the article, well aware that it was "using the resurrection image in a way that undoubtedly would have galled Bryan, who according to the article, was afflicted with 'intellectual incompetence' and 'bogus claims.'"[63] The *Nation*'s criticism was not always directed specifically toward Tennessee; rather, it often generalized the object of its denunciation, lumping small-town America into one homogeneous backwoods environment—a generalization that encouraged the regional discord.

Criticism came from within the South as well. Georgia reporters Julia and Julian Harris—he was the son of literary legend Joel Chandler Harris—had received national recognition, including the first Pulitzer Prize for a southern journalist, for their exposé of the Ku Klux Klan. Both developed a close relationship with Mencken, which led them to comment on the "Holy Rollers" that they, along with the "American Nietzsche," observed during their time in Dayton. The Harrises' commentary, carried in the *New York World* and in their own Georgia paper, the *Columbus Enquirer-Sun*, clearly encapsulates their overriding outlook: "What a barren and meager existence, what an ignorant and superstitious mentality must lead these poor 'Rollers' to find comfort and pleasure in such demonstrations! How much wiser and more human it would be if the power and energy which is being expended in the efforts of the fundamentalists to keep evolution out of the schools should be directed towards the education and physical uplifting of such people as these poor illiterates who exist in the backwaters of all Southern states."[64] The purpose of the Harrises' commentary, though stinging and somewhat condescending, was not merely to ridicule southern Christianity, but rather to grieve for the lost potential they could envision.

Responsible for much of the coverage of the trial that appeared in the *Nation*, journalist Joseph Wood Krutch proved particularly offensive to southern audiences. Krutch was, in fact, a native of Knoxville, Tennessee, and he had returned from his new home in the North to offer his impressions to the country at large. Of his hometown citizens, Krutch opined in *Commentary* that "Knoxvillians are defensive and indignant; they resent in various terms the publicity they have attracted and they protest against being judged by the laws their legislature passes; but these Knoxvillians will not admit that, fundamentally, they are to blame. In Tennessee bigotry is militant and sincere; intelligence is timid and hypocritical, and in that fact lies the explanation of the sorry role which she is playing in contemporary history."[65] Krutch primarily blamed the educated elite of his home state for surrendering to fundamentalism; he even titled one of his provocative and venomous critiques "Tennessee: Where Cowards Rule."[66] In the days immediately following the trial, Krutch surmised that Darrow's presence had had an immeasurable effect on the citizens of Dayton. He insisted that, "in Tennessee, as I said in a previous article, intellectual courage is almost dead. Whatever is done in the name of patriotism or religion may consider itself as exempt from any but the most respectful criticism, and anything like a vigorous liberal opinion seemed as unreal and remote in Dayton as the Daytonian psychology seems to a man who has spent his life in intellectual society. Even the State University had given the acquiescence of silence, but he, who came from afar, was a man who dared to do what no Tennessean had done—hold up a mirror that she might see herself as the world saw her."[67] And Krutch was specifically impressed with Darrow's closing speech, which extended beyond the judge's order for adjournment. "With flying banners and beating drums," Darrow warned the Dayton crowd, "we are marching backward to the glorious age of the sixteenth century when bigots lighted faggots to burn the men who dared to bring any intelligence and enlightenment and culture to the human mind."[68] The speech left an indelible impression on Krutch. In fact, the entire experience at Dayton haunted Krutch, and he grappled with the theological and philosophical repercussions of the fundamentalist collapse that he believed resulted from the spotlighting of Rhea County. Over forty years later, he continued to wrestle with the legacy of the trial and with his own frustration and toxicity, which, perhaps, tainted his view. In retrospect, Krutch insisted that he had overreacted to the anti-evolution advocates whom he had once seen as quite threatening. "Bryanism could not possibly have become the Wave of the Future," he surmised, because "it was only a backwashing ripple from the past."[69]

■ The same media writers who condemned Bryan and his fundamentalist followers trumpeted their demise in the weeks and months following the monkey trial. In fact, after the trial, when another anti-evolution bill was proposed in the Kentucky statehouse, the media ridicule resurfaced and the statute was "laughed out of existence."[70] Such instances convinced many scholars that the media and the advocates of modernity had successfully squelched this religious uprising. Scholars have disagreed on the effects of the critical spotlight. Ray Ginger, for example, connected the public ridicule of the trial to the demise of anti-evolution fervor; while others, such as southern historian Willard Gatewood, argued that religious fundamentalists turned their attention elsewhere, specifically to defeating the presidential candidacy of Catholic Al Smith. Religious historian George Marsden insisted that the fundamentalists continued to enjoy a brief surge of support south of the Mason-Dixon Line, where "the rural, southern image of the anti-evolution movement popularized by Scopes became self-fulfilling."[71] By the end of the decade, many southern states had initiated some type of restriction on the teaching of evolution by way of legislature or executive pen. In Texas, for example, Governor "Ma" Ferguson had the section on evolution removed from state-adopted science textbooks.

More recently, Joel Carpenter, professor of History at Calvin College in Michigan, offered a revisionist perspective of fundamentalist history, suggesting that the evangelical fervor displayed at the Scopes Trial did not fade or change focus.[72] Abandoned and rejected by their parent traditional denominations, fundamentalists sought to develop an aggressive and expansive counterestablishment, including a network of Christian colleges, which is exactly what happened in Dayton. The public criticism resurrected the oppositional or negative aspect of identity construction. Southern whiteness now extended beyond race, absorbing proreligion, antiscience, and antimodernism elements that have proven resurgent today. Moreover, Richard Hofstadter has insisted that during this particular moment in American history, "advertising, radio, the mass magazines, the advance of popular education" had forced "the old mentality into a direct and unavoidable conflict with the new."[73] This was never more true than for the rural, not particularly religious citizens of Dayton, Tennessee, who, in the wake of the Scopes Trial, confronted the new mentality and its accompanying public judgment.

According to southern writer and member of the Fugitive literary circle Donald Davidson, the ridicule that engulfed Rhea County in the summer of 1925 did "irreparable damage,"[74] and "the discredit that fell upon Tennessee was extended to the South in general and embittered sectional relations."[75] Tennessee governor Austin Peay had feared and had come to lament what the trial did to his state. He believed that reporters had exaggerated the case and "ridiculed Tennessee, 'until I [Peay] fairly boil.'"[76] His anger and embarrassment was echoed by many citizens of his state and throughout the South. Thus, despite the conviction of John Scopes, the fundamentalists seemed to have lost and Dayton seemed to have become "the laughing-stock of much of the western world."[77] In response, these newly radicalized southern white fundamentalists would retreat from the society that judged them, create their own educational enclave founded on a campaign to reclaim victory for William Jennings Bryan and his followers, and combat the collective sense of inferiority that united them.

CHAPTER 3

REACTIONARY FUNDAMENTALISM

THE FOUNDING OF

WILLIAM JENNINGS BRYAN COLLEGE

More than any episode of this century, the antievolution crusade dramatized the conservative religious temper of the South and popularized the Bible Belt stereotype. It did more than this, however. For nonsouthern ridicule solidified southerners and activated defensive psychological mechanisms.
—Kenneth K. Bailey, *Southern White Protestantism in the Twentieth Century*

This desperate plunge backward took the form of an offensive, often fanatical in intensity, to fortify the orthodox, traditional order of rural, small town America against the encroachments of the emerging urban-industrial society.
—Willard B. Gatewood Jr., *Preachers, Pedagogues, and Politicians: The Evolution Crisis in North Carolina, 1920–1927*

Indeed, fundamentalism became a byword in American culture as a result of the Scopes trial, and fundamentalism responded by withdrawing. They did not abandon their faith, however, but set about constructing a separate sub-culture with independent religious, educational, and social institutions.
—Edward Larson, *Summer for the Gods: The Scopes Trial and America's Continuing Debate over Science and Religion*

Until the Scopes Trial erupted on the world stage in July 1925, criticism of backwater religion seemed almost clichéd to educated urban dwellers in the North. Even Woodrow Wilson claimed that he could not believe that there was anyone by the 1920s who still questioned evolution. For the citizens of Dayton, for whom the trial began as a publicity stunt to attract tourism and spur the economy, the media disparagement was perhaps even more shocking. At stake for Bryanites, as they were dubbed, stood both their acceptance as a respected element of American society and their entire faith-based cosmology. If evolution survived as fact, and if fundamentalism was proven false, then humans, noted historian Paul Conkin, "all alone in a world ever beyond their full understanding, [would] have to take full responsibility for their moral standards. They cannot appeal to any authority. They live in a world without providential guidance, a world full of not only irony, but often also with tragedy, for it is a world that exhibits no purpose, moves toward no preordained goal, and provides no promise of human redemption."[1] The victory of science over religion would result in a type of "virtual despair," a phrase used by presidential candidate Barry Goldwater nearly half a century later. Walter Lippmann defined the phrase as "the unease of the old Adam who is not ready for the modern age." He further explained that virtual despair resulted from "being lost in a universe where the meaning of life and of the social order are no longer given from on high and transmitted from ancestors but have to be invented and discovered and experimented with, each lonely individual for himself."[2] Such chance, such a gamble, would undoubtedly be accompanied by grave anxiety, leaving the believers of Dayton, Tennessee, and other like-minded communities throughout the South overcome by the judgments of their jury of peers and, even more so, their jury of foes.

William Jennings Bryan's embarrassment on the stand under the grueling examination of Clarence Darrow and the acute media ridicule of his faith and campaign activated a deep sense of inferiority for himself and his followers. For white southern fundamentalists, in Dayton and throughout the region, the defeat was only one among many, but this time, due to the huge presence of mass media, the stereotype proliferated. The cause of anti-evolution merged with the other great lost causes of the South, and the southern white Christians, to whom Bryan was divine intervention, were left to grapple with their reprised status as American fools. According to Scopes historian Ray Ginger, the international and domestic rebuff, from northern and some southern journalists, proved particularly difficult for homogeneous, like-minded communities because "rejection is especially rare in closed societies like the rural South, where the frame was consistent and unvaried, where it was persistently hammered home, where competing frames were seldom heard." He continued, "For most Southerners a suspension of judgment was almost impossible and when they had judged they tended to become intolerant of other judgments. They wanted their children to think as they did."[3]

This sense of defeat and loss intensified dramatically when William Jennings Bryan died only days after the Scopes verdict was delivered. At this point, what Bryan meant to white southerners—what the whole trial meant to white southerners—became abundantly clear. Specifically, the public reaction to his death revealed just how painful the ordeal had been for the religious community that had elevated him to the status of martyr. And the second wave of ridicule that characterized Bryan's eulogies revealed just as clearly what his opponents thought of him and his followers as well. The community in Dayton, Tennessee, a microcosm of the white South, was transformed by the media criticism that accompanied Bryan's death and the trial, and its response reflected a growing, collective sense of inferiority.

Those who became the butt of the media's jokes lived the experience of the trial for decades after the grandstands were disassembled and the "cranks and freaks" had flown the coop. The power of this public criticism lay in the way in which it extended elements of southern whiteness—including an opposition to modernism and science. The community in Dayton, and other sympathetic white southerners, assuaged their humiliation and overcame this growing sense of inferiority by retreating from their critics, isolating themselves, and recasting the Scopes narrative to valorize both the fundamentalist position and its late leader. Bryan, himself, had set quite an example. The tangible result of their efforts was a memorial to the Great Commoner that would provide a protected space for fundamentalists, one that would remain unshakable by modern science and unexposed to media critics, duly named William Jennings Bryan College.

THE DEATH OF BRYAN

Despite the fact that Bryan suffered from diabetes and indulged his voracious appetite, his demise only five days after the trial was quickly linked to his strenuous performance, mythologizing the anti-evolution crusader as martyr number one.[4] The Great Commoner did not live long enough to give his final oration, meant to redeem him in the eyes of his evangelical beholders. But his death—and the subsequent dissemination of his opus posthumous—did the trick all the same. Historian George Marsden, when assessing the transformation of American fundamentalism, once wrote that "it would be difficult to overestimate the impact of 'the Monkey trial' at Dayton, Tennessee," and Bryan's death only made this impact greater. William Jennings Bryan's effort to "slay single-handed the prophets of Baal"[5] begot a deluge of derision that did not end upon his death. And his death did not dilute H. L. Mencken's ridicule; his eulogy for Bryan, considered by many to be his most biting writing on the whole affair, rubbed salt in the wounds of southern fundamentalists.

The Sage of Baltimore knew what Bryan had come to mean to his southern white flock. He had witnessed the almost mystic and divine regard in which Bryan had been held in this country pocket of Tennessee: "The news that he [Bryan] was coming was enough. For miles the flivver dust would choke the roads. And when he rose at the end of the day to discharge his Message there would be such breathless attention, such a rapt and enchanted ecstasy, such a sweet rustle of amens as the world had not known since Johann fell to Herod's ax."[6] Even though Mencken clearly recognized that the crowds in Dayton were moved by Bryan's defense of their way of life, he never shied away from insulting their very nature and existence, insinuating that they were mere pawns in Bryan's power game: "There was something peculiarly fitting in the fact that his last days were spent in a one-horse Tennessee village, and that death found him there. The man felt at home in such simple and Christian scenes. He liked people who sweated freely, and were not debauched by the refinements of the toilet. Making his progress up and down the Main street of little Dayton, surrounded by gaping primates from the upland valleys of the Cumberland Range, his coat laid aside, his bare arms and hairy chest shining damply, his bald head sprinkled with dust—so accoutered and on display he was obviously happy."[7] Mencken's obituary for Bryan revealed what many of the lifelong friends and colleagues of the Great Commoner had begun to fear. His last stand in Dayton, Tennessee, would cloud the progressive legacy and example that had distinguished the bulk of his career. In the end, most who had known the young crusader, the dynamic orator who championed the rights of farmers and laborers and demanded direct democracy for the common man and woman, would turn away.

Furthermore, Mencken clearly saw that Bryan's individual life had become a key component of white southern identity, a connection forged through Populism, white superiority, and religious fundamentalism. Mencken argued that "in the presence of city folks he [Bryan] was palpably uneasy. . . . He knew all the while that they were laughing at him—if not at his baroque theology, then at least at his alpaca pantaloons. But the yokels never laughed at him. To them he was not the huntsman but the prophet, and toward the end, as he gradually forsook mundane politics for more ghostly concerns, they began to elevate him in their hierarchy. When he died he was the peer of Abraham. . . . His place in Tennessee hagiography is secure. If the village barber saved any of his hair, then it is curing gall-stones down there today."[8] In the wake of the public denunciation of his faith, and in conjunction with a lifetime of falling short of great achievements, Bryan—suggested Mencken—suffered from his own inferiority complex.

Moreover, toward the end of his life, Bryan visibly rejected the society that deemed him inferior, choosing instead to surround himself with like-minded evangelicals who would extol his values rather than mock his ignorance. His own disdain for his critics drove his behavior, which Mencken characterized as self-destructive:

His last battle will be grossly misunderstood if it is thought of as a mere exercise in fanaticism. . . . There was much more in it than that, as everyone knows who saw him on the field. What moved him, at bottom, was simply hatred of the city men who had laughed at him so long, and brought him to so tatterdemalion an estate. He lusted for revenge upon them. He yearned to lead anthropoid rabble against them, to punish them for their execution upon him by attacking the very vitals of their civilization. He went far beyond the bounds of any merely religious frenzy, however inordinate. When he began denouncing the notion that man is a mammal even some of the hinds at Dayton were agape. And when, brought upon Clarence Darrow's cruel hook, he writhed and tossed in a very fury of malignancy, bawling against the veriest elements of sense and decency like a man frantic . . . upon that hook, in truth, Bryan committed suicide.[9]

Bryan's demons, his ambition, had gotten the best of him in front of an audience who considered him infallible; such a lapse was unthinkable for a talent like his. After all, Bryan "knew mob psychology as well as he knew his A. B. Cs, and the mob adored him."[10] A seasoned veteran and man of faith, Bryan was well versed in resurrection. But the crowds would not even need the final speech over which Bryan labored during his last days on earth; rather, his death alone, coupled with the rage and disillusionment brought on by the media spotlight, proved sufficient for full resurrection. Though Dayton had not been, in the days before the Scopes Trial, excessively religious or self-conscious, in its aftermath the small town "seemed to conform to the image thus imprinted."[11]

REACTIONARY FUNDAMENTALISM

What resulted from the black eye of the Scopes Trial was a new type of religious fervor, more organized, more insulated, and coping with this sense of inferiority, labeled here as reactionary fundamentalism. In the wake of the evolution controversy, the very nature of fundamentalist belief proved uncompromising. The reactionary southern evangelical fundamentalism of the 1920s became devoted to a literal reading of the Bible, to a sense of textual authority that was not based on rationality or a logical theology but rather on passion and a personal relationship with a revelatory god. Some have labeled the combination of fundamentalism and regionalism as a neurosis of sorts, which, "when threatened in its time and place, rejected any prospect of change from outside."[12] But this stalwart rejection of modernism, of science, of any northern encroachment, became increasingly entrenched as a result of the public denunciation that it received that summer. Whether conscious or not, the community under siege followed Bryan's lead, choosing to surround itself with like-minded people of faith, who would judge not lest they be judged. Fundamentalism, scholar Eric Sandeen notes, had "to secure its existence outside the old-line denominations where its members could hope for no more than tolerance."[13] Hence, fundamentalism actually initiated its retreat during the early days of the anti-evolution crusade.

German theologian Paul Tillich discerned that "whenever a movement is under attack, it withdraws into what it considers an impenetrable fortress." The 1920s fundamentalist movement did indeed withdraw, creating a doctrinal fortress of sorts, constricting all belief to what was labeled the Five Points. Emphasis was placed on belief in the Virgin Birth, the divinity of Scripture, the saving grace provided by the Messiah's death, the Resurrection, and the Second Coming. But oftentimes the oversimplification of these limited tenets led to distortion of the fundamentalist cause, particularly by rural and evangelical congregations.[14] However, this theological recoil served as an example of what Bryanites would mimic in the aftermath of the media assault on Rhea County. Reactionary fundamentalism in Dayton, Tennessee, was simply fundamentalism that went underground and, in this case, switched tactics, choosing to establish its own institution of higher learning rather than trying to influence the public school system. Its fortress, rather than being conceptual, was physical— a series of buildings devoted to the gospel truth of Genesis, aptly named William Jennings Bryan College.

Within one month of Bryan's death, a group of his closest political friends and followers established the William Jennings Bryan Memorial Association. The committee immediately set out to raise funds to establish the Christian college that Bryan had envisioned and discussed with Dayton citizens during the trial. This national association did not automatically choose the rural Tennessee location for the college. After all, Bryan had a long history of campaigning for numerous political causes—populism and women's suffrage, to name a few. And, of course, he had served as secretary of state under President Woodrow Wilson. His death drew numerous notes and telegrams of condolence from world leaders and American politicians. But Bryan's last stand in Dayton had altered his reputation as a progressive; and although many supporters from earlier days spoke highly of Bryan's past championing such causes, the burden fell to the fundamentalists, who had chanted his name and filled the many lecture halls in which he spoke during his anti-evolution campaign, to immortalize his legacy. It was Dayton locals, desperate to create a home for fundamentalists, who jump-started the campaign. Walter White and F. E. Robinson each offered $1,000 to support the effort. A final nod from Bryan's widow fulfilled the wish that Bryan had made, and in November 1926, the soon-to-be-named

"Bryan Hill" in Dayton was purchased for $6,654.33. Only four days after offi- cially acquiring the land, 10,000 spectators gathered to watch Governor Austin Peay break ground.[15] *Outlook* magazine carried an article by Don Wharton, "The Lord's College," which described the eventful day:

> Jerusalem in the sprightliest days of King Solomon never entered upon a grander day than did Dayton when it shoveled the first dirt and laid the fine cornerstone of Bryan Memorial University. The townspeople had seen other great days, had heard longer speeches and had grown accustomed to newspapermen. But trial openings had meant trial closings; here they were starting a university which would run on forever. A veritable mint it was to be, turning fundamentalism into the brightest gold, increasing in production with each matriculation, bringing unending fame to the town. . . . They put on their best Sunday clothes that morning and went out to hear the ruddy face governor "make a speech. . . ." Now Governor Peay was, like Joshua, leading his people into the promised land, happy as he turned the first dirt, his face glowing as he daubed a little cement on the stone, his eyes brightening as he heard the cheers.[16]

The Bryan Memorial Association was thus charged with raising the money nec- essary to fulfill the promise that started that day. Members chose as their slogan "Fifty Thousand Fundamentalists for the Faith of Our Fathers" and included numerous pastors such as John Roach Stanton and the Reverend Bob Jones.[17] The statement of their purpose, as repeated on their numerous publications, read "Bryan Memorial Association, Dayton, Tennessee: An Institution Founded upon the Conviction That the Bible Is the Word of God."

In response to the public ridicule that accompanied the trial, the association exhibited what W. J. Cash called the "histrionic urge to perform in splendor."[18] It made the bold move to proclaim its mission and intentions nationally, ini- tiating a "Dime a Day" subscription campaign and soliciting donations from some of Bryan's long-standing political friends and foes. U.S. congressman Cordell Hull of Tennessee, who would go on to serve as secretary of state dur- ing World War II and found the United Nations, agreed to contribute.[19] But oth- ers proved cautious in light of the direction that Bryan's politics had taken. One signed pledge card belonged to future president Franklin Delano Roosevelt, who had already served as assistant secretary of the navy and was preparing to run for governor of New York. According to a handwritten notation on the donation card, however, the money was never received due to conditions set by the donor: "Mr. Roosevelt—requests $ not to be used as he wants to see how the teachers and the teaching work out." The association targeted southerners specifically, circulating a press release to Virginia dailies and weeklies that pointed to Bryan's prominence in the South.[20] Only one short year after the trial, the director of the association, Malcolm Lockhart, received an encouraging letter from A. W. Murray, secretary of the Knox County Knights of the Ku Klux Klan. Murray complimented the fund-raising group, proclaiming that "I know of no other association or organization that is rendering a more needed service at this time in preserving 'God's greatest thought in speech.'" Additionally, Murray promised the loyal and unwavering support of his local chapter and of those throughout the world: "I am sure that you will find each and every Klansman ready to help as well as their local unit, as Klansmen of the Nation know and realize what William Jennings Bryan stood for, as well as they know that he went down fighting for a good cause, and while he is laying at rest and his voice can no longer be heard, that warm and heart-felt spirit still reigns in the hearts of millions, and I am only sorry that we did not have the opportunity to help more as time did not allow, but at any time we can be of help to you, or to the proposed University, do not hesitate to call on us."[21] Within four years of the groundbreaking ceremony, the association succeeded in garnering three-quarters of a million dollars in subscriptions, approximately $200,000 of which was received as cash. Bryan may have lost favor among the political elite, but along with other fundamentalist preachers such as Mordecai F. Ham, Bryan had used the anti-evolution issue to attract an estimated 1 million converts (including a sixteen-year-old boy from North Carolina named Billy Graham).[22] The association had also acquired a total of eighty-four acres for the campus and had laid the roads, water mains, and foundation for the main building. According to active member and future president of the university George Washburn, such progress "had seldom been equaled in this country in the raising of money for memorial purposes."[23]

In an effort to preserve the dignity of Bryan's legacy, and the dignity of fundamentalists as a whole, Washburn kept a close eye on the accomplishments of the anti-evolution crusade after the Scopes verdict and reported his observations to Lockhart. Mississippi was one of the few states where the anti-evolution campaign peaked after Bryan's death. Washburn insisted that "it was the Bryan influence that extended into Mississippi and helped to secure the passage of the anti-evolution bill through the Mississippi Legislature. It is even now the Bryan influence and example that stands like the 'Rock of Gibraltar' for the highest ideals in morals and religion based on Biblical authority."[24] Washburn's vision—and the Klan's for that matter—of Bryan's legacy was not unique to members of the Memorial Association, most of whom still saw the Great Commoner as the kind, warm protector of rural America. One such Kentucky supporter, P. H. Callahan, did not want to see Bryan's national legacy forgotten or his image tainted by his last bursts of frustration and anger in Dayton. Callahan was part of a group attempting to build a statue of Bryan to be placed in Washington, D.C. Minutes from a 1932 meeting of this committee reveal that the location for the likeness was to be somewhere along Constitutional Avenue, facing south toward the Lincoln Memorial and Arlington Cemetery, where Bryan was buried.[25] Regarding the design of the sculpture, Callahan offered several aesthetic suggestions based on a preliminary image. In a letter to fellow committee member Clifton C. Berryman, he wrote: "The upraised arm of Bryan is more characteristic of Roosevelt and, in my opinion, there ought to be a radical change there. Furthermore, I never did see Bryan use that gesticulation of force and power, but on the contrary it was always a plea of a pleading approach. Then again I have seen Mr. Bryan under fire on many occasions and even at Dayton, but never did all the soft lines of his face disappear, no matter how great the provocation or the earnestness of his appeal, and am afraid Borglum [the artist] has been reading Henry Mencken."[26] Apparently legacies were not exclusive to Bryan; Mencken seems to have continued to incur the wrath of the Great Commoner's supporters. Lehman Johnson of Memphis, nearly nine months after the Scopes Trial, wrote to Governor Peay, complaining about the radical material that continued to be published by Mencken.[27] Peay responded quickly, condemning Mencken as a "word juggler without personal or moral responsibility" and, in one final punch, "an intellectual skunk."[28] Emotions obviously persisted.

In addition to raising money, the Memorial Association worked diligently to craft the image of William Jennings Bryan College and to attract prospective students. In the process of conceptualizing the new institution, Memorial Association director Lockhart attempted to justify the decision to build a separate college in a letter to his staff. In describing a recent Walter Lippmann lecture at the University of Virginia and noting that Lippmann opposed "their viewpoint," Lockhart summarized Lippmann's take on Thomas Jefferson's views of taxation. Lockhart wrote that Jefferson, "in formulating his famous Bill of Rights stated that to assess through taxes or otherwise citizens of a state and use the money thus procured in the propagation of that which the tax payers do not believe, was sinful and indefensible."[29] Thus, Bryan College was portrayed as a moral obligation endorsed by a founding father, who would have, according to Lockhart's interpretation, been on the side of majoritarianism. This internal campaign to gather voices of support from the likes of Jefferson was a direct attempt to combat the media critics and to assuage a collective sense of inferiority. Endorsements also came from leaders of state and national organizations, such as the Alabama president of the Woman's Christian Temperance Union and the national World's Christian Fundamentalists Association, which issued a proclamation of support at its 1927 annual convention.[30]

The Bryan Memorial Association used these endorsements to establish a sense of community among Bryanites. It tinkered with slogans with the same intention, including "Agnostics call us 'Yokels': Bryan Memorial University, Dayton, Tennessee."[31] Perhaps most telling are instructions to association members written by Lockhart regarding fund-raising techniques. "The best method," Lockhart wrote, "is what you call 'Personal radiation.' When you find an aggressive militant Christian, who is interested in protecting the faith of our young people, ask him for the names of several others." He envisioned this growing army as the "beginning of an effort to set up a great counterstream . . . against the enemies."[32] His vision confirms that in their retreat from the society that rejected them, fundamentalists were committed to building a network among themselves. The media ridicule during the Scopes Trial had pitted Bryanites against civilization, giving rise to a consciousness of inferiority that galvanized local citizens to reclaim the Scopes narrative and preserve Bryan's legacy.

Numerous pamphlets were published and disseminated among Christian churches and organizations to promote this redemptive institution, this "city on a hill" that Bryan had once imagined. The chairman of the Richmond, Virginia, office of the Bryan Memorial Association, J. H. Chappell, circulated posthumous copies of Bryan's undelivered speech, along with a cover letter that called Bryan a "protagonist" fighting for the "eternal truth at Dayton."[33] The association's first manifesto included a section entitled "The Birth of the Idea," which recounted the events of the Scopes Trial and characterized what many fundamentalists believed had been at stake that summer—which was not merely the cause of evolution but even the entire existence of a faith they now saw as persecuted. Bryan's own words were used to express what can only be seen as the desperation of a community to maintain its culture and cosmology, and his sentiment was echoed by Bishop W. T. Manning, who proclaimed: "The present movement does not mean only rejection of the Virgin Birth, or this or that miracle of the Gospel. . . . It has at its roots in a determined presupposition against the possibility of miracle, against the supernatural as such, and so against the very message of the Gospel as declared in the New Testament. A Christ who was not born of the Virgin, who did not rise in the body on the third day, and who did not ascend into Heaven, is not the Christ in whom this Church believes and has always believed."[34] Thus, the Memorial Association, despite all of Bryan's progressive reforms, required all of its trustees to "believe in the historicity and infallibility of the Holy Bible" and to affirm that belief "to the satisfaction of the Association."[35] And members created and listed in the university charter a statement of beliefs that included a clear-cut position on creationism: "We believe that the origin of man was by fiat of God in the act of creation as related in the Book of Genesis; that he was created in the image of God; that he sinned and thereby incurred physical and spiritual death."[36] In order to define further the institution, early administrators chose the byline for the college to be "An Institution Which Recognizes Revelation and Accepts the Supernatural."[37] All of this material used language that reflected the fundamentalist cause and directly rejected the modern embrace of science and logic, as opposed to faith. Additionally, the association republished in pamphlet form several of Bryan's key anti-evolution speeches, including "The Modern Arena," which focused primarily on the threat that Darwin's theories posed to young people—an argument particularly relevant to university fund-raisers. Bryan's own words maintained their effectiveness and clarity:

> Darwinism attacks the faith of the student just at the time when the spirit of dependence is giving way to the spirit of independence. This is the age when self-confidence reaches its maximum. It is the time when he is inclined to think his parents are old fogy—he does not need to have men like the President of the University of Wisconsin ridicule the beliefs of his father, mother, and grandparents. . . . When the evil influence of Darwinism is understood it will be sent to oblivion and these college combats so fatal to students, however pleasant they may be to their instructors, will be remembered as we now recall the bloody gladiatorial contests that took place in ancient arenas.[38]

Obviously, these "college combats" were not remembered as Bryan would have liked them to be. Evolution was not driven from the American consciousness, except, of course, at William Jennings Bryan College.

In an attempt to appeal further to their fundamentalist community, the early founders of Bryan College recast the story of the Scopes Trial in a more favorable light, offering their own brand of public criticism and scrutiny of their antagonists such as Clarence Darrow. Bryan was, of course, depicted as almost a prophet, the true believer who fought "for the faith which was once delivered unto the saints."[39] The defense, on the other hand, was demonized. Included in a publicity pamphlet, "A University in the Making," distributed by Bryan College as construction on the main buildings began, was an article written by J. H. Hunter that called Darrow an atheist three times and insisted that he had come to Dayton "bent on destroying" the scriptures.[40] Yet another Bryan College press release, "In Order That You May Know," opened with this aggressive retaliation against the modernists: "The William Jennings Bryan University exists for a purpose. This memorial to William Jennings Bryan is a 'Testimony' against those that would make God a liar." The document elaborates still further on the mission of Bryan College, stating that "even if the evolutionary belief is not dislodged from the public mind before the Lord's return, some will heed the warning, and many are being strengthened spiritually through the ministry of the Word."[41] In order to further still distinguish themselves from their critics, the Bryan Memorial Association published yet another pamphlet, which included both a reprint of the speech that Bryan was planning on making regarding the outcome of the Scopes Trial before his unexpected death and a seven-point list of differences between fundamentalists and modernists that had recently appeared in a Boston journal.[42] Conscious of crafting its image, the Bryan Memorial Association specifically placed William Jennings Bryan University in the New Testament narrative, promoting a ministry preparing for the Second Coming, appealing to fundamentalists, particularly to those who felt the modern world had rejected both religion and the religious. University president Leo E. Guille gloated in a 1931 letter to donors, writing, "The Institution is in operation now—for Freshmen—and our President [Guille] is teaching Genesis as the inspired Word of God in the very classroom in which John T. Scopes taught Evolution as accounting for Creation."[43] The fundamentalists, by retreating from their critics and opening their own school, perceived themselves as having come full circle.

Additional promotional material for the college continued to express the fundamentalists' theme of redemption and resurrection. One such historical sketch of the new Christian college on Bryan Hill proclaimed that "little did the actors in the now world-famous Dayton evolution trial realize that from the ashes—Phoenix-like—would spring a nationally known institution of higher learning."[44] Even more revealing are typescript internal memoranda listing the reasons, possibly talking points, for building William Jennings Bryan University. Vivid evangelical language permeates the documents, including much discussion of salvation as a key purpose for supporting the institution. Number three on the list reads: "God's people need to be stirred in activity in combating the Devil and the forces of evil as manifested in modernism, and the associated 'isms.' Since 'Evolution,' as science, falsely so called, is at the root of these false 'isms,' it merits increasing attention."[45] In anticipation of future criticism, administrators at Bryan College apparently held on to articles and clippings regarding challenges to evolution, even some dating back to the turn of the century. A typescript of an article, for example, written by John T. S. Blackburn in 1903 discussed the flaws in Darwin's theories. Exclamation points and excited statements such as "Darwin began writing on this subject to break down the belief in OUR BIBLE" exemplify the many documents kept in the early college press materials. Blackburn's informal lecture of sorts includes a list of books that he read that shaped his skepticism regarding evolution and natural selection.[46]

Comments from the Reverend James Jefferson Davis Hall made in the *Southern Churchmen* have also been typed and filed among the archived documents. Hall's argument, laid out in "The Falsity of the Theory of Evolution," hinges on recorded quotations of famous figures who rejected Darwin's work. Lord Kelvin, president of the Royal Academy of Learning in England, is remembered for saying, "That man could be evolved from inferior animals is the wildest dream of materialism, a pure assumption which offends me alike by its folly and its arrogance."[47] And Thomas Carlyle is quoted as having announced that evolution "is a Gospel of dirt."[48] Still another document, "Jonah May Have Occupied Air Chamber, Placed at His Disposal by Whale," written by Dr. Ransom Harvey and published in an issue of the *Jewish Forum*, has been retyped and added to publicity material produced in support of Bryan College. And Bryan College itself has generated a list of potential criticisms that it might face, along with arguments that could counter such ridicule as that which the people of Dayton and fundamentalists endured in the summer of 1925. The memory of the Scopes Trial was long, and the administration and early founders of Bryan Memorial University did not hesitate to arm themselves with any and all possible proof of their faith and with any arguments that would disprove Darwin's science.

THE SCOPES LEGACY AT BRYAN COLLEGE

Across one entire wall of the bookstore at Bryan College (the name was shortened from William Jennings Bryan University in 1993) stand pamphlets, xeroxed articles, and cassette tapes, all devoted to reeducating the public and students on the Scopes Trial, with additional materials available for a small copying fee. Many of the articles are written by Richard Cornelius, a retired English professor and the leading Scopes archivist at the college. Such materials include, for example, a list of factual misrepresentations in the film version of the trial, *Inherit the Wind*, the transcripts from the Symposium on the 70th Anniversary of the Scopes Evolution Trial, and a selected annotated bibliography of the trial and of evolution and creationism in general. Most recently, a DVD entitled "The Scopes Trial: Inherit the Truth" has been released, which features a two-hour trial reenactment that attempts to counter the negative publicity the original conflict attracted.[49]

Bryan College has held steadfast to its original mission—to champion the cause of biblical literalism and, in a sense, to answer Darrow's questions about creationism that had tripped up Bryan on the stand. In an effort to publicize and maintain its fundamentalist cosmology, Bryan College has established the William Jennings Bryan Center for Law and Public Policy (CLPP), the Center for Worldview Studies (CWS), and, most significant, the Center for Origins Research (CORE).[50] The primary purpose of CORE as described in its mission statement is to develop a creationist model of biology, which requires research and teaching in what are labeled the "five foundational areas of biology." These areas include "design, natural evil, speciation, biogeography, and biosystematics," the study of which is intended to "bring glory to God by understanding His revelation of Himself in creation."[51] Faculty active in CORE are regular guest speakers at various churches, and they teach one of the primary science courses offered at Bryan College, Biological Origins. Bryan College also offers a minor in Origin Studies, for which the Biological Origins class is required, along with Pentateuch, Elements of Hebrew I, and History of Life.[52]

CORE's reach extends beyond the local religious community and the classroom through its publications. The center offers a regular periodical, *enCORE: Educational Notes on the Center for Origins Research* and maintains an active bibliography of creationist publications.[53] It also maintains several key databases for creation scholars and advocates, including CELD, which contains articles from journals such as *Creation Science Quarterly, Origins,* and *Transactions of the Victoria Institute,* and the Hybriddatabase (HBD), which includes references to interspecific hybrid animals. Additionally, a third database, BDISTMDS, explains the theory of Baraminology, which classifies species based on "kinds" as dictated in the book of Genesis.[54] The theory was cofounded by Kurt Wise, the former director of CORE at Bryan College. As part of the methodology of Baraminology, taxidermied animals are observed for like traits, and Bryan College has recently established the William Henning Natural History Museum to house specimens, which were increased by a gift of African taxidermy donated by a Tennessee family in 2002. CORE director Todd Wood (Ph.D., University of Virginia) maintains a blog with a tagline from Proverbs, "It is the glory of God to conceal a matter; to search out a matter the glory of kings,"[55] and serves as president of the Creation Biology Society. Wood, along with Professor Roger Sanders (Ph.D., University of Texas), executive editor of the *Journal of Creation Theology and Science,* oversees a library that includes 2,000 books and "papers related to Biblical studies, creationism, and evolution spanning the past 400 years."[56] The library even includes the archive of Dr. Wayne Fair, creationist zoologist (Ph.D., Rutgers), who corresponded with Henry M. Morris and Frank L.

Marsh, noted creationist advocates. Their efforts signal a retreat from society. Rather than combat evolutionary biology directly, Bryan College has insulated itself among like-minded believers, networked and organized around a single principle made infamous in 1925.

The contemporary struggle of a century-old debate—the great clash of science and religion that once took place on the courthouse lawn—lives and reverberates atop Bryan Hill. The university did show some movement outside of the separate sphere of fundamentalist higher education, particularly when the controversy on which it was conceived resurfaced. Motions to appeal the Butler Act in 1935 and in 1952 elicited passionate objection in the forms of letters from members of the Bryan College community.[57] The president of Bryan College, Judson A. Rudd, actually sent a copy of Bryan's posthumous speech from the Scopes Trial to every Tennessee legislator.[58] Even as late as 1973, Tennessee attempted to pass legislation mandating that evolution be referred to as a theory and taught alongside creationist accounts of human development. The law was challenged and declared unconstitutional immediately.[59] Though legal challenges to the teaching of evolution have not fared well in the late twentieth and early twenty-first centuries, the hearts and minds of Americans have been heavily influenced by these once underground, now resurgent, fundamentalists. A July 2005 Pew Research poll revealed that 64 percent of those surveyed nationally believed that creationism should be taught alongside evolution, with 38 percent supporting the teaching of creationism exclusively. Moreover, on at least four occasions between 1993 and 2004, the General Social Survey has asked respondents to indicate whether they believe that the statement "human beings developed from earlier species of animals" is true or false. In 1993, less than half (48 percent) of those polled believed evolution to be false, a number that increased to 54 percent by 2004.[60]

The popularity of the new theory of Intelligent Design has reignited not only the evolution question but also the peripheral partisan political issues concerning the environment, the role of religion in public life, and even the rights of gays and lesbians. In 2004, the commissioners of Rhea County—a county that gave Republican presidential nominee John McCain one of his largest margins of victory, 74 percent of the vote to Democratic nominee Barack Obama's 25 percent—voted unanimously to recriminalize sodomy in an effort to discourage gays and lesbians from living in the area. Media outrage and an equally resurgent critical spotlight led to the quick reversal of the decision.[61] Bryan College has also remained politically active in the debate tangentially related to the historic evolution controversy, inviting various speakers (and providing recordings of these lectures online) on topics such as "Global Warming,"

"A Christian Response to Left/Right Environmental Ideologies: Bearing Witness in a Post-Modern Culture," and "Politicized Science: A Challenge to Evangelical Thinking."[62]

■ Scopes historian Jerry Tompkins characterized the brand of fundamentalism displayed in Dayton as a neurosis, arguing that at its core, "fundamentalism is emotive, a bias, a provincialism that new information cannot change."[63] And emotions ran high that summer of 1925. Florida philanthropist George Washburn, who promised $10,000 to Bryan College at first mention of its possible existence, insisted that the memorial campaign was "the beginning of the battle that will encircle the world." Washburn, perhaps more clearly than most, recognized the mental devastation that accompanied the public ridicule and the death of Bryan, predicting one proactive way that fundamentalists would attempt to counter the negative construction of white religious identity and respond to this cultural, collective anxiety. Writing to Dayton school superintendent Walter White, he claimed that "this was a psychological moment to establish a Fundamentalist university."[64] The fundamentalists in Dayton and those who shared their faith, or were at least sympathetic to their cause, needed a way to cope with and react to this sense of inferiority and the anger and rejection that accompanied it. Building, planning, crafting an image for William Jennings Bryan College gave them just such an outlet, providing a protected space for fundamentalists, sheltered from the brutal pen of journalists and the judging gaze of modernists, liberals, scientists, and nonbelievers. Having officially opened its doors in the fall of 1930, Bryan College continues to promote its vision of providing young Christians with a biblically founded education and to maintain faithfully its version of the trial. Over eighty years later, what began as a publicity stunt, and in many ways as a personal battle between Bryan and Darrow, has become a reactionary, defining mission.

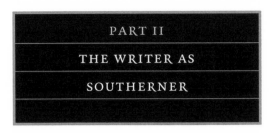

With one stroke the Agrarians thus countered the tendency to regard the rise of a new class of southern intellectuals as commensurate with the development of liberalism in the region. Now there suddenly was—or appeared to be—an active conservative voice ready to affirm Old South values in twentieth-century terms.
—Daniel Joseph Singal, *The War Within*

When journalist H. L. Mencken, upon observing the Scopes Evolution Trial, described the South as the "bunghole of the United States, a cesspool of Baptists, a miasma of Methodism, snake-charmers, phony real-estate operators, and syphilitic evangelists,"[1] he did more than insult the religious faithful of Dayton, Tennessee. To the reading public of the South, the Sage of Baltimore came to embody the barrage of public criticism that accompanied the myriad of "causes célèbres" intended "to agitate metropolitan newspapers and to bring to Southern capitals protesting telegrams, eminent attorneys, and roving bands of petitioners, investigators, and missionaries."[2] For one specific group of talented southern intellectuals, self-titled the Fugitives and gathered at Vanderbilt University, these attacks on the South and the negative identity construction that followed would catalyze their transformation, not once, but twice. Talent does not inherently insulate one from ridicule, but it did give this group, which included John Crowe Ransom, Allen Tate, Robert Penn Warren, and Donald Davidson, a vital tool to overcome the disparagement. Nicknamed for the literary journal, the *Fugitive*, that they published from 1922 to 1925, these writers originally intended to throw off the sentimentality of southern romanticism and bring modernism to southern arts and letters. However, the blistering coverage of the Scopes Trial awakened a dormant historical consciousness among the young writers, who realized that their individual identities were part of a larger regional identity at odds with American national identity.

Davidson personally referred to the media that descended on Dayton as "shock troops,"[3] revealing a "new mood of defensive anger."[4] In an effort to respond to this public criticism, the Fugitives abandoned their emotional and psychological flights from their homeland, morphing into a community intent on reclaiming the southern past and using it specifically to garner recognition in the literary world. This transformation resulted in a series of publications, including biographies of the likes of Jefferson Davis, poetry infused with local lore and nostalgia, and critical essays championing tradition, authoritarian religion, and self-determination. However, this effort to resuscitate southern art and revise southern history failed to effectively counter the public denunciation of the South. C. Vann Woodward argued that for the Fugitives, "the best defensive was an offensive"[5]—and so it was, at least momentarily. In an effort to prove that intellectual life in the South did exist and to seek recognition from the critics, Ransom collected and published individual articles by his fellow Fugitives, promoting the integrity and purity of the white southern experience. The regional manifesto, titled *I'll Take My Stand* (1930), aggressively defended the agrarian lifestyle against industrialization, offering an idyllic picture of the white southern way of life. The South that Ransom and his fellow contributors described, however, never really existed, for they brushed over most aspects of the atrocities of slavery and sharecropping. Ransom's essay in the collection was appropriately titled "Reconstructed, but Unregenerate," and in his version "the South was a fine spun living dream . . . rosy, romantic, and unreal."[6] Close readings of *I'll Take My Stand* and the published and unpublished correspondence among the contributors, as well as the critical reviews of the book, expose further evidence of this striving for recognition.

The Fugitives-turned-Agrarians did not get the respect that they sought. Despite promoting their white southern cosmology in a series of five public debates, as well as in countless essays and even in a sequel entitled *Who Owns America*, Agrarianism failed to succeed as a real alternative to American capitalism. Nor did it resurrect the South or prove its culture to be more genuine, if at all viable, in the new modern temper. In fact, more criticism and public ridicule from journalists from both the North and the New South followed. Characterized as southern apologists and delusional neo-Confederates, the Agrarians, despite their best efforts, seemed only to initiate a "second phase of the Fundamentalist campaign."[7] The resulting wave of criticism was followed by a transformation as distinct as that which initially turned these Fugitive poets toward the cause of Agrarianism.

Recognizing the futility of their efforts, Ransom encouraged his former students and fellow writers to return to their authentic field of expertise, the English departments of universities throughout the South, cultivating, penning, and promoting a distinct type of literary analysis that came to be known as New Criticism. Named after the title of Ransom's book, *The New Criticism*,[8] this modern, yet reactionary, method of evaluating literary techniques and artistic value emphasized the critical, yet nonscientific, knowledge that was accessible only to poets and writers. According to Terry Eagleton, New Criticism insisted that "rescuing the text from author and reader went hand in hand with disentangling it from any social or historical context."[9] And these southern New Critics encouraged an almost-fundamentalist close reading of the text, while giving less importance to the historical and social context of the work. Though the New Critics' attention to form and the text was primarily driven by their aesthetic vision, the method, which so directly contrasted with their Agrarian views, can also be seen to some extent as a compensatory response—the drive for recognition and superiority—to this second wave of public criticism. New Criticism not only offered these embattled Agrarians a place of significance as artists within the modern, industrial world; it also handed these Nashville-bred critics the gavels of judgment, while downplaying the southern culture that they once had argued deeply affected their worldview and their creative process.

Solidifying their place in American literary history, Robert Penn Warren and Cleanth Brooks wrote two best-selling textbooks, *Understanding Poetry* (1938) and *Understanding Fiction* (1943), which taught numerous generations of both teachers and students the methods of evaluation fundamental to New Criticism. In general, scholarly explanations of the transformation from Agrarianism to New Criticism either attempt to locate some core element shared between the two expressions, thus downplaying the dramatic nature of the shift, or simply note that Agrarianism was abandoned in favor of a return to art and critical theory. Their essays, including Ransom's collection *The New Criticism* (1941), as well as the correspondence among Ransom, Warren, and the other New Critics, reveals New Criticism to be part of a larger and more complicated regional response to the well-documented denunciation of the South. Moreover, this transformation had significant political consequences. By championing white southern economic values, the Agrarians established a rhetoric of rural southern superiority and resistance to modernization. And the New Critics, by championing white southern aesthetic values, stripped the American literary canon of any diversity or challenge to their southern perspective for decades following their emergence. Though there are aspects of the New Critical attention to form and text that surely benefited the generations that followed, this specialized vision of American art belied the true complexity of the southern and national experience. Thus, examining the evolution of but a fraction of this particular cohort of successful writers sheds new light on their metamorphosis as a group and also reveals the effects of the expansive reach and pervasiveness of public criticism on the formation of southern white identity.

CHAPTER 4

FUGITIVES CAPTURED

THE WASTELAND OF

SOUTHERN IDENTITY

I can hardly speak for others, but for John Ransom and myself, surely, the Dayton episode dramatized more ominously than any other event easily could, how difficult it was to be a Southerner and also a writer. It was horrifying to see the cause of liberal education argued in a Tennessee court by a famous agnostic lawyer from Illinois named Clarence Darrow. It was still more horrifying—and frightening—to realize that the South was being exposed to large-scale public detraction and did not know or much care how to answer.

—Donald Davidson, quoted in Thomas Daniel Young, *Waking Their Neighbors Up: The Nashville Agrarians Rediscovered*

For the Fugitive poets of Nashville, Tennessee, the experience of white southern identity began in the wake of the "cold Civil War,"[1] when the Dayton evolution trial, according to Donald Davidson, "broke in upon our literary concerns like a midnight alarm."[2] During adolescence, acknowledged Allen Tate, "we knew we were Southerners, but this was a matter of plain denomination; just as we knew that some people were Yankees. . . . This was our long moment of innocence."[3] This midnight alarm, however, somehow catalyzed in the minds of these writers an awareness of the South's alienated status within the nation as a whole. This recognition of southern "otherness," of a South that has been defined in opposition to American culture, resulted in a skewed self-perception, muddying both the white southerner's sense of regional identity and his or her American identity. Such inner conflict resulted predictably in an artistic regional culture that often proved resistive, frustrated, and self-absorbed. Though these writers and critics had the benefit of education and innate talent, they were not immune to the public criticism of the South. In fact, their awareness of historical precedent only deepened the wounds inflicted in Dayton. And the attacks, particularly H. L. Mencken's, were not limited to religious fundamentalism, but spread to southern art and letters and culture in general. For these promising young writers, who thought they would rescue southern literature and put it on the map, the Scopes Trial criticism made them realize the depth of disdain for the South.

In an unpublished essay draft titled "The South and the Nation: A Historical Essay, No. 2," Davidson pointed to the repercussions of this historical awakening that transformed the Fugitives, locating in the 1920s' public denouncement of the South a pattern reflecting the "days when abolitionism first began to be militant." According to Davidson, in the War between the States and thereafter, "the South has repeatedly served as a stalking-horse for bagging game that in the last analysis had little to do with pious rewards and humanitarian reforms. Whenever the Northeast has felt a threat against its power or has wished to gain new power, the familiar story of the Southern 'outrage' begins to flood the press."[4] Thus, the experience of criticism in the 1920s seemed part of a unique regional heritage; one conflict seemed to merge into the next. The bloody clash between slaveholders and humanitarians, between high tariff and low tariff advocates, now snowballed to include the cultural collision of science and religion, industry and agrarianism, urban and rural, and, of course, North and South.

The contemporary drama, for the Fugitives, now played out against the backdrop of its historical ancestry or heritage. Such damnation, concluded Davidson, not only served to "discredit Southern opinion, and prevent it from making headway in the nation, but it also indoctrinate[d] the South, under present conditions, with a feeling of its own inferiority and so divides the South against itself."[5] In order to appreciate fully the way in which negative identity construction transformed this group of writers, it is necessary first to understand what their collective intentions were in their first incarnation as the Fugitives and what motivated their efforts. Unlike the community in Dayton, the Fugitives expressed, in their correspondence and in their writings, their sense of alienation and their striving for recognition. Eventually, Davidson, Tate, John Crowe Ransom, and Robert Penn Warren would go their separate ways, but for the decades of their collaboration, their aesthetic and political choices, in some measure, reflected a shared sense of inferiority and their struggle to overcome it and to secure acceptance and acknowledgment in the literary world.

THE CIRCLE FORMS

Led by Sidney Mttron Hirsch, a professor of English and respected aesthete, this informal gathering of gentlemen poets offered both their latest attempts at verse and their philosophies of art, experience, and the nature of poetic knowledge. Donald Davidson, a student at Vanderbilt before the war, was drawn into the circle through his acquaintance with Goldie Hirsch, the daughter of this local man of letters and Fugitive founder.[6] Inspired by his Shakespeare instructor, John Crowe Ransom, Davidson soon extended his mentor an invitation. Ransom's scholarly reputation—he graduated first in his class from Vanderbilt in 1909 and was soon thereafter awarded a Rhodes Scholarship—quickly made him the academic captain of the troupe. Ransom had returned to Nashville after serving as an artillery officer in France and published a small volume, *Poems about God* (1919). The collection had been encouraged and praised by Robert Frost, consequently elevating Ransom's status among the participants in the evening discussions. After completing his service as an infantry company commander in France, Davidson also returned to Vanderbilt. He was now a member of the faculty, and it was at this time that he met Allen Tate, whom he considered to be one of the most talented and well-read students of his teaching career.[7] Naturally, Davidson encouraged Tate's affiliation with the Saturday night critics, and Tate was happy to join. Reminiscing about the invitation, Tate acknowledged that his excitement resulted from his own vanity: "Don and John were professors; and when I got there the next Saturday night, being the only undergraduate present, I was flattered."[8]

Robert Penn Warren arrived on campus in the fall of 1921 at the age of sixteen and enrolled in two composition classes taught by Ransom, whose work and teachings would ignite Warren's passion for poetry. According to biographer Joseph Blotner, when Warren read Ransom's *Poems about God*, he "felt a shock of recognition."[9] "For the first time," Warren confessed, "I saw the world that I knew around me to be the stuff of poetry, because that book was a book with the same background of the upper South. It was strange and even disturbing, that discovery."[10] To his fellow teachers, Ransom would confide that "Warren was the brightest student that they had ever seen around here."[11] "Red" Warren, nicknamed for his infamous fiery locks, joined the Fugitive community in 1924.[12] At that point, the group was already fairly well established, with a publication of the same name, the *Fugitive*, backed by donations from the Nashville community and garnering some recognition in the local literary community. In addition to Davidson, Ransom, Tate, and Warren, several other local academics and artists rounded out the membership. The list included Hirsch's brother-in-law and local host for the meetings, James Marshall Frank; Nashville banker Alec Brock Stevenson; local businessman Jesse Willes; mathematician Alfred Starr; Boston psychiatrist Merrill Moore; English instructor Stanley Johnson; well-regarded literary scholars Walter Clyde Curry and William Frierson; political science scholar William Yandell Elliott; creative writer Andrew Lytle; and a Kentucky homemaker, Laura Gottschalk Riding.[13] Cleanth Brooks Jr., who later worked extensively with Warren at the *Southern Review* and in coediting the popular New Critical textbooks, *Understanding Poetry* and *Understanding Fiction*, enrolled at Vanderbilt just as the Fugitive journal ceased publication, though he is often considered part of the creative swell of this period.

In its new setting, Dr. Hirsch—according to Tate, "attendance at the meetings seemed to confer upon us all the degree of Doctor, but Doctor of what I never knew"[14]—called on his colleagues to read aloud their respective works while carbons were passed out to the audience. On one such night in 1922, Dr. Hirsch first suggested a magazine, an outlet for all the manuscripts that these evenings had produced. Though the group seemed to be unanimously agreeable to the endeavor, Tate and Davidson were cautious. Tate, specifically, regarded the idea as one "of the utmost temerity; if not of folly." Davidson, although thrilled with the notion, insisted that he "could not believe, at first, that my friends would really go through with this undertaking." "I thought it was bold," Davidson conceded, "but not folly."[15] Davidson felt sure that the poetry being discussed in closed session on Whitland Avenue would rival any work being published in a burgeoning young band of southern journals, including the *Reviewer* of Richmond, Virginia, and the *Double Dealer* of New Orleans. The project quickly materialized, with poems chosen democratically by group members,[16] and the most economical printing company was selected, which in this case was an African American–owned business.[17] The cost was shared by these Nashville "doctors," and public copies sold for 25 cents per issue. The selected contributors adopted pseudonyms for the first issue, a tactic that, according to Tate, was "less for concealment, I believe, than for the romance."[18] Perhaps more significant than their choice of romantic aliases was the title chosen for their journal—contradicting accounts credit the title to both Hirsch and Stevenson. The name conjured feelings of flight and escape, but to Tate the intent was clear. "For a Fugitive," he proclaimed, "was quite simply a Poet: the Wanderer, or even the Wandering Jew, the Outcast, the man who carries the secret wisdom around the world." In the foreword to the first issue in April 1922, Ransom "announced rather majestically that one hope of the contributors was to open the channel so that Southern literature, which had expired, 'like any other stream whose source is stopped up,' might flow again."[19] The hard work and creative discipline required to produce the magazine seemed to indicate a promising literary future for the young southerners.

ESTABLISHING AN OASIS IN THE DESERT OF DIXIE

In truth, the triumph, as Davidson called the publication of the inaugural issue of the *Fugitive*, signified a turn in southern letters, or so it seemed to the contributors, who were well aware of the accusation of southern cultural aridity made by Mencken. The Baltimore journalist had actually espoused his disdain, pity, and scorn for the South as early as the first decade of the twentieth century. In a 1907 essay titled "The Passing of a Civilization," Mencken argued that "the Old South had been failing for years."[20] Less than two years later, in his new position as the book editor for the glossy Smart Set, Mencken observed that southern books were growing increasingly scarce. The appearance of Montrose J. Moses's The Literature of the South elicited an intensely visceral Mencken review featured in the Los Angeles Times. According to southern historian and Mencken biographer Fred Hobson, this 1910 review foreshadowed Mencken's future commentary on what he considered countless southern deficiencies: "Not until the Southerner overcame the cult of hero-worship, Mencken stressed, would he stop producing 'shameless mush.' Not until he forgot the nineteenth century and concentrated on 'the dilemmas and difficulties which confront the southern people today' would he be taken seriously outside the South. To be of any value at all, Mencken maintained, Southern literature had to be 'first of all, a criticism of life.'"[21] This, of course, was not the intent of this group—the Fugitives—who were seeking to flee the sentimental culture of the Old Confederacy.

Mencken's most frequently cited essay, "The Sahara of the Bozart," published in 1917, reiterated his perception that southern literature was virtually nonexistent. Yet this piece, unlike the Times essay, did not offer a theory as to how a regional revival could be fashioned; rather it vilified Dixie for its comprehensive cultural and artistic sterility. His tone had changed; upon observing the South in the new century, Mencken insisted that "the picture gives one the creeps." At the center of Mencken's contempt for rural religion demonstrated during the Scopes Trial lay the South's complacency and anti-intellectualism. This perceived cultural stagnation had actually prompted this verbal beheading for the South, one that was not aimed solely at the unschooled bucolic masses. "The Sahara of the Bozart" portrayed the South as a wasteland that would not be missed if it were to dissolve into the sea. This piece incensed educated southern artists and academics, particularly the Fugitives. According to Mencken, the essay "made me a dreadful bother to the South, and brought me a great deal of violent denunciation, but all the more enlightened Southerners had to admit its truth."[22] Linking the southern past with the contemporary moment, Mencken further explained:

It is as if the Civil War stamped out every last bearer of torch, and left only a mob of peasants in the field. One thinks of Asia Minor, resigned to the Armenians, Greeks and wild swine, of Poland abandoned to the Poles. In all that gargantuan paradise of the fourth-rate, there is not a single picture gallery worth going into, or a single orchestra capable of playing the nine symphonies of Beethoven, or a single opera-house, or a single theater devoted to decent plays, or a single monument worth looking at, or a single workshop devoted to making beautiful things. Once you have counted James Branch Cabell (a lingering survivor of the ancient regime; a scarlet dragonfly imbedded in opaque amber) you will not find a single Southern prose writer who can actually write.[23]

The essay was read widely throughout the South, and many considered it an unwarranted assault. More important, the attack came from someone whom, despite being a native of the peripheral southern state of Maryland, many considered to be an outsider.[24] His scathing essays on the South and his personal elitism further dissolved any perceived empathy for the region. For the Fugitives, Mencken's diatribes served merely as a challenge of sorts, and they positioned themselves to be the exception to the cultural lag highlighted by the journalist. Mencken was a mighty antagonist, and his influence on the growing self-conception of the region that the Fugitives called home would become a profound and debilitating one.

As counterintuitive as it may seem in retrospect, Mencken was actually popular at one time on the Vanderbilt campus, and Tate was known to carry some of Mencken's writings with him.[25] Even Davidson, who would eventually attack Mencken publicly in the years following the Scopes Trial, seemed to hold the journalist in great regard in the early days of the Fugitive project. The group was so anxious to impress Mencken—he was, after all, the foremost cultural critic of his day—that they quoted him in the advertising copy for the Fugitive[26] and sent him a copy of the first issue, accompanied by a letter from Tate that emphasized the purpose of the magazine. The foreword also made a similar argument:[27] "Official exception having been taken by the sovereign people to the mint julep, a literary phase known rather euphemistically as Southern Literature has expired, like any other stream whose source is stopped up. The demise was not untimely: among other advantages, THE FUGITIVE is enabled to come to birth in Nashville, Tennessee, under a star not entirely unsympathetic. THE FUGITIVE flees from nothing faster than from the high-caste Brahmins of the Old South."[28]

The Fugitives were obviously determined to aggressively distance their work from that which had been deemed so lacking, so unnoticeable as to be virtually nonexistent in Mencken's Sahara.

Tate actually agreed with Mencken's depiction of the South, not only with the alleged infertility of southern literature, but also with the general intellectual vacuum that had become the New South. In his "Last Days of the Charming Lady," written only months before the Scopes Trial and carried in the *Nation*, Tate went so far as to express his own frustration with the growing fundamentalist movement, which he would defend against southern critics in only a few short years: "And so it is not surprising that the second generation after the Civil War is whooping it up in boosters' clubs along with the veritablist descendant of carpet-bagger and poor white. For this second generation, like its forebears, has no tradition of ideas, no consciousness of moral and spiritual values, as an inheritance."[29] Louise Cowan's early history of the Fugitives reinforces this antisouthern sentiment, though she insists that their disdain was subconscious: "Surrounding them in their native territory they could see only the ugliness, the ignorance, and the insensitivity of many of the people with whom they dealt. . . . At the time their topics of discussion were medieval, Elizabethan, Italian Renaissance, Oriental, or nineteenth-century French—anything but Southern."[30] But for the Fugitive band of writers, for whom "conventional Southern smugness and insensitivity to aesthetic values was a common point of departure" and for whom "a kind of wisdom the common goal,"[31] perhaps the sacrifice of their southernness seemed a small price to pay for acceptance in the significant modern literary circles of the North. But the Fugitives would reverse course abruptly and with great drama. By the time the "Last Days of the Charming Lady" reached newsstands in November 1925, Tate and his colleagues would embrace an all-consuming inspection of their white southern heritage. As a result, these poets would soon adopt a political stance that resembled nothing so much as self-appointed southern knights engaged in a duel to the death with Mencken, the dark knight himself.[32]

Mencken responded quite nonchalantly to the initial volume of the *Fugitive*, all the while insisting that the entire publication was "written by one man: its whole contents are the same key, and the names signed to the different power are obviously fictitious." He further announced, incredulously, "Why the author does not announce himself more frankly I do not know: his writings constitute, at the moment, the entire literature of Tennessee."[33] His inability to distinguish the various styles and aesthetics of the nine contributors could simply be Mencken's way of homogenizing the South once again; or, perhaps, Davidson's opinion that Mencken was not a discerning literary critic had merit. Hobson argues that in his original assessment of the Nashville writers, Mencken's "chief weakness as a literary critic had been exposed." Hobson concluded that "although he [Mencken] could detect the movement of a national or regional literature, he often could not recognize distinctions in the individual poem—and he could not distinguish one poet from another when the two poets happened to belong to the same broad 'school.'"[34] Mencken's initial support of a rebirth in southern literature was intended to spark a regional consciousness that would force southern intellectuals to respond to the socioeconomic and political aspects of their diseased society. He was, first and foremost, an instigator, as well as an extraordinarily gifted polemicist. And he could muckrake, when muckraking was called for, with the best of them.

Mencken's role as catalyst for spawning southern critics within the South was noted by the northern and eastern media. Hobson records a specific example: "When T. S. Stribling of Tennessee wrote *Birthright* (1922) about racial prejudice in a small town, the Charlotte *News* charged that he was 'strongly under the Mencken influence.'"[35] But not all southern writers, particularly Ransom, Tate, Warren, and Davidson, followed in Stribling's shoes. Rather than expose the very real southern problems finally coming to light around them, the Fugitives chose effectively to eliminate all southern references—and especially socioeconomic issues—from their verse. Even Harriet Monroe, editor of the influential *Poetry* magazine, suggested that the Nashville circle embrace the local that she considered "so rich in racial tang and prejudice, so jewel-weighted with heroic past." Tate voiced his disagreement to Monroe, insisting that "we who are Southern know the fatality of such an attitude."[36] Their efforts to escape would not impress a certain journalist.

Mencken supported the efforts of similar southern projects such as the *Reviewer* and *Double Dealer*, commenting on their value in his own journals such as *Smart Set* and the *American Mercury*. The *Double Dealer* had declared specifically—and one year earlier than the *Fugitive* proclamation regarding its intention to flee the Old South—that "the traditions are no more. . . . The Confederacy has long since been dissolved."[37] But Mencken saw a vast distinction between the critical analysis, or the prose, that the New Orleans publication was generating and the poetry embraced by the Nashville writers. The Fugitives were committed to breaking free from the "mint julep and magnolia stream of literature,"[38] but this was not the oasis in the desert for which Mencken was looking. He saw it only as "a stage in the Southern literary revival."[39] He insisted that poetry was "much easier to write than prose, and so it is always turned to by young writers and young literatures."[40] Ransom clearly delineated the journalist's position: "H. L. Mencken, with damnable iteration, declares that poetry is nothing but paregoric of lullaby, good for making him go to sleep, two teaspoonfuls of the drug doing the work if it is sufficiently pure."[41] The Fugitives had been unwilling, and perhaps uninterested, in commenting on Mencken's animosity toward their homeland; but they took the bait, so to speak, when he disparaged poetry in general. And, despite their recognition of Mencken's influence on the intellectual world, the Fugitives did perceive that they were actually succeeding at dismantling the Old South's "genteel tradition" and the "sentimentality, cant, and intellectual softness" that defined their regional predecessors.[42]

Although the Fugitives believed that they were destined to create an oasis in the Sahara of American literature below the Mason-Dixon Line, not all southern intellectuals supported the new journal. Edwin Mims, arguably the most senior member of the Vanderbilt English department, attempted to persuade the members of the group to submit their work to established scholarly and creative journals in the North, publications that would heighten their reputations (and thus the reputation of the Vanderbilt English department) more substantially than publication in a local project.[43] The need to gain approval from the traditional sources of academic validity located outside the region further emphasized the potential inferiority of any independent southern literary project. Chancellor James Hampton Kirkland did not support the magazine, and he rebuffed Tate in person when he arrived at the administration's office to sell him a subscription.[44] To Kirkland, the endeavor "smacked of rebelliousness— against the university, against status distinctions between students and faculty, against conventional moral seriousness, against sentimental evocations of the Old South." Moreover, the journal's "bohemian overtones" troubled the chancellor; after all, "plans for The Fugitive emanated from the off-campus home of a Jew," and "there were rumors that women had been seen emerging from the windows of some of the young poets' quarters."[45]

Though the Fugitives did make a conscious effort to break ties with the traditional culture of their Old South upbringings, they had other reasons for focusing specifically on poetic form and aesthetic theory. In part, such a focus seemed to be the subject of a mature and educated community of letters, while regional subject matters seemed narrow and a hindrance to gaining the national audience and recognition to which they aspired. Paradoxically, northern intellectuals praised southern writers and journalists who exposed their local plagues such as the Ku Klux Klan or the ever-expanding evangelical movement, which was just the kind of self-criticism that Mencken wanted from the Fugitives as well. Their desire to separate from society suggested an alienation from their environment that was not merely a response to southern condemnation, but also, quite notably, to the tidal wave of modernism. The opening poem of the first issue of the Fugitive, entitled "Ego," was attributed to Roger Prim (Ransom) and espoused the desire to flee from this culture to which the writer does not belong, finding refuge only with this community of poets in their safe haven on Whitland Avenue: "I have run further, matching your heart and speed / And tracked the Wary Fugitive with you."[46] Ransom and his fellow writers would be heavily influenced by the burgeoning modernist literary movement, a move-ment that insisted upon their rejection of their southern identity. However, as modernism grew increasingly opposed to the white southern tradition—a battle that is much in evidence during the Scopes Trial—Ransom and his fellow writers would have to choose sides.

THE MODERNIST DILEMMA

In order to appreciate fully the transformative choice that these white southern Fugitives would make—and in order to see how complete this transformation would be—it is necessary to understand how attractive and powerful the mod-ernist example was in their early creative years.

Many intellectuals and writers of the 1920s, not to mention everyday men and women, sensed that the Victorian value structure had collapsed, leaving a vacuum where once a definable tradition had stood with clear standards of judgment. World War I had moved people across continents and exposed them to a diversity that suggested new realities. Additionally, advances in science pro-moted a more relative and dynamic universe constantly changing and evolving, heightening this sense of instability. Christianity and the nature of revelation came under scrutiny by critical historians and practitioners of biblical exegesis; moreover, the new human behavioral sciences such as psychology and psycho-therapy insisted that one's actions were somehow biologically or scientifically driven, and that human motivation, as noted by Nietzsche, operated as a bur-ied and unseen force of nature. Practically speaking, in American daily life, the post–World War I era witnessed the "development of corporate capitalism, the rise of consumer culture, changes in the position of women, and the growth of scientific management."[47] In the arts, the rise of impressionism, as opposed to consensus and collective judgment, signaled dramatic change. As William Butler Yeats famously proclaimed: "Things fall apart; the centre cannot hold; / Mere anarchy is loosed upon the world."[48] The year 1922 marked the publication of two landmark modernist works, *Ulysses* by James Joyce and *The Waste Land* by T. S. Eliot. Joyce broke modernist ground for the novel, while Eliot, more signifi-cant to the Fugitives, ushered in modern poetry.

For Warren, Eliot's poem, which appeared in the *Dial* on November 22, was a watershed moment in his young career as a poet. Warren recalled standing in line to buy every issue of the *Dial*, specifically the copy with Eliot's *Waste Land*,[49] but his biographer claims that Davidson lent Warren his copy of the issue. In any case, "its effect was stunning,"[50] and Warren insisted that he "was completely overwhelmed by it."[51] Nevertheless, the impressionable Red claimed that he and his fellow students "memorized the poem and went about quoting it all the time" and confessed that "we intuited the thing as belonging to us"[52] (Warren was known to have recited the entire 434-line poem at a speakeasy with his fellow teaching assistants years later in California).[53] Part of the impact of *The Waste Land* lay, for the Fugitives, in its utter lack of regionalism. Though edited substantially by his friend Ezra Pound, Eliot's *Waste Land* manages to merge various religious and mythological symbols as well as languages (including the famous Sanskrit line "Shantih, Shantih, Shantih") into a transnational denouncement of the disillusionment and chaos of the modern existence.

The sources for Eliot's poem were particularly influential among this southern cadre of writers, who were looking for the kind of antiregionalism that Eliot's poem exhibited. Eliot juxtaposed references to Arthurian legends, Chaucer's *Canterbury Tales*, the *Satyricon*, the Bible, and two contemporary works, specifically Jessie Weston's *From Ritual to Romance* and Sir James Frazier's *The Golden Bough*, from which he draws his title, all sources obvious and well known to literary scholars. Both Weston's and Frazier's works examine the influence of fertility and reproduction mythology on modern culture; and both note the significance of the Fisher King, a figure prominent in ancient lore, who has been wounded in his genitals and is unable to populate his dying kingdom. Legend attests that whoever can cure the Fisher King thus saves the country from becoming a virtual wasteland. But perhaps more significant was the tone of gloom and futility, the pessimism that suggested there was no way to save the Fisher King in this postwar era, a tone completely devoid of the sentimentality and emotion that tainted Victorian verse. Southern historian and literary critic Louis D. Rubin emphasized the Fugitive attraction to modernist literature, insisting that for this community of writers, "the flaccid language convention and the evasive platitudes needed to be discarded." They subscribed to Eliot's pronouncement that the poet "must force the intellectual and emotional complexity of contemporary experience into the poem, at the risk of ignoring a general, middle-class audience."[54] Like the multitude of voices in *The Waste Land* all crying out for an audience, Eliot had found his. And the Fugitives, in turn, set about finding theirs; they envisioned themselves as part of a worldwide angst well beyond Dixie. Poetry now rang important, valuable, elite, and, above all, transcendent of geographic limitations in this new world order. Eliot had shown the Fugitives how to transcend the South.

Warren, Davidson, and particularly Ransom and Tate would debate Eliot's contribution as both poet and critic in the years that followed the birth of their magazine, and they would not always agree. But Eliot, a midwesterner reared in St. Louis, shed his American identity by moving to England, marrying an

English governess, adopting an English accent, and eventually becoming a British citizen. Eliot was more than just an example of literary modernism; he was, in fact, the ultimate Fugitive, an escape artist able to transcend his roots and garner national and international recognition as a substantial literary contributor. Tate envisioned that the project and conversations in which his Nashville friends were participating could result in a greatness that would mirror that of Eliot and Pound. When reflecting on his Fugitive experience, Tate declared: "I may disregard the claims of propriety and say quite plainly that, so far as I know, there was never so much talent, knowledge, and character accidentally brought together at one American place in our time."[55] Tate's confidence is not entirely misplaced, or arrogant for that matter. The Fugitives, in their efforts to break free of southern convention and to embrace the complexity of literary modernism, actually made substantial advances in their careers. They were not, by any means, poets of national rank and power yet, nor had their aesthetic critiques reached the heights they would under their future manifestation as the New Critics; nevertheless, their artistic production during the years in which their journal was published proved impressive.

First and foremost, the magazine provided a consistent outlet for their poetry, allowing Ransom, Tate, Davidson, Warren, and their colleagues to experiment with poetic form, and as nonsouthern modernists they garnered some success. In the three years of its publication (the last issue appeared in 1925), Ransom saw several of his most acclaimed poems grace its pages, including "Philomela" (1923), "Bells for John Whiteside's Daughter" (1924), "Captain Carpenter" (1924), and "Piazza Piece" (1925), to name a few. Additionally, Ransom's Fugitive years saw the publication of two books of poetry by major presses. *Chills and Fever* (1924), with Alfred A. Knopf, was reviewed in prominent journals, including the *New Republic*, the *New York Times Book Review*, and the *Saturday Review of Literature*. Meanwhile, Davidson's poetry, under the title *The Outland Piper* (1924), found an outlet with Houghton Mifflin, and he was named editor of "The Book Review and Literary Page" for the *Tennessean*, where he would begin to sharpen his critical claws. Allen Tate, in his student days at Vanderbilt, published the poems "Red Stains" (1919) and "Impossible" (1920) in *American Poetry Magazine*, as well as "Calidus Juventa," "Euthanasia," and "William Blake" in the *Double Dealer*.

Ransom and Tate had an exchange of letters regarding the significance of *The Waste Land* that was published in the *Literary Review*. Additionally, when Tate left Nashville for New York only months after graduation, not only had he secured freelance assignments with the *New Republic*, the *Nation*, and the *Herald Tribune*, he had "already been called 'the White Hope of the South,' in poetry, and would soon be deemed as 'the only critic worth reading in the United States.'"[56] Even Warren, the youngest of the group but whose major contributions would surpass those of his Tennessee friends, had the distinct pleasure of seeing his earliest poems in print on the pages of the *Fugitive* alongside Robert Graves, William Alexander Percy, Louis Untermeyer, and John Gould Fletcher, all up-and-coming American poets.[57] The journal clearly benefited from the networking efforts of the Fugitives as well as the lack of publishing opportunities available for young, unknown poets. Despite the success of the new journal and of its core members, the workload involved in editing and producing the *Fugitive* grew increasingly burdensome for the writers, who wanted to focus more on their own work—and jobs and fellowships were pulling them in various directions, both literally and artistically—and thus the journal ceased publication in 1925. On the eve of the greatest media spectacle in Tennessee history—the Scopes Evolution Trial—the Fugitives sat poised to make a major contribution to American letters. Mencken's Sahara now seemed a budding garden at first spring.

THE BURDEN OF PUBLIC RIDICULE

The Fugitives did not comment on the passage of the Butler Act outlawing the teaching of evolution in the Tennessee public school system when it made headlines in January 1925. But Tate seemed to recognize the brewing storm that was to come in the great showdown the following summer. In a handwritten postscript to a letter that Tate wrote to Davidson on May 27 of that year, he mentioned that he was currently in negotiations with the *Nation* to cover the trial.[58] He was, in fact, hoping to be sent to Dayton, but he lost the job to fellow Tennessean and southern expatriate Joseph Wood Krutch. No one, particularly the Fugitives, could have predicted the media sensation that would forever alter the image of the South, particularly of the Protestant faithful, to the world at large. Such a sensation would ultimately capture and resurrect the historical imaginations of these southern writers, forcing them to critically examine their heritage. What was once a war fought by their grandfathers against the Yankees now became not only a war of geography, not only a war of slavery versus freedom, but a war of city versus country, the educated (and a specific type of scientific education) versus the rural and ignorant, or the modern versus the antimodern. The observations made by Mencken regarding the cultural wasteland of the South now read less as observation and more as judgment. For the first time, this intellectual and elite community of writers envisioned themselves as part of that which Mencken and Krutch, among others, were ridiculing; they realized that they "belonged to a scorned minority and that their own lives and careers were ineluctably enmeshed with the history and the future of their re-gion."[59] The wasteland of modern life was now not merely a world of exhilarat-ing and disorienting chaos, it was a world against which these Fugitives would position themselves.

This white southern consciousness began to outweigh their literary and aesthetic visions. Cultural critic Mark Jancovich argues that this introspection began collaboratively, confessed in letters to each other in the immediate years following Scopes. "It is within these communications," Jancovich declares, "that they begin to identify themselves consciously as Southerners for the first time."[60] For example, Ransom wrote to Tate that "our fight is for survival. . . . I can see clearly that you are as unreconstructed and unmodernized as any of us, if not more so."[61] This burgeoning consciousness would be inextricably linked to feelings of inferiority generated by the trial and its coverage around the world. Prior to this awakening of sorts, "the gallantries of the Lost Cause, the legends of southern history," Tate insisted, had been "mouthed over and cheapened."[62] They had not been passed down with any real comprehension of their significance or meaning. Cowan argues that the underlying defensive attitude that the poets would express in the years following the events in Day-ton was present all along. "What happened to them involved no real change of heart and character," Cowan insisted. "Instead it was a movement toward wholeness, toward accepting with their minds something they had known all along in their poetry."[63] However, when viewed within the broader context of their entire careers, Cowan's argument seems short sighted. Their reaction, rather than being a "movement toward wholeness," was a sharp and radical transformation; rather than passively accepting their white southern heritage, they initiated a campaign for southern credibility. They thought they could gar-ner respect nationally by glorifying an idealized Agrarian vision of the South.

The Scopes Trial and the subsequent condemnation of the "Savage South" instigated a dramatic shift in the Fugitives' worldview, as they themselves noted publicly at the well-known Fugitive reunion of 1956 and in published interviews and personal memoirs. The writers knew that their magazine, the *Fugitive*, had failed miserably in New York bookstores;[64] they knew that Mencken was encour-aging the southern self-critics, rather than those who sought to escape their roots. Daniel Singal, in his extensive work *The War Within: From Victorian to Mod-ernist Thought in the South, 1919–1945*, insists that "many writers have unfortunately connected these events"—the Fugitive turn toward southern Agrarianism—"to the Scopes trial." But such critics simplify the Fugitive reaction to Scopes, not-ing that it "was simply a case of the 'old atavism' bursting forth in response to the infamous mockery of the South by northern journalists covering the trial."[65]

Singal downplays the role of the Scopes Trial by noting that "Davidson had already drafted his seminal article, 'The Artist as Southerner,' by May 1925, two months before the trial began."[66] The article, in which Davidson tackles the place of the white southern writer within the modern temper, would eventually be deemed by its author as his "spiritual Secession."

The influence of the episode in Dayton, if one bases it narrowly—as Singal does—on the comments made during that two weeks in July 1925, would not seem great. But considered within the broader context of the barrage of public criticism that accompanied not only the trial but also the anti-evolution movement and the death of William Jennings Bryan, the significance seems undeniable. For example, the passage of the Butler Act in January 1925 alone received considerable attention from the *New York Times*. The lead-up to the trial, including Mencken's efforts to secure Darrow as lead counsel for the defense and the effort to convince William Jennings Bryan to make one last stand as the great orator of the common man, was hyped in media outlets across the country. And all such reports would have reached and interested the Nashville writers. Likewise, the Fugitive poets were well aware of the entirety of southern faults that were exposed in reports throughout the country in the months preceding the trial. But the Fugitives were not just reacting to a textbook controversy in Rhea County, Tennessee. The Scopes Trial was perceived, in effect, as the symbolic final blow against the benighted South—the culmination and pinnacle of national rejection.

■ In his 1958 tome, *Southern Writers in the Modern World*, Davidson labels the decade of the 1930s as the period of "Counterattack," a reaction to the benighted South of the 1920s, and he notes the recognition by himself and his colleagues of the subtle shift in the intensity of the public criticism of the South that seemed to emanate from Dayton. Prior to the 1920s, Davidson insists that the "northern criticism of the South was couched in the dainty and still fairly plausible language of nineteenth century liberalism." But, "gradually," he observes,

> the criticism became a little more bitingly specific. We were religious bigots. We were Ku Kluxers. We were lynchers. We had hook worm, we had pellagra, we had sharecroppers, we had poll taxes, we had poor whites, we had fundamentalists. We did not have enough schools, colleges, Ph.D.'s, Deans of Education, paved roads, symphony orchestras, public libraries, skyscrapers—and not near enough cotton mills, steel mills, labor unions, modern plumbing. But we had too many U.D.C.'s, D.A.R.'s, W.C.T.U.'s, too many Methodists and Baptists, too many one-horse farms, too many

illiterates, too many Old Colonels. Our women were too hoity-toity about ancestors. Our men all chewed tobacco or drank mint juleps and our preachers encouraged our flocks to indulge in religious orgies. That was, it was claimed, the only relief we could get from our dull rural life—except the lynching of negroes. We were a bad lot, a disgrace to the United States—and the only possible salvation for us was through instruction from Northern sources.[67]

Davidson's memoirs and rhetoric grew defensive and vitriolic as he grew older. But his general point still sheds light on the transformation of the Fugitive writers from those who fled the South artistically to a political community attempting to make a case for the southern way in the modern world. It is a point worth repeating: knowledge of the criticism of the South was not the same as coming to terms with one's southern consciousness. The "dainty" censure of the Gilded Age was not internalized to the same extent as the benighted condemnation that would follow. The early disapproval of Mencken and others did not seem to apply to these gentlemen poets, who, for a brief time, saw themselves as the solution to the sentimentality of southern literature.

But as the attacks did, indeed, become increasingly specific, not to mention all-consuming, they grew much more difficult to ignore, until finally the Fugitives witnessed the evolution spectacle in their own backyard, in the Tennessee that had not only been their intellectual home but for many the place of their birth and the birth of their ancestors, and, in fact, the only home they had ever known. Though the pronouncement of the guilt of John Scopes may not have been the exact moment upon which the Fugitive energy changed course, its significance as a capstone of sorts is evident. "The war on the South," professed Fred Hobson, "was conducted on several fronts: Mencken, in general command, his special domain being cultural sterility; [Frank] Tannenbaum concentrating on social ills; Oswald Garrison Villard and *The Nation* crusading against lynching; and [W. E. B.] Du Bois filling the paces of the *Crisis* with bitter indictments of the Southern white."[68] The cup runneth over, so to speak, and with it came a rush of self-knowledge and an incredulity that southern voices seemed all but silent in the wake of this verbal abuse. Moreover, the timing of the Fugitive engagement with the South resulted not only from this personalization of northern criticism but also from the realization that such attacks were just as profuse from southern journalists. Historian George Tindall argued that exposés of the South by its own citizens became a genre in and of itself in the 1920s. All in all, Hobson notes, "southern newspapers rode the theme of the benighted South to a total of five Pulitzer prizes between 1923 and 1929."[69] Their efforts were lauded by Mencken but would be deplored by the Fugitives, who saw the southern self-critics as succumbing to the New South vision of progress as defined and dictated by northern industry and values.

To see the Fugitive turn to Agrarianism as merely a knee-jerk reaction to the public ridicule that accompanied the Scopes Trial is short sighted. As previously mentioned, the Vanderbilt poets were well aware of the opinions of northern journalists and southern critics regarding the state of white southern culture in the interwar years. But this criticism only heightened a deep-seated sense of inferiority and insecurity that accompanied the rush to modernism that seemed inevitable, insatiable, and relentless, uprooting the Victorian value system and the Christian cosmology without compromise. For these talented southern writers, the change was all the more disconcerting because the physical changes in the South were all the more extreme. The volatility of the post–Civil War period included, abstractly, a stifling of intellectual ideas in the South, a cultural lag. Thus, the explosion of literary modernism, of science, of institutes of higher learning, of psychology and behavioral studies was more dramatic by comparison.

Davidson's primary complaint in "The Artist as Southerner," in fact, addresses the cultural anxiety that such a radical juxtaposition elicits. The southern writer in such an environment is burdened with "a set of complex inhibitions that make him extremely self-conscious in his attitude toward his own habitat. And the more completely he is aware of the phenomena of modern literature—the more nearly he approaches a perfection of his technical equipment—the greater these inhibitions will become. He is obliged to realize the incongruities of his position as artist in the South."[70] Despite their early and future success, the sense of inferiority lurked within the Fugitive experience. The suppression of their white southern identity became a part of what Matthew Arnold described as "The Buried Life,"[71] that which gets lost by the artist as he or she becomes increasingly alienated from the modern world. And in this case, this sense of alienation was heightened by the confrontational image of the savage South.

CHAPTER 5

A KNOCK AT MIDNIGHT

THE AGRARIAN PLEA

FOR THE SOUTH

I believe that religious myths, including those of the Bible, are unhistorical and unscientific, precisely as our gallant historians and higher critics have recently discovered; but that their unhistorical and unscientific character is not their vice but their excellence, and that it certainly was their intent.
—John Crowe Ransom, *God without Thunder: An Unorthodox Defense of Orthodoxy*

Nobody now proposes for the South, or for any other community in this country, an independent political destiny. That idea is thought to have been finished in 1805. But how far shall the South surrender its moral, social, and economic autonomy to the victorious principle of Union? That question remains open. The South is a minority section that has hitherto been jealous of its minority right to live its own kind of life.
—"Statement of Principles," *I'll Take My Stand: The South and the Agrarian Tradition*

The national and international denunciation of the South during the Scopes Trial and the negative associations of white southern identity that followed activated a collective response from southern writers, including John Crowe Ransom, Robert Penn Warren, Allen Tate, and Donald Davidson, who could no longer ignore their shared regionalism under attack. The result, the anthology *I'll Take My Stand: The South and the Agrarian Tradition* (1930), is more than simply an apology for the South, more than simply a reassertion of the myth of the Lost Cause. Rather, the Fugitives morphed into their new status as Agrarians, attempting to establish an expanded mythology of the white South, characterized by a veneration of the sacred, a demonization of the urban, industrial wasteland, and an association of white southern culture with both high European culture and a singular, authentic Americanism. This assertion of authenticity as artists and as southerners was yet another example of this striving for recognition. Yet this time these talented writers turned away from their modernist icons and sought acceptance and praise from reactionaries both inside and outside the South.

Reexamining their efforts as young artists, those attending the Fugitive reunion of 1956 "generally agreed that the two endeavors [the Fugitive and Agrarian movements] really were phases of a single movement, the one growing naturally out of the other, and that the artistic concerns of the Fugitives could not be separated from the social and political concerns of the Agrarians."[1] Despite the general assumption concerning the common ground shared by the two movements, the transformation was drastic. The products of each movement's efforts were radically different—modernist poetry as opposed to economic, political, and theoretical essays championing traditional regional values at odds with a burgeoning modernism in America. Perhaps the only commonality lay in the motivation behind each movement and not in an abstract aesthetic way as noted by literary historians. The Fugitives-turned-Agrarians had always wanted to be taken seriously as American writers, to become prominent figures on the literary stage. In the wake of the criticism echoing from Dayton, Tennessee, such motivation took a strange turn. Ransom, Davidson, Warren, and Tate, each in his own way, attempted to salvage a growing list of determinants of white southern identity—God-fearing religion, an imagined European hierarchy, and a sanctified genealogy—all of which they believed provided stability in the turbulent onslaught of industrialism and progress. In an effort to convince northern and southern audiences of the superiority of the white southern way of life, they were, in effect, masking their own sense of inferiority. They were no longer fugitives fleeing the South. They embraced it and tried to convince others to do the same.

The publication of I'll Take My Stand marked the culmination of these efforts, and it was exactly that—a final stand. In the five-year interim between the Scopes Trial and the publication of this southern manifesto, Ransom, Davidson, Tate, and Warren tackled their newly embraced and somewhat problematic white southern identity and the growing sense of inferiority associated with it. Unlike the fundamentalists creating William Jennings Bryan College, whose identities must be gleaned from early college pamphlets, the thoughts, intentions, and feelings of the Fugitives-turned-Agrarians are revealed directly in their writings and correspondence. And they applied their considerable talents and education to their efforts to combat these critics. Ransom and Tate sought recognition for a "cultured" southern ancestry and attempted to convince northern audiences that southern culture was highly civilized, descended from the highly mannered European system that the new American elite emulated and envied. And Ransom and Davidson championed the structure and function of fundamentalism at a theoretical and, in Davidson's case, confrontational level. Warren and Tate, through biographies, drew attention to southern historical icons; and Tate and

Davidson resurrected their "gallant" Confederate ancestry, in both their post-Fugitive poetry and their fictional works. And all of this before their ultimate decision to present the Agrarian alternative to northern industrialism—a superior alternative, at that, which would unfortunately become yet another point of ridicule, eliciting peals of critical laughter and disdain and indelibly marking each with the southern label.

RANSOM'S SEARCH FOR DIVINE AUTHORITY

According to Fugitive historian Louise Cowan, Ransom was less attached to the South than Davidson, feeling somewhat sentimental about his homeland rather than defensive. But the Dayton trial, insisted Cowan, "and the arrogant and ill-natured attacks on the South had involved him more deeply with his society, placing him in the somewhat surprising position of defending Fundamentalism."[2] Perhaps his convictions were more theoretical or less public, but in the immediate aftermath of the trial, Ransom began fleshing out the ideas that would eventually constitute his controversial book *God without Thunder: An Unorthodox Defense of Orthodoxy* (1930). The book, which was considered by fellow Agrarians to be profound but was dismissed as "theological homebrew"[3] by critics, would eventually be seen as a spiritual companion to the more political tract *I'll Take My Stand*. The original impetus for the book—although Ransom had undoubtedly been wrestling with the core concepts in the confusion of the post–World War I mood—resulted from a direct confrontation with Edward Mims, his chair in the Vanderbilt English department. Mims, who voiced his humiliation regarding the dark shadow cast on Tennessee after the Scopes Trial, called for his fellow southern intellectuals to denounce fundamentalism, showing the world that such blind belief, such intolerance, did not characterize the state majority.

Ransom rejected Mims's request, "arguing that the issue at Dayton was not tolerance versus free inquiry but rather science versus religious mythology."[4] He admittedly wrote the book in a "hot and hasty"[5] manner, but the breadth of its argument proves the long germination of its ideas. John L. Stewart sees a natural transition from Ransom's attention to poetry during his Fugitive days to his focus on the relationship between science and aesthetics:

> The more he thought about them, the more it seemed that poetry was but one of a number of analogous means of representing man's sense of the character and value of his experience. Among these were the other arts, religious rituals, public ceremonies, traditional codes of conduct, and, supremely, myth. All of these brought order and meaning into the flux of

life without denying the presence and even the charm of contingency and particularity in the local scene—and without denying the mysteriousness and uncontrollableness of the universe. They had the pluralism he missed in science and the monistic philosophies.[6]

Thus, art (and specifically poetry) seemed for Ransom, as well as for many artists, to be an anchor in the modern world, and he praised it and encouraged its presence in society. Perhaps such feelings would seem a natural evolution, considering what writers in the 1920s encountered, but for Ransom the revelation had a second, more pressing purpose. His elevation of the role of myth as counter to the post-Victorian disorder seemed to shed light on the controversy that erupted at the Rhea County Courthouse in Dayton, Tennessee. The media frenzy and the unquenchable thirst of the spectators, radio listeners, and readers worldwide seemed to indicate a collective anxiety. The fundamentalists had gotten a bad reputation, Ransom concluded, from the egregious depictions made by journalists. But at the root of their belief system lay the structure and ritual that eluded modern culture. "Suddenly," claimed Stewart, Ransom "saw that he had an answer to the North." The epiphany resulted in a furious nine-week writing stint that produced the completed version of the book in the summer of 1929, in which, ultimately, Ransom praises "southern fundamentalists for clinging to their myths as more sufficient and satisfying representations of life than the new rationalism."[7]

Though Ransom rarely mentions the South specifically in *God without Thunder*, critics generally recognized that Ransom was "transmuting the spirit of Dayton" into what literary scholar Richard King has labeled "a rather dubious historic-theological generalization."[8] The primary problem with the book, King has argued, resulted from the fact that Ransom was not a fundamentalist, nor was he a scholar of religion or science, a fact pointed out by hostile reviewers such as John S. Middleton, who titled his review "Thunder without Light."[9] In *God without Thunder*, Ransom criticizes, for example, all American sects that, regardless of their stance on biblical literalism (with which Ransom did not agree), have lost their fire and brimstone as well as their reverence for the mysterious and the supernatural. "Little by little," Ransom, echoing William Jennings Bryan, articulated to Tate, "the God of the Jews has been whittled down into the spirit of science, or the spirit of love, or the spirit of Rotary; and now religion is not religion at all, but a purely secular experience, like Y.M.C.A. and Boy Scouts."[10]

Ransom's philosophical glorification of the abstract cultural benefits of a god with thunder, of a "god that invites fear and trembling, that created both good and evil," was a more sophisticated and highly learned response to the same sense of inferiority that confronted the citizens of Dayton and the faithful founders of William Jennings Bryan College. Ransom focused on the ontological differences between science and religion, on the danger of worshipping what he considered the "God of Progress" or the "God of Evolution," or the "God of Machines" (all of which he saw as growing out of the same evil),[11] and on the dehumanizing effect of the "scientific ordering of our experience."[12] Ransom's theoretical argument, in which he connected the battle of science and religion with the growing battle between progress and tradition, grew out of his frustration with the New South advocates and the industrial culture he perceived as being forced upon the South. He rejected "the new gods and the modern liberal religion of a Kirkland or a Mims," which he considered the "products of essentially impious men, of men who denied evil, defied fate, and foolishly claimed human omnipotence."[13] Ransom produced a somewhat confusing book, and his efforts to map the advantages of the "old-style" religion over onto the empirical relationships of science "remained loose and imprecise."

Though Ransom's primary intent was to resurrect the God of the Old Testament and champion the necessity of institutionalized myths, he succeeded in adding a new layer to southern whiteness. Now the white southerner was defined in opposition to the onslaught of industrialism—the crux of the Agrarian movement. "Industrialism," Ransom asserts, "assumes that man is merely a creature of instincts. That is, he is essentially an animal with native appetites that he must satisfy at the expense of his environment."[14] For the Vanderbilt professor, progress, as defined by the capitalist industrial system, was one such dangerous appetite. It would, in his mind, destroy his idealized rural and agricultural South. Immersing himself in the abstractions of the southern conflict— the war between scientific rationalism and authoritarian religion as well as the threat of an industrial, mechanical coup—Ransom's sense of the South's alienation from the country at large intensified, as did his sense that this latest battle was part of a historical struggle for existence. Furthermore, in a letter to Tate, Ransom proclaimed that "the more I think about it, the more I am convinced of the excellence and the enduring vitality of our common cause. . . . Our fight is for survival." He wrote to Tate: "I see clearly that you are as unreconstructed and unmodernized as any of us, if not more so."[15] Ransom's defense of fundamentalism at a philosophical level—though perhaps his most thorough and provocative—would not constitute his only attempt to reconcile the southern experience, of which he was acutely aware, with the industrial North and the increasingly urban New South.

In addition to his most intellectual tactic of highlighting the potential consequences of living in a society devoid of myth and ritual, without a Christian hierarchy, Ransom tried to explain and rationalize the provincialism of southern culture, which had become a driving factor in the negative identity construction of southern whiteness. In two separate essays, Ransom historicized white southern culture by highlighting its similarities to European culture in an effort to elevate the agrarian social system and give it credibility. In "The South—Old or New," which appeared in the *Sewanee Review* in April 1928 and was reprinted as a pamphlet, Ransom argued that the program to industrialize the South and to bring it in "line with our forward-looking and hundred-percent Americanism" could constitute a "charge of treason."[16] His primary thesis, stated clearly and forcefully in the essay, espouses a white southern exceptionalism based on the perception that "the South in its history to date has exhibited what nowhere else on a large scale has been exhibited on this continent north of Mexico, a culture based on European principles."[17] In an effort to combat the criticism of the savage South, Ransom turned the criticism back on its source, declaring that the obsession with materialism and ambition is a "dream of youth," beyond which European and southern culture had matured. The paternalistic and violent image associated with the Ku Klux Klan, lynching, and, of course, the southern slave system was subtly combated by Ransom, who depicted the North as aggressive and belligerent, as a culture that, although it had enjoyed a military victory in the Civil War, had suffered a spiritual defeat. The northerner was now, like the biblical Adam, cursed by Eve, analogized Ransom; he was resigned "every morning to keep up with the best people in the neighborhood in [taking] the measure of his success," and such ambition promoted "personal advancement at the expense of the free activity of the mind."[18] Thus, he posited that the leisure of white southern life was not characteristic of an illiterate or lazy culture but was superior, and particularly well suited for the artist, who required an authentic and creative intellectual freedom.

Ransom reiterated his argument in his essay "The South Defends Its Heritage," which appeared in *Harper's Monthly* the following year. This time Ransom called on European audiences to support the southern way of life, which he saw as suffocating under the authoritative definition of Americanism advanced by industrial capitalists. Southern historian Ulrich B. Phillips noted that Ransom unearthed in the white southern condition the type of stability that characterized European culture in American eyes—a stability, both physical and intangible, for Ransom, that was absent in modern society.[19] Ransom chastised the southerner who dwelled exclusively on the past, "who persists in his regard for a certain terrain, a certain history, and a certain inherited way of living. He is punished as his crime deserves."[20] And he even acquiesces to the inevitability of industrialization—though in moderation—but his conclusion reveals his personal truth. In his effort to see southern culture preserved, Ransom called on the Democratic Party, which at this time still enjoyed the loyalty of the Old Confederacy, to redefine itself as "agrarian, conservative, profoundly social." If this major party was to make a defensive stand against the modern North, Ransom concluded, "then the South may yet be rewarded for a sentimental affection that has persisted in the face of many betrayals."[21]

Rather than rely solely on his argument of the aesthetic superiority and creative functionality of the yeoman South, here Ransom sounded a call for an almost populist political movement, and such a call signified loudly the desperation with which Ransom wanted to get his ideas across to a national audience. Eventually Ransom would incorporate his defense of the white South with those of his fellow colleagues in the southern symposium I'll Take My Stand. Clearly, they were not now fleeing the "Old Brahmins" of the South—the antebellum, traditional intellectual elite whom they chastised in the original issue of the Fugitive—as they had done in their youth. The shift away from the aesthetic arena toward the pulpit of economic politics revealed a new desire for credibility and recognition, a desire that directly reflected a heightening sense of inferiority.

TATE'S AND WARREN'S SEARCH FOR A USABLE PAST

Allen Tate and Robert Penn Warren proved less defensive and perhaps more deliberative than Ransom in their responses to public criticism of the South. As writers, they both tried to make sense of the southern narrative that had given rise to the current moment, and both felt compelled to recast the white South as the recognized source of American authenticity and morality. Tate, who had moved to New York after completing his studies at Vanderbilt, was heavily influenced by Ransom's Euro-southern model and his general defense of the region. After reading a 1927 draft of Ransom's "The South—Old or New," originally titled "Pioneering on Principle," Tate wrote to Davidson, declaring: "I've attacked the South for the last time."[22] Ransom's correspondence with Tate also began to consider their shared white southern identity and its persistence. In a letter to Tate composed later that year, Ransom expressed his conviction that "something ineradicable in Southern culture" existed and was made manifest in his interaction with his fellow southern writers, particularly those like Tate who "'exhibit the same stubbornness of temperament and habit' [and] go North but cannot bring 'themselves to surrender to an alien mode of life.'"[23] Tate, perhaps more than his fellow Fugitives, had accepted the superiority of the established, dominant New England literary models such as Hawthorne, Melville, and Emily Dickinson,[24] making his transformation to a committed student of the South all the more striking.

Tate's introspection was not merely literary or personal—though perhaps it began that way. Rather, his efforts to discover a redeemable South as both an alternative to northern industrialism and an affront to the public ridicule of the 1920s, were also clearly political. Tate's biographer, Thomas A. Underwood, describes Tate as confronting his own feelings of alienation in New York: "He began wondering instead whether Northern values dating back to the Civil War era were responsible for the feelings of emotional fragmentation that were plaguing him—and whether those values had caused the disintegration of his own family. Although he had never been pious, he was beginning to feel not only a need for religion, but also for a hero for the South."[25] Just as fundamentalists desired to memorialize William Jennings Bryan and what he represented after his death, Tate was looking for a southern conqueror. And just as the events in Dayton had sparked Ransom's defense of the South, so too did the attacks inspire an identity crisis in Tate (his original essay concept for I'll Take My Stand included a historical interpretation of the Scopes Trial). Like Ransom, Tate would make several attempts to redeem some aspect of his benighted southern heritage, including revising southern history, highlighting the European influence of southern culture, and eventually championing a reinvented notion of southern tradition that provided him with a "monistic principle," which would give him "a feeling of belonging to the universe."[26] Moreover, "in response to his crises of identity and art," surmised Robert Brinkmeyer, "Tate began a vigorous exploration of his white southern heritage. Hoping to discover a rationale in history for order and community, he pored over books of the southern past and became an expert on the Civil War, even on the intricate battle strategies." Brinkmeyer noted that "sometime during the period of these studies, Tate began to assume the stance of a southern gentleman, both to gird himself against what he now saw as the chaos of New York and also to assert his allegiance to his southern identity."[27] In only a few short years, Tate would not only look to his band of poet brothers, all struggling with their own heritage, for support in his status as the prodigal southerner, but would also call for a symposium to answer the charges at Dayton. But first he would undertake a quite productive journey deep into Civil War history.

Despite their shared dislike for the public criticism that befell the South in the 1920s, Tate's fellow Fugitives, whom he would refer to in correspondence as "Confederates,"[28] admitted their surprise at Tate's first prose effort: a biography of southern general Stonewall Jackson. The biography, Stonewall Jackson: The Good Soldier (1928), resulted from Tate's immersion in southern history and his resulting obsession with the Civil War and the altered course of southern history that accompanied surrender. Writing to Davidson in April 1927, after successfully placing the proposed biography with publishers Minton, Balch and Company, Tate announced that "since I'm convinced that the South would have won had Jackson not been killed, I'm doing a partisan account of the Revolution. The Stars & Bars forever!"[29] Like *God without Thunder*, Tate's biography of Jackson was written with great speed and intensity, with Tate producing close to 40,000 words in ten days.[30] He visited Civil War graveyards, including Gettysburg, where his own grandfather had fought for the Confederacy.[31] The experience was intensely personal. In a radical revisionist account of the Civil War in general, Tate "took pleasure in reversing the roles conventionally assigned by historians. Tate's southerners were 'Constitutionalists,' his northerners 'Rebels.'"[32] His agenda is strikingly clear. Jackson, from childhood, is characterized as moral: "Tate's young Stonewall is a cloying composite of Honest Abe (reading borrowed books) and Tom Sawyer (stripped of mischief and humor)."[33] As a general, Jackson is praised for his single-mindedness and authoritarianism, a certainty in great demand in the modern world. Warren scholar William Bedford Clark argues that "most disturbing, perhaps, is Tate's determined preference for Jackson's monomaniacal religiosity (a concomitant willingness to shed blood) over the balanced restraint of the more morally circumspect Lee, who drew distinctions between 'war' and outright 'massacre.'"[34] The hagiographic narrative, according to Allen Huff, "turned Jackson into an icon of the fierce Christian warrior."[35] Jackson is, in a sense, the historical and military version of the God with Thunder that Ransom desired.

Perhaps more significant in exposing Tate's revised perception of his homeland was his depiction of northern culture as contrasted to the southern culture that composed the background of the Jackson biography. In an effort to invalidate historically the damnation of the South in the 1920s, Tate shone the critical spotlight on the mind of the North during the mid-nineteenth century: "There were people in New England who wanted to destroy democracy and civil liberties in America by freeing the slaves. They were not very intelligent people; so they didn't know precisely what they wanted to destroy. They thought God had told them what to do. A Southern man knew better than this. He knew that God only told people to do right: He never told them what was right. These privy-to-God people were sending little pamphlets down South telling the Negroes, whom they had never seen, that they were abused."[36] Tate glorified the organization of the Confederate military, and he depicted the southern cause as an admirable defense of self-determination and federalism. The madness that Jackson faced on the battlefield seemed symbolic of the modern culture that confronted Tate in New York; and Jackson himself embodied the type of decisive man to which Tate aspired. Michael O'Brien has argued, in fact, that

Tate's "view of the Civil War was the mirror image of the warfare in Tate's mind between religious temperament and an atheist mind, a conservative view of culture and a modernist training." O'Brien concluded that "Tate was as divided against himself in 1928 as had been the Union in 1861," and he further explained that "the Confederacy stood for what he [Tate] wanted to be, the Union for a pessimistic diagnosis of what he feared he was."[37]

The resurrection of the southern past further contributed to the contemporary relationship between region and nation. And Tate believed the North acted on abstract principles with no regard for tradition and history and that such moral absolutism and a blind faith in progress had resulted in the turmoil of the interwar years. Tate quickly followed his successful biography of Jackson with a similarly hagiographic portrayal of the Confederate political leader in *Jefferson Davis: His Rise and Fall* (1929). He wrote the book while living in France on a Guggenheim fellowship, and the underlying theory of the work reflected his experience abroad. Just as Ransom argued that southern culture was the only European social system to be re-created in the Americas, so too did Tate attempt to position the conflict between North and South on the world stage. He recounted in detail the efforts of the Confederacy to attain ally status with France and England and concluded that the lack of success in these efforts ensured southern defeat.

Tate needed to find a replacement for what Charles Reagan Wilson has called the Lost Cause civil religion that would be authoritative and structured but void of the sentimentality of antebellum Dixie, and he personally found such a faith in Catholicism—to which he converted. His effort to redesign the region as a sacred landscape required Tate to reconstruct a mythical South, which scholars have noted did not actually exist (this would be one of the most prominent criticisms of *I'll Take My Stand*). Willard Arnold made precisely this point: "It was not the real South of that era which he looked to but rather a myth, a convenient symbol of an aristocratic tradition based upon moral order and benevolent democratic aristocracy. It was a culture which Tate once called a 'buried city'—yet one they must defend and whose example they were ready to apply in the face of all those forces that once destroyed it."[38] This mythologized southern tradition allowed Tate to embrace his regional culture, despite the public denouncement of it in the 1920s. Such a tradition was superior, implied Tate, to the industrialist vacuum of the North, and it offered the writer a stable perch from which he could create.

For Tate, the mythology of the South would also begin to figure prominently in his poetry, specifically his "Ode to the Confederate Dead" (1927), as well as in his novel, *The Fathers* (1939), in which Tate investigated his family genealogy and transformed it into a source of inspiration. In "Ode to the Confederate Dead," Tate showed early signs of his inability to escape his southern past, and he mourned the inability of modern southerners to connect fully to their regional history, which he felt was being ridiculed and wiped out of contemporary culture. But personally Tate was torn between the choices to protect and preserve the traditional culture of the South or to embrace the present, modern temper and turn his back on his regional heritage. His angst regarding this choice figured prominently in his ode. He catalogs the battlefields, "Shiloh, Antietam, Malvern Hill, Bull Run," and confesses in his final line that the past "Smothers you, a mummy, in time."[39] Tate clearly believed that the southern dead and the Confederate memory continued to influence the generations that followed. But just as surely as he appreciated the rich and dark history of the South, he recognized the suffocating burden that remained just as constant. This internal conflict would trouble Tate repeatedly throughout his career.

Tate's success in publishing two biographies in such a short period of time convinced him to encourage his friend Red Warren to undertake a similar attempt at narrating their shared regional history. With Tate's help and introduction, Warren too secured a contract with the newly established press of Payson and Clarke for a biography, but this time not of a likely southern hero. Even so, Warren's *John Brown: The Making of a Martyr* (1929) was just as reflective of the antinorthern sentiment expressed in Tate's portrayals of Jackson and Davis and shared by his fellow Agrarians. While Tate's biographies functioned primarily to mythologize his southern heroes, Warren's biography of John Brown attempted to deconstruct the martyrdom of the northern abolitionist who killed five proslavery advocates in Kansas and led the raid on Harpers Ferry in Virginia. Warren describes Brown as an egomaniac of sorts; he embodies the Puritan vision of the selectman and attaches himself, somewhat obsessively, to the abstract concept of freedom with no regard for the practical application of his passion. In Warren's version, Brown is "blissfully untroubled by self-knowledge." Charles Bohner, another of Warren's biographers, notes that "in his stiff-necked resistance on being right, he [John Brown] represents a type which has fascinated Warren ever since: the man who possesses or develops 'an elaborate psychological mechanism for justification.'"[40] Brown's vision of justice allows the end to justify the means, and the more abstract the goal, the more readily comes the justification.[41] This new emphasis on biography reflected not only the Fugitives' need to control the historical narrative but also their desire to establish a pantheon of white southern heroes and American demons who could be moral archetypes for modern audiences.

Perhaps more so than the other Fugitives at this particular crossroads in their struggles with self-identification, Warren understood the complexity of southern identity and the powerful influence of history, which remained both a burden and an inspiration. William Bedford Clark argues that "Tate's 'Agrarian' biographies are thesis books," while "Warren's account of the ambiguous career of John Brown, in spite of the youthful author's unabashed biases, is something more—an evolving meditation on history."[42] Such a meditation, which began in response to the public denunciation of the South in the 1920s, would extend throughout Warren's creative life, and history would become "the thematic core of all of his writing."[43] The Fugitives-turned-Agrarians longed to stand on the right side of history, on the side of vitalization. Each was attempting to locate something in their shared regional identity of value and significance, an identity marked with a scab of inferiority, picked at every turn by yet another public denunciation of the South.

DAVIDSON'S SEARCH FOR SECTIONAL FIRE

Not surprising, Davidson's frustration with northern critics and their southern counterparts had reached full throttle by 1927. In a letter to Tate dated May 9, 1927, he declared that upon sight of the magazine entitled *The New South*, "I get sick with the black vomit and malignant agues." His reaction to the *New Republic*, which he also saw as trumpeting science, modernism, industrialism, and racial progress, proved equally visceral. Upon reading it, he was "willing to take to my bed and turn up my heels,—except that I am too mad to die just yet, and itchin for a fight, if I could only find some way to fight effectively. If genuine sectional feeling could be aroused there might be some hope."[44] Davidson was less entranced with modernism than his fellow Fugitives, but he proved much more attached to his southernness, proclaiming his identity loudly, not only in the aftermath of the Scopes Trial but throughout the racial controversies of the civil rights movement.

At the 1956 Fugitive reunion, Davidson insisted on the centrality of the Scopes Trial to his resurrected regional sympathies. However, just as Ransom, Tate, and Warren offered variations on their defense of the southern past, so too would Davidson. His reaction to the benighted South was not instant or consistent. Davidson's overarching position was to point to the right of self-determination for the southern states (an opinion that he would reassert during the integration crisis that followed the 1954 *Brown v. Board of Education* decision): "To contend that there are different ways of progress is not to be a foe of progress. The Southerner who takes such a journey may well ask himself what sort of progress he is going in for. To make Charleston over into the image of Pittsburgh or Akron would be a crime worse than the Dayton crime. And those who advocate progress without any positive regard for the genius of the South may presently find themselves in the unenviable position of the carpetbaggers and scalawags of the First Reconstruction."[45] Davidson's praise for this "genius of the South" would appear in his critical reviews, personal essays, and poetry, as he simultaneously attempted first to explain the South, then to justify its way of life, and finally to promote its superiority. "The Southerner," Davidson argued, "has been obliged to live in a world that he never made."[46] Living as an alien of sorts, Davidson, not unlike his colleagues, began to see the South as a culture in recoil. He was desperate for a supportive voice to be found somewhere in "the organized wrath of the outside world."[47] To Davidson, the fundamentalists had been one of the most vulnerable targets of this wrath, and so, similar to Ransom, Davidson jumped to their defense.

In an undated essay draft titled "The South and Intellectual Progress," which would appear in 1928 in Forum magazine as "First Fruits of Dayton," Davidson actually mimics his New South nemesis and former department head at Vanderbilt, Edwin Mims, insisting that the diversity of the South was clearly demonstrated by Chancellor James Hampton Kirkland's reaction to the Dayton affair. In the wake of the criticism, Kirkland promised to fund the construction of more labs on campus in an effort to prove that Vanderbilt University embraced modern science. Despite Davidson's disclaimers, his true intention—to fire back at Mencken and the press—quickly surfaced. These fundamentalists, demanded Davidson, are merely pawns in a broader cultural "cold Civil War,"[48] instigated by condescending northern intellectuals against southern conservatives. Davidson continued by outlining his rationalization for the William Jennings Bryan side of the great monkey debate. "Anti-evolution legislation," he contended, "may even be taken as a kind of progress, for it signifies that Fundamentalism appeals to an issue of battle, already lost elsewhere, to law-making bodies, and that sort of appeal is characteristic of the American idea that law can effect what society in its innerworkings cannot." Or Davidson encourages: "Consider, too, that Fundamentalism, whatever its wild extravagances, is at least morally serious in a day when morals are likely to be treated with levity; and that it offers a sincere, though a narrow, solution to a major problem of our age: namely, how far shall science, which is determining our physical ways of life, be permitted also to determine our philosophy of life."[49] The essay also gives way to Davidson's historical interpretation of the significance of the region's agrarian economic system, which he believed incorporated ethics and accountability, rather than the greed and profit motives of industrialists of the twentieth century. Colonial Virginia had adopted the chivalry of the Cavalier archetype and established a solid southern business practice:

> The South has never blushed to acknowledge that the good life has its foundation in economic matters. But the plantation masters of the old days and even the factory builders of the late nineteenth century mixed a considerable amount of civic responsibility and generous paternalism with their business affairs. The Southern business men of to-day seem to be out of touch with this tradition. . . . They are ready to egg on their industrial revolution enthusiastically without ever counting the evils they may be dragging in with it, and without considering whether they are hurrying the South into an artificial prosperity.[50]

Davidson even depicted the northern train stations as dirty and ugly, while positing the Garden of Eden vision of the South.[51] He was likewise preoccupied with the actual definition of progress for the South, encouraging his fellow southerners to think critically about what they were losing if they blindly accepted the northern model at the expense of regional integrity.[52] The dangers of industrial decay and the New South lust for "artificial prosperity" permeated I'll Take My Stand, which would take shape in only a few short years as the Agrarian politics of these once-Fugitive poets reached fruition.

The defense of fundamentalism that appeared in one portion of "First Fruits of Dayton" was not Davidson's first attempt at equating fundamentalism with moral gravity. The idea had reached mass audiences in a 1926 essay, "The Artist as Southerner," which appeared in the Saturday Review of Literature.[53] Its appearance, nonetheless, shocked many of its readers, whose memories were still fresh with the accounts of Holy Rollers dancing wildly in Rhea County, Tennessee. Careful reading of the piece, however, reveals that Davidson was not solely or wholeheartedly defending the actual practices or beliefs of the Bryan followers or even biblical literalists; on the contrary, Davidson tried to locate in the phenomenon of fundamentalism a usable past for the southern writers (much as Tate had tried to excavate the same gem in southern history). Davidson urged his fellow artists to embrace the fundamentalist cause as indigenous to the South: "Fundamentalism, in one aspect, is blind and belligerent ignorance; in another, it represents a fierce clinging to poetic supernaturalism against the encroachments of cold logic; it stands for moral seriousness. The Southerner should hesitate to scorn these qualities, for, however much they may now be perverted to bigoted and unfruitful uses, they belong in the bone and sinew of his nature as they once belonged to Milton, who was both Puritan and Cavalier. To obscure them by a show of sophistication is to play the coward; to give them a positive transmutation is the highest function of art."[54] Just as Tate sought a tradition and Ransom a thunderous god as necessary for the production of high art, so too did Davidson portray his support of fundamentalism as an aesthetic concern. And surely their concerns were aesthetic to a certain point, but the Fugitives-turned-Agrarians were also angry at the hypocrisy of the northern media and the cultural treason of their fellow southern turncoats.

The essay, as its title suggests, also pointed to the dilemma of the southern writer, for whom, Davidson declared, there were only two paths. Writers such as himself, in the face of the benighted South stereotypes, could either reject their southern identity and embrace "the remote, austere approach of the uninhibited modern," or they could fall into the habit of local colorists and their southern predecessors and choose "the empty provincial approach of the inferior writers who have 'mooned over the Lost Cause and exploited the hard-dying sentimentalism of antebellum days.'"[55] Inferiority, of one sort or another, was much on Davidson's mind during these years, and it is an obsession that fundamentally organized this period of southern history, in both its political and its aesthetic formations. Davidson yearned for a middle ground, a ground that he saw as promoting the vision of Agrarianism that counters northern industrialism without directly attacking the North. Such a stance would also have the benefit of avoiding race altogether. He would soon find, however, that critics did not make room for a southern compromise.

Warren, Tate, and Ransom all spent time away from Nashville, even abroad for that matter, in the years between the Scopes Trial and the publication of I'll Take My Stand, but Davidson stayed close to home, perhaps accounting for the intensity of his regional commitment. On September 7, 1924, Davidson became the editor of "The Book Review and Literary Page" of the *Tennessean* and "The Weekly Review—A Page about Books." The position put Davidson in constant contact with forthcoming histories, sociological studies, and new novels about the South. His new status as literary critic was empowering for a young English professor, and he contributed reviews to numerous journals in addition to the regular column. Davidson took the opportunity to promote consistently what he deemed to be the correct type of southern fiction, and his reviews suggested that Stark Young's work fulfilled these lofty ideals (Young would later contribute to I'll Take My Stand). For example, in an October 6, 1929, review carried by the "Critic's Almanac," Davidson explained why Young was particularly deserving of praise:

Of the many people writing novels about the South, Stark Young is, so far as I know, the only one who sees the Southern way of life as a whole and communicates it with the grace and conviction that it deserves. Others, no matter what their distinction, too often seem special pleasers; bright or gloomy features distract them. They are not able to see beyond the case of the Negro, the poor white, the mountaineer. Like Ellen Glasgow, they are stricken with a contrary itching to deride; or, like Cabell, they achieve a bitter escape to romance, or like William Faulkner, they become terribly conscious of pain and decay.[56]

In retrospect, Davidson's track record as a reviewer would be questioned, considering that many of the authors, such as Faulkner, that he dismissed remain irreplaceable in the field of American literature. Yet another future fellow Agrarian and Vanderbilt colleague, Frank Lawrence Owsley, found his book *State Rights in the Confederacy* (1925) reviewed by Davidson. In an extra review printed in the December 20, 1925, issue of the *Tennessean*, Davidson admitted his Confederate biases regarding the history of the Civil War, though he credits Owsley with revealing some credible flaws in the Confederate psychology: "Like every other Southerner, I was brought up to believe in the gallantry and invincibility of the Confederate armies during the Civil War. The defeat of the Southern armies was to be attributed to the obscure manipulations of incomprehensible fate, or, at most to pressure of numbers and resources. There was furthermore a picture in the mind of admirable and desperate loyalties, all the men and all the women of the South were beyond measure devoted to the Cause, and in the great drama of the Civil War the only villains were Yankees."[57] The process of offering critical judgments of these works sharpened Davidson's position regarding the place of the South in the larger American historical narrative. His anger at the actions of the North's Reconstruction policies fueled his anger at Mencken and his fellow northern journalists, whose disparagement of the South in the 1920s now seemed part of an unrelenting pattern.

Reviewing these historical works resurrected southern history for Davidson and connected the struggles of the Confederacy with the twentieth-century battle for white southern traditional values. For example, in his review of Claude Bowers's *The Tragic Era: The Revolution after Lincoln* (1929), Davidson declared the Radical Republicans of the post–Civil War era to be the devil himself. Their Reconstruction plan, proclaimed Davidson, was "a conspiracy of made partisans willing to go to any length for power, a complete subversion of American institutions, a crime to which the slightest gilding of mistaken idealism cannot possibly be applied."[58] Southern novelist T. S. Stribling also stood on the receiving end of Davidson's anger and frustration. His 1926 novel *Teeftallow* contained, according to Davidson, "a check list of all the matters on which Tennesseans need to be admonished, for the book clicks these off neatly as an adding machine, with a very unpleasant sum-total."[59] For Davidson, southern writers such as Stribling were pandering to the New South audience, an audience that he deplored. His frustration resulted not only from the barrage of public attacks that the South was receiving (particularly from many of its home-grown intellectuals and journalists), but also from his struggles as a "provincial," as he described it, book page editor. Davidson was handicapped by a meager editor's salary, which was less than the compensation received by the more important southern sports writers and society column editors—yet another sign of the inferior status of the South's artistic culture.

Moreover, Davidson considered his post extremely trying, due to the national consensus that seemed to make offering a counter opinion to northern critics a virtual literary suicide.[60] In his time as book page editor, Davidson did, however, present one surprising review. Upon reading James Weldon Johnson's *Autobiography of an Ex-Colored Man*, in which the main character is able to pass between white and black society due to the ambiguous color of his skin, Davidson claims to have felt a kinship with the author. In the September 11, 1927, review, Davidson announced that the book was "the autobiography of a traitor," a traitor to oneself. Biographer Mark Winchell describes Davidson's empathy:

> Within the larger intellectual community, defenders of the southern tradition were a maligned and ridiculed class. Only those southern writers who were willing to abandon that tradition and embrace the cosmopolitan values of the North would be allowed full citizenship into the dominant culture. Such writers were in a position analogous to that of the mulatto who "passed" for white. Although Davidson would surely have been amused, perhaps even offended, by the metaphor of the southerner as nigger, it is clear that by the time he read *The Autobiography of an Ex-Colored Man*, he was determined not to sell his own birthright for a mess of pottage.[61]

In a sense, Davidson understood the instinct of wanting to pass for something else—to escape the burden of one's own besieged identity. Though it was something he could never do, and although his situation was in no way comparable to what African Americans experienced, he boldly announced the connection all the same. Thus, he continued to express his opinions on all things southern both through his book page reviews and in his own creative efforts, but he was moving quickly toward a political stance, envisioning a symposium that would register with northern critics and pack a substantial punch.

Davidson's collection of poems *The Tall Men* (1927), in a sense, embodied all of the arguments made against his fellow gentlemen poets. In his own words,

Davidson described the book as "a dramatic visualization of a modern South-erner, trapped in a distasteful urban environment, subjecting the phenomena of the disordered present to a comparison with the heroic past."[62] The disor-der that Davidson articulated centers primarily on the machine and industrial culture that he saw as overtaking the cities of the South. Once again, in his poem "Geography of the Brain," he waxes sentimental as he details the beauty of his pastoral homeland, a beauty slowly eroding in the modern era. "Over the Southern fields green corn is waving, / Husky and broad of blade," writes David-son, and "pollen falls in my heart, / A dust of song that sprinkles fruitfulness, / Mellowing like the corn in Southern fields."[63] More than simply reflecting on the splendor of the regional landscape, Davidson's *Tall Men* "was sounding the bugle call of Agrarianism,"[64] a return to the mythical southern Eden that echoes loudly in *I'll Take My Stand*. Davidson, in line with Tate and Warren as biogra-phers, looked to the past for evidence of the southern heroic spirit. Contempo-rary southerners, according to Davidson, demonstrated a "spiritual and moral softness," as compared to the "common devotion of his pioneer forebears."[65] Despite its local color, *The Tall Men* was published by a northern press—the lack of southern publication houses was a constant complaint made by many of the Agrarians. However, Davidson's anger at what he considered the discrimination against southern authors was mounting. According to Daniel Singal, Davidson as late as 1925 had considered moving to New York, the place he considered the American literary "Mecca." But after the *Nation* selected a modernist poem rather than Davidson's submission for a 1926 literary prize, Davidson became deeply agitated, complaining to Tate "about 'midwestern jackasses' and 'Yale-Harvard-Princeton pretty boys' dominating the New York literary scene." Davidson con-tinued, "'As a Southerner egad, and a gentleman (I hope) of independent mind, I hate these cliques and Star Chambers.'"[66] In truth, Davidson wanted his own southern clique, which is exactly what his Fugitive band of poets had been. This time, however, they would take a political stance, denouncing the northern and New South culture of their detractors. "I propose to fight 'em like hell,"[67] Da-vidson proclaimed.

THE AGRARIAN INTENTION

Literary scholars naturally look to the published works of Ransom, Davidson, Tate, and Warren to identify their inner struggles with modernism and their growing attachments to their southern identities. Additionally, Tate's corre-spondence with his fellow Fugitives and Agrarians reveals a distinctly political effort to counteract the mass criticism of the South and the cultural inferiority complex that followed. Such criticism obviously contributed, perhaps dominantly, to Tate's newfound Dixie pride, as can be clearly seen in his 1929 call for a symposium to defend the South. Tate had originally proposed an anthology of essays intended to draw together the ideas about southern religion, southern history, and the threat posed by science and industrialism that his fellow Fugitives had been exploring since their magazine ceased publication. As their individual interests in the South gathered steam, Davidson mentioned the notion to Tate, who responded with a detailed plan. Historian Thomas Daniel Young characterizes the exchange of letters between Tate and Davidson as a new phase in the group's history: "Instead of a vague notion of wanting to do something to counteract the bad publicity the South was getting from the Northern press, what they now had in mind was a defense of their sectional heritage, which only a few years before they were either oblivious to or felt a compelling urge to escape."[68]

However, Tate was not satisfied with the publication of one southern manifesto; rather he proposed a three-pronged attack to restore and increase the credibility of southern intellectuals and to create a formal club to which they could belong and in which they dictated the rules of membership. In a letter to Donald Davidson dated August 10, 1929, he outlined his plan:

1. The formation of a society, or an academy, of Southern positive reactionaries made up at first of people of our own group.

2. The expansion in a year or two of this academy to this size: fifteen active members—poets, critics, historians, economists—and ten inactive members—lawyers, politicians, private citizens—who might be active enough without being committed at first to direct agitation.

3. The drawing up of a philosophical constitution, to be issued and signed by the academy, as the groundwork of the movement. It should be ambitious to the last degree; it should set forth, under our leading idea, a complete social, philosophical, literary, economic, and religious system. This will inevitably draw upon our heritage, but this heritage should be viewed, not in what it actually performed, but in its possible perfection. Philosophically, we must go the whole hog of reaction, and base our movement less upon the actual old South than upon its prototype—the historical, social, and religious scheme of Europe. We must be the last Europeans—there being no Europeans in Europe at present.

4. The academy will not be a secret order; all the cards will be on the table. We should be secretive, however, in our tactics, and plan the campaign

for the maximum of effect. All our writings should be signed 'John Doe of the _____ _____,' or whatever we call it.

5. Organized publication should be looked to. A newspaper, perhaps, to argue our principles on the lower plane; then a weekly, to press philosophy upon the passing show; and third, a quarterly devoted wholly to principles. This is a large scheme, but it must be held up constantly. We must do our best with what we can get.

"The advantages of this program," Tate continued, "are the advantages of all extreme positions":

It would immediately define the muddling and *unorganized* opposition (*intellectually* unorganized) of the Progressives; they have no *philosophical* program, only an emotional acquiescence to the drift of the age, and we should force them to rationalize into absurdity an intellectually untenable position. Secondly, it would crystallize into opposition or complete allegiance the vaguely pro-Southern opinions of the time. These two advantages of my proposed academy seem to me decisive. Without the academy we shall perish in two ways: (1) under the superior weight of metal (not superior strategy) of the enemy (Progressives); and (2) our own doctrine will be diluted with too many shades of opinion.

In short this program would create an intellectual situation interior to the South. I underscore it because, to me, it contains the heart of the matter.

For the great ends in view—the end may be only an assertion of principle, but that in itself is great—for this end we must have a certain discipline; we must crush minor differences of doctrine under a single idea.[69]

Obviously, Tate's concern with his southern image, as well as the reputations of his friends and colleagues, extended well beyond their literary interests or their internal dissent with the modern mood of the country. Tate clearly intended to reestablish the southern hierarchy—or some version of it—beyond the boundaries of influence once sought by the Fugitives. Davidson thought Tate's idea for a Southern Academy of Arts and Letters, as he called it, was modeled after the French Academy, which Tate had revered during his time abroad and that such an idea was "an act of vast presumption."[70] But the book would come to fruition and irrevocably alter the public image of the Nashville poets and writers.

The individual essays written by Ransom, Tate, Warren, and Davidson in I'll Take My Stand reflect this sense of inferiority and its corollary, the striving for recognition. "Reconstructed but Unregenerate," Ransom's contribution, devotes much of its content to repeating the mantra that white southern culture is European culture. He does find fault with the Old South for not establishing an intellectual culture that would have rivaled ancient Rome or Greece. And, of course, he warns of the impending industrialization of his homeland, conceding that "the South at last is to be physically reconstructed; but it will be fatal," Ransom prophesies, "if the South should conceive it as her duty to be regenerated and get her spirit reborn with a totally different orientation toward life."[71] The sectionalist spirit must be revived, urges Ransom, and "it will be fiercest and most effective if industrialism is represented to the Southern people as— what it undoubtedly is—a foreign invasion of Southern soil, which is capable of doing more devastation than was wrought when Sherman marched to the sea."[72]

Tate took an equally defensive stance, theorizing that the South, particularly southern religion, had collapsed under the cultural prescription of the North. The South had failed, according to Tate, to develop and render viable a religious tradition capable of sustaining its way of life. "The South, as a political atmosphere formed by the eighteenth century, did not realize its genius in time," reasoned Tate, "but continued to defend itself on the political terms of the North; and thus, waiting too long, it let its powerful rivalry gain the ascendancy." Tate further complained that the South's "religious impulse was inarticulate simply because it tried to encompass its destiny within the terms of Protestantism, in origin, a non-agrarian and trading religion; hardly a religion at all, but a result of secular ambition." This failure, remarked Tate, meant that southern defenders "could merely quote Scripture to defend slavery . . . and this is why the South separated from the North too late, and so lost its cause."[73]

While Tate blames his abstract South for a lack of backbone, Davidson blames industrialism solely for the suffering of the artist. But for Davidson there is a solution: "The supremacy of industrialism itself can be repudiated." He continues: "Industrialism can be disposed as a regulatory god of modern society." Davidson predicts that the artist in this type of culture "has no reason to hope that those who hold the machine will ever subdue it." "Lonely exile though he be," Davidson advises, "he must be practical enough to distrust the social philosophers who promise him a humble corner in the Great Reconstruction that they are now undertaking to produce for our age."[74] The South, Davidson insists, is the only region that can provide the leisure and sanctuary that the artist requires, but only if it refuses to bow to the capitalist machine. Warren's argument against industrialism begins with his exploration of the position of freed African Americans in the post-Reconstruction South. He questions why African Americans should be educated, though he supports Booker T. Washington's Tuskegee model of vocational instruction, which Warren insists is not "a piece of white man's snobbery."[75] He warns that industrialism and the opportunities for low-paying unskilled jobs for African Americans will heighten the animosity of poor whites, and from that hostility will "come much of the individual violence, such as lynching, which sometimes falls to the negro's lot."[76] In an effort to educate the reading public on the complication of industrialization in a racially charged society, Warren concludes that "the Southern white man may conceive of his own culture as firmly rooted in the soil, and he may desire, through time and necessary vicissitude, to preserve its essential structure intact. He wishes the negro well; he wishes to see crime, genial irresponsibility, ignorance, and oppression replaced by an informed and productive negro community. . . . The chief problem for all alike is the restoration of society at large to a balance and security which the industrial regime is far from promising to achieve."[77] Warren clearly desires, along with his fellow Agrarians, a reinstatement of the old southern hierarchy. Such structure and rules would provide artists with a clear place in society, rather than forcing them to fit into a modern culture in which they are not valued.

The Agrarians obviously saw their efforts as an authentic expression of regional concern, though they most assuredly did not see it as related to economics in the least. Davidson even proclaimed that the "symposium *I'll Take My Stand* can be taken as a defense of poetry as it can be taken as a defense of the South,"[78] a statement with which Tate publicly agreed. Lewis Simpson points to the inherent contradiction of the book: the type of culture that the Agrarians—specifically Tate in his letters—sought to reconstruct would have inevitably collapsed. Simpson contends that Tate wanted "to join a movement of men of letters in the American South to the central motive of modern Western letters: a paradoxical and aggressive movement of mind against itself."[79] Tate advocated a nearly cerebral utopia in which the critical mind developed, controlled, and regulated the landscape of southern life. Along with his fellow Agrarians, Tate wanted to emphasize the intellectualism of southern men of letters, but to what extent they desired a reversal of the roles of mind and society for the masses is unclear at best. For surely such a critical self-assessment of the region in the 1920s and 1930s would have produced exactly what the Agrarians loathed: treasonous denouncements from their native countrymen. After all, the Agrarians were neither social workers nor economic theorists. They were literary men, and their collective endeavor was political at its core. The manifesto was written to acquire recognition and power for their region; it was a direct attempt to refute the criticism of the benighted South, to respond to this crippling sense of cultural inferiority, and, thus, to overcome such alienation by proclaiming the white South to be, paradoxically, more American than the progressive regions that lay glaringly to the North. The authentic impact of *I'll Take My Stand* lay not in its content but in its motivation.

Perhaps the most obvious example of the contrived nature of the southern manifesto was not in what it argued but in what it excluded. These educated contributors sought recognition for the superiority of white southern culture but failed to address the institution of human slavery and the post-Reconstruction wall of Jim Crow. Other than Warren's essay, "The Briar Patch," which commented on southern race relations directly, *I'll Take My Stand* made few allusions to the plantation system. The overarching sentiment echoed the old paternalistic argument of the notorious nineteenth-century Confederate polemicists, secessionist John Calhoun and proslavery social theorist George Fitzhugh. When forced to defend the enterprise, the Agrarians were quick to redirect the attention to the inhumanity of industrial labor. "According to Tate," notes Alexander Karanikas, "the Negro slave of the Cotton Kingdom was better off than the modern wage-earner because he could never join the ranks of the unemployed."[80] Richard Gray argues that race, or in this case the absence of attention paid to the "peculiar institution" of slavery, was the defining feature of the book. *I'll Take My Stand*, he proclaims, "is not just Southern as a matter of historical accident but distinctly and determinately so." He further demands, "It belongs first and last to a body of writing for which the constitutive absence, the invisible or at best marginal character, is and always has been the black."[81] The failure of the authors to apply the same, though somewhat amateur, historical and economic analysis that permeates the rest of the book to their own past, choosing instead to highlight simply their perception of northern hypocrisy, makes the authenticity of their cause less credible.

And the Agrarians were, indeed, tapping into larger national and international forces, including a developing inward appreciation for regional distinction—in this case southern nationalism—and an outward trend toward disillusionment with modern society. In his book *Revolt of the Provinces*, Robert Dorman argues that the rejection of a homogeneous America was expedited by the perception by many Americans "that Western culture in general was being left behind, as it were, by the abstract and fragmenting urban-industrial order."[82] Thus, not only did many white southerners attempt to define their agrarian Eden, but Native Americans sought cultural distinction, as did African Americans active in the Harlem Renaissance. These movements were characterized, insists Dorman, by "backward glances" and were demonstrated in significant historical events and movements such as "prohibition, the Scopes Monkey Trial, the 1924 immigration laws . . . Henry Ford's Greenfield Village, the Ku Klux Klan, the 1928 gubernatorial victory of Huey Long, Rockefeller's Williamsburg." In each, "all had constituencies, audiences, or visitors clinging confusedly, swearing allegiance to, wistfully remembering, an older America."[83] But the southern Agrarians were not only dealing with a sense of estrangement between the national culture and the local culture. They were responding to a public denunciation of their regional culture. Their collective response, thus, was not wholly a search for a usable, distinct past, but rather a defensive outpouring of regional propaganda.

Alexander Karanikas envisions the resurgent Nashville circle as part of a larger community of disillusioned American artists, and it is this link that gives their work broader significance. He cites Solomon Fishman's *The Disinherited of Art*, which suggested that "the key to the cycle of American literature is the term 'alienation.'" Fishman contends that this consistent impulse incorporates a "whole constellation of attitudes associated with the literary twenties: isolationism, individualism, bohemianism, dissidence, rejection, rebellion, disillusion, pessimism, defeat, decadence, disintegration, escape, exile." "Alienation in brief," Fishman asserts, "implies a centrifugal impulse, the detachment of the particle from the mass."[84] Unlike many of their more successful fellow writers, the Agrarians chose not to pursue their art in the heady cafés of Paris or the streets of Barcelona, but they were equally political in their commentary on American values. Moreover, their alienation was distinct, for they found themselves at odds not only with the dominant cultural course of the North but also with the southern business developers and southern journalists who, each for his or her own reason, chided the Agrarian system. Why these former Fugitives from the South did not expatriate themselves, as did many of their contemporaries, is a matter of speculation. But their alienation was uniquely personal. Theirs was not a general angst or a universal reaction to the horrors of trench warfare. Nor was it the common anxiety of defining what it means to be American in the twentieth century. Their anger and frustration was harnessed, directed, and executed at an unambiguous target in a futile attempt to gain recognition as political critics, of sorts. "Although the Fugitive-Agrarians never renounced their American citizenship or entertained serious thoughts of expatriation," insists Karanikas, "*I'll Take My Stand* did signify a spiritual secession from the national as a whole."[85]

THE AGRARIAN RECEPTION

The reactions to *I'll Take My Stand* were mostly damning, although a few supportive voices—mostly from regional reviewers—championed the symposium's advocacy of traditional southern values as a welcome alternative to industrial progress. An editorial review in the *Leaf Chronicle* of Clarksville, Tennessee, pinpointed the source of the book's title, the song "Dixie," which includes a line that rings "In Dixie Land, I'll Take My Stand," and waxed philosophical on the practical application of the manifesto's charge. "There is no doubt," the column read, "that the South as it is at present is a better place to live than an industrial South would be."[86] The *Nashville Tennessean*, which had carried Davidson's book review page, found in *I'll Take My Stand* a resurgence of regional passion. "They are singing it again—Dixie," noted the local paper, "the song that has always brought its wild surge of feeling in Southern hearts. But it is sung in a more thoughtful way." The article further contends that "its strains may not sweep the crowd off its feet but they are sung with the oldtime fervor and love of homeland."[87] An editorial appearing in the *Advertiser* of Montgomery, Alabama, "A Militant Indictment of Progress," echoed a similar sentiment, though with greater intensity. Signed only with the initials W. J. M. Jr., the piece concluded that *I'll Take My Stand* would touch southern hearts directly. "In it," the author decreed, "he [the southerner] will find expressed a concept that had long flinched, inarticulate, before the scowls of industrialism. It is a militant Agrarianism whose followers need not be ashamed."[88]

In addition to the mostly southern applause, the collection did receive notable nods from Fugitive hero T. S. Eliot, as well as from John Peale Bishop, who appreciated the critical lens focused on the capitalist machine. Writing for the *Criterion*, Eliot remarked that Tate and his fellow authors were inspired by "a sound and right reaction." Bishop wrote Tate specifically and claimed that he agreed with the chief principle of the symposium.[89] Even William S. Knickerbocker, who had criticized Ransom's *God without Thunder*, admitted in the *Saturday Review of Literature* that *I'll Take My Stand* was a significantly challenging book.[90] And Harry Hansen's column, "The First Reader," carried by papers such as the *New York Morning World*, actually called the twelve contributors "valiant," with Hansen surmising that "the machine age is making dummies of us all and the exploitation of industrial products has no other object than to heap up useless profits."[91]

But even the few receptive audiences, whether southern sympathizers or anti-industrialists, questioned the practicality of the Agrarian plan. Their efforts were deemed praiseworthy but essentially irrelevant, all charges that led directly to a gnawing sense of inadequacy. James I. Finney echoed this sentiment. Writing for the *Journal* of Knoxville, Tennessee, he chronicled the doom of industrialization, all the while chastising the authors for failing to offer any real solution: "There is no denial of the devastating effect of this materialistic view of life from which we suffer today upon its amenities, upon religion, arts and social relations. But after the reader has been taken to the high peaks and looks down upon a world seemingly lost to an appreciation of all the cherished ideals of life, he is plunged into the deepest gloom of pessimism. For the writers failed to enumerate the practical and specific measures which we believe must be adopted in order to recover the things that we have sacrificed to this mad, hurried scramble after so-called material rewards."[92] The *Chattanooga News* admitted kindly that those who had followed the careers of these poets-turned-polemicists were greatly antici-pating the new book. But the ideological crux of the collection, noted the article, was merely a resuscitated point of view that had once belonged to the French Physiocrats, the "economic philosophers who flourished in Eighteenth Century France" and "who put forward a framework of economic organization in sharp contrast to the commercial tone of Adam Smith and the English Manchester school."[93] It is at once a brilliant and devastating remark that gets just right that peculiar note of privileged alienation, characteristic of both the French and the southern elite. Rather than endorse the stance taken by the Twelve Southerners, the review chose only to historicize their argument. Perhaps more memorable, the piece referred to the group as the "Young Confederates," a title that stuck but that many of the contributors deplored, despite the fact that Tate had actually used the term to refer to his colleagues in his correspondence.

John G. Neihardt of the *Post Dispatch* of St. Louis noted in his column that the debate inherent in *I'll Take My Stand* was of the utmost importance and insisted that many of his readers "would be sure to be astonished not only at the resul-tant revelation but at the fascinating character of the inquiry as conducted by 12 brilliant Southerners." However, regardless of Neihardt's personal praise for the southern Agrarians, his enthusiasm turned sour when assessing the practi-cal application of the theories hence discussed. "Furthermore, the hope for a triumphant 'agrarian movement,'" contended Neihardt, "which appeared to be cherished by these 12, is to be regarded as pathetic. If the book's value were to be judged by the reasonableness of that hope, the work, for all its obvious bril-liance and persuasive humanness, could be ignored as practically worthless."[94] But for many critics, the pragmatism of the work would be a minor vice among many. Still, it is worth noting that this peculiar tactic of acknowledging the work's brilliance while insisting on its clear irrelevance to modern life proved to be a large and debilitating thorn in the Agrarians' sides. Diffidence, inferiority, alienation—all of these self-destructive emotions surface continually through-out the collection.

The negative reviews echoed the criticism of the Scopes Trial fundamental-ists, criticism that had initially been the catalyst for the symposium. *Publisher's Weekly* printed a small notice but poignantly identified the essays as "attacks."[95] Moreover, Henry Hazlitt's review of *I'll Take My Stand* for the *Nation*, "So Did

King Canute," regarded the book as wholly reactionary, condemning Ransom for his trepidation toward modernism. If Ransom's "fear of Progress had always prevailed," argued Hazlitt, "we should still be in the savage state—assuming that we had at least accepted such technological advancements as flint and the spearhead."[96] "This book," he declared, "is in the main, the rationalization of a nostalgia for ancestral ways rather than a rational approach to real problems."[97] Writing for the *New York Times Book Review*, Arthur Krock also argued against the nostalgia that permeated the southern manifesto. To make his point, Krock quoted from the other book examined in his combined review, *The Industrial Revolution in the South* (1930), by Broadus Mitchell and George Mitchell. Reflecting on the Old South, the Mitchells asked, "Why embalm his [the Old South's] remains and keep his few belongings like relics at the shrine of a saint? We paid him too much honor while he lived, and furthermore sad reminders are all about us in the South this long time afterward: poverty, race hatred, sterile fields, the childish and violent crowd gulled by the demagogue."[98] For many of the northern critics, and in fact for several southern journalists as well, it was impossible to separate the Agrarian call for a return to a traditional farm culture from the provincialism that had caused so many regional atrocities.

The *Macon Telegraph* published perhaps the most visceral review of all, mockingly titled "Lee, We Are Here!" "The Neo-Confederates have seen the shadows of the smoke stacks," it read, "and have become as alarmed as ever did a Kluxer at the sight of a healthy-bodied Negro." The review drew a clear connection between the reactionary nature of southern fundamentalism and the desperation of the Agrarian plea: "They are as offended by automobiles and radios as the late John Roach Straton was offended by public dance halls and the theater. Their opinion of mill owners would read like William Jennings Bryan's idea of Charles Darwin. Bryan wanted the supremacy in the community to rest on the heads of the orthodox preacher; the Neo-Confederates want supremacy to rest on the head of a stately old plantation owner with chivalrous intentions."[99] For the Agrarians, this was a perilous place to inhabit, and it only got worse. "We marvel," the paper proclaimed, "that there is such a group in the South today."[100] Gerald Johnson, who had been considered, even in the Fugitive days, to be a treasonous journalist, decried the ignorance of the twelve contributors in the *Virginia Quarterly Review* (VQR), an act that only added to the perception of him as a traitor. He was incredulous that such educated men would see Agrarianism as an honest and authentic answer to the problems facing the South in the wake of the Great Depression, most notably the 1929 textile strike in Gastonia, North Carolina, which Johnson mentioned directly: "But that the Twelve should turn to agrarianism as a remedy would seem to indicate that their sole knowledge of the South has been gleaned from the pages of Joel Chandler Harris and Thomas Nelson Page."[101]

Here, then, was an attack wielding the hard edge of social realism, and it must have pained, even embarrassed, some of them deeply. "Have they never been in the modern South," he asked, "especially in the sections still completely ruled by agrarianism?" Such willful blindness fueled Johnson's outrage. "If the things that happen under their noses are unknown to them," he pronounced, "it is hardly worthwhile to point out that the fine civilization of the ante-bellum South was already falling into ruin in 1860, and was merely given the coup de grace by the Civil War; and that it was falling into ruin because no purely agrarian polity can maintain a fine civilization for any length of time."[102] The entire premise that the South was being swallowed wholly by industrialism, Johnson insisted, was "a figment of the imagination." But it was not an unconscious figment of the imaginations of these Fugitives-turned-Agrarians. Regardless of its feasibility, their manifesto, and specifically their choice of the banner of Agrarianism, was deliberate and political, an effort to combat the public criticism that deemed them an inferior breed among their fellow Americans.

Tate had initially worried that the title of the collection would ensure rapid-fire public ridicule, and in a sense he was right. But the group admitted to being taken off guard by the publication of such scathing reviews as Johnson's in southern journals such as the VQR. Stringfellow Barr had assumed editorship of the VQR in October 1930, and he was already an acquaintance of Ransom and his colleagues. Barr had authored an article titled "The Uncultured South" in a 1929 issue of the VQR that opened with the following question: "Has the South been buffaloing America for half a century into thinking it was a second Athens wrecked by a Northern barbarian democracy, when actually the second Athens drank mint juleps, ate batter-bread, and thought up a moral defense for the institution that made life comfortable?"[103]

What would surely have attracted the attention of the former Fugitives was Barr's declaration that in order to answer his initial question one could not ask a southerner, for "the South has been on the defensive for so many decades that it has lost the art of self-examination." Ransom and his fellow southern writers would have obviously wanted to prove Barr's statement false; they had actually invited Barr to contribute to I'll Take My Stand, an offer that he considered and for which he submitted an outline. His 1929 article, despite its aggressive nature toward southern culture, had faulted the New South campaign for many of the region's problems. "And since the World War," Barr declared, "the South has been sold on progress, with the result that under the guidance of its Young Men's Business Clubs it has deserted its glorious past for a rosy and profitable future." Despite a suspected sympathy for the Agrarian cause, the former Fugitives were rejected by Barr because he claimed to be unable to endorse the "Statement of Principles" in the opening pages of the symposium.

Moreover, Barr instead published the essay "Shall Slavery Come South," which was carried on the front pages of the VQR the same month that he became editor and the same year that I'll Take My Stand reached audiences. The article called for the regulation of industry, rather than whole-scale rejection, and it ridiculed one particular group of southerners called "Traditionalists," or Neo-Confederates, for their nostalgic ideals. According to historian Edward Shapiro, "Davidson, Ransom and Tate correctly assumed that Barr had them in mind and publicly protested."[104] Barr's mockery noted the weakness and inexperience of the traditionalist vision: "The traditionalists, frightened by the lengthening shadow of smokestacks, take refuge in the good old days and in what I have called the apotheosis of the hoe. They make a charming but impotent religion of the past, make idols of the defunct horse and buggy, and mutter impotently at the radio. They themselves no longer think they are going to do anything about it, and this cheapens their veneration for the past."[105] Perhaps the Agrarians were already conscious of their insincerity or, at least, of their inability to reverse the American trajectory toward progress and industrialism. But they would put up a fight for a bit longer.

The conflict between Barr and the Agrarians sparked great public interest, inciting George Fort Milton of the Chattanooga News, as well as the Richmond Times Dispatch, to propose a public forum for debate. On November 14, 1930, Ransom and Barr squared off in front of an audience of approximately 3,500 at the Richmond Civic Auditorium to debate the question, "Shall the South Be Industrialized?" Moderated by Sherwood Anderson, the debate was given substantial publicity in newspapers throughout the country.[106] Davidson covered the event for the Chattanooga News and quoted Ransom as accusing Barr of fashioning his southern identity "as a gardenia to stick in his buttonhole when he goes traveling in New York."[107] Barr maintained a moderate position that encouraged the regulation of labor through collective bargaining. Barr's history with the Agrarian group, particularly his refusal to contribute to I'll Take My Stand and his publication of negative reviews of the book, ensured extreme tension. While Ransom delivered an address that was "carefully organized, sober and persuasive," Barr "abandoned consecutive argument for a fiery, witty series of abrupt retorts which won the good humor of the audience."[108]

Barr mocked the Agrarians and, as Davidson reported, "warned southerners against encouraging an attitude of mind toward industrialism that resembled

Harriet Beecher Stowe's attitude toward Negro slavery."[109] Such a comparison, equating the Agrarians with the abolitionists, added fuel to the fire. According to Davidson's account, though no victor was declared, Ransom claimed to appreciate the level of discussion and desired to continue expounding his Agrarian beliefs where he thought the southern masses might finally take notice—or perhaps where he might be taken seriously regarding his ideas for the South. He was clearly a man who wanted to be redeemed. He then agreed to a series of three debates: against Barr again, this time at the University of Chattanooga on January 9, 1931; against William S. Knickerbocker, editor of the *Sewanee Review* on December 15, 1930, in New Orleans; and against William D. Anderson, a noted industrialist at Emory University, in Atlanta on February 11, 1931. Davidson would fill in for Ransom for a repeat performance against Knickerbocker in Columbia, Tennessee, on May 21, 1931.

Unlike Ransom's formal presentation—Ransom hoped to quell the criticism that *I'll Take My Stand* offered no pragmatic solutions to the South's problems—Davidson decided to appeal to the raw emotion of the southern audience, a strategy that he confessed in a letter to Tate. "I shall talk about perfectly familiar and immediate things that folks can take to heart," he planned. Despite the best efforts of these "Young Confederates," their attempt to convince the southern masses that the hoe and the plow were superior to the industrial machines, including the creature comforts that such a system could potentially produce, would yield few results, especially as New Deal programs lurked on the horizon—the Tennessee Valley horizon, specifically. Although their efforts gained steam for a brief moment, they failed because the theories they offered were precisely that—theories adopted by poets to respond to the public attacks on their region. Theirs was a political campaign waged against their critics in an effort to compensate for a regional heritage from which they had once been Fugitives. Though it is impossible to assess if there was any authenticity in their personal commitment to southern farmers and to the rural culture that they championed, it is essential to uncover their motivations.

H. L. Mencken reportedly attended the first debate in Richmond, and although he was not quite as hostile as he had been to the fundamentalists of Rhea County, he did not refrain from taking shots at the Agrarians. His initial review of *I'll Take My Stand*, titled "Uprising in the Confederacy," appeared in the *American Mercury* in 1931 and was comparatively tame—for Mencken, that is. The Sage of Baltimore implied that he agreed theoretically with the general premise of Agrarianism but believed a turning back of the clock to be ludicrous. This was yet another version of what they had heard before, and it was equally debilitating: intelligent minds concocting ludicrous schemes and plans. Howard Odum, sociologist and leader of the Chapel Hill circle that attempted to find practical solutions to the South's problems through social science, had encouraged Mencken to read the book, noting in a letter the romanticism of *I'll Take My Stand*. This romanticism, according to Odum, had become a false reality of sorts for many southern artists,[110] and he tried to counter the notion in his book *An American Epoch: Southern Portraiture in the National Picture*.[111] "What we have to find now," wrote Odum to Mencken, "is the product of what was and what is—as a fact and not as an ideal."[112] Mencken replied that he would soon turn his attention to the symposium but that, "obviously, it is absurd to argue that the South should formally abandon industrialism. It would be no more nonsensical to argue that it should abandon heat spells and hail storms."[113] His review would reinforce the absurdity of the real-world application of the Agrarian solution for the South. "The present authors, for all their sincerity," he assured his readers, "show in their own persons most of the worst weaknesses that now afflict their homeland. There is something dreadfully literary and pedagogical about their whole discussion."[114] But Mencken was not finished assessing the validity of the twelve southerners' manifesto.

"The South Astir" appeared in the January 1935 issue of the VQR, nearly ten years since Mencken's time in Dayton and close to two decades since his initial rebuke of the South in "The Sahara of the Bozart." The publication of Mencken's piece proved to be controversial. Word of its impending arrival in the ten-year anniversary issue of the VQR came simultaneously with the news that Davidson's piece, "*I'll Take My Stand*: A History," was rejected. The rejection was significant because Davidson had intended to correct some of the misperceptions about the book and to answer its critics. Editor Lambert Davis attempted to assuage the Agrarians by including Warren's essay, "John Crowe Ransom: A Study in Irony," to offset Mencken's attack. The gesture, however, could not calm the brewing storm. Mencken accused the twelve contributors of fashioning a utopian South without any regard for the detail of the actual world—a common criticism by that time. Furthermore, Mencken supported and praised the regionalists of the day, referring to the Chapel Hill social scientists, for insisting that "the South should grapple resolutely with its own problems, and try to solve them in accord with its own best interests and its own private taste." And finally, in a move that would incur the wrath of the Fugitives-turned-Agrarians, Mencken singled out Davidson for condemnation. "But when they go on to argue," begins Mencken, "as Mr. Donald Davidson seems to do in a recent article, that it should cut itself off from the rest of the country altogether, then they come close to uttering rubbish."

Mencken's diatribe is relentless, but Davidson had continued in the years since the publication of *I'll Take My Stand* to denounce northern criticism of the South without apology:

> Mr. Davidson passes as an advanced thinker—and in many particulars his thought is advanced enough, God knows—, but whenever he observed an eye peeping over the Potomac his reaction is precisely that of the Mayor and City Council of Dayton, Tennessee. That is to say, he simply throws up his hands, and yields to moral indignation. All Northern accounts of Southern folkways are not more to him than libels invented by atheists in New York, "with Europe beyond" to afflict a Christian people whose only offense is that they are "believers in God." It would be hard to imagine anything more naïve—save it be some of Mr. Davidson's grave retailings of the arcana acquired in Freshmen History. He seems to believe in all seriousness that the Bryan obscenity at Dayton was a private matter, on which the rest of the country had no right to an opinion.[115]

The rhetorical technique used in *I'll Take My Stand*—of distracting the reader from the atrocities of the South by highlighting the atrocities of the North, and, of course, by blaming the North for all southern problems—proved equally persuasive in Mencken's hand. He concluded by promising that "I'll begin to believe in the prophets of Regionalism when I hear that they have ceased to fever themselves over the sins of New York, and applied themselves courageously to clearing the ground of their own Region. Let them begin at home."[116]

The reaction of the Agrarian circle to both Mencken's piece and Davidson's rejection signaled a more militant and self-indulgent phase of the campaign. Tate, according to Shapiro, questioned Davis's rebuff of Davidson's chronicle of *I'll Take My Stand*: "I suppose it comes down to this: whether you think the history of our group interesting and important enough to be published at this time."[117] John Gould Fletcher, one of the twelve contributors, immediately contacted Ransom, Davidson, Tate, Warren, and Frank Owsley and called for a boycott of the VQR. Fletcher, notes Shapiro, "had long been suspicious of what he saw as the lukewarm support of the VQR for the traditional South, and he had urged Ransom for some time to establish a southern literary and political journal modeled on the antebellum *Southern Review*."[118] Warren, Ransom, and Tate considered Fletcher's demands to be unreasonable, subjecting the author and his works to some sort of "loyalty oath."[119] Owsley and Davidson thought an investigation into what Owsley called the "scalawag publication" was more appropriate; their report could then be signed by their fellow southern writers, offering a censure to the "thoroughly vicious institution."[120]

The project seemed extreme to the former Fugitives and thus never materialized, but the proposals drew invisible boundaries. On his own, Owsley published a rebuttal, "The Pillars of Agrarianism," to Mencken in the *American Review*. Despite editing out an extensive personal assault on the Baltimore journalist at the encouragement of Ransom and Davidson, who feared the repercussions, Owsley could not resist a brief, but biting, jab: "The most recent, and perhaps, the most violent attack upon the advocates of an Agrarian state is that of H. L. Mencken. While Mencken's attack is so violent and lacking restraint that it does not fall short of libel, I have no desire to single him out as a critic worthy of answer."[121] The Agrarians were still consciously trying to shape their image, to counter the benighted South; clearly the old furor had not subsided.

In his account of Davidson's conservatism, biographer Mark Winchell explains that "although deeply offended by the whole affair, Davidson tried to mend fences with his old Vanderbilt colleagues while calming the apoplectic Fletcher, whom he feared he had inadvertently set off." Winchell noted that Davidson imagined the entire conflict with the VQR to be a conspiracy of sorts to break up the Agrarian group. Winchell further reveals through a study of Davidson's correspondence that he wrote both Tate and Fletcher on the same day, May 17, 1935, conceding to Tate that "there must be some almost psychopathic cause in F's [Fletcher's] intense rages, as you suggest."[122] Davidson then appeased Fletcher by confessing that "even if you or I should intensely dislike all the other 'Agrarians' (as we don't) we couldn't 'resign' because we couldn't stop being Southerners, ourselves, our fathers' sons."[123] *I'll Take My Stand*, the Agrarian movement, and the blistering public criticism that followed would again set these southern writers on a new course.

In the years after *I'll Take My Stand*, Ransom, Warren, and Tate returned to their roots in the world of literature, choosing to revive their careers by returning to where their careers had originated. Ransom had reached the end of his Agrarian rope, so to speak, while writing a collection of essays espousing his economic theories. He had entitled it *Land!* and had written it on a Guggenheim Fellowship in England in 1931 and 1932. Before heading abroad, Ransom submitted to *Harper's* one-third of the planned manuscript, under the heading "A Lion in Distress," which the magazine rejected. His Agrarian plan for rebuilding the South and the country at large received some attention at Rotary clubs and other community meetings that Ransom addressed both at home and in England. The spattering of support encouraged Ransom to submit an additional excerpt, "On Being a Creditor Nation," to *Scribner's*, which experienced the same fate as his first attempt.

Ransom persevered, continuing to sharpen his vocabulary as an economist, and tried to make an authentic contribution through his Agrarian philosophies. His chapters, including such titles as "Happy Farmers," "What Does the South Want," and "The South Is a Bulwark," reveal his attempt to reestablish credibility as a southern spokesman. He was temporarily pleased when two additional pieces, "The State and the Land" and "Land! An Answer to the Unemployment Problem," were accepted by the *New Republic* and *Harper's*, respectively. However, the book manuscript as a whole, which had been the focus of his creative energy in the somewhat disastrous aftermath of *I'll Take My Stand*, was rejected by Harcourt; Ransom confessed to Tate that he would not bother with revisions.[124] Just as quickly as Ransom had embraced Agrarianism, he would discard it.

Warren and Tate each took sharper turns back to poetry and literature in the wake of *I'll Take My Stand*, with Tate becoming the southern editor of *Hound & Horn* magazine, while Warren headed further south to the department of English at Louisiana State University, where he would ultimately cofound and edit the *Southern Review*—a dream of Davidson's—in 1935. He worked diligently on a novel, *God's Own Time*, which was rejected by Harcourt Brace in 1933.[125] Tate continued to write poetry, publishing his *Poems: 1928–1931* and penning "To the Lacedemonians" for the Confederate military reunion held in Richmond in 1932. His wife, Caroline Gordon, received a Guggenheim, which resulted in his return to France. In collaboration with his friend Herbert Agar, Tate even tinkered with the idea of founding a weekly on southern and midwestern politics. Moreover, just as Ransom tried to salvage his role as a southern intellectual, so too did Tate attempt to reshape his image, publishing the essay "The Profession of Letters in the South" in a 1935 issue of the *VQR*. In the article, Tate proclaims the need for southern presses.

Of all of the contributors to *I'll Take My Stand*, Davidson proved the most relentless in his effort to resurrect the South as the superior and true American culture. His essays, such as "Criticism Outside of New York," "Sectionalism in the United States," and "Still Rebels and Yankees," belabored his vision. In total, nine essays, all of them recognizably Agrarian, were published in the *American Review*, edited by Seward Collins, including the contentious historical narrative of *I'll Take My Stand*; and Warren's reestablished *Southern Review* would carry an additional six essays. Though Davidson's productivity proved admirable, his relationship with Seward Collins further damaged his reputation. Collins was an active critic of the New Deal—as were Tate and Davidson—but his conservatism in the 1930s grew increasingly entrenched as President Roosevelt's government programs expanded. In a 1936 interview, Collins confessed both his identity as a self-proclaimed fascist and his support for Mussolini and Hitler.[126]

According to Ian Hamilton, Tate was so desperate to "promote his 'spiritual' defence of the Deep South's traditions" that Tate was "more than ready to overlook the anti-Semitism and pro-Hitlerism of the *American Review*." Yet Tate himself proclaimed publicly in both the *Marxist Quarterly* and the *New Republic* that he would never write for the *American Review* again, even if it "were the last publication left in America."[127] And the following year, Tate insisted to Davidson that he "must become a creative writer once more."[128] Nonetheless, Davidson "soldiered on, alone."[129] Regardless of their varying commitments to the principles of the Agrarians, the contributors of *I'll Take My Stand* did reunite for a sequel.

Edited by Tate and Agar, the anthology *Who Owns America?* (1936) was intended, like much of the individual work that each had undertook in the intervening years, to revise and redeem their position. Tentative early notes describing such a manuscript bear the title "Counter-Revolution: The Sequel to *I'll Take My Stand*" or "The Agrarian Phalanx: Sequel to *I'll Take My Stand*." But many of the contributors wanted to broaden the Agrarian position, specifically to merge with the English Distributists, who promoted a similar philosophy, in an attempt to appear more worldly and to avoid the attacks of 1930. Ransom's essay "What Does the South Want?" was an elaboration of his essay that had appeared in a 1934 issue of the *American Review*, and the intent of the piece was to backpedal from the idea of one mythical South, by persuading the reader that "there are business men and laborers, equally with farmers, to be defended."[130] Despite this disclaimer, Ransom still blamed the loss of southern hegemony on the "insistent penetration of the region by foreign ideas."[131] In truth, Ransom had already retreated from his previous economic stances, and his primary occupation would be a return to aesthetics. This essay served as his Agrarian curtain call.

Always in tune with philosophy and increasingly interested in politics, Tate's contribution, "Notes on Liberty and Property," examined the nature of ownership as redefined by the Civil War—though he does not mention the institution of slavery. Tate's piece highlighted the concentration of wealth that accompanies capitalism, and he thus privileged the individual ownership of land that Tate believed ensures personal responsibility. Still pushing the Agrarian vision, Tate contrasted the experience for individuals, many of whom felt similarly disillusioned by the corporate machine and the stock market crash. Using his talent and experience as a historian, Warren planned to write a series of short biographies of prominent leaders of the English Agrarian movement, but severe headaches forced him to submit "Literature as a Symptom," a study of Victorian writers, instead. Only Davidson continued the polemics. His essay "That This Nation May Endure: The Need for Political Regionalism" still referred to

Reconstruction as the period of northern imperialism: the Fourteenth Amendment had been "'ratified' at the point of a bayonet."[132] He championed the doctrines of self-determination, majoritarianism, and states' rights, all forecasting the white southern defenses of the civil rights movement. Davidson insisted that "the land and the region belong to the people who dwell there, and that they will be governed only by their own consent."[133]

■ The rhetoric associated with Agrarianism and employed by the twelve southern essayists clearly delineated what they perceived to be the wickedness of northern progress and its New South followers from the authentically American, southern agrarian way of life—a rhetoric of good versus evil that again appealed to their white southern audience. The South is depicted as "mature and 'seasoned,' an old society and a society good because it is old," while the North "is dismissed as 'immature' and 'primitive.'"[134] In this sense, the contributors attempted to disarm public denunciations of the white South by turning the very criticisms with which they were negatively attacked on their attackers, defining each in opposition to southern whiteness. The word "modern" is written "as if it were a term of abuse," and the terms "industrial" and "cultural" are positioned "as though they were antonyms."[135] In retrospect, Davidson would explain the rhetorical devices of the book by admitting the intentions of the Agrarians: "We thought our fellow-Southerners would grasp without laborious explanation the terms of our approach to Southern problems."[136] Unfortunately for these southern gentlemen writers, Davidson was wrong.

Locating the exact moment when these Nashville Fugitives officially transformed into the politically driven Agrarians is difficult to determine at best. In truth, Ransom, Warren, Tate, and Davidson each brought to the Agrarian conversation a distinct perspective driven by equally distinct motivations. Ransom's vision was always shaped by his aesthetic values; Tate seemed desperate, both personally and as an artist, for a structure based on tradition and myth; Warren waded into historical waters in an effort to reconcile and contextualize his southern upbringing in a world hostile to it; and Davidson sought primarily to launch a counterattack against northern and New South criticism—to crown southern culture as superior. However, despite the divergent paths they took in the years after publication of the *Fugitive* ceased, they all stood in 1930 at the same crossroads. And for better or worse, as a collective group they used their talents as artists and cultural critics to defend their regional heritage at odds with American nationalism and to compensate for this heritage of inferiority. In an effort to counter the negative construction of southern white identity, the Agrarians compiled a new list of southern values that expanded the boundaries of whiteness in the twentieth century. And whether consciously or subconsciously, these Fugitives-turned-Agrarians began to look for a new campaign—one that would not provoke laughter and ridicule but would afford them the national intellectual influence they had desired ever since their Nashville days. But the war had been long, the damage certain. The recognition had not come. This time they would return to their subject of expertise, however, shedding their southern skin, chameleons once more.

CHAPTER 6

THE NOT SO NEW CRITICISM

RECONFIGURED,

YET UNREGENERATE

Like Beard's *Whither Mankind* (a symposium of civilization), *I'll Take My Stand* is
the collected thought of a group of leading writers. But [to] the Southerner it
will have a more specific meaning and interest. In it he will find expressed a
concept that had long flinched, inarticulate before the scowls of Industrialism.
It is a militant Agrarianism whose followers need not be ashamed.
—W. J. M. Jr., "A Militant Indictment of 'Progress,'" *Advertiser*,
Montgomery, Alabama

The New Critics' distaste for modern society and their desire to isolate the
world of literature from it mirrored and extended the Agrarian rejection of the
modern South and its yearning for an earlier, imaginary version of the antebellum South. Their rejection of history was matched by history's rejection of
their vision.
—Richard King, *A Southern Renaissance*

Just as the Fugitives had transformed themselves in an effort to cope with the
criticism of both a lack of southern art and an abundance of southern fundamentalist religion, the Agrarians undertook a second metamorphosis in the
aftermath of the criticism that befell their political efforts. In a letter to Tate
dated February 23, 1940, Davidson admitted that he could not participate in
what he called the "Third Revolution," now undertaken by his Fugitive-Agrarian
friends.[1] Determined to continue their campaign for intellectual credibility and
recognition, Ransom, Warren, and Tate entered into perhaps their most well-
known endeavor, the development of what Ransom would call the New Criticism. And indeed, the New Criticism was a revolution of sorts, redefining the
very nature of imaginative literature and reforming the process by which such
literature was read and judged. After two decades of being subjected too often
to the condemnation of northern and New South critics, John Crowe Ransom,
Allen Tate, and Robert Penn Warren positioned themselves as both judge and
jury, armed with a strict code of aesthetic hierarchy and searching for the means
to disseminate their ideas.

Returning to their literary roots, Ransom, particularly, felt more authoritative and confident in the artistic vision that he explained in the numerous essays that make up the origin of New Critical thought in America; no longer did he feel out of his element, as he had in the economic and political writings that had consumed him in the years following the Scopes Trial. His early musings in correspondence with his own father and with his fellow Fugitives reveal an aesthetic concern predating his Agrarian sympathies, ideas that Ransom would fully articulate in the turbulent wake of the critical reception of I'll Take My Stand. Ransom's two primary collections, The World's Body (1938) and The New Criticism (1941), along with Tate's Reactionary Essays on Poetry and Ideas (1936) and Warren's textbooks, Understanding Poetry (1938) and Understanding Fiction (1943), edited with Cleanth Brooks, established and institutionalized this "Third Revolution" in American English departments, granting these aspiring southern gentlemen the critical acclaim—albeit temporary—that I'll Take My Stand had not.

In general, the New Criticism has been credited with refocusing attention on the language of the text, envisioning it as a literary object, a verbal icon, worthy of examination independent of the author's intentions or the reader's response. New Criticism rejected the romantic literary attitude that preceded it, as well as the meticulous biographical criticism that centered wholly on historical context at the expense of close textual analysis. By avoiding history, the New Critics were able to shed their individual identities as southerners and their collective identity as Agrarians battling against the national embrace of modernism and industrialism. Ransom, most extensively, though Tate as well (and utilized by Warren as critic), developed a rigid system for analyzing these resurrected classical components of literature. Consequently, they developed nothing short of a definitive formula for assessing the greatness of a work of literature.

According to the New Critics, the perceived greatness of poetry hinged upon several intangibles such as the harmony of poetic language—a kind of transcendental sonics—and the ability of the verse to juxtapose and balance contradictory realities. Setting at equilibrium the force and the restraint of emotion, the sensory and the rational perceptions, the practical experience as well as the abstract, New Criticism valued a structured, organic whole, which the New Critics believed most accurately reflected the human experience. From such balance arose the pure meaning of art. Ransom insisted that "true poetry has no great interest in improving or idealizing the world, which does well enough. It only wants to realize the world, to see it better."[2] Clearly Ransom the Agrarian activist, even public debater, had changed his political tune. American art, as defined by the New Critics, contained new abstract elements of an expanded southern whiteness, including complexity, purity, and tradition. In many ways, this new aesthetic theory reflected the motivations and intentions that drove both the Fugitive movement and the Agrarian movement—including the desire for recognition and national acceptance and the effort to construct a positive identity in the wake of negative public criticism.

THE THIRD REVOLUTION

It is difficult to define New Criticism precisely, since its founding principles have been so worked and reworked in the theoretical vineyards of the late 1940s and 1950s. Moreover, the movement had roots in both England—influenced abroad most notably by Matthew Arnold and T. S. Eliot—and America, specifically the South, and thus counts as its advocates an odd group of bedfellows. Arnold, writing in a series of essays that composed his influential work *Culture and Anarchy* (1869), foresaw the challenge that modern science would pose for faith and the arts. He argued for the advancement of poetry—in his case, classical and Victorian verse—in society to take the place of religion.[3] Moreover, he insisted on the important role of the critic, a notion echoed by Ransom and his colleagues nearly seventy years later. And Arnold believed critics could assess "the best that has been thought and known in the world"[4] and should canonize those works—a concept that was significant to the southern New Critics of the next century, who also aspired to positions of judgment. Arnold's principles proved particularly influential to I. A. Richards and T. S. Eliot. Richards experimented in his classroom by giving students unfamiliar poems and asking for their intuitive judgment of the poem's value. He demonstrated the technique of reading literature in isolation, an experiment documented in his 1929 book *Practical Criticism*.[5] Eliot also saw the potential application of Arnold's original beliefs about poetry to the modern era. In his 1923 essay, "The Function of Criticism," Eliot defines criticism as "commentation and exposition of works of art by means of written words," and he insists that valuable criticism will result in the "elucidation of works of art and the correction of taste."[6] Writing simultaneously from the mid-1910s through the 1930s, the Russian Formalists, including Viktor Shklovsky and Roman Jakobson, also proclaimed the distinctiveness and independence of poetic language and argued for a methodical approach to literature.[7] Building on the works of Arnold, Richards, Eliot (who was called at times the "Father of New Criticism," despite personally rejecting the label), and the Russian Formalists, the former southern Agrarians actually coined the name, New Criticism, and initiated the American movement.

In his seminal work, *American Literary Criticism from the Thirties to the Eighties*, Vincent Leitch contended that "we can effectively summarize the panoply of formalist protocols that conditioned and directed New Critical 'close reading,' keeping in mind the usual provisos which accompany such reductive idealizations." Leitch instructs the New Critical reader and critic to follow sixteen enumerated guidelines—a list that clearly defines the legacy of the principle of New Criticism. A selection of these commandments, of sorts, reveals the empirical confidence that underlies much of the New Critical doctrine:

(1) Select a short text, often a metaphysical or modern poem;
(2) rule out "genetic" critical approaches; [Leitch uses the term "genetic" to refer to the type of criticism that is concerned primarily with the context— biographical, historical, sociological—that generated the work]
(3) avoid receptionist inquiry; [the personal response of the reader was deemed irrelevant by the New Critics]
(4) assume the text to be an autonomous, ahistorical, spatial object;
(8) focus continually on the text and its manifold semantic and rhetorical interrelations;
(10) eschew paraphrase and summary or make clear that such statements are not equivalent to poetic meaning;
(12) subordinate incongruities and conflicts;
(16) try to be the ideal reader and create the one, true reading, which subsumes multiple readings.[8]

Sometimes labeled "aesthetic formalism,"[9] New Criticism's disciplined method seemed at times so empirical that Art Berman defined it as a "form of scientific analysis of unscientific meaning."[10] Ransom, specifically, had chastised what he saw as the cultural obsession with science and progress, which he considered inextricably linked to industrialism and northern values. However, in an effort to unify and promote the study of literature in university English departments, Ransom paradoxically created a system that mirrored the scientific method that he had once sought to discredit. Tate, too, emphasized the separate spheres of science and art—a kind of secessionist aesthetics.

Despite the initial attraction of New Criticism, its wholesale institutionalization throughout American English departments tended to oversimplify the initial intentions of Ransom and his colleagues. Though successful and popular for several decades, the rigid method of interpretation inevitably came to seem arcane and overly formal. New approaches, such as Semiotics, Reader-Response criticism, Feminist criticism, Marxist interpretations, New Historicism, and Deconstructionism, no longer insisted on the primacy of the text alone. Moreover, the postmodern cultural criticism of the 1960s, 1970s, and

1980s championed the interpretative lenses of race, gender, ethnicity, and class, which required again incorporating the political, historical, and economic contexts. By the late 1950s, even T. S. Eliot, who had in many ways inspired the New Criticism and whose essays, most notably, "Tradition and the Individual Talent," had contributed to the rise of this literary perspective, would reject the method, mocking it as "the lemon-squeezer school of criticism."[11] And Eliot was not the only one to see the efforts of the New Critics as being too narrow and constricted. Northrop Frye's seminal work, *The Anatomy of Criticism* (1957), accused the New Critics of missing the forest for the trees, so to speak. Frye envisioned literature as a genealogy with patterns and common themes branching from a universal trunk; as a proto-structuralist of sorts, he argued that literature was a vast interplay of systems. Though valuable insight could be gained from close readings of individual texts, many scholars, including Frye, "grew tired of paradox and ambiguity, and began to look for new sources of inspiration."[12] Frye insisted that the critic should consider the conversations between texts across time and by various artists.

The trend against the New Criticism was by no means limited to the restrictiveness of its application; rather, New Criticism would actually be vilified as conservative, moralistic, and self-serving. Robert Gorham Davis insisted that under the New Critical system, terms such as "authority, hierarchy, catholicism, aristocracy, tradition, absolutes, dogma, truths became relation terms of honor, and liberalism, naturalism, scientism, individualism, equalitarianism, progress, protestantism, pragmatism, and personality became related terms of rejection."[13] Jonathan Culler, one of the early American structuralists, did not reject the technique of close reading, but he argued that the process of reading and understanding the text comes with subjective baggage and unexamined assumptions. Terence Hawkes has argued that a work of literature ultimately consists of everything that has been said about it and that any attempt to identify one pure interpretation constitutes an act of selective violence against the teeming masses of opinion.[14] The New Critics, like many evaluators of literary merit, were rarely self-reflective; they failed to, or decided not to, question their own intentions and motivations in crystallizing their American canon.[15]

For the Agrarians-turned–New Critics, poetry had to fill the vacuum left by modern skepticism. This particular agenda led the New Critics to value certain writers as opposed to others. The Italian poet Dante, for example, would be favored for depicting in his work a Christian worldview, entrenched in the doctrine and cosmology of Original Sin. William Blake, who attempted to deconstruct the Christian value system, would have been dismissed as a lesser talent. Despite the apparent flaws, the moralistic and dogmatic nature of New

Criticism left a substantial legacy with which future critics would have to contend.[16] Frank Lentricchia, in *After the New Criticism*, claims that New Criticism was never a monolithic entity, but as a didactic institution, which it surely became in American university English departments, it resulted in an almost monolithic reaction, an intense disavowal of New Critical conservatism. The schools of criticism that followed Ransom, Tate, Warren, and Brooks continue to wage war on the value judgments and the canon established by the New Critics. Lentricchia remarked that "the New Criticism is dead—in an official sense, of course, it is—I must stipulate that in my view it is dead only in the way that an imposing and repressive father-figure is dead."[17]

Perhaps a contributing factor behind the Agrarian embrace of New Criticism was the opportunity that it provided for redemption and national recognition in the wake of the failure of the regional manifesto, *I'll Take My Stand*. Returning to the art of criticism and elevating the stature of the critic and poet gave these talented writers the chance to redefine the standards of literary achievement while discarding their southern identity. In other words, regardless of their intentions, the very nature of their southern white identity became irrelevant under the precepts of New Criticism and thus freed them from the ridicule of the past. Traditionally, southern literary scholars fall into one of two camps. Either they find a natural, though wholly abstract, connection between the Agrarian movement and the New Criticism, or they contend that the Agrarians simply abandoned their political positions and reinvested their talents in the separate field of literature. Richard Gray, generally representative of the first group, argues that the New Critical emphasis on harmony and the organic nature of the whole text derives from the Agrarian vision of the natural balance of man and earth, as well as a focus on the concrete as opposed to the abstraction that Agrarians associated with the North's value system. Additionally, Gray distinguishes a sense of loyalty and a penchant toward tradition as common elements between the Agrarian philosophy and the New Critical enterprise. Robert Brinkmeyer, in his review of Gray's book *Southern Aberrations: Writers of the American South and the Problems of Regionalism*,[18] surmises that "the New Critics' stranglehold on the southern canon led to the elevation of their chosen literature (particularly that which pitted a noble traditionalism against a crass modernism) and a devaluation of everything else." Brinkmeyer directly quotes Gray's summary of the "southernist New Critical thinking."[19] Gray argues that "to write as a traditionalist is evidently to write objectively about 'flesh and blood Southerners' and to write something of aesthetic importance; while to write in a way that interrogates traditionalism is to fall victim of [to] polemic and propaganda.'"[20] Gray sees a clear link between the Agrarian vision, which is traditional and concrete, and its opposition, the industrial, self-critical, and abstract, deemed by the New Critics as propaganda.

On the other hand, John Fekete, in *The Critical Twilight*, a book in which Fekete focuses on the New Critical essays of John Crowe Ransom, insists that the transition from Agrarian politics to aesthetics was a trade-off. "All possibilities of reshaping the exterior world," proclaimed Fekete, "are renounced to gain social sanction for the perfection of the interior world, the sensibility, through the strictly literary experience of life."[21] Moreover, Fekete suggests that key components of the Agrarian manifesto would simply dissolve into the "established reality." "We find, too," he argues, that "the strong Agrarian critiques of industrialism are reduced to a critique of science, then to a critique of abused science, until, finally, peace is made altogether in the New Critical period, and the primacy of science is acknowledged."[22] Perhaps later generations of New Critics released their antagonism toward science and the type of culture that is produced when it is held up as the ultimate source of knowledge, but for the southern Agrarians first promoting New Criticism in America, such a release never occurred.

Still others, such as Richard Godden, draw connections between the Agrarian assault on industrialism and the machine age on the one hand and the New Critical efforts on the other hand, to offer an alternative to the commodity culture that exploded in the interwar years. Thus, their notion of the verbal icon is most beneficially seen as a response to commodity culture, and commodity culture comes up with a means of representing itself that is in no way instructional, moral, ethical, or enlightening. It serves one purpose: to sell the product. The New Critics see the South becoming industrialized, and they attempt to show a different form of human representation that is uplifting, moral, and ethical. The New Critics established a value system that excluded concerns of marketability or material success, and such a value system, Godden claims, was naturally derivative of the Agrarian vision of a southern Eden that cherished leisure and supported the artist.[23]

Robert B. Heilman recognizes a clear link between the New Critic Cleanth Brooks and the original Fugitive impulse in his book *The Southern Connection*. A fan of the Tennessee community, Heilman asserted that no other group with such literary talent had existed in one place at one such productive moment in history. His more poignant point, however, is his contention—similar to Gray's—that the southern fixation on the concrete, as opposed to more abstract ideals such as progress and freedom, the very ones that had driven the minds of the North, merely manifests itself in the New Critical fixation on the text as object and verbal icon.[24] Gerald Graff echoes a similar note in his analysis of the transition from Agrarianism to New Criticism that took place in the aftermath of the publication of I'll Take My Stand, arguing that the method of close reading adopted by the New Critics functioned not merely as a rejection of contextualization of literature, but was intended, rather, to refocus the reader on the language, a concrete concern in a modern world of abstraction and chaos. Moreover, Graff counters that although such textual analysis could appear limited, the alternative—a sentimental and subjective reader response—was worse.[25]

The arguments made by Gray, Godden, Heilman, and Fekete, however, fail to examine the political motivations of the Agrarian relationship to New Criticism. Only a handful of scholars, such as Paul A. Bové and Norman Podhoretz, have delved into the politics of the New Critical method and its establishment of an American canon. Bové and Podhoretz are not kind to the New Critics, writing that their efforts to reshape American criticism were self-motivated attempts to restore their regional value system in the wake of the triumph of northern progress over southern Agrarianism. Michael Kreyling, author of Inventing Southern Literature, traces Bové's argument: "'PROFESSIONAL SOUTHERNERS,' Bové's label for the purveyors of the formalist aesthetic, induced cultural amnesia, not the historical knowledge they claimed to be explaining."[26] Bové accused the Agrarians of turning their "politics into the political quietism of conservatism of New Critical orthodoxy," which, Kreyling adds, allowed the New Critics to "effectively 'forget' any and all connections to history by stressing the formal, aesthetic qualities of literary works over their social and cultural conditions."[27] Podhoretz, a New York critic, expressed his suspicion regarding the entire Southern Literary Renaissance, a large portion of which was the success of the New Critics: "One would like to think that the whole thing is a case of innocent literary misjudgment. But we are already dealing here not with a group of people so impressed by Southern literature that they feel impelled to study it, but rather with something closer to a political movement."[28] Podhoretz concluded that there was a more sinister implication and motivation for such a political movement, and it concerned the canonization of certain works over and above others that might be equally deserving of critical attention. According to Kreyling's assessment of the critic, this political movement, for Podhoretz, served only to "thwart change in the legal and social relations between the races in the South."[29] Such a claim fueled the negative image of New Criticism, with Ransom, Warren, Tate, and Brooks reduced to racist southern neo-Confederates holding steadfast to a lost cause for which they were taking one last stand. Mark Jancovich prefaces his extensive analysis, aptly titled The Cultural Politics of New Criticism, by noting the peculiarity of the Agrarian transformation. "What struck me at this time was that the positions which I had identified in the works which

Ransom, Tate and Warren had produced during the Southern Renaissance seem to contradict the positions attributed to them as New Critics," wrote Jancovich. He further confessed that he "intended to illustrate that the New Criticism developed out of certain Southern critiques of modern society; that contemporary interpretations of the interest and practices of the New Criticism were largely inaccurate; and that the New Criticism had actually established the terms within which contemporary theory had defined."[30] Despite his efforts to examine all three points, however, Jancovich claims that he was "persuaded to concentrate on the second of these arguments."[31] He thus sets out in the bulk of his monograph to debunk the myths of New Criticism, but he does include a poignant observation regarding the critics' drive for recognition. Denying the claims of Fekete, Jancovich declares:

> They [Warren, Tate, and Ransom] did shift from Agrarianism to an involvement in the debates over the teaching of English, but the goal of the latter activity was only seen as an intermediate one. It was hoped that the transformation of the academy would enable the distribution of their social and cultural criticism, and so encourage further social and cultural changes. The shift was not one of political position, but merely a tactical maneouvre. They had simply identified a more immediate and practical way of promoting their position. . . . They consolidated their ideas in books, established organs of publication, and organized and agitated for institutional change.[32]

Jancovich does not undertake an explanation of this "tactical manoeuvre,"[33] but conceivably it is yet another manifestation of the efforts made by these talented artists to combat the public criticism of the South and the collective anxiety and sense of inferiority that followed.

THE IDENTITY POLITICS OF NEW CRITICISM

The failure of Agrarian politics directly influenced the system of values adopted and advanced by the New Critics. Such a radical transformation was preceded by an equally influential experience, and in this case, the Agrarians were the subject of widespread public condemnation after the publication of I'll Take My Stand, similar to the ridicule they experienced as Fugitives during and after the Scopes Trial. The arc from Fugitives to Agrarians to New Critics must be considered in its entirety in order to expose fully the identity politics common to these manifestations. Public criticism served as a key catalyst in the first conversion, and it was influential, at least to some degree, in the second. Simply put, the Agrarians walked away from a fight that they could not win. However, rather than retreating into isolation and creating a world unto themselves, as did the southern fundamentalists in Dayton, the New Critics established new rules by which literature would be judged, allowing the work that reflected their moral and cultural viewpoint to be praised, while suppressing their indigenous and authentic southern identities, which had proved costly to their reputations as intellectuals. When seen in this way, New Criticism represents an elaborate entrenchment of sorts, a way of disguising one's real position, one's real identity, under a highly wrought, deeply intellectualized, aesthetic camouflage. And though claims of racism and quiet violence were perhaps repercussions of an overly moralistic literary system, they were not the burning impetus behind the New Critical vision, which turns out, of course, to be not so new. They are indeed, however, predictable side effects of a community of southern traditionalists who, though educated and gifted, are attempting, in some way, to reconstruct their culture and their reputations.

Four key elements of the New Critical position as developed by Ransom, Tate, Warren, and eventually Brooks reflect their southern heritage as well as a heritage of inferiority: the argument for the special knowledge of poetry; the demand for close readings and textual authority; the support for formal rules of interpretation; and the demotion of historical and biographical context. The first initiative of New Criticism—regarding the special knowledge of poetry— has its roots in Ransom's early work. In the latter half of 1926, Ransom began writing a manuscript titled "The Third Moment" in which he attempted to distinguish three aspects of cognition—it is, of course, deeply philosophical in nature. The First Moment comprised the sensory reception of immediate experience, free of analysis, and Ransom linked this phase to early childhood. The Second Moment, corresponding to a coming-of-age period, focused on rationality, explaining reality pragmatically and often scientifically. Maturity enabled the Third Moment, intended to marry the First and Second Moments, meshing raw experience with human logic, reflecting the true complexity of knowledge. "This was the blessed state Ransom longed for," claimed Daniel Joseph Singal, "in which the liberated sensibility would coexist with the discipline of rigorous logic—much as the poet's feelings were to harmonize with the requirements of meter and rhyme."[34] And this is exactly the next step that Ransom would take one decade later when he applied the basic tenets of "The Third Moment"—the manuscript was never published and was ultimately destroyed by its author—to his New Critical definition of the special knowledge of poetry. If Ransom could apply his theory effectively, perhaps the New Criticism could signal the maturity of the southern Agrarians, now engaged in a movement intended to capture fully the human condition in art, despite the cultural chaos of the modern era.

"The Third Moment," in fact, is political in its intention, though aesthetic and literary in its application. Singal concludes that in Ransom's view, implementation of the Third Moment meant that "the whole mind would thus be engaged and the rift in the modern psyche healed, at least temporarily."[35] Such healing offered Ransom and his colleagues a clean intellectual slate, freed from the responsibility of defending the Agrarian culture, which seemed an unfruitful endeavor.

One of the fundamental texts associated with the establishment of the New Criticism, Ransom's *The World's Body* (1938), included an essay titled "Forms and Citizens," in which he professes the importance of literary form using John Milton's "Lycidas" as his case study. Additionally, Ransom injects his concept of civilization into the essay, claiming that societies naturally progress through two phases: the Pioneering phase and the Maturity phase. Ransom's cataloging of civilization is wholly regional; his independent perspective produces a regional characterization based on his opposition to and alienation from northern and American culture. He cites the antebellum South as an example of a mature society—he claims that the North never developed a mature society— one that is no longer wholly occupied with survival but rather has the luxury of reflection. "The mature society knows the value of traditions, manners, rituals, ceremonies, myths, rites, and poetry,"[36] remarks Ransom scholar Thomas Daniel Young.

Clearly Ransom's position was influenced by not only his early aesthetic principles but also his experience in the Agrarian movement, though now his focus was primarily on the way in which a culture such as that of the Old South would influence art and literature, as opposed to debating the agricultural social and economic policy. It is also important to note that Ransom's argumentative method is based on general categories—Pioneering, Maturity—and such categories are useless in determining the needs and goals, the value systems, of those who might not fit into those categories. So, from the beginning, Ransom's New Criticism, while seeming to claim a kind of inviting inclusiveness with its broad categories, can just as easily be seen as exclusive and highly selective in its evaluative procedures. To be realistic, as many critics ultimately would become, it might profitably be asked, "Who precisely is allowed to go through the Pioneering and Maturity phase and finally arrive at the highly valued Third Moment?"

Still another essay in *The World's Body*, "Criticism, Inc.," which appeared independently in 1937, echoed the separate status of poetry—thus the need for prominent literary critics—as part of Ransom's Third Moment. Since poetry for Ransom "tendered the fullest image of human experience,"[37] its interpretation required specific training, reasoned Ransom. Modern society had destroyed any sense of myth and tradition, and thus it fell upon men of letters to reconstruct some sense of morality and standards. Only three types of people were eligible to decipher the true meaning of a poem and to judge it accordingly: the artist, the philosopher, and the English professor at the university level. Negative identity construction had activated a defensive response from Ransom, and, along with his fellow New Critics, he advocated a need for expertise that he could then fill. The artist's critical sensibilities, Ransom further argued, were driven by instinct and thus were too personal and emotional; and the philosopher, he remarked, was not inclined to undertake literary analysis. Thus, the professor of English, Ransom insisted, must take on this great responsibility to interpret literature for the masses and to judge its failure or greatness. Thus Ransom conveniently appoints himself and his colleagues as architects of a new literary canon, a position of authority denied to him both as a Fugitive and as an Agrarian.

In order to explain fully this sacred status of poetry, Ransom not only theorized about the various types of cognition, he also directly commented on the differences between poetry and science, a sentiment consistent with his ideas in *God without Thunder*. Literary historian and critic Art Berman describes the historical context regarding scientific knowledge in which New Criticism arose: "Given enough time, it seemed science would fully explain whatever there might be to know about the universe and humankind and would bring beside this knowledge, equitable government, prosperity, health, and general well-being. It has been argued, convincingly, that with science in command of exploring the world around us, poets more and more claimed subjectivity, the contents and potential of the individual mind, as their domain of interest."[38] The acceptance and popularity of science, evident in the criticism of the Scopes Trial, contribute to Ransom's claim to the exclusivity of poetic and artistic knowledge, as would Tate, former student and trusted confidant. Tate's vision was less concerned with the special cognition of poetry and more explicitly concerned with the intangible elements of the human condition. As Jancovich notes, Tate "maintained that the aesthetic acknowledges the complexities of the world and does not reduce it to a mere object of use."[39] For Tate and Ransom, privileging paradox justified the inner conflict of their southern identity. The burden of lost cause anxieties from which they fled as Fugitives had proved too heavy, and they had returned home, intellectually and emotionally, to defend their way of life. Their defense proved costly. Oversimplified and dismissed as pathetic, the Agrarians-turned–New Critics naturally championed complexity, particularly in a transitioning southern culture that languished under the microscope.

Ransom's most recognized contribution to the movement appeared in 1941 in a collection of four long essays published under the official title *The New Criticism*. Having already expressed his opinion regarding the danger of science worship and having previously encouraged the professional and didactic responsibilities of critics, Ransom attempted to clarify his particular definition of a New Critic in the final essay, "Wanted: An Ontological Critic." In this essay, Ransom sounded a call for a new type of critic, one that would explore the specific existence of poetry as a source of knowledge in a modern world with a "definable content" and distinct in some way from prose writing. Having examined the differences and shortcomings of three eminent critics, I. A. Richards, T. S. Eliot, and Yvor Winters, in the three preceding essays, Ransom explained his perception of the unique nature of poetry: "It is my feeling that we have in poetry a revolutionary departure from the convention of logical discourse, and that we should provide it with a bold and proportionate designation."[40] Ransom corresponded with Tate during the writing of the manuscript, and although his confidence in the project, particularly the writing, waned, he still elicited Tate's critique. In a letter dated January 16, 1941, addressed to "brother Tate" (the group sometimes addressed each other as such), Ransom explained this final essay: "When I look for what is 1) universal in all the works of art, including non-moralistic works, abstract works, and music, and at the same time, 2) absent from the scientific discourse, it is texture; or the extra-dimension; or particularity."[41] It is another example of Ransom's generalities: seemingly inclusive and universal, but actually opaque and exclusive. Though Ransom had some trouble articulating this "extra-dimension"—he shied away from using the term "metaphysical" because of its broadness and susceptibility to misunderstanding—he seemed to trust that Tate, with his shared experience, would recognize and appreciate the revered space he was carving out for poetry. Poetry, for these southern New Critics, ascends to the role of civil religion, and with it the New Critic is self-ordained as a non-pathetic, blessed judge.

The second and third components of New Criticism that reflect the Fugitive-Agrarian–New Critic experience with mass public criticism are inextricably linked. The New Critical demand for close reading was part of the system of intricate rules that the New Critics developed to perform such close readings. Ransom first remarked on his appreciation for close scrutiny of language in a letter written to his father in February 1914 as he began his teaching career after returning from Oxford. He confessed to his father that he recognized "a good translation of Virgil with no difficulty, and I [Ransom] like it because even the translation is poetry."[42] But his appreciation for careful translation would reach the status of dogma. The New Critics eventually regarded the practice of paraphrasing as heretical. The meaning of the poem was "inseparable from the linguistic processes of the text."[43] Ultimately, the "heresy of paraphrase" discouraged the critic from making any sort of comment of political or historical significance. Thus, this tenet of New Criticism, in a sense, enshrines silence as the ultimate critical virtue. And silence is most closely related to quietism, or status-quo conservatism, the political view that refuses to examine the influence of the historical past on the present. The distaste for summary, moreover, is a reaction to the frustration that the Agrarians felt when their respective arguments, particularly those presented in *I'll Take My Stand*, were, in their opinion, misunderstood, not read closely, and oversimplified. In many ways, the vision of the text as a precious object mirrored the fundamentalist commitment to a literal translation of the Bible. Words and language were sacrosanct.

Though the New Critics appointed themselves and their fellow English professors as the chosen interpreters, while the fundamentalist Christians shunned any type of interpretation, both relied on the text as a source of control. For the New Critics, channeling their energy into deciphering the language of the poem, "a linguistic revolution"[44] of sorts, allowed them to suppress the historical context of literature. Consequently, the New Critical approach was often chided as supporting "art for art's sake," particularly as literature became increasingly politicized in the years leading up to and throughout World War II. Ransom's dismissal of what he considered propaganda literature, Popular Front art, for example, reflected his belief that aesthetics should transcend social concerns. But transcending social concerns, when social concerns are the dominating subject of the day, is at least escapist, if not defensive. Such tactics lead to inconsistencies in both theory and performance. Jancovich wrote of his original research question as having been driven by the apparent inconsistencies in the New Critical position. The Agrarian movement and *I'll Take My Stand*, not to mention the bulk of post-Fugitive poetry, including Tate's "Ode to the Confederate Dead," were by no means a pure artistic expression, removed from politics. Despite Ransom's early theories regarding the primacy of poetic language, the New Critical and highly selective vision of the textual field served as a convenient distraction from the southern stereotypes, which, ironically, they themselves had reinforced. Vincent Leitch described this depersonalization of the task of the critic, which for the New Critic was "to judge the text, as one judges an object or machine, to determine whether it worked efficiently."[45]

In order to determine the efficacy of the work, the New Critics developed a system of explicit rules, previously categorized by Leitch. This system was intended to reestablish the strong moral tradition that Ransom associated with the Old South; for Tate the New England Puritan cosmology was the quintessential example of tradition against which an artist could create. In one of his New Critical articles, collected in the book *Reactionary Essays on Poetry and Ideas*, Tate discussed the theocratic society within which Emily Dickinson composed. The article originally appeared in 1928 and reveals the continuity of Tate's obsession with social order. In a way similar to the Agrarian distrust of industrialism, Tate cited the establishment of the earliest mills in the late eighteenth century as the beginning of the end for the Puritan way of life. Jancovich claims that in Tate's opinion, the first rumblings of capitalism "destroyed the tragic vision of Puritanism which was the distinguishing feature of the New England theocracy."[46] Without cultural rules, enforced by a god with thunder, the artist would lose the power of self-definition, a power that the failed Agrarian poets intended to recapture. Consequently, and despite their collective skepticism toward the scientific method, Tate and Ransom—and soon Warren and Brooks in textbook form—defined a nearly mathematical prescription that measured poetic harmony and value.

In "Wanted: An Ontological Critic," Ransom's desire for control takes on an almost fundamentalist insistence on the formula for literary evaluation. He offers the following analogy as an indication of how the critic should weigh poetic meaning and meter:

> Let us suppose a lady who wished to display a bowl of fruits upon her sideboard and says to her intelligent houseboy: "Go to the box of apples in the pantry and select and bring me a dozen of the biggest and reddest ones." The box contains a hundred apples, which vary both in bigness and in redness. . . . He ranges the apples first in order of their bigness and denotes the biggest as B_1, the next as B_2, and so on down to B_{100}. Then he ranges the apples in order of their redness, and denotes the reddest as R_1, the next reddest as R_2, and so on down to R_{100}. Then for each apple he adds the numerical coefficient of its bigness and the numerical coefficient of its redness; for example, the apple which is tagged B_1 is also tagged R_{36}, so that its combined coefficient is 37. He finds the twelve apples with lowest combined coefficients and takes them to his mistress.[47]

Such a formula, argued Ransom, demonstrates the responsibility of the critic, who will have to decipher the text and judge the balance of its literary elements. Additionally, in the same essay, Ransom presents a graph detailing the interaction between what he labels the determinate meanings (DM), the intended meaning (IM), the determinate sound-structure (DS), and the indeterminate sound-structure (IS).[48] There was little, if any, flexibility, a manifestation of the southern New Critics' desire to control the interpretation of American literature and to, thus, reconstruct a conservative culture. The chart reflects an algebraic method accessible only to the professional expert, which made poetic knowledge exclusive, with the New Critics as gatekeepers. In many ways, Ransom's numerical mania, a true rage for order, seems paradoxically closer in spirit to the mechanized society he abhorred.

In addition to the New Critical elements previously discussed—the special knowledge of poetry, the close reading of texts, and the adherence to formal rules of interpretation—still one key component, perhaps most directly, reflects this heritage of inferiority that confronted these southern poet-critics. Their desire, whether conscious or not, to shed their southern identity, as they had once proclaimed in the foreword to their first published issue of the *Fugitive*, clearly influenced the New Critical theory they espoused. Though they indeed had their own aesthetic reasons for relegating historical context to the sidelines of literary criticism, the effect, particularly since they were critiquing their own work, was to render invisible the baggage of the benighted South. Ransom actually took a job at Kenyon College in Ohio, giving up his long tenure at Vanderbilt. Outraged by the university's failure to submit a counteroffer to try to keep Ransom in Nashville, Tate and Davidson organized a campaign of protest on their teacher's behalf.[49] The move gave Ransom the opportunity to edit the *Kenyon Review*—he, along with his colleagues, had longed for such an outlet, although this one was clearly not in the South. Much of the theoretical debate concerning the New Criticism would appear in the pages of the *Kenyon Review*, as well as in the *Southern Review* at Louisiana State University, where Warren, as editor, fulfilled an Agrarian dream of sorts. It is not difficult to find a tragic element in all of this. The cultural amnesia promoted and institutionalized by New Criticism allowed, at least for awhile, these men of letters, blinded by their cultural assumptions and allegiances but driven by their undeniable intelligence, to avoid engaging with some of the greatest complexities of their day. Even during their own time, the New Critics came to seem oddly eccentric, somehow refusing to acknowledge the major upheavals of their region and all the while evaluating the IM, DM, IS, and DS of a poem.

In his 1940 essay "Miss Emily and the Bibliographer," Tate condemned the historical critic as deficient and the historical method as flawed. He insisted that the literary critic was charged solely with judging the objective elements of the work, which was limited, he reasoned, to the formal qualities of the poem. These formal elements transcend time and place and constitute the "poetry" of the poem, contended Tate, and they must be assessed in the present, removed from their historical circumstances. This perspective has merit in and of itself and seems only to suggest that literature be reinterpreted by each successive generation. However, Tate had a secondary purpose in championing the demotion of historical analysis, and it is inextricably linked to his perpetual striving for recognition. He lamented that literary greatness is conveyed by the passage of time. "Perhaps the same scholar acknowledges the greatness of Dryden and the even more formidable greatness of Milton and Shakespeare," Tate wrote, "and if you ask him how they became great he will reply, as I have heard him reply, that History did it and that we have to wait until History does it, or declines to do it, to writers of our own time."[50] Tate did not want to wait, nor did his fellow New Critics. Focusing on the structure and texture of a poem allowed them to avoid history and social issues, for in that arena they could not win. Thus, inherent in the New Critical method was the ability to reconstruct the canon and to include themselves.

SELF-PROMOTION

The foremost source of both the success and the mass appeal of New Criticism lay in the publication of two textbooks, Understanding Poetry (1938) and Understanding Fiction (1943), coedited by Warren and Brooks, colleagues at Louisiana State University. The books began with a preface titled "Letter to a Teacher," which shared what Brooks and Warren considered the total vision of literature.[51] It encouraged students and professors alike to focus their attention on the text and to follow three maxims:

1. Emphasis should be kept on the poem as a poem.
2. The treatment should be concrete and inductive.
3. A poem should always be treated as an organic system of relationships, and the poetic quality should never be understood as inhering in one or more factors taken in isolation.[52]

It is in some ways the closest thing this country has ever had to a popular aesthetics. Under the Brooks and Warren method, English professors, and high school teachers to whom the New Critical method had trickled down, did not have to provide historical background, author biography, or linguistic etymology in order to investigate the formal elements of meter, rhyme, metaphor, and so on. Though their theories were inevitably simplified (even oversimplified), they were popular in the classroom. These theories solved problems by redefining the notion of complexity, and in complex times, this is a dangerous maneuver. The New Critics were concerned primarily with defining "'the poetic in poetry,' and 'the prosaic in prose'; to say nothing of 'the literariness of literature.'"[53] Walter Edgar, in his analysis of Warren as a critic, wrote, "I have seen

Mr. Warren's colleague Cleanth Brooks criticized, in the course of a single polemic, both for being uninterested in the historical dimensions of literature and for conducting a covert apologia for the Old South, which is a pretty neat trick if you can pull it off."[54] And indeed, that is exactly what the Warren and Brooks textbooks accomplished. Their popularity institutionalized their canon, one that reflected a southern, white, male sensibility. According to René Wellek, *Understanding Poetry* accomplished "more than any other single book to making the techniques of the New Criticism available in the classrooms of American colleges and universities and to present the techniques of analysis as something to be learned and imitated."[55]

Reflecting the ahistorical nature of their method, *Understanding Poetry* included close readings of forty poems, which were not grouped by time period, but rather by form. Major divisions included "implied narratives," "metrics," and "tone and attitude." The strong reputations of "great" writers were not spared from the New Critical attack. For example, scenes in Edgar Allan Poe's "Ulalume" are dismissed as "merely good for frightening children." And Poe's effort is further characterized as "too transparent, too obvious," and the rhythm of the poem is labeled "monotonous and unexpressive."[56] Percy Bysshe Shelley's "The Indian Serenade" is judged unconvincing and sentimental. The New Critics were, of course, not required to accept the literary assessments of the past, and criticizing the "greats" cleared room for new voices. Their denunciations, however, were not as telling as their inclusions. A noticeable and significant portion of the works included in the textbook were from southern writers, including Donald Davidson, John Crowe Ransom, and Allen Tate. In fact, Ransom and Tate appeared twice and were featured alongside John Dryden, William Butler Yeats, W. H. Auden, William Blake, John Keats, and Alfred Lord Tennyson.[57] Not only had the role of the critic and poet been elevated in the realm of New Criticism, but also the stature of these southern writers was equated with that of Shakespeare, Lord Byron, Matthew Arnold, Ezra Pound, and T. S. Eliot, to name a few. They inserted their friends and fellow southerners into a white male canon of world literature and advocated for an interpretive technique that justified their table of contents.

The self-promotional aspect of New Criticism extended beyond the popular Warren and Brooks textbooks, reaching their individual essays and edited volumes. Tate, for example, offered a New Critical reading of his own "Ode to the Confederate Dead" in a 1938 essay, "Narcissus as Narcissus." In the essay, he berates other historical and psychological critics (referred to in the essay as doctors) who fail to diagnose the poem's value—according to Tate, it is a meditation on solipsism—accurately. "According to its doctors," wrote Tate, "my one intransigent desire is to have been a Confederate general." What is important, demanded Tate, is "not where it [the poem] came from, or why";[58] only the finished poem itself should garner critical attention. So, for Tate, the bearing of the Civil War on his poem was irrelevant, which is not to say that a critical focus on language and form is not valuable, but in this case, it is convenient. And although it may not matter in terms of literary evaluation, the intention behind the New Critical approach is worth understanding. Just as the authenticity of the Agrarian intention was questioned, so too must the authenticity of the New Critical method for these southerners be considered. They did not abandon their advocacy for and defense of their southern way of life. In fact, their promotional efforts in many ways culminated in the publication of the landmark collection *Southern Renascence: The Literature of the Modern South* (1953), edited by Louis D. Rubin Jr. and Robert D. Jacobs, an anthology that canonized southern literature. It included entire sections promoting the contributions of Warren, Ransom, Davidson, and Brooks, and it cited Tate on no less than fifty pages. No African American writers were included in the first edition, and only in the 1961 revised edition did Ralph Ellison make the cut.[59] Though there were clear aesthetic visions at work, the former Agrarians' embrace of the "objective" New Critical method did provide them a way to cast aside their southern identity while promoting their own literary accomplishments and redrawing the literary canon in their southern likeness.

BEYOND THE NEW CRITICISM

In their third incarnation, the Fugitives-turned-Agrarians-turned–New Critics enjoyed great success, marked by their prominent employment. Warren and Brooks went on to teach at Yale, Ransom enjoyed a long career at Kenyon, and Tate established the creative writing program at Princeton. But, despite their efforts to remove the study of literature from specific historical contexts, they failed to suppress fully their collective southern identity. Eventually, the region's preeminent writers had to confront the racial injustice they had ignored for decades. In his essay "Pure and Impure Poetry," which was originally delivered as a lecture at Princeton and appeared in the *Kenyon Review* in 1943, Warren began: "Critics are rarely faithful to their labels and their special strategies."[60] Warren never truly abandoned his interest in history, and the burgeoning civil rights movement proved too formidable to ignore. In 1956, he published *Segregation: The Inner Conflict in the South*, a collection of personal conversations that he had had with southerners of all walks of life following the *Brown v. Board of Education* decision. The thin volume offers insight into the belief system of the southern white segregationist. Warren chronicled personal accounts of anti-miscegenation and mongrelization phobias, as well as scientific myths regarding the biological inferiority of African Americans. Though Warren offers no statistical assessment of southern opinions, nor claims of objectivity, he does profess to have witnessed the heart of the conflict—the internal struggle of the South against itself.

Warren continued to seek answers, publishing *Who Speaks for the Negro?* (1965), a historic collection of interviews with African American leaders such as Ralph Ellison, Stokely Carmichael, Malcolm X, and Dr. Martin Luther King Jr.[61] Warren resurrected Swedish sociologist Gunnar Myrdal's idea that Confederate slaveholders should have been compensated for lost land and freed slaves after the Confederate defeat in order to avoid the racial violence and Jim Crow system that defined the South in the twentieth century. He asked his subjects if they agreed, pushing them to offer counterperspectives. How could the South and the country as a whole have avoided such suffering? In the end, the South did not fare well in Warren's opinion, and he retreated to his home in Connecticut. His obituary in the *New York Times* in 1989 noted that Warren, after witnessing the racial conflict over integration as well as other issues central to the movement, felt "that he could not really return home again."[62]

Unlike his fellow writers, Davidson never abandoned his Agrarian politics or his zealous passion for the South that lay at the core of his anti-industrialist position. Perhaps his entrenchment resulted from a life spent at home in Tennessee, as opposed to his colleagues, whose careers took them beyond the Mason-Dixon Line. The book page that Davidson edited for the Tennessee newspaper had put him in direct contact with the burgeoning canon of southern condemnation. While his colleagues grappled with New Criticism, Davidson stayed invested in the political landscape of the South. Along with Jack Kershaw, a Tennessee sculptor and former student of both Ransom and Warren, Davidson campaigned actively for Dixiecrat Strom Thurmond's 1948 third-party states' rights candidacy, which broke from the Democratic Party because of the civil rights platform adopted at the national convention. Though Thurmond secured only one splinter electoral vote in Tennessee, Davidson's participation in the campaign revealed his commitment to the white supremacist hierarchy of his generation, a hierarchy that imploded in May 1954. Upon hearing the Supreme Court's unanimous decision in *Brown v. Board of Education*, Davidson proclaimed, "9 justices against how many millions of white folk in [the] South and elsewhere!"[63] Kershaw shared Davidson's views fully and exhibited complete loyalty to his friend, a quality Davidson found lacking in his fellow Fugitives, who had turned their attention to aesthetics.[64] Together they founded the Tennessee Federation for Constitutional Government (TFCG), which attempted to coordinate resistance efforts against public school integration. *I'll Take My Stand* was notable for the absence of attention to race, but Davidson's post-*Brown* opinions were considered by historian Numan Bartley to be a distorted continuation of his anti-industrialist politics; he claimed that the TFCG was "a Snopesian perversion of the aristocratic agrarian tradition."[65]

The TFCG never amassed the popular support that groups such as the White Citizens' Councils in Mississippi or the Virginia Defenders of State Sovereignty and Liberty did, establishing chapters in only fourteen of Tennessee's ninety-five counties.[66] Regardless of the TFCG's success or lack thereof, Bartley's point—the idea of a continued southern defensiveness apparent in Davidson's choices—exposes the power and longevity of the heritage of inferiority that he had battled since his youth. Davidson continued to blame those whom he considered to be northern agitators and southern traitors for their ridicule of the region, and he couched his defense in whatever terms were necessary at the moment—Fugitive, Agrarian, Constitutionalist. Unlike Warren, who eventually confronted the inner conflict of the South, Davidson never did.

■ Despite their success as New Critics, Ransom, Tate, Brooks, and even Davidson have not fared well over time. They are most often eclipsed by others with whom they had hoped to keep company. Warren, of course, has shown great staying power. He is still, after all, the only American to win the Pulitzer Prize in both fiction and poetry. And although a defining member of the Fugitive, Agrarian, and New Critical "revolutions," Warren seemed years later to see clearly the role that criticism and inferiority had played in the South. On the centennial of the outbreak of the Civil War, he published a long meditation, *The Legacy of the Civil War* (1961), on the psychological repercussions of the bloody conflict. In his analysis of the relationship between the South and the nation at large, the Agrarian side of Warren proves that old habits are indeed hard to break. He attempted to debunk certain myths about the benighted South, pointing out that the Confederacy "persisted [in protecting] to the point of mania" such civil rights as freedom of speech and due process of law. He further claimed that the Confederacy never suspended the writ of habeas corpus nor was any Confederate newspaper censored for its content.[67] Even in his later years, Warren could not refrain in his historical analysis from defending the South.

However, Warren did recognize the psychological toll that public criticism and ridicule had taken on his fellow southerners. He defined what he labeled as the North's "Treasury of Virtue" and the accompanying monopoly on morality that in turn created a dynamic in which southerners embraced a sense of victimhood. The defeat in the Civil War, he reasoned, provided the South a "Great Alibi" or excuse to stay stagnant, to blame others for the region's problems. He questioned the "guilt" that constant excuses and resistance creates. "Does he [the southerner] ever, for a moment, feel the desperation of being caught in some great Time Machine, like a treadmill, and doomed to an eternal effort without progress," asked Warren. This "Great Alibi," he argued, creates a conditioned response, "a neurotic automatism" in which "reality cannot be faced," and he predicted: "We all seem to be doomed to reenact, in painful automatism, the errors of our common past."[68]

Public criticism of the South in the twentieth century triggered among white southerners such an automated response. For the Fugitives-turned-Agrarians-turned–New Critics, the response was a collective striving for recognition, in various and conflicting manifestations, underneath which lay this common motivation. Their "third revolution" was in fact a coup d'état of sorts, leaving these critics and teachers in the positions of authority that had eluded them in their earlier efforts. They now had the power and intellectual clout to influence literary opinion; they were finally taken seriously as American artists. Their collective sense of inferiority, influenced heavily by the burden of mass criticism of the South and their defense of the South that they experienced, was one of the motivations that inspired them to change the rules by which they would be judged as southern artists. New Criticism incorporated much of the Agrarian and Fugitive theory, all the while deemphasizing their southern identity and championing textual authority, formal interpretation, and their select status as poets. If the New Critical movement had spiked and faded, existed as only a flash in the pan, then perhaps the cultural amnesia that it fostered would have had little effect. But, despite its seeming narrowness and its rigidity, it did indeed revolutionize the study of literature. The postmodernists would eventually deconstruct the bleached canon that the New Critics built and avowed, a canon that seemed no longer viable or sacred in the era of shifting racial and gender politics. Still their influence lingered as the conservative, white aesthetic rock against which the culture wars would break.

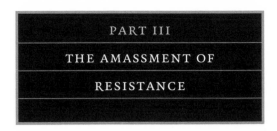

PART III

THE AMASSMENT OF

RESISTANCE

But however it is cast, no doubt is left that the South lies under moral indictment as certainly as it did in the days of the Abolitionists. This realization is
peculiarly lacerating to the Southern spirit, which is usually genial and gregari-
ous. . . . Humor has always been a great defensive weapon of the South's public men; a skillful raconteur can convert the most bitter conversation into an
amiable joke—and raise doubts that a gentleman so mellow and full of human
juices could actually be guilty of high crimes. But most Southerners simply retreat into unreality. It isn't so, they say (and with their hearts if not their minds,
believe).
—Harry Ashmore, *An Epitaph for Dixie*

Perhaps the most well-known and well-documented criticism of the South
accompanied the civil rights movement, which permanently altered the
southern landscape and dominated the political environment of the 1950s and
1960s. World War II, which had increased the economic production of the South
and ushered in a new era of American nationalism, had offered a reprieve,
albeit short lived, from regional criticism. However, the pressure to dismantle
southern racial boundaries increased significantly as American patriotism
focused on the atrocities of the German Nazi regime. And the founding of the
United Nations in 1945, C. Vann Woodward argued, opened "to the outside
world a large window on American race practices."[1] As representatives from
every corner of the globe descended on the United Nations headquarters
in New York, they were greeted, at times, by descriptions of racial atrocities
in the South as reported in national newspapers and journals. "To many of
these people," insisted Woodward, "the Jim Crow code came as a complete
shock. Those who had heard anything at all of the system before coming to
America often discounted the stories as propaganda. Now they witnessed its
workings daily."[2] As criticism of the South reached international audiences, the
United Nations launched investigations into these racial practices, publishing
numerous reports of the findings.

Pressure for change began to build inside the white southern community as well, as southern writers and journalists began to discuss the psychological damage that Jim Crow had caused not only African American southerners but their white oppressors as well. Specifically, Jim Cobb, in his essay "Does 'Mind' Still Matter?" claimed that the internal criticism of the 1940s and 1950s increasingly focused on the absurdity of southern behavior: "Works like Lillian Smith's *Killers of the Dreams* followed Cash's lead by presenting southern life as, in one reviewer's words, 'a schizophrenic invention without parallel, an insane dichotomy from the cradle to the grave.' Stetson Kennedy's *Southern Exposure* described the South as 'the nation's pathological problem No. 1' and warned that the insanity of the South 'infected the entire nation.'"[3] This growing emphasis on the psychology of racism was a clear repercussion of the exposure and defeat of Hitler's ethnic cleansing. What southern critics—internal, national, and international—began to assess would become the focus of the Supreme Court in the 1950s.

Most notable, the notion of inferiority actually appears in the legal language of the 1954 *Brown v. Board of Education* decision that desegregated American public education. The U.S. District Court of Kansas, which initially had heard the case in 1951, wrote in its decision that "segregation of white and colored children in public schools has a detrimental effect upon the colored children. . . . A sense of inferiority affects the motivation of a child to learn." Chief Justice Earl Warren would quote this exact passage from the Kansas district decision in his majority opinion in 1954. The inferiority complex thus gains additional credibility as a psychological reality endorsed by the American legal system. Scholars have labeled the period that followed the *Brown* decision as the decade of Massive Resistance, an all-out legal and political fight against integration that commenced with the 1956 Southern Manifesto authored by Virginia senator Harry F. Byrd and South Carolina senator Strom Thurmond, which declared such resistance. However, the intermittent years reveal a transformation from moderation to Massive Resistance that has been somewhat overlooked.

By contemporary standards, and as assessed by some scholars, the Virginia state plan for integration, developed by Virginia's Commission on Public Education—also called the Gray Commission—reads as a radical, programmatic, but legal, method to suffocate integration in its infancy. However, in light of the drastic measures taken only a few years later by Governor J. Lindsey Almond Jr., including the chaining of school doors and gates, the Gray Commission plan must be considered a moderate initial reaction. Moderation, though perhaps lacking true moderate intentions, characterized Virginia's primary stance, but over the course of several months in 1955, state leaders abandoned the moderate tenets of the Gray Commission plan entirely. By January 1956, when a constitutional referendum made its way to voters—an amendment necessary to alter state law that would allow the Gray Commission plan to be effectively implemented—an all-out anti-Gray campaign reverberated throughout the state. Over the course of one transformative winter, Virginia voters and leading politicians would demand that no integration be allowed in any county for any reason. "Within a year," journalist Harry Ashmore noted, "Virginia . . . was using the full weight of the state government not only to maintain segregation in those districts that desired it, but to prevent any degree of integration in those that appeared willing to accept it."[4]

This transformation was triggered, at least in part, by the increased criticism of southern racial practices that intensified while the Gray Commission deliberated the fate of the Virginia school system. Moreover, the public attention given to the protest initiatives of the African American community both inside and outside of the South must be read as yet another source of this criticism. What had once been empty and abstract rhetoric of inequality found concrete targets in the powerful narratives of the Emmett Till murder and the Montgomery Bus Boycott of 1955. These were only two examples of the explosive and history-altering civil rights events that erupted in the 1950s and 1960s. The media frenzy that surrounded this early tragedy and this early triumph of the civil rights movement, indicative of the scrutiny that would last for decades to come, resurrected the regional ghosts of an old war still raging on the American landscape. The public denunciation of the South disturbed the delicate balance practiced by Virginia governor Thomas B. Stanley, a balance between the national perception of his state and the devotion to the local desires of his constituency. Such media disparagement produced what Michael J. Klarman has called the backlash thesis. He insists that although *Brown* is generally recognized as the most significant Supreme Court decision of the twentieth century, scholars have failed to explore the exact nature of this significance.

Brown is often read as the event that catalyzes the civil rights movement; but Klarman contends that the catalyzer was twofold. "*Brown* crystallized southern resistance to racial change," he claimed, "which—from at least the time of Harry S. Truman's civil rights proposals in 1948—had been scattered and episodic."[5] Moreover, Klarman surmises,

> The unification of southern racial intransigence, which became known as massive resistance, propelled politics in virtually every southern state several notches to the right on racial issues; *Brown* temporarily destroyed

southern racial moderation. In this extremist political environment, men who were unswervingly committed to preservation of the racial status quo were catapulted into public office. These massive resistance politicians were both personally and politically predisposed to use whatever measures were necessary to maintain Jim Crow, including the brutal suppression of civil rights demonstrations. There followed nationally televised scenes of southern law enforcement officers using police dogs, high-pressure fire hoses, tear gas, and truncheons against peaceful, prayerful black demonstrators (often children), which converted millions of previously indifferent northern whites into enthusiastic proponents of civil rights legislation.[6]

The impact of the images of violence in the Deep South is well documented by historians, particularly its effect on northern moderates. As Klarman suggests, it is essential to assess the indirect impact of *Brown*, particularly the cultural and psychological ramifications that were, in this case, influenced heavily by the media denunciation of the South.

The backlash in Virginia transformed moderate leaders and communities into instigators and advocates of the movement for Massive Resistance. The public criticism that reached white southern audiences in the aftermath of the *Brown* decision proved to be a negative influence on white southern identity construction. Southern whites responded with predictable reactions to a growing sense of inferiority, including deeming another group inferior so as to secure one's own superiority (a familiar tactic in the South, but one that intensifies in reaction to the public criticism of the mid-1950s) and altering the rules by which one is judged as inferior. In the months following the moderate plan presented by the Gray Commission, key political and media leaders in Virginia began to revisit the original intentions of the founding fathers, establishing the Doctrine of Interposition, which was reminiscent of the nullification doctrines that provoked the Civil War. This sudden entrenchment into constitutional theory reached the mass public through relentless editorial columns and speeches by journalist James J. Kilpatrick.

Though born and raised in Oklahoma, Kilpatrick became a close friend and correspondent with leading Virginia politicians, including Senator Byrd, governors Stanley and Almond, and Garland Gray. He argued for a strict construction of the states' rights clauses, insisting that in general the federal government was limited solely to the enumerated powers granted specifically to it in the Constitution, and that all other powers, as noted in the Tenth Amendment, fell to the states. This strict constructionist interpretation of the Constitution mirrored the biblical literalism adopted by the fundamentalists and the New Critical devotion to the text and proved to be a lasting determinant of southern whiteness. Kilpatrick and others likewise grappled with the same heritage of inferiority that had judged the religious and Agrarian visions of the South as backward and un-American. The Doctrine of Interposition, a legal maneuver to protect the powers granted to the states as defined by the founding fathers, became the rallying cry of the Old Dominion, operating as a front that allowed moderate Jim Crow southerners a way to rebel against integration without resorting to physical violence or inflammatory language. With Interposition as their guise, white southerners remained obstinate in their efforts to fight integration at every turn, hoping to deplete the resources of the NAACP and the resolve of progressive advocates. It was, in effect, a polite, legalistic, and intellectual (or so many white southerners thought) racism, but no less violent in spirit. The new enemies that Kilpatrick would engage—the expanding federal government, judicial activists, and the liberal media—remain definitive foes of contemporary southern conservatism.

CHAPTER 7

BLACK, WHITE, GRAY,

AND BROWN

THE OLD DOMINION

CONFRONTS INTEGRATION

One needs only to read the decision of the Supreme Court in the case of *Brown v. Board of Education of Topeka, et al.*, with its fantastic references to the sociology of Myrdal and the psychology of "authorities" even more questionable, and then to compare it to Mr. Kilpatrick's summation of the evidence. Then one knows what has happened to bench and bar in what is supposed to be the United States, plural.
—Donald Davidson, "A Comment on James Jackson Kilpatrick's
The Sovereign States"

The people of Virginia will receive the opinion of the Supreme Court calmly and take time to carefully and dispassionately consider the situation before coming to conclusions on steps which should be taken. . . . This news today calls for cool heads, calm, steady, and sound judgment. I'm sure the people of Virginia and our elected representatives can find the right solution. I hope all will cooperate to afford this opportunity for the careful development of a program which will be in the best interest of the entire citizenship.
—Virginia governor Thomas B. Stanley, responding to *Brown v. Board of Education*

Virginia's reaction to the Supreme Court's decision was at first relatively moderate. Yet organization policy became very much like a canoe which, first drifting downstream in mild waters, soon followed more turbulent currents and eventually plunged over the waterfall.
—Harvey J. Wilkinson III, *Harry Byrd and the Changing Face of Virginia Politics*

The centuries-old practice of subjugating one race and proclaiming the superiority of another sensitized many white southerners to accusations that they were, themselves, inferior to liberal-minded Americans (both self-proclaimed and authentic civil rights supporters). Moderate Mississippi journalist Hodding Carter Jr. best described this general regional anxiety. "The angry Southern reaction to what is branded as outside interference," penned Carter, "is undeniably guilt-ridden, however subconsciously; and there are dilatory and hypocritical overtones to the plea that if they would only leave us alone we would work out our own salvation."[1] In the wake of the media wave, the *Brown v. Board of Education of Topeka* decision loomed unavoidable and more ominous than it had at first headlines. Virginia political leaders began to fear that even a gesture of integration would topple the state's delicate balance; if schools went, so too would an entire way of life. Moreover, public scrutiny brought on by the civil rights movement inspired for many white southerners a sense of inferiority, a sense of standing once again on the wrong side of history.

Virginia's influence on the South was not self-aggrandizement but fact, for Virginia inspired a mythology all its own within the complex mythology of the states of the defeated Confederacy. "Virginians were vastly important to the Old South, not so much because of what they did as because of the image they fixed in the Southern mind. The ruder men," noted Ashmore, "who were cutting down the trees and draining the swamps in Alabama, Mississippi, Tennessee, Arkansas, and Texas accepted the old Tidewater society as an ideal."[2] This cultural and ingrained idealization of the Commonwealth of Virginia made its decisions in the early months and years that followed the *Brown* decision acts of the greatest influence.

There were signs, at least rhetorically, that the state of Virginia might act radically when faced with the integration crisis of the 1950s. Three years prior to the *Brown* decision, the *Roanoke World News* prophesied that "the South is not now and is not likely to be anytime soon ready for an end to segregation."[3] The *Richmond News Leader*, a leading state paper, even dangled the strategy of school closings.[4] J. Lindsay Almond Jr., the Virginia attorney general at the time of the *Brown* decision, warned that integration would destroy the public school system. "That is not an idle threat," he vowed.[5] Almond would prove to be a man of his word. As governor, he would defy the Supreme Court in dramatic fashion, capping what would be called Massive Resistance with an official act to close the public schools in several counties in 1959.

However, though there were obviously early indications of dissent, the reactionary spirit that would engulf the state of Virginia—a spirit that would in time support these school closings and Massive Resistance—was slow to gain momentum. In the immediate aftermath of the *Brown* decision, the state press and key leaders promised patience. Thomas B. Stanley, Virginia governor during the *Brown* verdict, proclaimed upon the announcement of the Supreme Court's decision that "this news calls for cool heads, calm study and sound judgment." He further declared that he would be establishing a commission to which "views of leaders of both races will be invited."[6] After all, Virginia had actually been the last southern state to adopt the most visible Jim Crow law, the segregation of train passengers, famously upheld in *Plessy v. Ferguson* (1896), holding out until 1900.[7]

Other southern governors spoke out immediately as well. South Carolina governor James F. Byrnes confessed his personal shock regarding the *Brown* decision. William Bradley Umstead, the governor of North Carolina, acknowledged that he was "terribly disappointed." Though Umstead and Byrnes offered more emotional and affected statements as compared to Stanley, they were by no means antagonistic. In fact, in the immediate reaction to *Brown*, "there was little talk of the court decision's being 'illegal' or of the states' having the right, much less the duty, to resist." As historian Bob Smith noted, "The day of the Southern Establishment was not yet."[8] For example, the superintendent of schools in Mathews and Gloucester counties on the east coast of Virginia promised that "if we use good judgment, integration will take place smoothly and will be carried to a successful conclusion."[9] Even Dowell J. Howard, Virginia's state superintendent of public instruction, cautioned, "There will be no defiance of the Supreme Court decision as far as I am concerned. We are trying to teach school children the law of the land and we will abide by it."[10]

The *Richmond Times-Dispatch* actually called upon the Supreme Court to set a date for the implementation of state integration plans; and James J. Kilpatrick of the *Richmond News Leader*, who would become one of the most reactionary and vitriolic voices of Massive Resistance, conceded that "we accept the Supreme Court's ruling. We do not accept it willingly, or cheerfully, or philosophically. We accept it because we have to."[11] Anti-integration forces did exist in Virginia and did actively campaign, but even these forces envisioned themselves as moderate within the South as a whole. For example, the Defenders of State Sovereignty and Liberty staunchly opposed any and all integration, although they refused to engage in violence and deliberately sought to distinguish themselves from what they considered to be the extreme white supremacy organizations such as the Ku Klux Klan and the White Citizens' Councils. In order to appreciate fully Virginia's transformation and ultimate contribution to the defiant rhetoric and actions of Massive Resistance, it is necessary first to understand the context of the *Brown* decision within the state and, second, to understand the moderate nature of the state's initial response and plan.

A GLIMPSE OF SOUTHERN PROGRESS AND MODERATION

The white South in the 1950s seemed to be catching up in important socioeconomic markers to its northern counterpart. During the four-decade period between 1910 and 1950, the population of southern communities increased by 130 percent, as compared to a 40 percent hike for the rest of the country—and such growth came despite the fact that nearly 10 million southerners, both whites and African Americans, had left the region.[12] Moreover, rural populations in the South dropped dramatically, as farmers and sharecroppers left the fields for the booming industrial centers of burgeoning southern cities. By the 1950s, the death rate—including the infant mortality rate—for southerners had decreased substantially, putting the region closely on par with national statistics. African American southerners, whose average life span had been close to sixteen years shorter than white southerners, closed the gap to seven years. Moreover, the crime rate in the states of the Old Confederacy declined by approximately 15 percent, while such rates inched upward in the country as a whole.[13] Such statistics, many of which were reported in the southern media, gave many white southerners a sense of stability and national identity.

Some of the most dramatic changes were those made to the southern system of public education, although there is no doubt that white schools benefited most dramatically. The first wave of growth, measured from 1910 to 1930, witnessed the rise of school appropriations from $28 million to $415 million. Although stalled by the Great Depression, southern public education received a post–World War II increase, which included the construction of state-of-the-art school buildings, the value of which jumped exponentially. Higher education experienced a similar boost in the 1950s, with student enrollment figures that almost equaled the well-established universities of the North. Despite the population growth, southern colleges suffered from a lack of funding, which prevented them from competing for the most distinguished professors—indeed, Vanderbilt lost John Crowe Ransom to Kenyon College in Ohio.[14]

In Virginia, Thomas Jefferson had first proposed the idea of free schooling. He introduced the Jefferson Bill for the More General Diffusion of Knowledge in 1779. A part of the plan, which focused on elementary education (of course, for white students only), was adopted in 1796, and in 1810 the Literacy Fund of Virginia, which operated from a small endowment, was established with the express goal of fostering elementary education. Much of the Literacy Fund was eventually given to the building of a state university, while the remaining funds were offered to low-income students to attend private schools. By the 1820s, over $1 million had been funneled into higher education, as opposed to public elementary and secondary education in Virginia.[15] But the university, as well as a series of other colleges, became the pride of the state. The Southern Literary Messenger announced in 1840 that "only four states surpassed Virginia in the number of colleges, i.e., seven with a total of over one thousand students!"[16]

The spirit of free inquiry promoted by Jefferson took on a symbolic status during the early movement in the state to deal with impending integration conflict. The Southern Conference for Human Welfare (SCHW) held a meeting on November 20, 1948, in Richmond, with nearly 200 southern representatives, including teachers, students, lawyers, and clergymen. Their purpose was to pen a "Declaration of Civil Rights," reminiscent in name and spirit of Jefferson's Declaration of Independence. In fact, a large group of conference participants adjourned to Monticello to announce the adopted doctrine. The president of the Southern Conference Education Fund (SCEF), Aubrey Williams, claimed that he sensed "a growing feeling, even among the 'die-hards,' of the inevitability of the end of racial discrimination."[17] In language that reflected Jefferson's legacy, the declaration proclaimed: "We take these rights to include equality before the law, freedom from any discrimination bolstered for law; freedom of expression; and unrestricted access to all institutions supported by taxes for the public welfare, schools and hospitals not excepted; equal pay for equal work, and equal opportunity to receive training and to gain employment; and the right of unsegregated transportation, housing or assembly."[18] The document itself declared that many white southerners were "unashamedly advocating ideas of racism and white supremacy contrary to American democracy." It further announced that "truth and justice are not bounded nor divided by parallels of latitude. . . . This is one country and one people, governed under one constitution."[19] Little did this progressive group know that the Constitution itself, as well as the writings of Jefferson's fellow founding fathers, would soon be evoked as the prevailing source of anti-integration legal precedence, a strategy that proliferated and transformed much of moderate white Virginia.

The SCEF did not base its actions and declaration solely on the liberal and progressive opinions of its members and advocates. The organization intended to prove that a more substantial number of southern moderates existed than was portrayed by the media. James Dombroski of the organization distributed three sets of surveys in the spring of 1948, in the following fall, and in the fall of 1949. Each case study increased the number surveyed (which were primarily southern sociologists), and the results showed an increase in the number of participants that were open to the integration of graduate and professional schools. Though his sample group included primarily educated subjects with sociology degrees—often considered a progressive field—the results fueled the hopes of the SCEF.

WHAT BROWN MEANT TO THE OLD DOMINION

Despite growing moderate support in the South for integration, or at least a lack of violent resistance, early Supreme Court decisions such as *Sipuel v. Oklahoma*

Board of Regents (1948), which required the University of Oklahoma to admit an African American student to its law school, were circumvented by universities. In this case, the University of Oklahoma responded to the ruling by creating a small African American law school (with three teachers), hiding behind *Plessy v. Ferguson* (1896), which declared separate but equal facilities to be within the scope of the law.[20] The Oklahoma case, however, was not the only case that began to stir the segregation debate. In Virginia, specifically, a startling student protest in the Prince Edward County town of Farmville would put the state on a collision course with the Supreme Court and would make the eventual *Brown* decision all the more personal to many white Virginians.

Farmville represented the juxtaposition of the two distinct sides of Virginia's cultural identity. On the one hand, the middle- and upper-class white citizens of Farmville still followed an almost antebellum practice of either homeschooling (with private tutors) their children or sending them to private finishing schools, until the second decade of the twentieth century, when the county finally established a white public high school. An African American school, named Robert R. Moton High School after a Virginian who had succeeded Booker T. Washington as leader of the Tuskegee Institute, followed nearly twenty years later. Opening its doors in 1938, Moton High School could accommodate close to 200 students, but its enrollment tripled by the early 1950s. "A tacky string of poorly constructed temporary buildings—nothing more than tarpaper shacks," were constructed to house the overflow.[21]

In April 1951, on a Monday morning, Moton student leader Barbara Johns carried out a carefully orchestrated protest whereby the entire student population demonstrated frustration at the obvious inequity by striking. Johns, the niece of civil rights organizer Rev. Vernon Johns, had deliberately kept her plans secret from the school faculty so as to not implicate them in the protest. NAACP legal experts Spottswood Robinson and Oliver Hill were immediately contacted to advise the students and to ensure the efficacy of the demonstration. The African American community, inspired by the courage of the youth, agreed to endorse a lawsuit, particularly after the school board—all white—terminated the Moton High principal, who had not even been on school grounds the day of the walkout. The threat to students such as Barbara Johns grew so great that she left Farmville to reside with her uncle. The official lawsuit, *Davis v. County School Board of Prince Edward County* (named for one of the participating students), was submitted on May 23, 1951. In effect, it argued that separate but equal was inherently unequal.

Nine months after the suit was filed, it reached the state court in Richmond. The defense, which was overseen by none other than the state attorney general,

J. Lindsay Almond Jr., admitted the physical inequities between the all-white Farmville High School and Moton, but he assured the court that Prince Edward County would immediately address the problem. He, however, did not budge on the philosophical and ethical nature of the Jim Crow system of public education. Segregation was defended as "customary, moral, and lawful."[22] In Almond's closing statement, he addressed the judges, claiming to speak for "our people,"[23] implying the otherness or foreignness of the African American plaintiffs. The five-day trial was followed by one week of deliberation by three prosegregationist judges. The unanimous decision did order repairs and updates to be made to Moton High School, although no deadline was mandated; on the larger issue, the court insisted that "segregation in Virginia schools rested on the mores and traditions of the people, and was legal and harmless."[24]

The appeal to the Supreme Court would eventually be grouped with four other cases, *Briggs v. Elliot* (South Carolina), *Belton v. Gebhart* (Delaware), *Bolling v. Sharpe* (District of Colombia), and *Brown v. Board of Education of Topeka, Kansas*, and resulted in what southern segregationists would label "Black Monday." The *Davis* case did receive extensive statewide media coverage, so it should have been no surprise to Virginians that the segregation decision was working its way through the federal court system. But many white southerners expected the same pattern to continue—violations of separate but equal would have to be remedied. But simply spending money on African American school buildings was no longer enough, particularly because even court-mandated repairs were rarely accomplished. Though southern newspapers did cover these early desegregation cases, the part of the narrative that was often ignored was exactly this particular outcome. John Egerton concluded that "if there was one aspect of this story the papers didn't really cover or analyze (neither the southern press nor its upcountry counterparts), it was the extent to which the ruling elite of the region never seriously tried to deliver on either option."[25]

The lack of follow-up in the media created a false sense of security for many white southerners who expected Jim Crow laws to stand. But for the NAACP, the SCEF, and other human rights organizations, such as the progressive Southern Regional Council (SRC) and the Commission on Interracial Cooperation, anticipation of the ruling was palpable. The SRC actually hosted a conference in Williamsburg, Virginia, the week preceding the Supreme Court verdict, which drew together members of like-minded councils and organizations; the intention of the meeting was to devise a course of action to help southern states cope with the outcome of the case.[26] For southern liberals and African American human rights advocates, "*Brown* was the beginning of that next step, the start of a cure. After a generation of preliminaries, the main event was about to begin.

Everything else had been yesterday. *Brown* was Tomorrow." And Prince Edward County, Virginia, was stepping onto center court.[27]

The interracial think tank that Governor Stanley first promised upon hearing the *Brown* decision did not materialize. Instead the governor simply waited, allowing public reaction and the media hype to run its course, while summoning his fellow southern governors to Richmond for a private meeting. Not until more than a full month after the May 17, 1954, *Brown* decision did Stanley's position and rhetoric intensify. On June 23, 1954, he proclaimed that "I shall use every legal means at my command to continue segregated schools in Virginia."[28] Despite his shift in tone, Stanley continued to act according to his initial plan. On August 20, 1954, he appointed a thirty-two-member commission—all white— to study the economic and social impact of the *Brown* decision on the state. The leader of the commission, Garland Gray, had met two months earlier with his fellow delegates from the Fourth District in Petersburg, Virginia, and they had concluded that as a district they were "unalterably opposed" to integration.[29]

Despite such vocal leadership, the Gray Commission was intended to represent the range of opinions on desegregation present in the state, which had great demographic variation from its northern to its southern borders. However, rather than appoint a mix of community leaders—political, religious, and educational—Stanley insisted the commission be legislative. Thus, of the thirty-two members, thirteen served as Virginia state senators and nineteen served as Virginia House delegates. Historian Robbins L. Gates, in his 1962 account of the rise of Massive Resistance, observed that the legislative makeup of the committee ensured the exclusion of African American representatives, since the legislative body of the Commonwealth included no African Americans.[30] These were men whose positions depended on the will of their Virginia constituents; thus, public opinion would inevitably weigh heavily. Moreover, although the distribution of the commission did cover all counties in the state, extra spots were allocated to districts with greater African American populations. While every legislative region received at least two members, the Seventh District was granted three slots, the Eight and Fifth Districts each held four slots, and the Fourth District received nearly one-fifth of the total membership of the commission with six slots.[31]

In his groundbreaking study, *Southern Politics in State and Nation* (1949), V. O. Key Jr. observed that the political representation of counties with large African American populations tended to be more ardent supporters of Jim Crow laws, hence the dramatic cultural images of the civil rights battles waged in Mississippi and Alabama. Such Deep South states were dominated by one-party political machines powerful enough to enforce the racial hierarchy at all costs. But Virginia's African American population was unevenly located across the state, with African Americans dominating fifteen Virginia counties, mostly in the southern part of the state. The more homogeneous white populations in northern Virginia proved somewhat less resistant to integration, since the effect in the public school systems would be less dramatic. Integration would also affect rural and more urban communities differently. According to the *Nelson County Times* (from the northern border of the state), rural counties would also be affected more dramatically by integration, because "in cities where Negro residents live[d] in certain sections an assignment plan would result in only a small percentage of integration."[32] The stacked committee, with the prosegregation leadership of its captain and the fact of more delegates from the rural counties with large African American populations, would surely produce a reactionary plan of action for Virginia. However, the initial Gray Commission plan, at least on paper, was moderate and more reflective of Stanley's original proclamation. The moderate nature of the plan reflected a false sense of security that gradual integration would be the acceptable norm. And this false sense of security made the ensuing onslaught of public denunciation of southern racial practices all the more biting and, ultimately, transformative.

Senator Gray, elected chairman, from southern Virginia, and Harry B. Davis, elected vice chairman, from Princess Anne County (present-day Virginia Beach) in the middle of the state, presided over the initial meeting of the committee. Fearing the influence of growing moderate sentiment, one of Gray's first initiatives was to establish a subcommittee, called his executive council, that was heavily stacked with delegates from African American–dominated counties. The Gray Commission adopted a privacy rule, which insisted that "all meetings of this commission shall be executive and its deliberations confidential."[33] The only exception was granted to public hearings, which would be expressly defined by the commission; such a hearing was held only once, on November 15, 1954, in a mosque in Richmond and was attended by over 2,000 people and lasted nearly fourteen hours. Of the 153 speakers, only 13 were African American, all of whom petitioned the commission for immediate implementation of *Brown*.[34]

For almost a year after that public hearing, the commission remained fairly inactive. Though the issue of public school integration was rarely absent from the news, most southern political leaders chose to wait for the Supreme Court addendum to be issued, in *Brown II*. Coming before the Court in April 1955,

Brown II hinged on the efficacy of integration and the uncertainty of the enforcement power and execution timeline of the original opinion. At the heart of the second hearing was the question of implementation of integration measures. Announced on May 31, 1955, Brown II dictated that integration should occur with "all deliberate speed." In greater detail, the Court further directed that "it should go without saying that the vitality of these constitutional principles cannot be allowed to yield simply because of disagreement with them."[35]

Most scholars credit Brown II with fueling southern resistance to integration. It is true that groups such as the Gray Commission delayed the formation of any integration plans until such a verdict was rendered. But the Supreme Court's carefully chosen phrase, "all deliberate speed," remained a vague deadline at best. Moreover, for many detractors, who vilified the Court for crossing boundaries into the legislative branch of governing, this second decision with its weak enforcement rhetoric seemed perhaps even less effective. Granted, the Court had not reversed its ruling by any means, and it had directly insisted that public opinion did not trump constitutional principles. However, the lack of details still gave Virginia much room to maneuver. For example, Prince Edward County, one of the cases that made up Brown, simply declared that integration for the 1955–56 school year would be impracticable.[36] Thus, the emotional explosion of Massive Resistance—which would sink the Gray Commission plan, yet to be submitted to Governor Stanley—was still to come.

What, perhaps, was more influential to the Gray Commission than the language of the Court's second decision were the early efforts of integration enacted in the parochial schools in Virginia and the enrollment of a handful of African Americans in higher education institutions in the state. These hairline fractures suggested a growing moderate community in Virginia and, along with the integration efforts in other former Confederate states, including Arkansas, Kentucky, and Texas, heightened the threat of change. Indeed, after conducting only that one public hearing, the Gray Commission, rather than offer any technical plans or even loosely defined plans, chose only to issue a statement regarding the unanimity of Virginia public opinion. In a letter addressed to Governor Stanley, dated January 19, 1955, Garland Gray declared that after considering the opinions voiced at the public hearing in Richmond, and after extensive discussion with state education leaders, school board members, and local citizens, the commission was convinced that the one hearing that they held had "brought into sharp focus the nature and intensity of the feeling as to the effect that integration would have on the public school system. Not only did the majority of persons speaking at the hearing feel that integration would lead to the abolition or destruction of the public school system, but some groups indicated, through their spokesmen, that they preferred to see the public school system abandoned if the only alternative was integration."[37] But Virginia public opinion was not as unified as Garland Gray portrayed it to be. Several prominent state newspapers, including the *Danville Bee*, the *Roanoke Times*, and the *Newport News Daily Press*, questioned the logic of issuing such a statement, not to mention the accuracy of its content. Specifically, the *Norfolk Virginia-Pilot* worried that the commission was too concerned with "establishing a point of view in Virginia."[38] The Gray Commission was obviously speaking for white Virginians, a point ironically made by Dr. E. B. Henderson, vice president of the Virginia State Conference of the NAACP. He argued that he knew 2,071 African Americans of northern Virginia who had "willingly signed a statement of opposition to all forms of segregation in public life."[39] What the state needed was a plan of action for implementing the Supreme Court ruling that would not destroy the public school system, rather than an opinion piece or Virginia manifesto on race relations.

The only hint that the commission revealed regarding its technical plan for integration was that it would find a way to avoid full implementation. Gray wrote: "I have been directed to report that the Commission, working with its council, will explore avenues toward formulation of a program, within the framework of law, designed to prevent enforced integration of the races in the public schools of Virginia."[40] The announcement seemed indicative of the emotional and national program of full-blown Massive Resistance that would spring from the Old Dominion in the years to come. But actually, the matter-of-fact tone of the letter read as unemotional. Moreover, Gray and his colleagues, at this point, were still insisting that the framework of the law would govern the plan. And the term "enforced integration" indicated a lack of resistance to unenforced integration; in other words, counties that chose to permit integration would, perhaps, be allowed to do so under the forthcoming Gray Commission plan. The true shift in rhetoric, emotion, and intensity of resistance was yet to come and would be catalyzed by the outpouring of public criticism toward Virginia and the South as a whole that would inevitably accompany the onslaught of the civil rights movement.

The Gray Commission on Public Education met again in August 1955, charged with laying out in detail a proposed solution to the integration debate in the state of Virginia. With the Supreme Court's vague language of *Brown II*, the commission had many options. Deliberations resulted in a three-point plan, submitted to Governor Stanley on November 11, 1955, that would emphasize local control while providing legal means for white students to avoid attending school with African Americans. First, the commission recommended that the state law of compulsory attendance be amended to no longer force white students to enroll in integrated schools. In other words, students (in the era before the growth of the home school movement) would not be compelled to attend school at all if their only option was attending an integrated school, a recommendation that was relevant primarily in rural communities. Second, the report recommended that a pupil assignment organization be established so that each county could determine how many African American students would be integrated into the white public schools. This local control option would, indeed, allow the geographic and population diversity between counties to be considered, as opposed to a statewide mandate. Finally—and what would become the most controversial recommendation—Gray reported to the governor that a system of tuition grants, made available by public funds, could be used at private schools, which remained outside of the reach of *Brown*.

The actual text of the Gray Commission report reveals much more than a three-pronged answer to integration; it sheds essential light on the cultural context in which the decision was made. The report begins with an indictment of the Supreme Court decision-making process regarding *Brown*. The influence of Swedish sociologist Gunnar Myrdal, whose landmark study, *An American Dilemma*, exposed the psychological effects of segregation, is dismissed as irrelevant. Specifically, Myrdal's nationality is accentuated, as is his lack of experience in America—he is depicted as foreign and other. His treatise, according to the commission, merely consisted of "a number of overlapping contributions made by a number of writers, many of whom were given their golden opportunity to voice their own preconceptions and prejudices."[41] Paradoxically, though the Gray Commission discredited the influences of psychology as an element of judicial review, it relied on such fundamental psychological functions as identity formation and collective memory in arguing for the maintenance of segregation and local control.

The report resurrected the memory of the destructive aftermath of the Civil War. "The public schools," proclaimed Gray, "have been built up slowly and painfully from the ashes of 1865." The paternalistic attitude that dominated defensive southern thought regarding the institution of slavery resurfaced as justification for the commission's decisions. "Our modern public school system," declared the report, "has been developed on a racially segregated basis and advancement of the Negro race has been a direct result of such a system." Gray added that "without segregation the white children would still be largely taught in private academies as they were in the early days in Virginia." Thus, he reasoned, "Public schools would have made no progress, and Negro children would have received little or no public education." This particular perspective promoting the generosity of white culture to an inferior African American populace served as a critical aspect of the social construction of whiteness in the Old Dominion.

Additionally, Gray invoked yet another historical element of white identity in Virginia by invoking the nation's founding fathers and other important and law-abiding citizens of the Commonwealth. In promoting the local county control of Virginia public education—which the commission insisted would require extensive labor for school boards—Gray remarked that such oversight would "call for unselfish service on the part of the best people of each community." "But this is not new in Virginia," Gray observed:

> In the years that preceded our Revolution, times of stress and danger, our best men contributed unselfishly and without compensation their thoughts and energies to local government, even while playing their parts on a larger stage. As county magistrates they legislated, adjudicated, and administered the laws of their people. George Mason, who wrote our Bill of Rights, was a magistrate of Fairfax County; Edmund Pendleton, who presided over the Virginia Revolutionary Convention and drafted the resolution calling upon Congress to declare Independence, was a magistrate of Caroline County; Richard Henry Lee, who moved the resolution to Congress, was a magistrate of Westmoreland; Jefferson, who wrote the Declaration of Independence, was a magistrate of Albemarle; and Washington, on whose broad shoulders the Revolution rested, was a magistrate of both King George and Fairfax. The Commonwealth is certain that the spirit that actuated our fathers during times of trial still lives in this Commonwealth, and that our best citizens will not fail to meet the challenges of their day.[42]

The reasoning and language laid out in the commission's report clearly invokes long-standing and powerful justifications for white supremacy and the Jim Crow system; it also seems to attempt to fortify the Old Dominion against its public critics. It is self-congratulatory and thus reveals a desire for self-preservation. Or, at least, preservation of a system of racial hierarchy threatened at every turn.

Prosegregationists knew that two of the three tenets of the Gray Commission plan could have destroyed the Virginia public school system. Tuition grants could have resulted in public schools that were "technically" integrated but without white students, who would have fled to private academies. Or students who did not want to attend integrated classes could simply drop out, under the revision to the compulsory attendance law. But moderates also recognized that the local control option would allow integration in counties where resistance was less intense (that is, in counties where African American populations were minimal). The state would thus be implementing some aspect of the Supreme Court decision, which would, in turn, reduce the damage to Virginia's national image. Within weeks of the plan's submission to the governor, interest groups on both sides began to push and pull the plan in their respective political directions. In order for the tuition grants to be viable, a state constitutional amendment would have to be passed to permit the use of public funds for private schools. Proposition 141 would have to be approved by a state constitutional convention and then voted on in a statewide referendum. Despite the efforts of the commission to come to a consensus and produce a plan of action over the course of eighteen months, the compromise seemed to disintegrate overnight, not only among government leaders but within the private community as well.

THE DEFENDERS OF STATE SOVEREIGNTY AND LIBERTY

At the same time that Governor Stanley appointed the Gray Commission, a group of private citizens from southside Virginia established the Defenders of State Sovereignty and Liberty.[43] Their primary intention was to represent the segregationist viewpoint and to express it nonviolently during the Gray Commission's decision-making period, although their purposes would expand greatly when negotiations in Virginia dissolved into all-out resistance. Robert B. Crawford of Farmville was selected to run the organization; his hometown had been the source of one of the five cases consolidated into Brown. He was admired for his sincere faith in the Jim Crow system and his paternalistic attitude toward race relations. He expressed clearly what many of his fellow committee members felt—that the racial hierarchy in the South was being exploited by northern Communist sympathizers. "He resented keenly that the political crises left an opportunity for that relationship to be misunderstood," explained Bob Smith, journalist for the Virginian-Pilot.[44] Crawford himself revealed this frustration: "The thing I hate most about it is that it has given the white man a sense of race guilt."[45]

Crawford was joined in leadership by J. Barrye Wall, the editor and publisher of the Farmville Herald. Wall's expertise allowed the Defenders to publish their own newspaper, the Defender News and Views, which helped strengthen their organizational structure throughout the state. They applied for a charter from the State Corporation Commission in which they stated their mission: "[To] seek by all honorable and lawful means the retention by each state of its full right and power to regulate within its borders, in the manner it believes to be most conducive to the happiness and good of its citizens, its own democratic arrangements."[46] They deliberately avoided any reference to segregation, couching their language in constitutional rhetoric that would be acceptable to "proper" Virginians. Their method would directly influence journalist James J. Kilpatrick, who attended many of their functions, as did attorney general and future governor J. Lindsay Almond Jr. Membership conditions were quite matter-of-fact, only requiring interested parties to sign a pledge: "I am a white, law abiding citizen of the United States of America, and a resident of the City / County of _____, Virginia. I am not a member of any organization detrimental to the peace and welfare of the U.S.A., nor do I ever intend belonging to any such organization. I believe the segregation of the races is a right of the state government, in the sovereignty of the several states and in the freedom of the individual from government controls."[47] The language was deliberately clinical and intended to promote the rational and nonviolent public persona the Defenders wanted desperately to portray.

Their campaign was thus centered on controlling public opinion. Historian Neil McMillen points out a significant difference between the Virginia Defenders and more infamous groups such as the Ku Klux Klan and the White Citizens' Councils: "What the Defenders could not stand for was as important as what they could stand for." Therefore, "Defender speakers bore down on the theme that violence would mean ruin for the movement."[48] A reporter for the *New Republic*, covering the mounting resistance in Virginia, directly quoted Crawford, who insisted that "if this community should suffer just one incident of Klanism, our white case is lost." "No matter who starts it," he concluded, "the whites will be blamed. We must not have it."[49] In addition to condemning physical acts of violence, the Defenders refrained from publicly using inflammatory or violent rhetoric. According to Smith, "Violence was not the only enemy the Defenders saw on the right. The White Citizens Councils and other racist organizations were spewing forth the seedy literature of race hatred, playing on the uncounted fears of ignorant white Southerners." "These men realized that the slightest taint could doom the organization in the eyes of the proper Virginians they must count on for support."[50] This notion of propriety and the determination of the Defenders to appeal to it exposed their anxiety regarding the power of public opinion.

In addition to maintaining a perception of integrity and propriety, the Defenders were committed to protecting their reputations outside of the Commonwealth of Virginia. According to McMillen, "The Defenders typically pitched their propaganda campaign on a relatively sophisticated plane, avoiding to a considerable degree the irresponsible Negrophobia that characterized the expressions of many resistance organizations."[51] As evidence, McMillen cited the rhetoric espoused in the *Defenders News and Views*, which focused on "the evils of centralized government—'one of the greatest internal dangers facing this nation'—and the virtues of that 'cornerstone of our Republic,' the tenth amendment."[52] The Tenth Amendment, or as it was often called, the States' Rights Amendment, was invoked in a manner similar to the anti-evolution fundamentalists, who claimed that the federal government had no authority to regulate public education since it was not an enumerated power listed in the Constitution.

As much as the Defenders attempted to distance their organization from radical extremists such as the Klan, they shared observable similarities. The Defenders, though they refrained from secret rituals and handshakes, did take their name from a Confederate monument in Farmville. Commissioned by the Daughters of the Confederacy in 1900, the statue of a soldier at attention bears the inscriptions "Confederate Heroes 1861–1865" and "Defenders of State Sovereignty."[53] Defender founder Wall insisted that the name was a coincidence, or at best a slip of the subconscious. Reviving the Confederate Lost Cause, whether intentional or not, inevitably revived the heritage of inferiority that plagued numerous variations of southern resisters. Sociologist James W. Vander Zanden, in his work on the Klan, argued that membership often functions as a psychological compensation: "One's own weakness, inferiority, and ambivalence are not infrequently concealed from others and even from one's self, and the substitute often is compensatory self-aggrandizement."[54] Moreover, he asserts that membership is further defined by creating a collective "enemy." Unlike targeted social movements, Vander Zanden argues, for the Klan, "the source of discontent is not seen as the social system, social conditions, or the government." He adds that "the difficulty is personified as an 'enemy'—as 'evil persons,' e.g., Eleanor Roosevelt, Richard Nixon, the justices of the Supreme Court, and Harry S. Truman; and 'evil groups,' e.g., Jews, Communists, Catholics, foreigners, the 'big-city' press, and 'scalawags.'"[55] Just as the Klan established an "axis of evil," so too did the Defenders—and in a manner similar to the southern Agrarians—constantly accuse Communist sympathizers and industrialists of instigating civil rights reforms.

Although Crawford and Wall attempted to keep the Defenders focused on the legal issues at hand in the public school crisis, other members could not help but connect the integration and the Supreme Court mandate with the long history of southern defeat and occupation. The Civil War did indeed enter the rhetoric of these Virginia conservatives. In a letter to FitzGerald Bemiss, a member of the Virginia House of Delegates and the Gray Commission, Defender Alfred P. Goddin requested Bemiss's support for resistance, "which is under fire from certain sections of our State which have been overrun in the

Second Yankee Invasion."[56] Goddin's comment signaled a second reality for the Defenders—that the state of Virginia initially was actually divided on the issue of integration. The Defenders were well aware that moderates and even some liberals in the northern part of the state (where populations were more homogeneously white) were advocating for the local control option of the Gray Commission plan. The Defenders, in response to the public criticism they experienced over the course of 1955, pushed the organization of Virginia senator Harry F. Byrd to reject this local control option: "The Defenders were fighting to prevent integration not only in rural communities but in the cities as well."[57] The group had actually submitted its own "Plan for Virginia" to the Gray Commission, which seriously considered and adopted two of the three tenets of the Defenders' plan—the use of public money for private academies and the termination of the compulsory education law. Finally, the Defenders insisted that the legislature ban all funding for any public school that chose to integrate.[58] This dramatic demand contradicted the final position taken by the Gray Commission, which had allowed for local choice. But, by the final weeks of 1955, the Defenders' last demand seemed possible. "By this time," historian Bob Smith observed, "it was becoming obvious that the 'freedom of choice' features of the plan were doomed."[59]

■ Between November 11, 1955, and January 9, 1956 (the date of the ballot referendum), something in Virginia finally shifted. The staunch anti-integrationists on the Gray Commission, including Gray himself, were no longer willing to back their own proposition, or at least the local control option. Integration allowed anywhere was a threat to segregation everywhere. This emotional and reactionary development was heavily and directly influenced by the media coverage of the civil rights movement. The murder of Emmett Till, for example, stamped the white South with a badge of violent resistance that seemed to encompass all of the racial atrocities that preceded that particularly tragedy. And the December 1955 Montgomery Bus Boycott, though not the first act of protest, was in itself a public denunciation of the white South. And this time the media and white audiences were paying attention. Criticism of southern racial practices did not focus on individual white southerners but rather accused the region as a whole of complacency and racism, as compared to a national image of progress and success. The negative construction of 1950s southern whiteness tapped into a well-established heritage of inferiority. And southern whiteness had an ever expanding list of forces against which it was defined, so it was no surprise that the root determinant—racial oppression—would usher in such resistance nearly one century after the Civil War.

While the governor considered the Gray Commission report, and while African American citizens and white sympathizers organized in Alabama, James J. Kilpatrick of the *Richmond News Leader* began a series of editorials detailing the Doctrine of Interposition. This would become the basis for the Massive Resistance movement, which would make the Gray Commission plan, in retrospect, seem liberal. Kilpatrick, although not a native southerner himself, resuscitated legal theories that would tap into the growing sense of anxiety, defensiveness, and cultural inferiority rumbling in the white communities throughout Virginia and the South. Encouraged by the seemingly invincible Senator Harry F. Byrd and evermore sensitive to the national public ridicule of southern white bigotry, Gray and his colleagues dug in their heels, dragging the Old Dominion along with them.

CHAPTER 8

BYRD WATCHING

THE SOUTH ON THE

NATIONAL STAGE

Of all the American States, Virginia can lay claim to the most thorough control by an oligarchy. Political power has been closely held by a small group of leaders who, themselves and their predecessors, have subverted democratic institutions and deprived most Virginians of their voice in government.
—V. O. Key Jr., *Southern Politics in State and Nation*

Virginia, famed for her moderation and conservatism, lent her prestige of leadership in historic cries of the South to the side of reaction.
—Marshall Williams Fishwick, *Virginia: A New Look at an Old Dominion*

The Northern viewpoint is drummed into our ears 24 hours a day. How many Northerners have ever—even ONCE—heard the Southern argument properly presented? How many of them subscribe to a Southern newspaper? How many of them have ever read even ONE magazine article giving the real Southern viewpoint—not the Southern viewpoint expressed by Ralph McGill or Lillian Smith or J. Waties Waring [his uncle] or Southern white female members of the NAACP? It is hardly a fair situation is it? And yet the average Northerner prides himself on being fair, on his willingness to listen to both sides of a question, on his lack of prejudice.
—Thomas R. Waring, Jr., "The South Has Lost Its Voice"

The celebration by liberals that followed the announcement of the *Brown v. Board of Education of Topeka* decision filled newspapers at home and abroad, and most assuredly reached powerful conservatives like Virginia senator Harry F. Byrd. One of the most disturbing aspects of the Supreme Court ruling for men like Byrd was that it seemed to reflect a change in national mood toward Jim Crow. The influence of Gunnar Myrdal's work, as well as the various investigations into southern racial practices made by the United Nations, signaled the rising international pressure on the United States to practice fully the doctrines of liberty and democracy that it preached. The decision may have lacked teeth and it required clarification in a second verdict, *Brown II*, but it opened the door to challenges of the separate but equal doctrine. Moreover, the year 1955 bore witness to two landmark civil rights events—one tragic, one triumphant. The murder of Emmett Till exposed the most violent, barbaric demons of white supremacy, while the symbolic and effective Montgomery Bus Boycott revealed the potential political and economic power of African Americans in the South. And both the boycott—which was, of course, a physical expression of public criticism—and the media denunciation of the South in the wake of the Emmett Till murder represented, among other events, a new onslaught of criticism facing the white South.

Writing nearly four years prior to the *Brown* decision, journalist Hodding Carter Jr. described this pattern of southern behavior, not only of southern extremists but also of moderate southerners, when reacting to public criticism. Carter himself occupies a unique position as both southern liberal and removed observer: "I know that much of this Southern resentment against distant criticism is dishonest. It is probably strongest among those groups which most deserve it, and its base is more emotional than rational. We in the South have not rights to say that what we do is no affair of the rest of the nation. An unpunished lynching mob is an affront to humanity everywhere. So is the persistent and calculated denial of constitutional rights to any segment of the population."[1] The twin descriptions of dishonesty and calculation are telling; the drive for superiority is an effort to cope with a sense of inferiority. Despite Carter's personal advocacy of civil rights progress, he clearly understood and effectively articulated the burden of public criticism and the heritage of inferiority that seemed to bombard southern communities without relief: "The Southern contradiction of democracy is the only one in the nation against which an aggressive demand for full, abrupt, and forcible revision is continuously directed. Ours is the only region in which an ethnologically distinct, repressed, and culturally retarded people are constantly told, through every available medium of communication, that the dominant majority is unqualifiedly evil in its behavior toward them."

And this constant assault, observed Carter, created "a historic and a present-day basis for suspicion and fear"[2] for white southerners. In the end, what got drowned out was what he considered to be the moderate voice. But this voice was moderate only in the fact that it did see that some progress had been made in some aspects of southern race relations.

However, this fragile moderate community was capable of being quickly radicalized. Carter noted that this fragility could and would be most easily disturbed and, even dramatically transformed, by the deafening voices that denounced the South.

This muted voice has something to say: *We have not gone far enough or fast enough, but we have already gone far. Your prodding has been in a measure responsible but not in principal measure or so we believe. We are not dealing in abstractions here. We know the meaning and the force of spectral fears and we are vying against them with unadmitted success. We will join you in the attainable. But if John Brown comes again there will be furious men to face him. If the imprecations of Garrison and Sumner and Stevens dominate elsewhere, there are as uncompromising Southern voices to contest them. If the spoilsmen of Reconstruction live in the political opportunists of the bloc vote, they can find their shameful match on the Southern hustings. It is not that we must be let alone, but that we must not be set apart as an incomprehensible, stubborn contradiction.*[3]

What Carter observed astutely or understood innately was that the line between moderates and extremists was paper thin and that the sense of inferiority that had shaped southern whiteness was not just in the past but in the present too.

Journalist Henry Savage, writing in *Seeds of Time: The Background of Southern Thinking*, noted the power of public criticism to elicit a reactionary backlash from southern whites, and to create, in effect, an endless cycle of resistance and violence. The "lack of understanding and intolerance of the South, on the part of the outside press," reasoned Savage, "tends to create a paralyzing defensive attitude in southerners and an emotional atmosphere in the nation which deters a calm approach to the South's problems."[4] Even a staunch segregationist such as Kilpatrick grew weary of what he saw as the public exploitation of the South. In a letter to Virginia governor J. Lindsay Almond Jr., Kilpatrick noted the extensive media attention to the NAACP. "I suppose that is the price we must pay for a free press," grumbled Kilpatrick.[5]

Charleston News and Courier editor Thomas R. Waring Jr. wrote a thorough analysis for *Harper's* entitled "The Southern Case against Desegregation," in which he, too, pointed out the influence of outside media scrutiny. "At the outset it is only fair to warn the Northern reader," cautioned Waring, "that he may be infuriated long before he reaches the end. This, I suspect, is just as inevitable as the outraged feelings of the Southerner when he reads the Northern press with its own interpretation of the American dilemma."[6] Perhaps these journalists were more sensitive to or aware of the public criticism because they were immersed in the industry itself, but nevertheless the denunciation of southern whites, though wholly deserved in many cases, as noted by Carter, clearly registered with these opinion makers. Some southern journalists, such as Waring, drew attention to what he called "the paper curtain," the silencing of southern white dissent—an accusation still made against the liberal media today. Waring would also attempt to point out various aspects of northern hypocrisy in order to dispel the myths of the distinctions between regional and national identities for his individual readers. Thus, public criticism, both after *Brown* and during the budding civil rights movement, made this one issue seem part of a larger regional alienation that made moderation unlikely and unpopular, if not downright impossible.

SPOTLIGHT ON JIM CROW

The media celebration in northern and western presses began only hours after the Supreme Court's verdict in Brown reached the airwaves. The New York Times produced a seven-page spread detailing the long history of the entire case and concluding that "the highest court in the land, the guardian of our national conscience, has reaffirmed its faith—and the undying American faith in the equality of all men and all children before the law." The San Francisco Chronicle announced succinctly that "the majesty of the democratic idea that men are created equal and are entitled to the equal protection of the law shined through yesterday's unanimous decision." The unanimity of the decision, remarked the Chicago Tribune, "should help a good deal to discourage resistance to the findings or attempts to evade its plain meaning." And the Washington Post jubilantly declared that the decision "affords all Americans an occasion for pride and gratification."[7]

Finally, the Detroit Free Press proclaimed that "those citizens of the United States who cherish the belief that the American concept of democracy is a vital, living, organic philosophy, slowly but inexorably advancing towards the ideals of the founders of the Union, will be heartened by the unanimous opinion of the Supreme Court in the historical school segregation case."[8] The media's common theme was that this decision had fulfilled an American promise, a new manifest destiny. By labeling those in favor of the decision as more authentically American, and by harping on the unanimity of the verdict, the media deemed white southern segregationists as "other" or inferior. Moreover, for Virginians, the Detroit Free Press's reference to the ideals of the founding fathers co-opted the likes of Thomas Jefferson, James Madison, and James Monroe, Virginia's most famous and beloved citizens.

African Americans responded with jubilation. Robert Jackson, an African American professor at Virginia Union University, claimed that "this is the most exciting moment. . . . A lot of us haven't been breathing for the past nine months." Jackson added, "But today the students reacted as if a heavy burden has been lifted from their shoulders. They see a new world opening up for them and those that follow them."[9] The African American Atlanta Daily World insisted that May 17, 1954, was "one of the most important days in the history of this country and the fight for freedom for all the citizens of the nation."[10] And perhaps most threatening to southern segregationists were the ramifications that African American leaders saw for this monumental case. Charles Johnson, the president of Fisk University, saw the decision as having far-reaching implications: "The principal enumeration was not merely that of the constitutionality of racially separate schools, but of the constitutionality of racial segregation. . . . If segregation is unconstitutional in educational institutions, it is no less so unconstitutional in other aspects of our national life."[11]

For many white southerners, even more threatening than statements such as these were the actual actions undertaken by the NAACP in the months following the announcement of *Brown II*. During the summer of 1955, the NAACP filed over eighty petitions in seven southern states to permit the attendance of African American students at formerly segregated public schools, most of which went unanswered.[12] But no longer was *Brown* simply legal rhetoric; it was now a tangible weapon that was fired without relief at every level of government, and implicit in these protests against segregation was a denunciation of southern white values. The *Pittsburgh Courier*, one of the top-selling African American newspapers, also commented on the far-reaching implications of *Brown*, not merely for the Jim Crow system but for the reputation of the United States abroad. "This clarion announcement," it noted, "will also stun and silence America's traducers behind the Iron Curtain. It will effectively impress upon millions of colored people in Asia and Africa the fact that idealism and social morality can and do prevail in the United States, regardless of race, creed, or color."[13] Indeed, the *Brown* verdict was heard around the globe within hours of its announcement, undoubtedly affecting America's position in world affairs, and particularly in the Cold War. Voice of America broadcast Chief Justice Earl Warren's opinion in thirty-five languages, and a message was sent to American diplomats in nearly sixty-five countries. *Die neue Zeitung*, of Zurich, Switzerland, complimented the court process, insisting that the overturning of the separate but equal clause in *Plessy v. Ferguson* was "an impressive example of the vitality of American democracy." But most international reports contained some subtle dig or reminder of how bleak the racial system in America had been. The *Indian Express* commented that the decision represented a "healthy change in enlightened American opinion," while the *Manchester Guardian* praised the fact that America would now "put behind it what has long been its worse reproach." The *London Times* echoed this sense of relief, calling segregation a "Black Stain" that had now been removed.[14]

This sense that America had redeemed itself was the natural and logical observation made by the international media, most of which had been covering the hypocrisy of American racial practices, as opposed to the anticommunist, procapitalist, egalitarian rhetoric that defined U.S. foreign policy. Historian Mary Dudziak recounts numerous instances of foreign media denunciations of Jim Crow. For example, in 1947, when Mohandas Gandhi's personal physician was banned from eating in an American restaurant while visiting, the story immediately made headlines in Bombay. The same year, the secretary of agriculture of Haiti, François Georges, had his hotel reservation canceled in Biloxi, Mississippi, when management insisted that he was colored.[15] And when word spread to London that two fourteen-year-old African American boys had been sentenced to death in Mississippi for the murder of their white boss, over 300 British citizens wrote letters of protest to the American embassy.[16] Such stories were so extensive that in 1950 James Ely examined over 500 such reports from European newspapers in an article titled "Black Tragedy in the United States Is No Myth," for the NAACP-sponsored magazine the Crisis.[17]

International attention on race relations in the United States had intensified dramatically in the years prior to the Brown decision, following the founding of the United Nations Human Rights Commission in 1946. The commission was expected to issue recommendations on "a) an international bill of rights; b) international declarations or conventions on civil liberties; c) the protection of minorities; d) the prevention of discrimination on the grounds of race, sex, language or religion."[18] Dudziak notes that American political leaders, such as Dean Rusk, were concerned that America would not fare well under such scrutiny, particularly if the United Nations focused its collective attention on the South. His trepidation was heightened by the fact that United Nations delegates from the Soviet Union proposed the establishment of a Subcommission on the Prevention of Discrimination and Protection of Minorities. Rusk conceded, as noted by Dudziak, that the "first session of the Subcommission is a very important one to the United States, principally because it deals with a very difficult problem affecting the internal affairs of the United States. United States problems concerning relationships with minority groups have been fully treated in the press of other countries. This Subcommission was established on the initiative of the U.S.S.R., and there is every indication that that country and others will raise questions concerning our domestic problems in this regard."[19] American leaders may have anticipated scrutiny from their Cold War foe, but the highly organized NAACP also took stock of the United Nations' new commitment.

The NAACP filed an "Appeal to the World," on October 23, 1947, authored primarily by W. E. B. Du Bois. The appeal exposed more clearly than any previous document the hypocrisy of American rhetoric of equality, freedom, and liberty. "It is not Russia that threatens the United States so much as Mississippi," proclaimed the NAACP. And "the disenfranchisement of the American Negro makes the functioning of all democracy in the nation difficult; and as democracy fails to function in the leading democracy in the world, it fails the world."[20] The appeal created an international sensation, and the NAACP was bombarded with requests for copies of the document from Russian, British, and South African citizens. Despite the global grassroots support of the appeal, member countries of the United Nations were hesitant to have the organization interfere in a sovereign country's domestic relations and did not respond to the petition. But the sting of accusation was still felt. For example, U.S. attorney general Tom Clark admitted that he felt humiliated.[21]

Journalists from outside the South wanted to disassociate the rest of the country from the Jim Crow racial practices that defined the South. Reporting in the *Nation* in 1955, Dan Wakefield focused on the dramatic rituals and philosophies of the most extreme prosegregationist groups, including the Ku Klux Klan and the White Citizens' Councils—and even the Virginia State Defenders, who tried to differentiate themselves from these other violent groups. He mocked the claim by members that they were "respectable" citizens, and he lumped all such organizations together as promoters of "Respectable Racism." Wakefield specifically focused on the Mississippi chapter of the Citizens' Council of America (the name was changed in 1956),[22] stating that "the movement, born in Mississippi and copied in Louisiana, Alabama, Texas, Arkansas, Florida, Georgia, and South Carolina (with similar but differently named organizations in Missouri, Tennessee, North Carolina and Virginia)."[23]

Moreover, Wakefield did not shy away from quoting Mississippi's most inflammatory orators, citing U.S. senator James O. Eastland's reaction to *Brown*: "We are about to embark on a great crusade. A crusade to restore Americanism, and return the control of our government to the people. . . . Generations of Southerners yet unborn will cherish our memory because they will realize that the fight we now wage will have preserved from them their untainted racial heritage, their culture, and the institutions of the Anglo-Saxon race. We of the South have seen the tides rise before. We know what it is to fight. We will carry the fight to victory."[24] Eastland's rhetoric was far removed from Virginia governor Stanley's more moderate initial acceptance. However, articles such as Wakefield's did not allow for such individual differences; rather they fostered the perception of a monolithic, white, resistant South at odds with a national norm. And Eastland himself seemed to speak not only for the current South but for the future generations of the entire region. Thus, the criticism of Mississippi became the criticism of Virginia, with all claims of "propriety" overshadowed and mocked, and the criticism became a self-fulfilling prophecy. And as

Virginia political leaders felt increasingly criticized, their political behavior gave way to irrationality.

MEDIA AND THE LYNCHING OF EMMETT TILL

Perhaps no event captured more public attention that fall of 1955 than the murder of a fourteen-year-old African American boy named Emmett Till. The tragedy riveted public attention because it was presented as a regional killing—a northern teenager lynched for violating some invisible southern and foreign racial boundary. The summer after public school segregation was declared unconstitutional by the Supreme Court, Emmett Till headed south from Chicago to visit relatives. Unfamiliar with the strict racial divide, not simply with regard to physical space but also with regard to the code of manners and interracial interactions, Till allegedly whistled at a white female cashier at a store in Tallahatchie County, Mississippi. Later that evening, Till was kidnapped from the home of his uncle, Moses Wright (also called Mose), by the cashier's husband and brother-in-law. His body was discovered three days later in the local river with a heavy cotton gin pulley tied to his legs and a bullet hole in his head. Media attention increased after Till's body was flown back to his home in Chicago, where his mother allowed his corpse to be viewed in an open casket by thousands of spectators over the course of four days. The graphic images and the insistence of Mamie Till Bradley, Till's mother, on making the tragedy an example of the southern bloodlust of white supremacy, caused a press frenzy.

According to historian James T. Patterson, the murder of young Emmett Till exposed the heightened racial tension that resulted from the Supreme Court ruling and was one catalyst for the major civil rights efforts to come. "White violence against blacks in the South had declined since its peak years between 1890 and 1920," wrote Patterson, but "now, after 1954, it surged again, perhaps reflecting rising white anxiety about blacks getting 'uppity' in the aftermath of *Brown*."[25] White supremacist judge Tom Brady had actually predicted the events of that Mississippi September in his racist polemic, *Black Monday*. Brady directed the attention of his fellow white citizens to the fact that African Americans in the North were becoming increasingly liberal and dangerous. He predicted that, "urged on by the radical leaders in the Communist labor organization, deceived by the agents of the NAACP and filled with arrogance by delusional and fanatical neo Socialist Christians, [young Negroes] will far exceed in their daily conduct the bounds of propriety and decency observed by the white men of the South. . . . The supercilious, glib young negro, who has sojourned in Chicago or New York, and who considers the counsels of the elders archaic will perform an obscene act, or make an obscene remark, or a vile overture or assault upon some white girl."[26] Till's alleged whistle was by no means an assault, although it resulted in his murder.

Roy Bryant and J. W. Milam were arrested shortly after the murder, and the speed of police action encouraged some observers. Marty Richardson of the *Cleveland Call and Post* reported that in "what is perhaps the shortest time on record in this state in a case where the victim was a Negro, two white men were indicted Tuesday for the lynch-slaying of 14-year-old Emmett Louis Till last Sunday."[27] Richardson also commented on the public shock and condemnation of the crime, reporting that "thousands of letters, wires and telephone messages to President Eisenhower, Attorney General Herbert Brownell and Congressman from all states, came over the fact that the murder of the boy was the third one since Mississippi first began showing a savage resentment over the Supreme Court ruling on segregated schools and Negroes began a stepped up-voting program."[28] Now readers outside of the South began to see the murder of Till as part of a violent pattern resulting from a unanimous Supreme Court decision. The *Yazoo City Herald* made the connection explicit for local readers, condemning the "nine ninnies who comprise the present United States Supreme Court," because "the young Negro's blood is on their hands also."[29]

As the trial got under way, between fifty and seventy reporters arrived in Sumner, Mississippi, to cover the proceedings for a watchful nation. As Stephen J. Whitfield notes in his account of the murder and its aftermath, a New Orleans radio reporter indicated that covering the trial was "the biggest thing we've ever done."[30] The media scrutiny, which appeared in such outlets as the *New York Times* and *Newsweek*, to name a few, "outraged" white southerners, who, prior to the public criticism, had been hostile to the suspected killers. Bumper stickers that read "Mississippi—The Most Lied About State in the Union" appeared, and local journalist Tom Ethridge reported that the "Northern denunciations of Mississippi constituted a 'Communist plot' designed to undermine the white South."[31] The old feelings were renewed again, and the animosity and anxiety radiated outward.

For advocates of segregation throughout the South, the most threatening aspect of the Till case was the eyewitness testimony offered by Mose Wright. In the past, one of the most difficult aspects of arresting and convicting white lynchers in the South had been the refusal of African American witnesses, who feared for their own lives and the lives of their families, to come forward. In the media, Mose Wright was heralded as unwaveringly brave, a strength surely encouraged by the outpouring of media criticism of white supremacist culture. In an article entitled "He Went All the Way," Pulitzer Prize–winning journalist

Murray Kempton, who had once worked as a copyboy for H. L. Mencken, described the courage of Wright. Kempton, who wrote for the *New York Post* and *Newsday* and went on to edit the *New Republic*, noted the dramatic appearance of Wright on the stand: "Mose Wright, making a formation no white man in his county really believed he would dare to make, stood on his tiptoes to the full limit of his sixty-four years and his five feet three inches yesterday, pointed his black, workworn finger straight at the huge and stormy head of J. W. Milam and swore that this was the man who dragged fourteen year-old Emmett Louis Till out of his cottonfield cabin the night the boy was murdered. . . . Mose Wright took all their blast straight in his face, and then for good measure, turned and pointed that still unshaking finger at Roy Bryant."[32] Kempton's praise of Wright, who headed north immediately following the legal proceedings, dominated the article, as it did most media coverage, with liberals finding hope in the attempt made by Mississippi prosecutors to actually take these white men to trial. Kempton recognized the historic nature of Wright's testimony and praised its potential implications:

> If it had not been for him, we would not have had this trial. . . . The county in which he toiled and which he is now resigned to leaving will never be the same for what he has done. Today the state will put on the stand three other field Negroes to tell how they saw Milam and Bryant near the murder scene. They came in scared; one disappeared while the sheriff's deputies were looking for him. They, like Mose Wright, are reluctant heroes; unlike him, they have to be dragged to the test. They will be belted and flayed as he was yesterday, but they will walk out with the memory of having been human beings for just a little while. Whatever the result, there is a kind of majesty in the spectacle of the State of Mississippi honestly trying to convict two white men on the word of four Negroes. And we owe that sight to Mose Wright, who was condemned to bow all his life, and had enough left to raise his head and look at the enemy in those terrible eyes when he was sixty-four.[33]

For white southerners committed to segregation, the bravery that Wright and his fellow witnesses exhibited that day revealed a crack in the armor of Jim Crow. What many southern whites, particularly those living in counties with a majority population of African Americans, had always feared was that the mental barriers of racial oppression would be overcome. Such fear resulted in a psychological phenomenon for southern whites, an increased sense of inferiority and anxiety that transformed moderates into supporters of Massive Resistance.

Wakefield also covered the verdict of the Emmett Till case, informing readers of the *Nation* that in only one hour and seven minutes the all-white jury had acquitted Milam and Bryant, and soon thereafter the town of Sumner, Mississippi, seemed to return to normal life. "The crowds are gone," reported Wakefield, "and this Delta town is back to its silent, solid life that is based on cotton and the proposition that a whole race of men was created to pick it." Just as the newly evangelized citizens of Dayton, Tennessee, grew weary and distrustful of the media attention that accompanied the Scopes Evolution Trial, the citizens of Tallahatchie County were relieved to have their streets clear, where "Chicago is once more a mythical name, and everyone here 'knows his place.'" Wakefield further claimed that "when the people first heard that there was national, even worldwide, publicity coming from Sumner and the murder trial, they wondered why the incident had caused such a stir." He observed that for most white Mississippians, "the feeling that it was all a plot against the South was the most accepted explanation."[34] But the site of "foreign" African Americans who descended on the small town on behalf of the NAACP, many of whom were business professionals, lawyers, or doctors, "has left a deep and uncomfortable mark on the whites of the Delta," concluded Wakefield.[35]

Adding fuel to the fire for liberals and moderates, *Look* magazine sent journalist William Bradford Huie to Mississippi to interview Bryant and Milam only months after their not-guilty verdict. The two men, under the protection of the double jeopardy clause of the Fifth Amendment, confessed to the murder and recounted the details, all of which were published in January 1956 in the article "The Shocking Story of Approved Killing in Mississippi."[36] The publicity could not have been worse for southern whites, who were no longer merely perceived by outsiders as using legal tactics to maintain the southern racial hierarchy but had stooped to violent acts for which they escaped legal responsibility. Journalist I. F. Stone, in his essay "The Murder of Emmett Till," summed up the mood of frustrated liberal observers throughout the country:

There is a sickness in the South. . . . Mississippi went through the motions [of seeking justice], and the motions were enough to muffle the weak conscience of the northern white press. . . . Those whites in the South and in the North who would normally have moved to act have been hounded out of public life and into inactivity. To the outside world it must look as if the conscience of white America has been silenced, and the appearance is not too deceiving. Basically all of us whites, North and South, acquiesce in white supremacy, and benefit from the pool of cheap labor created by it. . . . The

American Negro needs a Gandhi to lead him, and we need the American Negro to lead us.[37]

The legacy of the lynching of Emmett Till was the creation of a new journalistic beat that would reverberate throughout the region and, in the end, transform Virginia.

AND THEN MONTGOMERY

Although Emmett Till's killers walked free, the image of Till's beaten and mangled face marked the start of a new civil rights strategy for groups such as the Southern Christian Leadership Conference (SCLC). The gruesome photograph had appeared, with permission from Mamie Till Bradley (later Mamie Till Mobley), in *Jet* magazine, a leading African American publication. According to Sasha Torres, media and civil rights historian, "It would not be going too far to say that Mobley thus invented the strategy that later became the SCLC's signature gesture: literally illustrating southern atrocity with graphic images of black physical suffering, and disseminating those images nationally."[38] Thus, when organizers in Montgomery began what would be their successful yearlong bus boycott, they enlisted the help of the media. Torres noted that "both television and the movement were new enough that Montgomery whites apparently didn't think to censor televised representations of the protest."[39]

Specifically, Montgomery's local NBC station, WSFA-TV, covered the local story in detail. And news director Frank McGee, who recognized the national significance of one of the first successful organized boycotts to elicit tangible social change in the Jim Crow South, sought a partnership with the national NBC station. With a young charismatic Baptist preacher named Martin Luther King Jr. leading the charge, NBC was soon carrying McGee's own reports on its nationwide broadcast. Torres wrote: "Bridging local and national audiences, then, McGee's coverage allowed protestors to see themselves represented as social agents, both within Montgomery and within much larger struggles for human rights in the U.S. and internationally."[40]

Rosa Parks was well aware of her position as a social agent for change—she was secretary of the local chapter of the NAACP—before she refused to sit at the back of the public bus on December 1, 1955. Earlier that summer, as Virginia and other southern states struggled to respond to the ruling in *Brown II*, Parks was attending workshops at the Highlander Folk School in Monteagle, Tennessee. At the encouragement of her friend and employer Virginia Durr, Parks had taken advantage of the trip in order to be schooled formally in the methods of grassroots political and labor organization and nonviolent protest, patterned on the reform ideas of John Dewey and Jane Addams.[41] In 1955, Montgomery was not a city wholly resistant to racial change. It had, of course, been the site of the legal secession of the Confederate states from the Union in 1861, and for some whites a paternalistic antebellum attitude toward African Americans remained. Enough African Americans had begun to vote so that white politicians had to at least consider their support. And Governor Jim Folsom had ushered in a new era of moderation during his tenure from 1947 to 1951 and then again from 1955 to 1959. In this oasis of moderation, Jo Ann Robinson, an African American professor at the local Alabama State College, established a Women's Political Council, which went so far as to encourage black women to exercise their suffrage rights.

On the day after Rosa Parks was arrested for violating the segregation of public transportation, only one small news article ran in one of the two local papers, the *Montgomery Advertiser*. But Robinson felt the time was right to initiate a citywide boycott, and she had almost 40,000 pamphlets printed calling for mass participation by not only middle-class African Americans but poor blacks as well. An organizational meeting was called for the evening of December 5 at Holt Street Baptist Church, and Martin Luther King Jr. was selected to address the crowd, for he was perceived to be less militant than Robinson or local NAACP president Edgar D. Nixon.[42] Robinson's handbills drew a substantial crowd, who were rewarded with being in the audience for King's first major speech as a civil rights leader. King did not disappoint:

> The only weapon that we have in our hands this evening is the weapon of protest. That's all . . . and certainly, certainly, this is the glory of America, with all of its faults. This is the glory of our democracy. If we were incarcerated behind the iron curtains of a Communistic nation we couldn't do this. If we were dropped in the dungeon of a totalitarian regime we couldn't do this. But the great glory of American democracy is the right to protest for right. My friends, don't let anybody make us feel that we are to be compared in our actions with the Ku Klux Klan or with the White Citizens Council. There will be no crosses burned at any bus stops in Montgomery. There will be no white persons pulled out of their homes and taken out on some distant road and lynched for not cooperating. There will be nobody amid, among us who will stand up and defy the Constitution of this nation. We only assemble here because of our desire to see right exist. My friends, I want it to be known that we're going to work with grim and bold determination to gain justice on the buses in this city. And we are not wrong, we are not wrong in what we are doing. If we are wrong, the Supreme Court of this nation is wrong. If we are

wrong, the Constitution of the United States is wrong. If we are wrong, God Almighty is wrong. If we are wrong, Jesus of Nazareth was merely a utopian dreamer that never came down to earth. If we are wrong, justice is a lie: love has no meaning. And we are determined here in Montgomery to work and fight until justice runs down like water and righteousness like a mighty stream.[43]

By clearly contrasting the efforts of this community of African American protesters with the protest methods of segregationists and the violent actions of groups such as the Klan and the White Citizens' Councils, King positioned his followers as part of a true, authentic America and as a defining voice of public criticism (via actions and words) against white southern racial practices. They were on the right side of the law, the Constitution, and the Christian God.

The success of the boycott, helped greatly by white moderate support and organized by carpooling groups, prompted the African American newspaper the *Atlanta Daily World* to publish the headline "Alabama Might Take the Lead." The *Montgomery Advertiser*, although it initially supported the basic demands of the boycott, never took a strong stand. The editor, Grover C. Hall, did receive numerous letters, however, in favor of integrating the bus system. Historian David Chappell recounts that Frances McLeod, for example, wrote that "the treatment of Negroes on our city buses has caused us to bow our heads in shame."[44] Mrs. E. R. J., writing on Christmas Day in 1955, confessed that she "was born and reared in the Black Belt of Alabama, but I, like others, have been forced to do a lot of thinking on the race question lately." "I am afraid," she concluded, "the Negro is not now, nor has ever been as happy and content with his place as we southern white people have believed."[45] These sentiments were exactly what the Virginia Defenders were afraid would creep into the hearts of moderates in the state, who described themselves as models of gentility and southern propriety.

In the end, the Montgomery Bus Boycott succeeded when the courts overturned segregation on public transportation in Alabama (*Browder v. Gayle*). Media outlets from northern and African American newspapers covered the first integrated rides. Glenn Smiley, a white member of the Fellowship of Reconciliation (FOR) and an untiring aid to King in the cause of the boycott, remembered that day: "At 5:30 when we boarded the first bus—I've never seen so many TV cameras and radio reporters and lights and so on in my life—[there were] four of us, Dr. King and myself, the Rev. Ralph Abernathy and a Mrs. Bascomb. . . . And when Dr. King, being the first to get on, spoke to the bus driver, the bus driver smiled and said 'You're Dr. King aren't you?' and he said yes and [the driver] said, 'Well I am glad to have you aboard.'"[46] On the evening after the *Browder v. Gayle* verdict had been rendered, a parade of robed Klansman processed through the black neighborhoods in Montgomery. According to James McBride Dabbs, the "visitation was an obvious warning to blacks that they should not presume that a ruling from Washington would affect the racial status quo of the Deep South." However, Dabbs reported, "ordinarily, such a scene would have at least stirred uneasiness in the black community, but on this happy night, blacks greeted the Hooded Empire with applause and derisive laughter." In response, "the bewildered Klansmen sped off into the night."[47] The white supremacists throughout the South were surely now aware that something psychological had radically shifted, for both the parading Klan and the black protestors.

Several of Montgomery's moderate political leaders, such as Mayor W. A. Gayle, did not accept these changes quite as willingly as many had expected. By January 1956, Gayle and several of his colleagues had joined the local chapter of the White Citizens' Council, had denounced King, and were planning to host a rally for Mississippi senator Eastland.[48] Their radical transformation mirrored what was taking place simultaneously in Virginia. The media scrutiny of the South had revived an inherited sense of inferiority for politicians of the Old Dominion attempting to maintain the southern way of life. And the successful manipulation of the media by the civil rights groups in Montgomery only increased the threat of change. When journalist Joe Azbell attended that first meeting at Holt Street Baptist, this was exactly the impression that in many ways overwhelmed him. "The meeting was much like an old-fashioned revival with loud applause added," observed Azbell. "It proved beyond any doubt," he added, that "there was a discipline among Negroes that many whites had doubted. It was almost a military discipline combined with emotion."[49] What the coverage of the murder of Emmett Till and the Montgomery Bus Boycott meant for white southern moderates was that the status quo would no longer be accepted. Public criticism no longer was limited only to extremists. African Americans were encouraged and championed for their bravery in testifying against whites. And white violence, as seen in the Till case, was directed not just at southern blacks, but against outsiders, while black protest as demonstrated in Montgomery was proven successful in overturning Jim Crow laws. Though these were just two examples of historic civil rights events, they demonstrate how the civil rights beat evolved beyond merely chronicling racial suppression, to threatening, in a very tangible way, the nature of white southern life.

THE PAPER CURTAIN

As civil rights coverage exploded, white southerners began to complain about the one-sided nature of the coverage, adding yet another enemy—the liberal media—to the host of southern detractors. Editor and outspoken southern defender Thomas R. Waring Jr. published a series of editorials in the *Charleston News and Courier* that denounced what he labeled the "paper curtain," the media blackout regarding the prosegregation point of view held by many white southerners. The "one-sided reporting of race news in metropolitan newspapers and magazines of national circulation," argued Waring, was the fault of the "rich and powerful publications, which "seem to have made up their minds to attack any viewpoint that opposes the separation of the races."[50] Similar to the Agrarians-turned–New Critics, who complained that the publication industry was centered solely in the Northeast, Waring claimed that the same barriers remain fixed in the 1950s: "One of the ironies of our times is that in an age of miraculous means of communication, the South has lost its voice. The Southern argument on racial relations and states' rights is not heard in the North. It is not heard despite television, radio, moving pictures, newspapers, best-selling books and mass circulation magazines. Why? The principal reasons are these: the South is not a focal point for network radio or TV. It has no large movie studios and no newspapers or magazines of national circulation. There are no large Southern publishers of books."[51] The "paper curtain," Waring further claimed, resulted in an inescapable cycle in which the southern voice was silenced. Without access to a major media outlet in the region, northern audiences "are 'sold' on the belief that the Southern attitude toward Negroes is wrong." And this media attitude reaches southern audiences and further alienates them from the nation at large.

The other tactic employed by northern media in an effort to further ostracize segregationists from mainstream America, argued Waring, was its tendency to cite unrepresentative southern sources, such as liberals who advocated the mixing of the races. Such misleading reporting, argued Waring, gave "an impression to their readers that only demagogues and evil people who hate Negroes are holding back integration of public schools and other institutions." Waring further revealed that the takeover of the few media outlets that were indigenous to the South had exacerbated this problem. "In recent years," he wrote, "Northerners have bought newspapers in several Southern cities, including the largest and most prosperous. One or more of the newspapers in Miami, Atlanta, New Orleans, Charlotte and Birmingham—to name only five that readily come to mind—are now owned by Northern money." And, in an effort to revive the old sectional clash, Waring wrote that "we do not look with favor on a Carpetbagger Press."[52] Clearly, this popular and widely read South Carolina editor viewed the current struggle to preserve Jim Crow as part of ongoing southern oppression, defeat, and occupation.

African American communities embarked on their own media campaigns, a move that further alienated white audiences. Historian Brian Ward discussed the significant role that radio played in organizing the NAACP, as well as groups such as the Student Nonviolent Coordinating Committee (SNCC), observing that "the weekly even monthly publication schedules of most black news papers and magazines made them unsuitable vehicles for the rapid dissemination of breaking news."[53] He quoted Julian Bond, communications director of SNCC, who argued that "if you wanted to get to the large mass of people you had to go to radio. Radio was what they listened to and radio was where they got their information."[54] Walter White, director of the NAACP, used radio to inform African American audiences of the progress of segregation legal battles such as *Brown*. The direct access to the African American community allowed White to cast the battle against Jim Crow as a victory that would inevitably be achieved. For example, when reporting the early arguments in the *Brown* case to audiences only four months before the Supreme Court's verdict, White left "listeners in no doubt about who occupied the moral and constitutional high ground." His rhetoric clearly described his vision of the triumph of moral righteousness over segregation: "The 'shocking statements' and 'questionable taste' of the segregationists were contrasted with the 'immense amount of preparation' and 'unequivocal argument' of the NAACP chief counsel Thurgood Marshall."[55]

The use of print media and the airwaves by African American advocacy groups was not lost on journalists such as Waring and Kilpatrick, who recognized the power of Mamie Till Bradley's decision to publish photographs of her lynched and brutalized son, Emmett Till. "Already such incidents as the kidnapping of the Till boy in Mississippi are being blown up to inflame the public," wrote Waring.[56] And the power of organization supported by the media, whether through handbills or radio newscasts, proved vital to grassroots activists in Montgomery, Alabama. In fact, they seemed to have taken a page out of the NAACP's playbook, waging a media campaign that would recast this epic drama unfolding in the South, with their own people as the triumphant heroes who were authentically American and devoted to the Constitution as laid forth by the Virginia forefathers.

Waring turned to history to support his argument for the continued separation of the races. Waring focused primarily on attacking northern detractors and highlighting northern hypocrisy, an initiative that appealed to his conservative South Carolina audience. Specifically, and significantly for the citizens of Virginia, Waring cited John Brown's 1859 raid on Harpers Ferry, Virginia, as an example of "do-gooders stirring bloodshed." Waring began by stating that "in the 1850s, before the Civil War, Northern do-gooders gave money to stir racial strife in the South." He followed with this poignant dig: "Among the notable contributors [to the raid on Harpers Ferry] was Gov. Salmon P. Chase of Ohio. Later he was chief justice of the United States."

Moreover, in an effort to historicize the media ridicule of the South in the 1950s, Waring unearthed the century-old criticism that had precipitated the Civil War. "Wendell Phillips, New England orator, declared the State of Virginia a pirate and called John Brown a lord high admiral commissioned to sink every pirate." Waring continued: "Ralph Waldo Emerson, the poet and philosopher, compared the 'glorious' scaffold on which John Brown was hanged to the cross at Calvary." In response, as if to provoke the Virginians who were debating the fate of integration in their state, Waring reminded his readers that in the aftermath of the raid of Harpers Ferry, "the governor of Virginia announced that any further invasions from other states would be met with armed reprisals."[57] Waring was by no means the only journalist who would influence Kilpatrick's editorial stance against integration or who would share his beliefs that the South was the victim of a northern propaganda campaign. W. E. B. Debnam of North Carolina, author of *Weep No More, My Lady*, a defense of the South against Eleanor Roosevelt's observations of southern poverty, published a book in the summer of 1955 entitled *Then My Old Kentucky Home Good Night*, which laid out the facts, as perceived by the author, that supported the necessity for maintaining the Jim Crow system. "We have little hope," Debnam began, "that the presentation of these facts will silence certain critics of the South who, as were their forebears, are still hell bent on 'reconstructing' us." He continued, "But we do hope this little book will open the eyes of some, both White and Negro, who have been misled by NAACP propagandists and those who follow in their train."[58]

Kilpatrick's paper, the *Richmond News Leader*, solicited Debnam, its old "soul mate," to write an editorial on the fate of an integrated South. Debnam proclaimed dramatically that "integration, no matter how gradually it comes, is still integration and means the destruction of both races. . . . A man is just as dead if he slowly bleeds to death from slashed wrists as if his throat be cut from ear to ear." The paper announced: "We share Mr. Debnam's conviction entirely."[59] The graphic rhetoric may have echoed the sentiments of Virginia's radical segregationists, but Kilpatrick needed a way to inspire moderates to support what would become the campaign for Massive Resistance. Resurrecting the past would prove helpful. But rather than turn to the dark days of the Civil War and Reconstruction, Kilpatrick would return to the days of revolution in America and of the founding fathers of the Republic.

Waring, frustrated with the resurgence of what he perceived to be a northern media campaign against the South, reached out to Kilpatrick, writing to him personally in July 1955. He enlisted Kilpatrick to lead, along with himself, "a syndicate of Southern newspapers," which would "send a team of reporters into Northern areas to expose hypocrisy and other aspects of segregation outside the South." Waring's intention was to launch a counterstrike; he conceded that "nobody but our own papers would print the exposures," but he hoped that "if enough of us ran it, we might stimulate the AP, and possibly borderline newspapers, to report some of our coverage."[60]

Those in the news business were not the only southerners feeling the heat of the northern spotlight. Just as James Kilpatrick would wage a campaign of southern superiority and constitutional authority, others tried to highlight the positive aspects of the region in order to counter the growing civil rights coverage. A few years prior to the *Brown* decision, Louis Rubin Jr. wrote to Kilpatrick about establishing a southern book page in the *Richmond News Leader*. Rubin, who was working at the paper at the time, envisioned a page much like Donald Davidson's that was featured in the *Tennessean*. His purpose, similar to Davidson's, was to garner critical attention and secure intellectual and cultural credibility for the South. "My own opinion—I hope I'm not biased—is that it would be worth it in readership and in prestige to the paper," argued Rubin, and "I think we could easily get the best book page in the South out, and one that would have all the book companies quoting our reviews, all the schools and universities reading our reviews."[61] Rubin sensed the need to offer a better outlet for southern literary critics than was available at the time. "Our great advantage," he wagered, "over the [Richmond Times-Dispatch] is that we haven't just got a bunch of book-of-the-month ladies writing rhapsodies."[62] Even after Rubin left the *News Leader* to pursue his academic career, he stayed in touch with Kilpatrick, particularly on the issue of the "paper curtain" that he saw invading the academy as well. During his stint as executive secretary of the American Studies Association, Rubin reported to Kilpatrick about the infamous panel on segregation (on which William Faulkner appeared) that he attended at the 1955 Southern Historical Association annual meeting: "Even saw Faulkner in action—though on a screwball Segregation Panel with three points of view—all opposed to segregation! That's the way academics think when they try to show 'both sides.' Old Francis Butler Simkins and Frank Owsley [Agrarian contributor to *I'll Take My Stand*] wouldn't even attend. I went to hear and see Faulkner. They also had a non-partisan(!) discussant—fellow named James of the *Louisville Courier Journal* editorial staff—guess how non-partisan he was!"[63] Rubin clearly witnessed what he considered bias against the South, and it was not merely in the realm of public media. It was now infiltrating the southern educated elite in the academy.

Rubin's observations did not fall on deaf ears, for Kilpatrick considered himself to be not only a reporter but also a public intellectual. He commented specifically on this sense of media bias in the fall of 1955 in a speech given at the University of Richmond. "Within recent months," Kilpatrick informed the crowd, "two of the most influential magazines in the country have demonstrated how appalling [it is that] the problem [segregation] is misunderstood outside the South. One of these was *Harpers*, which carried a cheery little article some months ago, entitled 'When Negroes Entered a Texas School.' The other is the *Saturday Evening Post*, which carried a fatuous piece just last week under the remarkable heading, 'Southerners Will Like Integration.'"[64] He recognized that the "paper curtain" would have to be lifted by force, with a dramatic campaign that would transcend the argument of segregation, avoid the rhetoric of white supremacy, and give moderates in the South and states' rights advocates throughout the nation a charge they could support. Soon the scholarly work of a Virginia lawyer would reach Kilpatrick's desk, breathing new life into the old ideas that had once sparked the bloody and catastrophic War between the States.

■ The media celebration at home and abroad in response to the *Brown* decision, coupled with the press outrage and public criticism of the South that followed the lynching of Emmett Till, the acquittal of his confessed murderers, and the successful start of the Montgomery Bus Boycott, ushered in a new era of the Benighted South. According to Melvin M. Tulmin, in his 1959 study examining the influence of exposure to mass media on attitudes toward desegregation, "In the minds of many of the people in the northern sections of the United States there exists an image of the South as a single, homogenous body of people, all of whom do about the same thing in about the same way for about the same reasons and with about the same feelings." Individual white southern identities were referenced only as a collective regional problem that the nation at large had to overcome. In response, white southerners, particularly journalists, defined a new southern foe—the pro–civil rights and antisouthern media. Southern whites had to seek new outlets to get out their message, foreshadowing yet another element of southern conservatism still active today.

The research of Roy Carter Jr. of the University of North Carolina has exposed this "paper curtain" to be an imagined opponent. Carter's work examined twelve southern newspapers, concluding that the space allocated to the issue of segregation was fairly even, with 27 percent devoted to pro-integration stories, 12 percent to the progradualism position, 30 percent prosegregation, and 31 percent proving neutral in coverage. The paper curtain did not exist, but the perception mattered. For the advocates of segregation, public criticism heightened this ongoing sense of white southern persecution and activated a regional inferiority complex. But moderates still needed to be pushed. In the weeks to come, Kilpatrick would play on this growing sense of inferiority, giving southern white moderates a comfortable place on which to rest their hesitation toward change. What was at its core a racial issue became a constitutional question, adding yet another layer to southern white identity.

CHAPTER 9

EXCURSION INTO FANTASY

THE DOCTRINE OF

INTERPOSITION

The southern white man has also been damaged, although he is loath to admit it. He has been the victim of the fears and myths which he has created in order to justify the legal subordination of the Negro. In a real sense he has enslaved himself. . . . I suggest that basically what has happened to the South is that the generation which grew up after the coming of the Jim Crow system was so thoroughly "brainwashed" by its elders in the ideology of white supremacy and Negro inferiority that many of its members have never found their way back to the world of reality.
—Guy B. Johnson, "Freedom, Equality, and Segregation"

If the Virginia General Assembly should pass a resolution declaring the decision of the Supreme Court to be null and void, it might have one tangible result. The attitude of defiance might encourage those who believe that quick and complete integration of the schools should be forced upon the state. The legislators might recreate a shadow of the tragic play of extremism and fanaticism that brought on the Civil War. It is more likely that the legislators, if they pass such a resolution, will be made to look a little silly. The best thing to do is to lay the resolution aside and devote all attention possible to the heroic problem before it: how to abide by the law of the land and at the same time preserve the public schools and the public safety. The problem is hard enough without taking time out for an excursion into fantasy.
—*Virginian-Pilot*, "The Interposition of Fantasy"

James J. Kilpatrick, editor of the *Richmond News Leader*, was well aware of the expanding civil rights coverage in the fall of 1955. As a well-read man of letters, Kilpatrick, not a native southerner, recognized how the South was being portrayed as a region. Though staunch segregationists, such as the Defenders of State Sovereignty and Liberty, promised to maintain Virginia's traditional values while avoiding the lawlessness, violence, and lynch-mob mentality attributed to the Deep South, the national media failed to make the distinction. Kilpatrick, in response, grew increasingly insistent that the southern prosegregation position be heard. Thus, he too went through a transformation that echoed throughout the state and, in turn, transformed Virginia.

In a letter to Senator Harry F. Byrd immediately following the Supreme Court ruling in *Brown*, Kilpatrick urged following the law: "We have some fine legal minds in Virginia—indeed, we have some out-standing lawyers all through the South—and I feel certain they can come up with some solution to the problem that will permit segregated schools to be maintained where particular localities desire to maintain them, without doing violence to the Supreme Court or the Constitution."[1] At the end of the candid note, Kilpatrick's strong will surfaced. He assured Byrd that he was "not going to hold my breath until integration becomes a reality." Rather, Kilpatrick proclaimed that "within the bounds of the Supreme Court opinion (which is to say, that I am not about to advocate that Virginia secede from the Union), I would toss an old battle-cry back at the NAACP: Hell, we have only begun to fight."[2] By the time the Supreme Court issued its decree for integration "with all deliberate speed," in *Brown II*, Kilpatrick had amped up his defiance. In a blistering editorial that appeared on June 1, 1955, Kilpatrick revealed the extent of his frustration and exposed a budding rage, proclaiming: "In May of 1954, that inept fraternity of politicians and professors known as the United States Supreme Court chose to throw away the established law. These nine men repudiated the Constitution, spit upon the Tenth Amendment, and rewrote the fundamental law of this land to suit their own gauzy concepts of sociology. If it be said now that the South is flouting the law, let it be said of the high court, *You taught us how.* . . . Let us pledge ourselves to litigate this thing for fifty years."[3] And southern states in many ways followed Kilpatrick's suggestion, passing law upon law, many of which were inevitably declared unconstitutional when they were tested, which stalled integration for years.

The NAACP, however, organized a campaign equally resilient, equally determined, and more organized to test these laws relentlessly. And it soon recognized, in the aftermath of the 1955 murder of Emmett Till, that the media was an invaluable tool. Even William Faulkner, who had announced himself to be a moderate, seemed incensed by what he perceived to be media bias against the South. The criticism of the region as the black eye of the nation belied the complicated individual experience of integration. Faulkner argued that "the rest of the United States assumes that this condition in the South is so simple and so uncomplex that it can be changed tomorrow by the simple will of the national majority backed by legal edict."[4] *Life* magazine published Faulkner's remarks, titled "A Letter to the North." In addition to remarking on the complexity of southern race relations and illuminating the "mind" of the South, Faulkner also made a poignant case for the vulnerability of white southern moderates.

These moderates were the exact audiences to whom Kilpatrick would aim his Doctrine of Interposition, and Faulkner positioned himself as one such moderate on the verge of succumbing to reactionary resistance:

There are more Southerners than I who believe as I do and have taken the same stand I have taken, at the same price of contumely and insult and threat from other Southerners which we foresaw and were willing to accept because we believe we were helping our native land which we love, to accept a new condition which it must accept whether it wants to or not. . . . But where will we go, if the middle becomes untenable? If we have to vacate it in order to keep from being trampled? Apart from the legal aspect, apart even from the simple incontrovertible immorality of discrimination by race, there was another simply human quantity which drew us to the Negro's side: the simple human instinct to champion the underdog. But if we, the (comparative) handful of Southerners I have tried to postulate, are compelled by the simple threat of being trampled if we don't get out of the way, to vacate the middle where we could have worked to help the Negro improve his condition— compelled to move for the reason that no middle any longer exists—we will have to make a new choice. And this time the underdog will not be the Negro, since he, the Negro, will now be a segment of the topdog, and so the underdog will be that white embattled minority who are our blood and kin.[5]

Faulkner exposed the essential vulnerability of white southern moderates to feeling attacked by northern media or by the federal government and predicted this shift toward resistance. The negative construction of white southern identity by the increased public denouncement of the region threatened the precarious position of white southern moderates. Kilpatrick saw this vulnerability as an opportunity to garner support for maintaining segregation in Virginia.

The Doctrine of Interposition was outlined by Kilpatrick in an editorial for the *Richmond News Leader* on November 21, 1955. Simply put, the doctrine called for the state of Virginia to interpose its sovereignty against encroachments by the federal government outside of its defined limits as outlined in the Constitution. In addition to his own editorial, Kilpatrick also republished several historical documents, such as the Kentucky Resolutions of 1798 and 1799 and the Virginia Resolution of 1798, when a similar position was taken against the nation. Historian Joseph J. Thorndike has argued that Kilpatrick's campaign was "fundamentally rhetorical, not legal,"[6] and that its goal was to unite the Old Confederacy in a cause that was historically relevant to the region and at the same time one that served to avoid the racist and violent politics associated with the South. The timing of Kilpatrick's introduction to Interposition, an idea that spread like wildfire across the region, was intended to undermine the Gray Commission report, which many Byrd loyalists began to see as too moderate. Kilpatrick shared this vision, writing to Senator Byrd that "you can imagine how impatient I am to put aside the Gray commission's program, which is a hodge-podge of expediency and compromise."[7] But Byrd was not ready to dismiss all aspects of the Gray Commission report, particularly the government-funded tuition waivers for private academies.

The Old Dominion was set to vote by referendum on January 9, in favor or opposed to changing section 141 of the Virginia Constitution, which forbade the use of public funds for private organizations. Byrd needed the vote to test the waters for how resistant the state population was willing to be, and thus he asked Kilpatrick to shelve a vote on Interposition, as a piece of legislation, until after the referendum. Thorndike has argued that "Kilpatrick never conceived of interposition as an alternative to efforts by the state legislature to thwart the *Brown* decision." Rather, he saw it as the "intellectual, political and rhetorical solution to *Brown*—not the legal one."[8] Of course, Interposition garnered additional detractors, many of whom ridiculed Kilpatrick and the Virginia leaders for misrepresenting the intentions of the founding fathers. The *Washington Post* would later dispel what they called the myth of Interposition by claiming that it "really spells nullification" and by citing arguments against Interposition made by the likes of James Madison and Thomas Jefferson.[9] Kilpatrick had made the same misinterpretations of Jefferson and selective quotations of Madison as had the southern leaders of secession on the eve of the Civil War, claimed the *Washington Post*. Kilpatrick confessed to a reporter that he knew that Interposition, even if passed by the state, would not fare well in court. But he knew it was a powerful, if somewhat irrational, device to unite Virginians. By uniting them under the Doctrine of Interposition and Massive Resistance, Kilpatrick succeeded in prolonging segregation, and, perhaps more important, in radicalizing the state by manipulating the southern sense of inferiority. Interposition pierced the roots of southern whiteness while adding a new determinant—an opposition to judicial activism and support for strict constructionist interpretations of the Constitution—to this ever-expanding racial construct. At its core, Interposition reflected a regional desire to separate, to deny, to reject, and to refuse to participate, which still shapes modern southern conservatism.

THE ANATOMY OF INTERPOSITION

James J. Kilpatrick, nicknamed "Kilpo" by his friends and associates, grew up in Oklahoma and graduated from the University of Missouri School of Journalism in 1941. He immediately went to work for the *Richmond News Leader*, which offered him a one-year position at a salary of $35 per week. He quickly gained notoriety for his work ethic—he requested to shadow reporters on other beats on his days off—and for his vivid, detailed prose style. When the United States entered World War II less than one year after he moved to Richmond, Kilpatrick attempted to enlist in the Army Air Corps but was rejected because of his bronchial asthma. During the war years, Kilpatrick helped compensate for a depleted staff by covering the police beat, the city council, and most local news. In 1949, the esteemed editor of the paper, Douglas Southall Freeman, enlisted Kilpatrick to write editorials on significant political issues. Freeman was so impressed with Kilpatrick's work that he announced his own retirement; Kilpatrick, at the age of twenty-eight, was asked to replace him.[10]

According to historian James Ely, as an editor Kilpatrick was "a crusader against liberalism in all its forms," and he quickly succeeded in turning the *News Leader* into "the leading statewide paper in Virginia." He faced stiff competition from liberal Virginius Dabney, editor of the *Richmond Times-Dispatch*, who had won a Pulitzer Prize in 1948 for his editorial attacks on bus segregation and his call for the repeal of the poll tax. But even Dabney was eclipsed in the aftermath of the *Brown* decision by Kilpatrick's popularity, and his progressive position soon gave way to a weak, less than convincing, call for moderation. One of Kilpatrick's other critics, Robert Whitehead, who was part of the anti-Byrd community, once told him, "Certainly you are a very able editor with a remarkable command of the language and the touch to put it across."[11] Barrye Wall, who wrote for the *Farmville Herald*, admitted, in an interview years after the integration crisis had subsided in Virginia, that "most of the newspapers more or less followed Kilpatrick's lead."[12] And Francis Wilhoit, in his book, *The Politics of Massive Resistance*, categorized Kilpatrick as a "tutelary genius," capable with his pen and his speeches of influencing the course of Virginia history.[13]

Kilpatrick's power did not rest solely in his inflammatory prose or rhetoric. His close personal relationships with Senator Harry F. Byrd and Virginia state attorney general and future governor J. Lindsay Almond Jr., among others, assured him access to power. "So influential had Kilpatrick become by the mid-1950s," remarked Ely, "that Virginia liberals viewed him as the power behind the throne, the man who set the tone of the debate and effectively determined the course of public policy."[14] Throughout the course of Virginia's struggle to come to terms with the collapse of segregation, Kilpatrick counted among his social friends and frequent correspondents Byrd, Byrd's son, and Almond. Byrd, specifically, thanked Kilpatrick on several occasions for giving voice to the cause of white southern conservatives. After Kilpatrick's major editorial, "Interposition

Now," Byrd confessed to Kilpatrick that he had "read and reread it and am keeping it for future reference. It is beautifully written."[15] Attorney General Almond wrote to Kilpatrick to express his similar appreciation: "I am most grateful for your thoughtfulness in sending me a copy of your great editorials and other material relating to interposition. This will prove most helpful to me, and once again may I express my heartfelt gratitude for your splendid leadership in these days of trial." When Almond was elected governor in November 1957, he requested that Kilpatrick edit his inaugural speech, and he praised the journalist for his aggressive and relentless defense of segregation: "I thank God for the constructive leadership which you have given in presenting to the people the real essence of Virginia's stand against unwarranted Federal encroachments."[16] Clearly the boundaries of objectivity between public officials and reporters were absent in the cause of Massive Resistance.

Kilpatrick's primary motivation that fall of 1955 was to unite white Virginians in the cause of segregation in a time when such a cause was losing credibility in the eyes of the national media. Kilpatrick knew what Faulkner knew—that the political middle could not hold. However, in order to pull the middle to the right, he needed a distraction, a guise, a way for moderates to vote their conscience on defensible grounds while still retaining the old and indefensible traditions. In a speech given at the University of Richmond, Kilpatrick began to wave the banner of states' rights, championing self-determination. "When these changes are produced from below, out of the depths of public conscience and the deep waters of subtle attitudes," he insisted, "they can win peaceful acceptance. But they must come from below; they cannot successfully be imposed from above."[17] By above, Kilpatrick, of course, meant the Supreme Court, but he also meant the liberal media, which he believed was driving the civil rights movement. Kilpatrick confessed his own frustration with the media assault on the South in the opening of his book, *The Southern Case for School Segregation* (1962), in which he collected most of his prosegregation writings. "When this book was conceived," Kilpatrick wrote, "it was intended to be titled 'U.S. v. the South: A Brief for the Defense.'"[18]

Also apparent in this collection of writings is Kilpatrick's fear that the white South would be splintered by the media. He was concerned that moderate Virginians would fail to identify with the region, simply because they would choose to disassociate themselves from, for example, the Mississippi extremists exposed by the murder of Emmett Till. Kilpatrick resurrected the past to unite white Virginians in the present:

The Old Dominion is much closer to the "Old South" than say, North Carolina or Florida. Richmond was for four years the capital of a *de facto* nation, the

Confederate States of America; to this day, our children play soldier in the trenches and romp happily on the breastworks left from the bloody conflict in which the [Confederate States of America] were vanquished. The Confederacy, the War, the legacy of Lee—these play a role in Virginia's life that continues to mystify, to entrance, sometimes to repel the visitor to the State. Virginia's "Southernness" reaches to the bone and marrow of this metaphysical concept; and if Virginia perhaps has exhibited more of the better and gentler aspects of the South, and fewer of the meaner and more violent aspects, we nevertheless have shared the best and the worst with our Sister states. On questions of race relations, of school segregation, of a modus Vivendi tolerable to black and white alike, Virginia's views have been predominantly the South's views.[19]

In addition to reminding his audience of the unbreakable bonds shared by Virginia and the states of the former Confederacy, Kilpatrick defined the very nature of this bond, the shared spirit that he attempted to resurrect in the months that preceded Massive Resistance. He conceded that although there was not one unified South, white southerners did all share a "consciousness of the negro."[20] Kilpatrick believed that "it was, more than anything else, a state of mind that bound the states of the Old Confederacy together."[21]

Kilpatrick was not short of ideas for the rhetorical countercampaign that he planned to initiate, and he gathered sources in his private papers. For example, Senator James O. Eastland of Mississippi gave a speech on the floor of the U.S. Senate on May 26, 1955, in which he challenged the scientific evidence—a white southern tactic that began in the 1920s during the Scopes Trial—that had influenced Brown, a common point of contention at that time. The speech accompanied a resolution that Eastland submitted to the Senate that called for an investigation into the "alleged scientific authorities upon which the Supreme Court relied to make its decision." Eastland argued that such an investigation would reveal that "there is clear and unmistakable evidence that the Court chose to follow the insidious and false propaganda foisted by alien ideologies rather than rely on the Constitution as written and long established legal precedents."[22] Eastland proceeded to systematically interrogate the "so-called modern authorities on psychology cited by the Court," including sources cited in Gunnar Myrdal's influential book, An American Dilemma. In each instance, Eastland questioned the political loyalty of these experts and revived his allegations against a litany of southern enemies. Psychologist Theodore Brameld was accused of being a member of multiple Communist organizations and of having countless citations against him in the files of the Committee on Un-American Activities.[23]

E. Franklin Frazier, a member of the Southern Conference on Human Welfare, was discredited by Eastland for writing *The Negro in the United States*, which "was favorably reviewed by the Communist social journals, the *Worker* and *Daily People's Word*," and for glorifying "the brazen Negro Communist Paul Robeson."[24] Eastland left no stone unturned, detailing at length Frazier's associations with various groups, all of which, the senator insisted, were part of the Communist front. Franz Boas, Ruth Benedict, W. E. B. Du Bois, and Alain Locke were singled out for anti-American activity and demonized as traitors who had manipulated the Warren Court.[25] Thus, Eastland invoked two arguments that would potentially play well in the South—the distrust of science and the fear of Communism.

Kilpatrick also held onto documents that used a religious argument to defend the practice of segregation. For example, Dr. L. Nelson Bell, of Asheville, North Carolina, published an article, "Christian Race Relations Must Be Natural Not Forced," in an August 1955 issue of the *Southern Presbyterian Journal*, which outlined the biblical argument in support of segregation. Bell, the father-in-law of Billy Graham, insisted that "there is nothing Christian or natural in manufacturing situations for forced relationships."[26] Rather, Bell reasoned, real acceptance of racial equality would come only from Christians first freeing themselves of prejudice and hatred. Bell's argument supported Kilpatrick's assertion that change would have to come from the bottom up, not the top down. Perhaps in the days of the anti-evolution movement arguments against modern science and Christian interpretations of segregation would have been enough to unite southern whites in their resistance against *Brown*. But Kilpatrick knew that in order to fight the Supreme Court, he would need a legal argument capable of being easily understood by the public and able to tap into the southern heritage of inferiority that now weighed heavily on Kilpatrick and his fellow segregationist leaders.

In August 1955, as if by magic, Kilpatrick found the answer he was looking for. William Old, an attorney and circuit court judge from Chesterfield County, Virginia, published 1,000 copies of a pamphlet titled "The Segregation Issue: Suggestions Regarding the Maintenance of State Autonomy" with his own money.[27] Old suggested that the state of Virginia counter the Supreme Court with three actions:

1. Assert and invoke the inherent and lawful police power of the Commonwealth by appropriate legislation.
2. By resolution of the General Assembly, in the nature of the Virginia-Kentucky Resolutions, declare that the decision is an abortive attempt to amend the Constitution of the United States.

3. Withdraw from the County and City School Boards and from all state agencies and from the Commonwealth itself all consent that they may be sued in any matter concerning the operation of schools.[28]

Kilpatrick was immediately intrigued by Old's proposal, particularly his historical references to the Virginia-Kentucky Resolutions, and Kilpatrick turned to the legislation of the past for inspiration.

In the months after Kilpatrick presented what would be called the Doctrine of Interposition to his readers, and to the South at large, he was asked by Senator Eastland for a list of sources that supported the concept. Kilpatrick responded in an eight-page letter that began by thanking Eastland, as well as Judge Tom Brady, author of *Black Monday*, for their work on behalf of the cause of segregation in Mississippi. "I wish it were possible," Kilpatrick wrote, "for me to put together something really definitive for you, but the circumstances here are perhaps unusual." He continued: "It was not until six weeks ago that I professed even a cursory acquaintance with the doctrines of nullification; it was just one month ago yesterday that my first editorial on the subject appeared. There simply have not been enough hours in the day for me to put in the research-in-depth that ought to be done. About the best I can do is to pass along some comments on the materials I have read, with the suggestion that these will lead you to a wealth of helpful material."[29] Over the course of the remaining seven pages, Kilpatrick revealed just how much reading he must have done in the fall of 1955. He immediately directed Eastland to return to the *Federalist Papers*, particularly the discussion of the boundaries between federal and state powers as outlined in Federalist No. 39, as well as to considerations of the power of the courts featured in Nos. 78, 80, and 81. And Kilpatrick even turned to Jefferson's personal correspondence to John Taylor in 1798, published in *Jefferson's Writings*, to illuminate the question of states' rights. Madison's authorship of the Virginia Resolution of 1798 and the Kentucky Resolutions of 1798 and 1799 figure prominently in Kilpatrick's list of sources, as do the Alien and Sedition Acts and John C. Calhoun's writings of the 1820s, all of which he would excerpt in the *Richmond News Leader* during his rhetorical campaign to win the hearts and minds of the Virginia citizenry.[30]

Eventually, the inquiries to the *Richmond News Leader* regarding Kilpatrick's sources supporting Interposition became so plentiful that the paper published a final list—an extended version of the reading list sent to Eastland—to satisfy curious readers. This bibliography of Interposition was subdivided into seven categories: "Constitution Generally," "Supreme Court Generally," "Court Opinions," "Georgia Precedents," "Kentucky-Virginia Resolutions," "South Carolina

Precedents," and "Personal Liberty Laws." The list itself included some seventy items and seemed to indicate a level of historical and legal expertise as to prove very persuasive to a lay audience.[31] This list also reveals the strategy guiding Kilpatrick's invocation of Interposition. Similar to the transition made by the southern Agrarians in becoming New Critics, Kilpatrick aimed to shift the terms of the debate. Whereas the New Critics converted the political and economic vision of Agrarianism into an aesthetic formalism untainted by regional stereotypes, Kilpatrick and Virginia political leaders transformed an argument of racial superiority into a contest of constitutional intent. By grounding his theory in court precedents, as well as invoking southern icons such as Jefferson and Calhoun, Kilpatrick established a canon of resistance literature in which 1955 Virginia became the most recent incarnation. Kilpatrick himself recognized the movement that he was resurrecting and reshaping. At the end of his letter to Eastland, he gushed that "the delightful aspect of the little research I have been able to do is that one argument and exposition leads with such clarity to another; responses suggest themselves; the clear reasonableness of interposition becomes more evident the closer one examines the subject." He closed by expressing his solidarity with the segregationist senator, signing his letter, "With every expression of personal esteem, most faithfully yours."[32]

INTERPOSITION NOW!

Less than two weeks after the Gray Commission submitted its three-pronged response to *Brown*, Kilpatrick unveiled the Doctrine of Interposition on the editorial page of the *Richmond News Leader*. As if to signal that a fundamental shift was to occur, a move toward a legal and historic defense of segregation, Kilpatrick positioned a quotation from section 15 of the Virginia Constitution across the banner of his page: "That no free government, or the blessings of liberty can be preserved to any people, but by a firm adherence to justice, moderation, temperance, frugality and virtue, and by frequent recurrence to fundamental principles."[33] On that first day of Kilpatrick's campaign he discussed what he labeled the "Transcendent Issue" facing Virginia—the issue that rose above the deliberations over local control and pupil assignment. The transcendent issue was the right of the Supreme Court to alter wholly its interpretation of the Constitution (to reverse *Plessy v. Ferguson*) and, in Kilpatrick's opinion, to force the mingling of the races: "Can it be right, we have inquired, that binding 'law of the land' can be fashioned in this cavalier way? Was it ever intended by the founding fathers that such authority should be vested in the court? If the commission [the Gray Commission] correctly states that the degeneracy of constitutional process, does not Virginia have a right and a duty to interpose its sovereignty in a valiant effort to halt the evil?"[34] In place of making his own argument to the readers in Virginia, Kilpatrick chose to reprint the key sources that defined Interposition, filling the entire editorial page with legislation nearly 150 years old. Excerpts from the "The First Kentucky Resolution," passed on November 16, 1798, "The Second Kentucky Resolution," passed on November 14, 1799, and "The Virginia Resolution of 1798," passed on December 21, 1798, appeared on the right-hand side of the editorial page, accompanied by images of the U.S. presidents from the Commonwealth, Thomas Jefferson and James Madison. The presentation of these historic documents in their original text, under the watchful eye of these founding fathers, was intended, in a sense, to endorse defiance to *Brown* and to lend credibility and authenticity to the resistance movement. Whereas public ridicule of the South and of Virginia in the aftermath of *Brown* revived a sense of inferiority, Kilpatrick's crusade intended to overcome these feelings of inferiority by bombarding the reading public with the intellectual debates of their ancestors, regardless of the impracticability of their modern implementation.

For his lay audience, Kilpatrick offered his own explanation of the significance of these resolutions, all of which were introduced to protest the Alien and Sedition Acts, enacted by the Fifth U.S. Congress. These infamous acts empowered the government to deport all "aliens" deemed threatening to the United States, to apprehend, secure, and remove any "aliens" during wartime, and to deem it illegal for any person "to write, print, utter or publish . . . any false, scandalous and malicious writings against the government."[35] According to Kilpatrick, these acts had infuriated Jefferson and his colleagues, and those in the Old Dominion, Kilpatrick insisted, had been particularly offended. "Feeling ran especially high in Virginia," he argued, "where freedom of speech and the press had vital meaning." The General Assembly of the state of Kentucky solicited Vice President Jefferson to author a resolution nullifying the Alien and Sedition Acts, a resolution that James Madison edited and introduced at the Virginia General Assembly. Jefferson insisted that the acts were a "deliberate, palpable and dangerous exercise" and proffered the idea that "in such an emergency . . . a nullification, by these sovereignties, of all unauthorized acts done under color of that instrument" was necessary.[36] Kilpatrick, in turn, encouraged Virginians to learn from the past deliberations of their iconic forefathers and ask themselves, "in 1955, confronting a manifestly unconstitutional action not by the Congress but by the Supreme Court, whether the principles enunciated so forcefully by Jefferson and Madison may not have great validity today."[37] As if the connection had not been clearly drawn on November 21, Kilpatrick dedicated his entire editorial page the following day to spelling out the way in which the state was justified in reapplying the Doctrine of Interposition to reject the Supreme Court ruling.

Kilpatrick never lost sight of the public relations aspect of his campaign; he needed to unify Virginians in support of a cause that would not offend their traditional values or incite the radical violence of the Deep South. In his lead article, "The Right of Interposition," he flattered his fellow Virginians by appealing to their propriety and morality. "From the very day of the Supreme Court's opinion in the school segregation cases," he claimed, "the South, in searching for a wise course of action, has been handicapped by a fault that in ordinary times is among our highest values: It is our reverence for law, and our obedience to constituted authority."[38] In a series of additional persuasive essays, Kilpatrick questioned: "Is it reasonable to believe that the States, like Frankenstein, have created an agency [the Supreme Court] superior to themselves, and that they are utterly powerless to contest their own destruction."[39] And although Kilpatrick informed his audience that both Jefferson and Madison believed the Doctrine of Interposition to be a "right of last resort," he proclaimed that Virginia now faced a "deliberate, palpable, and dangerous threat," as ominous as the Alien and Sedition Acts of the late eighteenth century.

In the days and weeks that followed, Kilpatrick continued to strengthen his argument by excerpting additional historical endorsements. Particularly relevant to many white southerners was Kilpatrick's tribute to secession leader John Calhoun of South Carolina. In "'Interposition' Is Basic Right of Sovereign States, John Calhoun Believed," Kilpatrick printed a substantial portion of Calhoun's Fort Hill address, delivered in July 1831. "This Right of Interposition, thus solemnly asserted by the State of Virginia, be it called what it may—state-right, veto, nullification, or by any other name—I conceive to be," Calhoun declared, "the fundamental principle of our system, resting on facts historically as certain as our revolution itself."[40] And if bringing back southern Confederate heroes like Calhoun was not enough to unify his fellow Virginians, Kilpatrick found yet another way to manipulate the white southern heritage of inferiority by demonstrating how states outside of the South had invoked Interposition in the distant past. In a series of headlines, "New England Proclaimed the Right," "Wisconsin Proclaimed the Right," and "Iowa Successfully Challenged," Kilpatrick encouraged his readers to see their struggle not as a struggle of the South against the North, but as a universal struggle against the tyranny of the federal government. Delegates to a Hartford convention in a moment of strong opposition to the War of 1812, Kilpatrick reported, declared the following: "In cases of deliberate, dangerous and palpable infractions of the Constitution, affecting the sovereignty of a State and the liberties of the people, it is not only the right, but the duty of such

State to interpose its authority for their protection."[41] And the Iowa Supreme Court, in the aftermath of the Civil War, disregarded a Supreme Court ruling on state grants expanding railroads, Kilpatrick, somewhat vaguely, informed his audience.[42]

However, in a case of truly odd bedfellows, Kilpatrick turned to Wisconsin abolitionists for yet another example of the use of Interposition outside of the South. In response to the passage of the Fugitive Slave Act of 1850 and the subsequent upholding of the act in the 1857 Supreme Court *Dred Scott* decision, Wisconsin abolitionists waged a crusade of defiance motivated by the capture and arrest of fugitive slave Joshua Glover. The Wisconsin Supreme Court delayed his return via a writ of habeas corpus, and the Wisconsin legislature passed a resolution challenging the authority of the Supreme Court. Kilpatrick remarked that, "again, the voice of Jefferson and Madison, that time after 61 years; and this powerful statement of 'positive defiance' came not from the South, but from Wisconsin."[43]

On the final day of Kilpatrick's editorial crusade for the implementation of Interposition—on the eve of the meeting of the Virginia General Assembly, where Kilpatrick hoped a resolution of Interposition would be considered—he published his coda, "Interposition Now." Kilpatrick passed his torch to the Virginia legislature, and he quoted from the General Assembly of 1829. "For here," Kilpatrick noted, "is enunciated, in wonderfully clear terms, the tradition of Virginia's Assembly in the face of Federal encroachment."[44] Kilpatrick introduced the 1829 General Assembly's statement by writing, "Whenever an attempt has been made to pervert the Constitution, said the Assembly, 'Virginia has even been prompt to avow her unqualified disapprobation, and manifest her unqualified dissent.'"[45] The General Assembly was further quoted as proclaiming boldly that "to subject our local or domestic affairs to any other authority than our own Legislature would be to expose to certain destruction the happiness and prosperity of the people of Virginia."[46] After providing the historical context for Interposition, Kilpatrick did not rest on his editorial accomplishments. He embarked on a second phase of his campaign to spread his message directly to the state as well as to the sister states of the Old Confederacy.

His editorials focused wholly on the constitutional legitimacy of Interposition and the legislative history of its use in various states, but Kilpatrick revealed his true motivations more clearly in a speech delivered to fellow segregationists that same November. When discussing the repercussions of passing a resolution of Interposition, Kilpatrick confessed to the "strategy" of employing this new tactic:

We have suffered, in the South, from the disadvantageous position of defending a practice, racial segregation, which we believe to be sound but much of the country believes to be odious. That the South has excellent reasons for maintaining a dual society, and that both races have benefited enormously from the policies of separation, is unknown to the people of our sister States. If it were possible to elevate this controversy from the distasteful morass of racial segregation, and place it upon the high level of fundamental principles of government, we should gain perceptibly from the higher ground. In such a contest, it is Virginia and the South who would be defending state sovereignty from the usurpations of a Federal tyranny; like St. George, we would assail the dragon of usurpation, lest it devour the princess of our fundamental structure of government.[47]

The only negative consequence that Kilpatrick foresaw, according to his speech, was the "outraged cries of scorn and derision that would come from the National Association for the Advancement of Colored People, and the mockery and insult that would pour from the 'liberal' press."[48] But such mockery and ridicule were not new to Virginia or the South, and Kilpatrick recognized that placing resistance under the legal, historic, and constitutional umbrella of Interposition might be the only way to appeal to white southern moderates and, perhaps, nonsoutherners as well.

The General Assembly that convened that November and December of 1955 decided against introducing a resolution on Interposition immediately, opting instead to deal with the report submitted to Governor Stanley on November 11 by the Gray Commission. One of the primary tenets of the commission's plan—the tuition grant program that would provide students with public funds to attend private schools and thus avoid integration—would require a constitutional amendment. The Byrd organization, including Byrd himself, encouraged Kilpatrick to delay a vote on Interposition until after a state referendum, scheduled for January 9, 1956, could be held on the constitutional amendment. Byrd, Stanley, Almond, and Gray, among others, were by no means opposed to Interposition—they simply wanted to gage the support of the voting constituency before attempting this effort at Massive Resistance. Byrd's support of Kilpatrick's plan is well documented in the correspondence between the senator and the journalist during the month of December. Only two days after Rosa Parks was arrested in Montgomery, Alabama, Byrd confessed to Kilpatrick that "you certainly stirred up something when you brought out the interposition approach. I only wish we had gotten started on it earlier."[49] Kilpatrick updated Byrd on the progress of the Interposition campaign only a few weeks later: "This interposition movement is snowballing so fast I can scarcely keep up with the hour-by-hour developments."[50] And again, only a few days later,

Kilpatrick informed Byrd again that "this proposal for interposition is catching fire because it's right—it is basically and fundamentally sound, it transcends the race issue."[51]

Byrd was not the only U.S. senator being updated on the Interposition movement in Virginia. Senator Eastland of Mississippi remained in contact with Kilpatrick regularly. And FitzGerald Bemiss, a moderate member of the Gray Commission, even wrote to Senator Prescott S. Bush of Connecticut, father and grandfather of future presidents George H. W. Bush and George W. Bush, and enclosed copies of Kilpatrick's editorials. Bemiss encouraged Bush to read the editorials carefully due to the "solemn matter of these most fundamental principles." He continued: "I do hope you find the time to look at them. Jack has attracted a great deal of attention in the great public service of developing this series."[52] Whether or not Kilpatrick's editorials could be seen as a public service, they undoubtedly succeeded in altering the terms of the segregation debate, situating it on new ground that was more enticing to moderates. Eventually, on February 1, 1956, the General Assembly of Virginia, meeting in its regular biennial session, approved the Resolution of Interposition by a Senate vote of 36 to 2 and by a House of Delegates vote of 90 to 5.[53]

THE SPREAD OF INTERPOSITION AND THE
MANDATE OF JANUARY 9

Kilpatrick's editorials in the early winter of 1955 clearly touched a nerve, not only in Virginia but throughout the South, particularly for white southerners, who were watching the emerging and increasingly organized civil rights movement. The spread of Interposition throughout the South was aided by Kilpatrick himself, who consolidated all of his editorials into pamphlet form and began distributing them to the hundreds of citizens who wrote to him personally requesting a copy and to southern state leaders, including the governors of North Carolina, Texas, Arkansas, and Louisiana. Every member of the Florida legislature received a copy.[54] Kilpatrick also responded to letters from local chapters of the White Citizens' Councils that requested his services. Robert B. Patterson, the secretary of the Winona, Mississippi, chapter, requested a summary of Kilpatrick's plan for Virginia, which he hoped would inspire his state and others to undertake similar actions.[55] Kilpatrick responded by thanking Patterson, as well as Judge Tom Brady, for leading a similar charge in their home state, and he promised to write Patterson "a one page summary of the nullification proposal this week, and get it into the mail as soon as possible."[56] Kilpatrick refrained from using the term "nullification" in public or in his editorials, in an effort to avoid media ridicule by outsiders proclaiming this to be resurrected Civil War propaganda. A few days later, Kilpatrick sent another note to Patterson and informed him that 2,000 pamphlets were en route to the Association of Citizens' Council's office in Mississippi.[57]

The *Richmond News Leader* editor also kept in touch with fellow members of the southern media during that fateful December. He wrote a long letter to friend and fellow segregationist Thomas R. Waring Jr., editor of the *Charleston News and Courier*, informing him of the decision of the Byrd organization to hold off on a vote on Interposition. "As you know by now," Kilpatrick commented, "the General Assembly felt it inadvisable to take up the resolution of interposition at the regular session." He further explained to Waring that "this was wholly a matter of political expediency, for members of both the House and State Senate were wildly enthusiastic about the plan and might have gone off ill-prepared unless they have been restrained." He closed by instructing Waring to "hold down the fort."[58] Additionally, Kilpatrick sent copies of his statements on Interposition to Morris Cunningham at the *Memphis Commercial Appeal*, soliciting his support: "This proposal for a State to interpose its sovereignty may sound unbelievable at first glance, but on careful reflection, I believe you will find it has substantial merit. Some of the most outstanding attorneys of Virginia who approached it first as skeptics have since suggested to me that it may provide a valid and honorable approach to a problem of transcendent importance, far over-riding the school segregation fight."[59] Even television stations were supplied with copies of the Interposition pamphlet. Kilpatrick described the popularity of the Interposition idea in a letter to station manager Richard D. Morphew of WJDX and WLBT, NBC affiliates in Mississippi. "We ran completely out of the supplements until last night [December 27], what with the Christmas holiday weekend, that we were able to get press time to run off some more," wrote Kilpatrick. He further informed Morphew that "we first ran off 2,000 reprints, thinking that would be aplenty; then we ran off 7,000 more. Now, praise be, we have run off another 2,000 and today's mail alone brought requests for 480 copies."[60]

Kilpatrick was clearly breaking though the "paper curtain," and his campaign was having substantial effects throughout the South. Governor Luther Hodges of North Carolina wrote to Kilpatrick to request his assistance in implementing Interposition in his state,[61] and Kilpatrick approached Governor Allan Shivers, requesting that he too consider championing the cause in Texas. He assured Shivers that "you have many friends here in Virginia."[62] Judge Tom Brady forwarded to Kilpatrick a copy of the resolution being considered in Mississippi that would invoke Interposition against the Supreme Court's ruling. He thanked Kilpatrick for the editorials that were making such a step possible in Mississippi: "Your labors on the Right of Interposition are bearing good fruit and, in my opinion, within the next two or three weeks you will see ample proof thereof."[63] That December, Virginia governor Stanley joined Kilpatrick's outreach efforts, meeting with the governors of South Carolina, Georgia, and Mississippi to discuss the Interposition resolutions to be introduced in their state legislatures.[64] The cause did, indeed, seem to have "caught on fire," but in Virginia, a state referendum soon took center stage.

The attention and buzz generated by Kilpatrick's campaign for Interposition overshadowed the Gray Commission report. But Byrd organization members and prosegregationists did not abandon the January 9 referendum, because they believed it would provide a mandate for the next phase of resistance—Interposition. They did face organized opposition from the NAACP, the Virginia Council on Human Relations, and the newly established Virginia Society for the Preservation of Public Schools.[65] This group, specifically, argued that the state tuition grants for private schools proposed by the Gray Commission would result inevitably in the abandonment of the public education system in Virginia. They attempted to offer a countercampaign to the powerful politicians championing the tuition grant plan. They released pamphlets encouraging Virginia citizens to vote "no" on the referendum and cataloged the possible negative implications of a "yes" victory. They warned that the tuition grant program would eventually be declared unconstitutional and that it would prove costly. "There is no way to estimate the cost of the tuition grant program," the flyer read. "We would, in effect, be signing a blank check."[66] The Communist Party of Norfolk, Virginia, distributed its own anti–tuition grant program documents—a fact that did not go unnoticed by anticommunist Democrats. They listed the groups taking a stance against the referendum in an effort to counter the wave of support for resistance building in Virginia. They also listed the groups pushing for an affirmative vote: "For: the Byrd Political Organization and its numerous political appointees and wealthy contributors and supporters. Several small groupings of unashamed bigots. Some major newspapers that support the machine on all major questions."[67]

The efforts of the liberal and moderate groups, however, were no match for the Byrd machine. In a four-page typed memorandum, supporters of the referendum outlined their media campaign to reach voters throughout the state. Their purpose was twofold: to provide information on the Gray Commission plan and to get out the vote. They planned to counter the opposition accusation that tuition grants would destroy the public school system by focusing primarily on the local control aspect of the plan, which would allow individual counties to integrate or not integrate at their own speed. Referendum supporters established a seven-person executive board and created a publicity plan that included newspaper ads, pamphlets, radio spots, television panels, and public service announcements.[68] In the end, referendum supporters prevailed. The constitutional referendum passed on January 9, 1956, by a vote of 304,154 to 146,164.[69] The Byrd organization, as well as Kilpatrick and his supporters, believed that the vote signaled a mandate for greater resistance, particularly because of the organized opposition initiated by such groups as the Virginia Society for the Preservation of Public Schools. The greater resistance they had in mind was a Resolution of Interposition, which passed successfully less than one month later. Still, as a result of the affirmative vote on the January 9 referendum, a constitutional convention was called for March 5–7, at which delegates passed the Gray plan almost perfunctorily.[70]

MASSIVE RESISTANCE

In the spring of 1956, momentum in favor of all-out resistance to integration seemed overwhelming, and legislatures in South Carolina, Alabama, Mississippi, and Georgia, in addition to Virginia, passed over forty prosegregation resolutions.[71] Mississippi adopted a prosegregation measure that fined and jailed any white student who agreed to attend an integrated school.[72] Just as Kilpatrick felt the need to unify the state of Virginia against the Supreme Court, Senator Byrd wanted to unify the South against such federal encroachments. Along with senators Strom Thurmond of South Carolina and Sam Ervin of North Carolina, Byrd drafted a document, the Southern Manifesto, which was read on the Senate floor on March 12, 1956. John Egerton described the events: The bus boycott "was then in a critical stage in Montgomery (Martin Luther King's house had been bombed), and in Tuscaloosa, white students and their off-campus supporters had rioted at the University of Alabama to protest the admission of a single black graduate student, twenty-six-year-old Autherine Lucy."[73] As tensions heated up in Alabama and white segregationists began to realize the organizational strength of African American protest and the intensifying media indictment of southern racial practices, Byrd was able to capitalize on southern white fear of change. He secured signatures from nineteen southern senators and eighty-two southern representatives in the U.S. Congress on the Southern Manifesto.[74] It read in part: "This unwarranted exercise of power by the Court, contrary to the Constitution, is creating chaos and confusion in the States principally affected. It is destroying the amicable relations between the white and Negro races that have been created through 90 years of patient effort by the good people of both races. It has planted hatred and suspicion where there has been heretofore friendship and understanding. Without regard to the consent of the governed, outside agitators are threatening immediate and revolutionary changes in our public school systems."[75] Historian Francis Wilhoit enumerated ten motivations that underlay the Southern Manifesto, including the obvious denunciation of the *Brown* decision and the attempt to resurrect states' rights. But Wilhoit identified the intent of the authors as also being "to scare white southerners with threats of invasions by outside agitators."[76] Many white southerners were threatened not just by invasion; many, such as Kilpatrick, were concerned with media ridicule of the racist and backward South. For men like Byrd, liberal organizers were not the only source of blame; the "carpetbag press"—as labeled by Waring—shared the burden.

In the sweeping rhetoric of Massive Resistance and Interposition, the local control option of the Gray Commission plan was all but abandoned. And it was this aspect of the plan that referendum advocates had used to reassure the opposition that the public schools would be protected. Governor Stanley, encouraged by the passage of the Resolution of Interposition and pressured by the Byrd organization to resist any integration in any part of Virginia, announced in July that a special session of the General Assembly would be held the next month, at which point the Stanley plan to maintain segregation would be considered. Stanley couched his new plan in terms of the state's commitment and responsibility to fight against federal tyranny. Kilpatrick's rhetoric had, indeed, shifted the terms of the debate. Senator Byrd gave the governor his blessing, and, in a speech given at his apple farm in Berryville, Virginia, only two days prior to the opening of the special session on August 27, Byrd warned his supporters: "Let Virginia surrender to this illegal demand [the *Brown* decision] and you'll find the ranks of the South broken. . . . If Virginia surrenders, the rest of the South will go down too."[77] Central to Stanley's plan was the Governor's Fund Withholding Bill, House Bill No. 1, which would allow the governor to rescind all funding for any public school that chose to integrate.

In his private notes, FitzGerald Bemiss recorded the events of that special session. The governor's bill passed by a vote of 61 to 37 (a similar version also passed in the Senate), as did twenty-two other prosegregation pieces of legislation, signaling a radicalization of Virginia resistance.[78] Bemiss noted: "This victory for the Governor and his Southside supporters showed a very remarkable change in public sentiment." He continued: "This was not necessarily odd because the subject is one on which it is very easy to arouse the passions." Benjamin Muse observed that emotions did indeed run high that summer. He claimed specifically that in August 1956 "hatred of the NAACP had reached a high pitch in Virginia."[79] The gallery was overflowing on the opening day of the session, the result of a special issue of the *Virginian*, which called on white parents to travel to Richmond to voice their resistance. According to Muse, "This special issue of the *Virginian* carried a page of dubious photographs depicting 'integration as it really is';—from white and Negro children mingling on the playground to a white woman lying across the bed with a repulsive Negro man."[80] Virginia segregationists may have prided themselves on being nonviolent, but their threats and tactics were, increasingly, "deliberate, palpable, and dangerous."

The governor's plan, which virtually reversed or destroyed the Gray Commission's recommendations accepted earlier that year, was backed by members of the Gray Commission itself, including the chair, Garland Gray. Bemiss confessed that "one of the most intelligent senators who supported the [governor's] Plan told me privately that he thought the Plan was poor." Many others, noted Bemiss, believed it would only be another delaying tactic. However, as Bemiss explained, these Virginia representatives were now being held hostage by a reactionary and inflamed constituency. Of this senator, Bemiss recorded that "he said that the people had to see that their representatives had done everything possible to avoid any integration."[81] The result, Bemiss proclaimed, was that "'massive resistance' has so far satisfied the white populations of Virginia in that so far there is no integration."[82]

Stanley was succeeded as governor by Attorney General J. Lindsay Almond Jr., and it was Almond who made national headlines by invoking Stanley's Fund Withholding Bill. Aided by the public outrage over the events at Little Rock Central High School in Arkansas, Almond was elected in the fall of 1957 by 63 percent of the vote.[83] He claimed to be committed "to oppose with every faculty at our command, and every ounce of our energy, the attempt to mix white and Negro children in the classroom."[84] Kilpatrick wrote his inaugural address: "Against these massive attacks," proclaimed Almond, "we must marshal a massive resistance."[85] He followed this bold pronouncement by introducing the "Little Rock" bill to the General Assembly, which reconvened in January 1958. The bill would allow the governor to shut down any school that was policed by federal troops; it passed easily, along with an appropriations bill that shut off all funding to any school districts that planned to integrate their schools.[86] On Friday, September 12, in an action heard throughout the Commonwealth and the country at large, Governor Almond shut down Warren County High School and removed it officially from the public school system. One week later, Massive Resistance struck again when elementary schools in Charlottesville, Virginia, followed by public schools in Norfolk, were also removed from the Virginia public school system, pursuant to Chapter 9.1 of the Code of Virginia. The board of supervisors for Prince Edward County followed the governor's lead and closed all public schools in the county. The Old Dominion, which had once counseled caution and patience in the wake of *Brown*, had in only four short years been swept up into a vortex of hysteria and defiance.[87] Public criticism of southern racial practices had sparked the fire. The collective anxiety that followed would make white southerners particularly vulnerable, and opinion makers and leaders exploited this vulnerability, convincing white southern audiences of their own superiority. This illusion of superiority was built on the premise that southerners had a legitimate legal argument for continued segregation, endorsed by a pantheon of southern heroes—Jefferson, Madison, Calhoun, and others—and grounded in the textual authority of the Constitution.

Governor Almond's drastic act, particularly after the national media outrage regarding the Little Rock Central High School crisis a year earlier, shocked American progressives and moderates, as well as the liberal media. Famed newscaster Edward R. Murrow spotlighted the extreme behavior of Virginia segregationists in a national television exposé, *The Lost Class of '59*. The public ridicule, which was at least partially responsible for the radicalization of Virginia conservatives, had not subsided. The resuscitation of the Doctrine of Interposition had not convinced audiences outside of the South that southern segregationists were primarily concerned with the constitutional relationship between the federal government and the states. The jig was up. Interposition was merely a rhetorical campaign to justify a relentless opposition to integration, and although it may have been believed wholly by some or many white southerners, critics did not mistake it for a sincere constitutional argument. Virginia businesspeople were concerned that the public denouncement of Virginia fanaticism would hurt the state economically, and they expressed their frustration that Virginia's reputation was being ruined to the governor at a dinner held at the Richmond Rotunda Club in December 1958.[88] One month later, Almond faced the most substantial blow to Massive Resistance prior to the passage of the 1964 Civil Rights Act when the Virginia Supreme Court of Appeals submitted its ruling in *Harrison v. Day* (1959),[89] the case that challenged the closing of public schools as unconstitutional. Chief Justice John W. Eggleston ruled that "both the school-closing and the fund cutoff measures were contrary to section 129 of the Virginia Constitution which required the state to 'maintain an efficient system of free public schools throughout the state.'"[90] Eggleston noted in his majority opinion that the maintenance of the school system had to include "those [schools] in which the pupils of both races are compelled to be enrolled and taught together, however unfortunate that situation may be."[91]

The reversal of four long years of building toward Massive Resistance came on the anniversary of Robert E. Lee's birthday, January 19, 1959, and was not well received by Governor Almond, who had based his career on defying court-ordered integration. The following day, Almond denounced the ruling, proclaiming to radio and television audiences:

> To those in high places or elsewhere who advocate integration for your children and send their own to private or public segregated schools; to those who defend or close their eyes to the livid stench of sadism, sex immorality and juvenile pregnancy infesting the mixed schools of the District of Columbia and elsewhere; to those who would overthrow the customs, morals and traditions of a way of life which has endured in honor and decency for centuries and embrace a new moral code prepared by nine men in Washington whose moral concepts they know nothing about; . . . to all of these and their confederates, comrades and allies, let me make it abundantly clear for the record now and hereafter, as governor of this state, I will not yield to that which I know to be wrong.[92]

In the days that followed his blistering speech, Almond seemed to face what most segregationists in Virginia were beginning to face, namely, that the tactics of Massive Resistance were no longer feasible. Merely one week later, he again ascended to the podium on the floor of the General Assembly and, in a move that shocked the Byrd establishment, outlined his plan to end the defiance movement. On February 2, 1959, twenty-one African American students began attending classes in Norfolk and Arlington without interference.

Kilpatrick's response to the court reversals and the surrender of Governor Almond was simply to shift the terms of the debate once again. He embraced a policy of tokenism, hoping that selective integration would appease the federal government. "There are more ways of waging a war," Kilpatrick editorialized, "as we have remarked from time to time, than by stubborn defense of a single fixed position."[93] Historian Joseph Thorndike has insisted that Kilpatrick's dedication to the states' rights aspect of this campaign for Interposition was sincere, but by no means did it mask fully his views on race. His editorials were filled with accusations of the inferiority of the African American race. "The Negro race has never been able to build a civilization of its own, and it has debased every society into which its blood has been heavily mixed."[94] His goal had been to appeal to moderates and even to audiences outside of the South and, moreover, to provide white southerners who were demoralized and outraged by the public ridicule that engulfed their region in the 1950s with an intellectual and historical stance for defending the southern way of life. Interposition was motivated by a desire to exploit the cultural anxiety of Virginians and organize them against a national culture from which they were alienated. This desire reflected a growing awareness that civil rights groups such as the NAACP and the SCLC were more prepared and powerful than many white segregationists had realized prior to 1955.[95]

■ The insincerity of Kilpatrick's campaign for Interposition reveals the existence of an overwhelming sense of inferiority resulting from the media denouncement of the white South. According to James Ely, "No subject more infuriated the leaders of massive resistance than the coverage of events in Virginia that appeared in national newspapers and magazines and television." He continued: "Resisters smoldered with resentment at what they regarded as biased reporting of racial topics, and at the virtual exclusion of the southern point of view from national organs of opinion."[96] In September 1959, Kilpatrick echoed this sentiment, denouncing "the opaque paper curtain hung by the liberal press between the North and the South."[97] Kilpatrick had led the charge to combat this southern heritage of inferiority by pulling Virginia deep into the southern past. He had expanded southern whiteness to include anti–liberal media, anti–judicial activism, and anti–federal government elements, all of which remain to this day integral aspects of white political conservatism in the South. In the end, Virginia, Alabama, Georgia, Mississippi, South Carolina, and Louisiana all passed some version of a Resolution of Interposition, legally institutionalizing Massive Resistance, which would take several more years for African American leaders and progressive judges to untangle.[98]

On August 28, 1963, Interposition made headlines again, demonstrating its longevity as a concept, as hundreds of thousands of African Americans, liberal whites, and religious leaders marched on Washington to protest American racial inequality and violence. The event held on the National Mall and the ensuing speeches were originally intended to focus solely on economic opportunities for disenfranchised peoples, fulfilling a dream of early civil rights leader A. Phillip Randolph, who had conceived of such a march in the 1940s. Though Martin Luther King Jr.'s speech that day spoke to the "transcendent issue" of race in America, and though it is remembered primarily for the dream he described, King did not mince words for southern resistance leaders determined to maintain Jim Crow at all costs. "I have a dream today," rang King's chorus. "I have a dream," he proclaimed, "that one day, down in Alabama, with its vicious racists, with its governor having his lips dripping with the words of interposition and nullification; one day right there in Alabama, little black girls and black boys will be able to join hands with little white boys and white girls as sisters and brothers." It was a vision against which southern whiteness had been constructed and which was solidified by a collective sense of inferiority that surfaced repeatedly throughout the twentieth century.

THE POLITICS OF INFERIORITY

CONSERVATISM, CREATIONISM, AND

THE CULTURE WARS

The antics of Old Southern politics, although often eerily entertaining, were no laughing matter. They produced, or at least reinforced, a society that was the "sick man" of the country—uneducated, illiterate, unproductive, backward, poor, unhealthy, racist, and sexist—in a word, undemocratic. These conditions were not products of some distinctive, distorted Southern personality or culture; they were shaped and maintained by political institutions and leadership. Southern elites alone benefited from the politics of the Solid South. African Americans by and large were disenfranchised, as were many poor whites and women, and their needs were regularly ignored by Southern state governments. . . . The problems of ordinary Southerners that called desperately for new departures were neglected; the elites' stakes in the status quo were protected. . . . If our current national politics is coming to resemble Old Southern politics, we should take heed and act now.
—Augustus B. Cochran III, *Democracy Heading South: National Politics in the Shadow of Dixie*

This was a flight from reality, a movement not only behind the line but beyond civilization. It was a customary retreat for the South, shielding itself from the unpleasant burdens of its history—defeat, occupation, poverty, illiteracy, disease and alienation from humanity—only to have those burdens grow ever more onerous, inducing a deeper flight in a vicious cycle that strangled both black and white.
—David Goldfield, *Black, White, and Southern: Race Relations and Southern Culture, 1940 to the Present*

The South, then, has been a region with painful memories joined politically with other regions whose history has been until recent years little but an optimistic chronicle of victories and achievements. It has been an impoverished region in a nation of comparative plenty, a nation where the Horatio Alger myth was much recited. And it has been a region often held up to reproof and disdain in a nation prone to celebrate its high moral purpose.
—Kenneth Bailey, *Southern White Protestantism in the Twentieth Century*

Journalist and radio announcer W. E. B. Debnam lashed out at the liberal media and the Supreme Court following the *Brown* verdict handed down in May 1954. "There's a lot of propaganda being dished out in the press and on the radio and on television and from the pulpit," he complained, "to the effect [that] anybody who doesn't subscribe to this new Everybody's-Kissin'-Cousin gospel is an un-Christian bigot and not fit to associate with decent people."[1] Debnam, perhaps more directly than other southern journalists, expressed what he considered to be the majority southern opinion: "We have a tremendous regard for the White Race. We have a tremendous regard for the Negro Race. We believe we can all go to Heaven together . . . but we don't believe the only way to enter the Pearly Gates is sitting in each other's lap."[2] Debnam had become acutely aware, as had others such as James J. Kilpatrick, that the Supreme Court decision had serious implications that extended beyond the physical integration of the races, as dramatic as that action was in and of itself. The intangible, but powerful, consequence of the integration crisis was that it made many southern whites the "other" in American culture, or so it seemed to Debnam. It was not the first time. Indeed, what began as a battle over the institution of human slavery evolved over the course of the twentieth century. By the late 1950s, southern whiteness had developed in opposition to a host of modern American movements, dividing the country along social, cultural, and religious lines, with grave political consequences.

The anti-evolution fundamentalists and Bryanites of the 1920s had demonized modern science and the cult of expertise, while the Agrarians-turned–New Critics of the 1930s and 1940s had vilified industrialism, Communism, and the singular definition of American progress. The segregationists of the 1950s positioned themselves against judicial activism, an expanding federal government, and what was deemed the "liberal" media. The public denunciation of "the Benighted South," was, at least partially if not directly, responsible for the polarization that pitted the Old Confederacy against a growing array of enemies. Reflecting on the question of regional distinctiveness in his essay "Why Was the South a Problem to America," Larry Griffin noted the negative structure that underwrote southern identity: "In the contestation over the meaning of nation and region the South became defined, sometimes quite strongly, sometimes less so, by southerners and nonsoutherners alike 'in opposition' to America and therefore experienced, intimately or vicariously as something profoundly (if only periodically) 'opposite to' the broader culture."[3] With every onslaught of public ridicule, southern whites added a new enemy to their list of attackers, shifting their own ideology and belief system to directly counter any new threatening force. Early publicists for William Jennings Bryan College revealed their opposition to a growing litany of American sins. Again, it is important to reconsider the proclamation of one of their pamphlets: "God's people need to be stirred in activity in combating the Devil and the forces of evil and manifested in modernism, and the associated 'isms.' Since 'Evolution,' as science, falsely so called, is at the root of these false 'isms,' it merits increasing attention."[4] And then it is critical to juxtapose this revealing sentiment against Thomas Waring's noted defense of southern racial practices published in Harper's: "At the outset it is only fair to warn the Northern reader that he may be infuriated long before he reached the end," he warned. "This, I suspect," Waring continued, "is just as inevitable as the outraged feelings of the Southerner when he reads the Northern press with its own interpretation of the American dilemma."[5] This sense of outrage and alienation exacerbated a regional heritage of inferiority and, over time, proved transformative.

The Tennessee fundamentalists retreated into isolation, where they established their own sub-society, marked by the founding of a fundamentalist college that sought not only to control the historical narrative of the Scopes Trial but also to maintain a belief in and an advocacy of biblical literalism and creationism. The Fugitive poets of Vanderbilt University responded by publishing I'll Take My Stand and arguing for the superiority of the rural lifestyle of the Jeffersonian yeoman farmer, while demonizing the modern temper of the machine age and questioning the humanity of industrial progress. And when a second wave of criticism by liberal intellectuals and New South promoters made a defense of these Agrarian values impossible, they redirected their attention to the establishment of the New Criticism and its institutionalization in American university English departments. Finally, the Virginia politicians charged with constructing a plan for integration in the aftermath of Brown changed course in the wake of media coverage of the civil rights movement, invoking James Kilpatrick's Doctrine of Interposition and calling for Massive Resistance, including the closing of several public schools.

Not only did each community under scrutiny follow this pattern, they also shared a critical commonality, the impact of which has shaped not only the modern South but the country as a whole. In each case, communities that perceived themselves to be under siege retreated physically, artistically, or politically and established a new defiant reality. They also grounded this reality in the textual authority of the Bible, the literary work, or the Constitution, respectively. This alternate sense of authority acted as an anchor, to which these white southerners held tightly, in a storm of change and uncertainty. The text functioned as proof, provided validation, encouraged righteousness, and propped up tradition. Consequently, this privileging of a text ensured the longevity of these alternative realities, even after the media spotlight had turned elsewhere.

So southern whiteness turns out to be broader and more enduring than simply a racial label. And despite the passage of time and generational shifts, the persistence of this generally homogeneous constituency and its ability to reinvent and realign itself as political winds change demonstrates clearly how and why inferiority still matters. Though there are abundant examples of this dynamic at play in the southern past, none is more instructive than the political realignment of the region from blue to red, which in many ways turns out to be not only the most important story of the twentieth-century South but also an example of the politics of inferiority. The story is well-trod ground with profound implications, and many scholars have offered their analyses of the catalysts for this change, including race-baiting, Sun Belt suburbanization, and political evangelism. All are major players, supported by an ensemble cast of public criticism, negative identity construction, the overdetermination of southern whiteness, and a southern inferiority complex. When reconsidered in light of this pattern of criticism and reaction and with a broader understanding of the true nature of southern white identity, the dramatic political realignment of the South seems predictable.

■ For Republican strategists in the 1960s, the vulnerability of the white South offered a political opportunity, a chance to compete for votes in the states of the Old Confederacy for the first time since Reconstruction. The civil rights movement was becoming increasingly associated with the Democratic Party— via the legacy of John F. Kennedy and the administration of Lyndon B. Johnson. To oppose the 1964 Civil Rights Amendment was to oppose Johnson; and to oppose Johnson was to align oneself against his other initiatives. Political scientists Thomas Byrne Edsall and Mary D. Edsall surmised that the broader campaign included not only "civil rights for minorities," but also "reproductive and workplace rights for women, constitutional protections for the criminally accused, immigration opportunities for those in developing countries, free-speech rights for pornographers, and the surfacing of highly visible homosexual communities."[6] The Equal Employment Opportunity Commission, Medicaid, welfare, and subsidized public housing required a dramatic tax increase, which also came to be associated with the new liberalism. Many white southerners, in particular, feared that liberal Democrats under Johnson's leadership would "raise taxes from the largely white lower-middle and middle classes in order to direct benefits toward the disproportionately black and Hispanic poor—benefits often seen as wastefully spent."[7] If the threat of their children being educated in a classroom sitting beside an African American child caused a panic in states such as Virginia, then the idea of their tax dollars paying for buses that would physically accomplish integration or fund public housing for African American families was enough to shatter southern loyalty to the Democratic Party.

Republican presidential campaigns, exemplified by those run by Senator Barry Goldwater and Vice President Richard Nixon—as well as the third-party campaign of George Wallace—manipulated the perception held by many white southerners that much more than Jim Crow was being reconstructed. The Republican Party of Lincoln defined the realignment of its own party and that of its opposition "by pitting taxpayers against tax recipients, advocates of meritocracy against proponents of special preference, the private sector against the public sector, those in the labor force against the jobless, and those who bear many of the costs of federal intervention against those whose struggle for equality has been advanced by interventionist government policies."[8] Not only were white southerners now battling a sense of inferiority from being constantly demonized for the ongoing support of segregation, they were now dealing with what many considered to be the superior treatment of minorities. Republican strategists tapped into this resurgent notion of inferiority in a series of conscious political acts that, over the course of several elections, formed a strategy[9]—Operation Dixie, or as it was later called, the Southern Strategy.

In 1961, Arizona Republican senator Barry Goldwater released "A Statement of Proposed Republican Principles, Programs, and Objectives," which, in a sense, initiated the Southern Strategy of the Grand Old Party. Goldwater's manifesto invited his "forgotten" countrymen, "who quietly go about the business of paying and praying, working and saving,"[10] to speak loudly in one voice for conservative, traditional American values. In comments such as these, Goldwater used racial fears to attract white southern voters, and he appealed to moderates who were feeling increasingly alienated from a changing national culture. Goldwater further recognized that in order to take advantage of the growing anxiety and anger regarding the tide of "liberal" legislation and court rulings, he would have to appeal to the "traditional virtues of individual enterprise and self-reliance."[11] For white southerners, the phrase "traditional virtues" was, by the 1960s, a loaded concept. The traditional belief in white superiority remained strong, but a commitment to religious fundamentalism, home rule, and agrarian authenticity, as well as to the sentiments of anticommunism, anti-intellectualism, and antiscience, became key as well. A virtuous white southerner shared these values, many of which seemed at odds with the national vision of American progress.

The Republican National Committee launched Operation Dixie, a plan to attract southern voters to the GOP to fill the void of a dwindling moderate wing of the party and to take advantage of an imploding opposition party. Alienated southern whites, grappling with a heightened sense of inferiority and a rapidly changing cultural landscape, were ripe game, and the Arizona senator had just the right ammunition. Goldwater's rhetorical strategy—the groundwork for which was outlined in a book ghostwritten under his name, The Conscience of a Conservative (1960)[12]—included four primary components, most notably his call for small government, code for his opposition to federal intervention. Additionally, he waved the banners of fiscal conservatism and anticommunism. The latter played especially well below the Mason-Dixon Line, where many white southerners, including the Agrarians, had railed against Communism in an effort to gain national acceptance and to prove their patriotism. Moreover, Communists, as demonstrated poignantly in Mississippi senator James Eastland's speech following the Brown decision, were perceived to be working in conjunction with the NAACP. Finally, Goldwater took a stand against what he labeled the "permissiveness" of American society. This "vague" enemy could be interpreted as America's softness on crime, the loosening of sexual norms, shifting gender expectations, or even the growing popularity of ethnic art and culture, all developing during the turbulent 1960s.[13] This message was well received by southern audiences, who at that point had experienced dramatic examples of racial confrontation and who sensed that the wave of change accompanying the civil rights movement was yet to crest, looming larger and encompassing more facets of southern life with each passing year.

Goldwater, who decided that "we're not going to get the Negro vote as a bloc in 1964 and 1968, so we ought to go hunting where the ducks are,"[14] succeeded in capturing five southern states, including 87 percent of the ballots cast in Mississippi. And Operation Dixie increased Republican Party membership in the states of the Old Confederacy. By 1968, southern delegates to the Republican National Convention totaled 356, over half the number needed for a candidate to secure the nomination.[15] Moreover, Goldwater's efforts, though they failed to halt Johnson's reelection to the White House, inspired influential young conservatives, including future president George H. W. Bush. As historian Dan Carter has noted, Bush during his early campaign years "labeled the Civil Rights Act an abuse of federal power, one that 'trampled on the Constitution.'"[16] He also exploited the alienated status of white southerners and the fear that their jobs would be given to minorities; this threat of displacement, of an inverted social hierarchy, was reminiscent of Radical Reconstruction, which Bush was now pinning on the Democratic Party. On the stump in Grand Prairie, Texas, he informed hundreds of white workers at the Ling-Temco-Voight Corporation that "the new civil rights act was passed to protect 14 percent of the people. I am also worried about the other 86 percent."[17] Portraying white southerners as oppressed victims activated a collective response that would eventually help the young Bush get elected to the U.S. House of Representatives from the Texas Seventh District.

Despite his loss in the general election, Goldwater's sense of what Stephen Skowronek has called "political time" proved prophetic.[18] In 1963, when Lyndon Johnson succeeded John Kennedy following the assassination in Dallas, 31 percent of surveyed Americans believed that the country was attempting to integrate "too fast." Only five years later, this fear of the pace of "all deliberate speed" had increased to include more than half of American voters. And this anxiety, though perhaps more pronounced, or at least more reported, was not regionally limited. The divisive nature of this oppositional structure of white southern identity helped to establish an "us versus them" political culture. The longer the list of "threats," the broader the appeal became to audiences outside of the South. Alabama governor George Wallace made national headlines in January 1963 when he uttered this famous sentence of Massive Resistance in his inaugural speech: "In the name of the greatest people that have ever trod this earth, I draw the line in the dust and toss the gauntlet before the feet of tyranny, and I say segregation now, segregation tomorrow, segregation forever."[19]

Wallace's primary persuasive technique was to convince his audience that it was under siege, persecuted by an enemy hell-bent on destroying its way of life, and that there was no middle ground. Perceiving themselves to be ostracized and demonized by the "liberal media," white southerners were energized by the governor's message. He cautioned the crowd that "communism was winning the world" and blamed liberals, who supported a "false doctrine of communistic amalgamation." He used international atrocities as apocalyptic warnings. The "national racism of Hitler's Germany persecuted a national minority to the whim of a national majority," argued Wallace, although the "international racism of the liberals seek to persecute the international white minority to the whim of the international colored majority."[20] In Wallace's analogy, whites would suffer the fate of Jews, exploited and destroyed by the Nazi-like coalition of liberals and African Americans. Wallace also resurrected the oldest terror scenario of the southern white memory—the threat of black violence reminiscent of the slave revolt. Pointing to the recent black-on-white violence that had erupted in the Belgian Congo, Wallace warned his audience that the white survivors were not allowed to "present their case to a 'war crimes commission.' And neither, he added, could the citizens of Oxford, Mississippi."[21]

Only six months later, Wallace further sharpened his national reputation when he stood in the doorway of the University of Alabama to block the admission of two African American students, Vivian Malone and James Hood, and denounced defiantly the "illegal usurpation of power by the Central Government."[22] Only a few short hours later, a federalized Alabama National Guard enforced the enrollment, but the governor had cemented his resistance with the whole country as witness and jury. Though many outside of the South would have found him guilty of crimes against humanity, others lauded his persistence and his dedication to states' rights. Wallace, like Goldwater, believed in a silent white conservative majority, bunkered somewhere beneath the dominant liberal denouncement of southern racial practices. He railed against the "paper curtain" that kept the southern conservative voice isolated and demonized the American South. Moreover, he thought the Democratic Party had moved too far to the left, and that he too could go "hunting where the ducks were" and land himself a consolidated regional and budding national following among angry and alienated white Democrats. Wallace entered the 1964 presidential race in a bid for the Democratic nomination, and he won nearly one-third of the vote in the Wisconsin, Maryland, and Indiana primaries.[23]

In 1968, Wallace entered the presidential race as an Independent and further honed his method of positive polarization. He was constantly drawing lines between what kind of person would support him and what kind of person would not, invoking the familiar oppositional and negative construction of white southern identity. At speeches when he was heckled by what he called "long-haired hippie agitators," he goaded them into continuing their attacks. He claimed that every time they ridiculed him, they secured him a million votes. When Wallace was ridiculed, he was automatically aligned with this silent majority; positive polarization defined who Wallace was by exposing who he was not. At its core, the method required a black-and-white, definitive vision for the future of the country, which is exactly what the culture of inferiority has created. For example, Wallace had once insisted that, in terms of segregation, "you're either for it, or you're against. There's not any middle ground as I know of."[24] Just as he had drawn a line in the dust on the issue of integration, he drew a line between himself and a host of other groups in a manner in which no one could confuse who was friend and who was enemy. In his stump speeches, he lashed out at "intellectual snobs who don't know the difference between smut and great literature," at "hypocrites who send your kid half way across town while they have their chauffeur drop their children off at private schools," and at "briefcase-carrying bureaucrats."[25]

And the Alabama governor had yet another weapon in his arsenal, an insight into the psychology of southern whites. Wallace knew that his fellow southerners struggled to overcome a sense of inferiority, a heritage passed from generation to generation that resurfaced when public criticism intensified. He turned the criticism on the critics, condemning journalists and "pseudo intellectuals" who were constantly "looking down their noses at the average man on the street, the glassworker, the steelworker, the autoworker and the textile worker, the farmer, the policeman, the beautician and the barber and the little businessman."[26] Wallace resurrected the old enemies—the liberal media and the "expert," first established during the Scopes Trial—and revealed their common target to be the white southern worker. The Alabama governor returned to the spirit of the underdog made famous by William Jennings Bryan and regenerated by the Nashville Agrarians. According to Carter, he "skillfully pulled from the American political fabric the strands of xenophobia, racism, and a 'plain folk' cultural outlook that equated the cosmopolitan currents of the 1960s with moral corruption and weakness."[27] In turn, he captured his "listeners' sense of betrayal—of victimhood,"[28] the white, southern burden of inferiority. "No Wallace speech," insisted Carter, "was complete without the defensive claim that he and his supporters were 'just as cultured and refined' as those 'New York reporters.'"[29] The "victims" carried Wallace and his American Independent Party to general election victories in Arkansas, Louisiana, Mississippi, Alabama, and Georgia.

In a similar vein, and perhaps more effective, Richard Nixon's southern strategy capitalized on white resentment of the civil rights legislation that many believed had gone too far, particularly as early elements of affirmative action surfaced. He recognized that many white southerners needed a moral justification for supporting candidates that would stem the tide of civil rights changes and maintain the long list of white southern values established over the course of the twentieth century. It helped Nixon that personally he could empathize with this southern sense of inferiority, as he struggled himself to conquer feelings of paranoia and poor self-worth. "Although as a Republican he represented the party of privilege," noted Richard Mason, "he harbored a sense of identity with ordinary Americans. The identity was absolutely at odds with the dominant image of his party and represented an asset in seeking to improve its fortunes."[30] George Wallace had proved too extreme for those outside of the Deep South, but his ability to transform the terms of the debate had garnered him significant support.[31] Likewise, Nixon made broad, general statements regarding his support for equality for African Americans, while simultaneously coming out against big government. The message to the South was that Nixon, if elected, would not use the federal government as a means to enforce social change. Vice presidential candidate Spiro Agnew was heavily involved in pitting white southerners against African Americans, driving conservatives to the polls. In their 1992 work, *The Vital South: How Presidents Are Elected*, Earl and Merle Black quote an unnamed Republican strategist who detailed the plan:

> You start off in 1954 by saying "Nigger, Nigger, Nigger." By 1968 you can't say "Nigger"—that hurts you. Backfires. So you say stuff like forced busing, states' rights, and all that stuff. You're getting so abstract [that] you're talking about cutting taxes, and all these things you're talking about are totally economic things and a by-product of them is that blacks get hurt worse than whites. And subconsciously maybe that is part of it. I'm not saying that. But I'm saying that if it is getting that abstract, and that coded, that we are doing away with the racial problem one way or the other. You follow me—because obviously sitting around saying, "We want to cut this," is much more abstract than the busing thing and a hell of a lot more abstract than "Nigger, Nigger."[32]

Nixon also found a way, beyond the use of coded language, to appeal to white southern voters concerned with the enforcement of Johnson's legislative agenda. Channeling the language made popular by Kilpatrick, Nixon promised southern delegates to the 1968 Republican National Convention, with whom he met in a closed session, that he would appoint conservative justices. "I want men on the Supreme Court who are strict constitutionalists," promised Nixon, "men that interpret the law and don't try to make the law."[33]

He nominated two southern judges, Clement Haynsworth and Harrold Carswell, to the Supreme Court, and "when the Senate rejected both of them, Nixon angrily and hypocritically accused the Senate of bias and discrimination against the South."[34] According to Murphy and Gulliver, Nixon's decision to play up the fears and insecurities of many white southerners "was a cynical strategy." His administration publicly denied that any such strategy existed. George McGovern, Democratic presidential nominee in 1972, reflected on the nature and existence of the Republican efforts in the South. "What is the Southern Strategy," he asked, answering: "It is this. It says to the South: Let the poor stay poor, let your economy trail the nation, forget about decent homes and medical care for all your people, choose officials who will oppose every effort to benefit the many and the expense of the few—and in return, we will try to overlook the rights of the black man, appoint a few southerners to high office, and lift your spirits by attacking the 'eastern establishment' whose bank accounts we are filling up with your labor and your industry. It is a clever strategy."[35] In 1969, GOP strategist Kevin Phillips prophesied that the new conservative coalition, including the South, would dominate American politics for decades to come.[36] His book, *The Emerging Republican Majority*, encouraged Republicans to engage Wallace supporters in the future.[37] In 1968, Richard Nixon won the presidency with the support of the Southeast, winning Florida, South Carolina, and North Carolina, as well as with the support of southern peripheral states such as Tennessee, Kentucky, Missouri, Virginia, and West Virginia. If this block could be added to Wallace's victories in the Deep South, a conservative stronghold would result that could stem the tide of change in bifurcated America.

In their documentary, *Settin' the Woods on Fire*, Steve Fayer, Daniel Mccabe, and Paul Stekler include a poignant interview with Tom Turnipseed, executive director of Wallace's 1968 campaign. In his commentary on Wallace's popularity, Turnipseed described the power of class consciousness to splinter the Democratic Party in the South. He recounted one of Wallace's stump speeches:

> He'd [Wallace] say "You ever heard of Mountain Brook, Alabama?" And they'd say, "No, Geor—Governor, tell us about it." And he said, "Well, Mountain Brook is an all lily-white town. It's over across the mountain from Birmingham. You know, Birmingham, as you know, has got all the steel mills and all. And, and you got the blue collar working class people there and, of course, they're faced with their schools, their kids being bussed from here there to yonder to kingdom come to integrate the schools." And he says, "But you take the fellows, that, that—the executives of the mills, the big shots of the mills, they get into air-conditioned Cadillacs and their chauffeurs drive on back up to Mountain Brook where the average home is worth about $300,000 a piece and some of the homes have 15 bathrooms in 'em." [laughs] And he says, "And they drive up there and they sit up there at the Country Club, the Mountain Brook Country Club, and they got these little martinis and they hold their little fingers up in the air, and they sip on the martinis. And you know what they say? 'Oh, we've got to be progressive, we've got to have some of this integration, says, it's good.' You know, to bus your children from here to there to kingdom come and back again and guess where their children go to school? To all-white private schools up in Mountain Brook."[38]

In one story, Wallace paints pro–civil rights Democrats as elitist, portraying himself as the opposite, a man of the people. But the technique had broader implications because it also described a southern upper middle class where racial integration was avoided and white privilege was maintained at all costs. The draw was powerful, and so the Silent Majority moved to the suburbs, as Matthew Lassiter has shown.[39] Private schools and gated communities accompanied the rise of the "superior" Sun Belt South, and a new southern middle class sought recognition, challenging the elite control that had dominated regional politics. By tapping into the cultural sense of inferiority shared by many white southerners in the 1960s, the GOP was able to convince southern voters, as

Joseph Aistrup has noted, "to identify psychologically as Republicans."[40] Only by appealing to an emotional aspect of white southern identity could Republicans break the Democratic label that, though twisted and stretched over time, had blanketed the region for nearly 150 years.

The allegiance only strengthened during what Darren Dochuk has called the second Southern Strategy,[41] when Republicans, most notably Ronald Reagan, added a new layer to the Red South by appealing to fundamentalists and evangelical Christians once driven underground in the 1920s and 1930s. In this instance too, negative identity construction appealed to many white southerners, who were comfortable defining themselves against an outside threat. In 1983, Reagan addressed the National Association of Evangelicals, whom he considered the "ground troops for his revolution."[42] Specifically, he believed that the evangelical faith in the institutions of the church and the family would "put us in opposition to, or at least out of step with a prevailing attitude of many who have turned to a modern day secularism, discarding the tried and time-tested values upon which our civilization is based."[43] The appeal to an authentic America included support for traditional gender roles, which was not limited to specific definitions of marriage. In the decade following the 1973 *Roe v. Wade* decision, "more and more of the Christian conservatives, including a lot of homemakers and noncollege-educated women, stepped forward to defend marriage, their views on motherhood and the special world of the family."[44] Reagan recognized that this religious subculture of modern Americans was highly organized, and he took his message directly to them. Using the technique of positive polarization, Reagan was able to inject faith into the Republican Party while insisting on its absence in the liberal demagoguery of the Democratic Party.

Reagan, to the delight of Christian evangelicals, who had begun their fight over the public education curriculum, supported prayer in American public schools. William Jennings Bryan would have surely approved. The new leaders of the fundamentalist cause such as Pat Robertson and Jerry Falwell also saw the opening of politics to faith as a potential opportunity to advocate once again for causes long since lost. William Jennings Bryan College had never wavered from its support of creationism as the counter to what it believed to be the unproven theory of evolution. The Monkey Trial never really ended, as H. L. Mencken would have liked his readers to believe; it just took a vacation from the public consciousness. In truth, Arkansas had followed Tennessee's lead only three short years after the circus in Rhea County. But in the 1960s, a young biology teacher from Little Rock named Susan Epperson challenged the statute, believing the time was finally right for the Supreme Court to rule in favor of science. Creationists, connected through a network of religious colleges, much like the memorial university established in Dayton, Tennessee, feared the liberal Court would strike down one of the only remaining bans on the teaching of evolution.

In 1966, California superintendent of public education Max L. Lafferty encouraged two Baptist mothers, Nell J. Seagraves and Jean E. Sumrall, to petition the California State Board of Education to require equal time for the teaching of creationism. Lafferty interpreted the newly passed 1964 Civil Rights Act to be a measure of protection for religious communities that believed that the science of evolution was being privileged over what was being called the science of creationism. Fundamentalists were right to be concerned; the Supreme Court did overturn the Arkansas ban on the teaching of evolution in its ruling in *Epperson v. Arkansas* in 1968. And in California, Seagraves and Sumrall did not succeed in injecting creationism into the biology textbooks, but they did succeed in portraying evolution as one theory, as opposed to a science.[45] The contemporary advocacy of Intelligent Design results directly from the challenge in California and has now swept through the evangelical and religious homeschool movement. Embarrassed by Clarence Darrow and the media ridicule that accompanied the Scopes Trial, fundamentalists licked their wounds and collected their thoughts in like-minded company. And, in turn, they lived to fight once again nearly eighty years later. An issue that was settled for Europeans and many scientists in 1859 with the publication of Charles Darwin's *Origin of Species* has not been put to rest in America. In the 2008 and 2012 Republican primary campaigns, several key contenders, such as former Arkansas governor Mike Huckabee, Texas governor Rick Perry, and former U.S. senator Rick Santorum, proclaimed proudly in numerous televised debates that they did not believe in evolution.

These candidates, as well as President George W. Bush, among others, centered their campaign on the issue of American values. This too became a defining feature of the Republican strategy, one that evolved from Operation Dixie in 1964 and helped ensure the support of traditional and religious white southerners. The trend began with George Wallace, who constantly ridiculed the values system of the 1960s counterculture, a culture that many believed reflected a nationwide societal permissiveness.[46] The Alabama governor and presidential contender believed there had been a "fundamental decline in the traditional cultural compass of God, family, and country, a decline reflected in rising crime rates, the legalization of abortion, the rise in out-of-wedlock pregnancies, the increase in the divorce rate, and the proliferation of 'obscene' literature and films."[47] These southern values voters, in truth, were New Critics of postmodern

America. They wanted a return to tradition, a canon of social norms that was definable, recognizable, fixed, permanent, and superior.

■ The Tennessee fundamentalists did not vanish in the wake of the Scopes Trial or the untimely death of leader William Jennings Bryan; rather, they withdrew from the society that had ridiculed them with such vigor. Their energy built a fundamentalist college that still attempts to control this historical narrative of the "Monkey" debate. James Kilpatrick waved the banner of Interposition, and Virginia politicians followed his lead, questioning the very nature of federalism and equality. And the Fugitive poets of Vanderbilt University, who were initially determined to flee the traditions of the Old South, became advocates for the superiority of the rural lifestyle of the Jeffersonian yeoman farmer, demonizing the modern temper of the machine age and questioning the humanity of industrial progress. And when relentless criticism made their Agrarian values indefensible, they did not abandon their belief in the South. Rather, they transformed their ideals into the literary aesthetics of the New Criticism. All were influenced by a heritage of inferiority passed from one generation to the next by a constant public airing of southern ills and the subsequent reawakening, again and again, of the white, conservative, southern awareness of their national estrangement. And whether biblical, literary, or constitutional, their canons became their armor.

The abstract idea of canonicity is intrinsically related to the notion of homogeneity—a safe and clear sameness that ensures a status quo and insulates a community from criticism. The Fugitives-turned-Agrarians-turned–New Critics were values voters in the world of art and literature. Those that challenged the New Criticism under the banners of deconstructionism, poststructuralism, feminist criticism, black aesthetics, cultural criticism, and even transnationalism were activists promoting pluralism and diversity, similar to those who questioned biblical literalism or argued for a judicial activist interpretation of the Fourteenth Amendment. Even a diverse canon is in and of itself, as Stanley Fish has asserted, a series of political decisions;[48] and it is also a source of control. The fundamentalists wanted command of the education of their children; the New Critics fought for the aesthetic power of university English departments; and the Virginia Defenders of State Sovereignty and Liberty sought to dictate who would and who would not sit next to their children in the classroom. Each battle was waged in an effort to combat a cultural inferiority complex and to control, in effect, the hearts and minds of the next generation.

Over the past several decades, southern historians and journalists such as John Egerton and Peter Applebome have argued that southern distinctiveness has either vanished or enveloped the rest of the country.[49] Clearly, the explosion of technology and the global community that has resulted makes regional boundaries superficial, and the advances made in all of the civil rights movements of the late twentieth century have established a more politically correct public culture. But if whiteness in the South had only been about racial difference and superiority, then this post–civil rights environment should have, at the very least, diminished the power and cohesiveness of the label. However, because southern whiteness became a multilayered and overdetermined identity over the course of the twentieth century, it remains pervasive today. The South is red for the foreseeable future. And new groups, such as the Tea Party protesters, the Birthers who challenge the constitutionality of Barack Obama's presidency, and the anti-environmentalists, among others, are not new, but are old spirits that will not die. Such communities predominate in the South and have been maintained, at least in part, by the blistering media spotlight that resuscitates the unforgivable mistakes of the southern past. And these resistant and radical communities must be understood in all their complexity—their intentions, motivations, and compensations—rather than being solely denounced and dismissed. Their existence and longevity sheds essential light on not only the deep and enduring attachment to southern whiteness, but also the divisive religious, political, and cultural debates that are the inheritance of all Americans.

NOTES

Abbreviations Used in the Notes

APP   Austin Peay Papers (Governor), Tennessee State Library and Archives, Nashville, Tennessee

DDP   Donald Davidson Papers, Jean and Alexander Heard Library, Special Collections, Vanderbilt University, Nashville, Tennessee

FBC   FitzGerald Bemiss Collection, Virginia Historical Collection, Richmond, Virginia

JJKP   James Jackson Kilpatrick Papers, Albert and Shirley Small Special Collections, Mary and David Harrison Institute for American History, Literature, and Culture, University of Virginia, Charlottesville, Virginia

RVHD   Records of the Virginia House of Delegates, Office of the Clerk, 1956 Constitutional Convention, State Library and Archives, Library of Virginia, Richmond, Virginia

WJBCP   William Jennings Bryan College Papers, Office of Richard M. Cornelius, Scopes Archivist and Professor Emeritus of English, William Jennings Bryan College, Dayton, Tennessee. This unarchived material was accessed and copied via permission from Professor Richard M. Cornelius in January 2006. Author and publisher have retained copies.

Introduction

1. Eleanor Roosevelt, quoted in Debnam, *Weep No More*, 10.
2. Leggett, "Between You and Me."
3. Debnam, *Weep No More*, 19.
4. Ibid., 9.
5. Ibid., 4.
6. Hobson, *Tell about the South*, 11–12.
7. Green, "Resurgent Southern Sectionalism," 225.
8. Gerald W. Johnson, "Critical Attitudes North and South," 575.
9. Tindall, "Benighted South," 281.
10. Anderson, *Eyes Off the Prize*, 74–77; Dudziak, *Cold War Civil Rights*, 43–44; Woodward, *Strange Career of Jim Crow*, 132–33.
11. Odum, *Southern Regions of the United States*, 13–15.
12. Adler, *Superiority and Social Interest*, 54.
13. Orgler, *Alfred Adler*, 64.
14. Woodcock, Foreword to *Alfred Adler*, 6.
15. Stepansky, *In Freud's Shadow*, 242.

16. Lundin, *Alfred Adler's Basic Concepts and Implications*, 147.

17. Grey, *Alfred Adler*, 55.

18. Rattner, *Alfred Adler*, 37.

19. Frank, *Routledge Historical Atlas*, 128, 131.

20. John Shelton Reed, *Enduring South*, 67.

21. Carson and Holloran, *Knock at Midnight*, 167.

22. Way, "Psychology of Prejudice," 249.

23. Guindon, Green, and Hanna, "Intolerance and Psychopathology," 167.

24. Powers, "Myth and Memory," 271.

25. Ibid., 274.

26. Ibid., 277.

27. Other studies, such as Dhirendra Narain's "Indian National Character in the Twentieth Century," which appeared in *Annals of the American Academy of Political and Social Science* in 1967, and more recently in Yan Wang's article, "Value Changes in an Era of Social Transformations: College-Educated Chinese Youth, published in *Educational Studies* in 2006, and Joanna Kurczewska's piece, "What Is Likely to Happen to Polish Collective Consciousness after Accession to the European Union," from a 2003 issue of the *Polish Sociological Review*, continue to examine the idea of a collective cultural inferiority complex.

28. Brachfield, *Inferiority Feelings in the Individual and the Group*, 269.

29. Ibid., 270.

30. Ibid.

31. Ibid., 271.

32. Orgler, *Alfred Adler*, 81.

33. Whitehead, "Man to Man Violence," 416.

34. Killian, *White Southerners*, 26.

35. Ibid., 111.

36. Ibid., 112.

37. Cobb, *Redefining Southern Culture*, 44.

38. Kirby, *Media-Made Dixie*, 83.

39. John Shelton Reed, *Enduring South*, 89.

40. Cobb, *Redefining Southern Culture*, 4.

41. Woodward, *Strange Career of Jim Crow*, 119.

42. Howard Odum, quoted in ibid.

43. Wilson, *Baptized in Blood*, 1.

44. Connelly and Bellows, *God and General Longstreet*, 22.

45. Wilson, *Baptized in Blood*, 7.

46. Calhoun, "Speech on the Reception of Abolition Petitions," 12.

47. Woodward, *Burden of Southern History*, 66.

48. Ibid., 67.

49. Ibid., 110.

50. Grantham, *The South in Modern America*, 333.

51. Ibid., xv–xvi.

52. Silber, *Romance of Reunion*, 94.

53. Kirby, *Media-Made Dixie*, 1.

54. Woodward, *Burden of Southern History*, 2.

55. Woodward, *Strange Career of Jim Crow*, 72.

56. Grantham, *The South in Modern America*, 39.

57. Ibid.

58. Woodward, *Burden of Southern History*, xii.

59. Link, *Road to the White House*, 2.

60. Quoted in Grantham, *The South in Modern America*, 63.

61. Quoted in Wilson, *Baptized in Blood*, 180.

62. "Lynchings: By Year and Race," www.law.umkc.edu/faculty/projects/ftrials/shipp/lynchingyear.html.

63. Tindall, *Ethnic Southerners*, 53.

64. Ibid., 50.

65. Ibid., 49.

66. Mencken, "Sahara of the Bozart," 229.

67. Debnam, *Weep No More*, 29.

68. Ibid.

69. Mencken, quoted in Cooper and Terrill, *American South*, 664.

70. Roosevelt, "My Day."

71. Duck, *Nation's Region*, 3.

72. Woodward, *Burden of Southern History*, 229.

73. Taylor, *Cavalier and Yankee*, 17–18.

74. Cash, *Mind of the South*, 68.

75. Ruffin, "Political Economy of Slavery," 76.

76. Fitzhugh, "Sociology for the South," 69.

77. Degler, *Place over Time*, 60.

78. Graves, *Fighting South*, 15.

79. Warren, *Legacy of the Civil War*, 54.

80. Hackney, "Southern Violence," 924.

81. Ibid.

82. Ibid., 924–25.

83. Nakayama and Martin, *Whiteness*, vii.

84. Supriya, "White Difference," 131.

85. Du Bois, *Black Reconstruction in America*.

86. Roediger, *Wages of Whiteness*, 8.

87. Nakayama and Martin, *Whiteness*, vii.

88. Fanon, *Black Skin, White Masks*; Morrison, *Playing in the Dark*.

89. Freud, *Interpretation of Dreams*.

90. Althusser and Balibar, *Reading Capital*, 315.

91. Richards, *Philosophy of Rhetoric*.

92. Watts, *White Masculinity*; Friend and Glover, *Southern Manhood: Perspectives on Masculinity in the Old South*; Friend, *Southern Manhood: Perspectives on Manhood in the South*.

93. Watts, *White Masculinity*, 3.

94. Ibid., 8.

95. Crespino, *In Search of Another Country*, 9.

96. Sokol, *There Goes My Everything*, 10.

97. Ibid., 9.

98. John Shelton Reed, *Enduring South*, 89.

99. Howard Zinn, quoted in Cobb, *Redefining Southern Culture*, 73.

100. Lasch, *Culture of Narcissism*, xviii.

Part I

1. Kemper, "Evolution on Trial," 52.

2. Tindall, *Emergence of the New South*, 205.

3. H. L. Mencken, quoted in Cooper and Terrill, *American South*, 664.

4. Ibid.

5. Karen Armstrong, quoted in Valpy, "God Is Big These Days," www.shambhalasun
.com.

6. Marsden, *Fundamentalism and American Culture*, 184–85.

7. Larson, *Summer for the Gods*, 233.

8. William Jennings Bryan, quoted in Coletta, *Political Puritan*, 280.

9. Hofstadter, *Anti-intellectualism in American Life*, 130.

10. H. J. Shelton to Jason Blankenship. This letter was provided to the author by the recipient, Jason Blankenship, who wrote to Mr. Shelton for a class project as a student in the Melbourne Public Schools, in Melbourne, Arkansas.

Chapter 1

1. Levine, *Defender of the Faith*, 271.

2. Kazin, *Populist Persuasion*, 43–44.

3. William Jennings Bryan, quoted in Reid, *Three Centuries of American Rhetorical Discourse*, 602–3.

4. Josephson, "Bryan Campaign," 34.

5. Quoted in ibid., 40–41.

6. Ibid., 41.

7. Porter and Johnson, *National Party Platforms*, 104.

8. Glad, *McKinley, Bryan, and the People*, 169.

9. Burnham, *Critical Elections*, 1, 6–10. Burnham defines "critical realigning elections" as those that exhibit four key characteristics. First, critical realignment occurs when there are "short-lived but very intense disruptions of traditional patterns of voting behavior." Second, critical realigning elections are unusually intense election cycles, and this intensity is associated with (a) the party nomination and platform writing process and (b) a heightened polarization of ideology between major parties. Third, critical realignment does not occur randomly (it can be anticipated). And, finally, critical realignment, though most easily viewed through party outcomes, is initiated by constituents. Burnham argues that the national elections of 1800, 1828, 1860, 1896, and 1932 exhibit these elements of critical realignment.

10. Woodrow Wilson, quoted in Kazin, *A Godly Hero*, 238.

11. Ibid., 285.

12. Ginger, *William Jennings Bryan*, 218; excerpted from *Official Report of the Proceedings of the Democratic National Convention*, 303–9.

13. Ginger, *William Jennings Bryan*, 219–21.

14. Stephen Wise, quoted in Willard H. Smith, *Social and Religious Thought of William Jennings Bryan*, 50.

15. Coletta, *Political Puritan*, 275.

16. Quoted in Willard H. Smith, *Social and Religious Thought of William Jennings Bryan*, 49.

17. Ibid., 52.

18. Ibid., 53.

19. William Jennings Bryan, quoted in ibid.

20. "They Sang 'Dixie's Land.'" The *New York Times* covered the New York Southern Society's annual "Dixie Dance," which was attended in some years by over 1,000 members. The 1893 ball was described in the paper as the seventy-second annual event, thus dating the founding of the organization to as early as 1821. The membership of the organization as reported in 1893 was 1,550, which the president of the society claimed made it the largest club in New York. Mrs. Jefferson Davis is known to have attended the 1893 dinner, where she was cheered upon arrival.

21. Bryan, "Bryan Says North Would Act as South on Negro Question."

22. Kazin, *A Godly Hero*, 278.

23. Bryan, "Bryan Says North Would Act as South on Negro Question."

24. Ibid.

25. Ibid.

26. William Jennings Bryan, quoted in Willard H. Smith, *Social and Religious Thought of William Jennings Bryan*, 61–62.

27. William Jennings Bryan, quoted in Russell, "William Jennings Bryan," 103.

28. Willard H. Smith, *Social and Religious Thought of William Jennings Bryan*, 54.

29. Modisett, *Credo of the Commoner*, 72–73.

30. Bryan, "Bryan Says North Would Act as South on Negro Question."

31. Willard H. Smith, *Social and Religious Thought of William Jennings Bryan*, 63.

32. Ashby, *William Jennings Bryan*, 189.

33. Ginger, *Six Days or Forever*, 32–33.

34. Ashby, *William Jennings Bryan*, 189.

35. Ginger, *Six Days or Forever*, 33.

36. Lisby and Harris, "Georgia Reporters at the Scopes Trial," 786.

37. Ginger, *Six Days or Forever*, 33.

38. Willard H. Smith, *Social and Religious Thought of William Jennings Bryan*, 193.

39. Ibid.

40. Larson, *Trial and Error*, 46.

41. Bailey, *Southern White Protestantism*, 46–52; Gatewood, *Controversy in the Twenties*, 8–13; Larson, *Trial and Error*, 44–45.

42. Coletta, *Political Puritan*, 204.

43. Thomas Ivey, quoted in Israel, *Before Scopes*, 136.

44. Ibid.

45. Smout, *The Creation/Evolution Controversy*, 99.

46. Moran, *The Scopes Trial*, 67.

47. Cash, *Mind of the South*, 339.

48. Moran, "Reading Race into the Scopes Trial," 899. Moran also suggests that the perceived racial implications of evolution were influenced by the rise of antimiscegenation legislation that was also occurring in the 1920s.

49. Gatewood, *Preachers, Pedagogues, and Politicians*, 154.

50. Hofstadter, *Anti-intellectualism in American Life*, 127.

51. Levine, *Defender of the Faith*, 271.

52. Coletta, *Political Puritan*, 209.

53. Bryan, "A Very Present Help in Trouble," 8–9.

54. Hibben, *Peerless Leader*, 370. This section of the book is attributed to C. Hartley Grattan, who completed the biography after the death of Paxton Hibben.

55. Dewey, "American Intellectual Frontier," 303–5.

56. Coletta, *Political Puritan*, 218.

57. Ibid., 218–19.

58. Darrow, "Darrow Asks W. J. Bryan to Answer These," 1.

59. Bernabo, "Scopes Myth," 158.

60. William Jennings Bryan, quoted in ibid., 118.

61. Clarence Darrow, quoted in ibid., 115.

62. Larson, "Scopes Trial in History and Legend," 252–53.

63. Ibid., 253.

64. "Dayton: Good Advertising for the South," 353.

65. Higdon, *Leopold and Loeb*, 19–20.

66. Nietzsche, *Portable Nietzsche*, 486–87, 303.

67. Willard H. Smith, *Social and Religious Thought of William Jennings Bryan*, 191.

68. Ibid.

69. Koenig, *Bryan*, 645.

70. Allen, *Bryan and Darrow at Dayton*, 187.

71. Larson, "Scopes Trial in History and Legend," 253.

72. Tierney, *Darrow*, 356.

73. Ibid.

74. Darrow, *Story of My Life*, 150. Darrow sometimes used this sarcastic nickname for Bryan. The phrase also references Bryan's first public lecture by the same name, "The Prince of Peace" (1904), which contains his initial warnings against the dangers of evolution and social Darwinism.

75. Ibid., 250.

76. Tierney, *Darrow*, 357.

77. Mencken, *Gist of Nietzsche*; Mencken, *George Bernard Shaw*.

78. H. L. Mencken, quoted in Fecher, *Mencken*, 105.

79. Mencken, "Invitation to the Dance," 278–79.

80. Teachout, *Skeptic*, 213.

Chapter 2

1. Ginger, *Six Days or Forever*, 191.

2. Owen, "Dayton's Remote Mountaineers Fear Science," 23.

3. "Europe Is Amazed by the Scopes Case," 1.

4. Lloyd George, quoted in ibid.

5. Sir Arthur Shipley, quoted in ibid.

6. "Tennessee vs. Civilization," 220.

7. Israel, *Before Scopes*, 145–46.

8. Bailey, "Enactment of Tennessee's Anti-Evolution Law," 477.

9. Coletta, *Political Puritan*, 200.

10. Lippmann, *American Inquisitors*, 84.

11. Coate, "Evolution Disproved," 90.

12. Martin, *Hell and the High Schools*, 8.

13. Israel, *Before Scopes*, 160–61.

14. Rosser, *Crusading Commoner*, 310.

15. De Camp, *Great Monkey Trial*, 4.

16. Ibid., 5.

17. Ginger, *Six Days or Forever*, 68–69.

18. Ibid., 69.

19. William Jennings Bryan, quoted in Koenig, *Bryan*, 639.

20. Ibid.

21. Levine, *Defender of the Faith*, 327.

22. Allen, *Bryan and Darrow at Dayton*, 40.

23. Ibid., 37.

24. Quoted in ibid., 8.

25. Rev. Howard G. Byrd, quoted in ibid.

26. Darrow, *Story of My Life*, 257–58.

27. Ben McKenzie, quoted in Irving Stone, *Clarence Darrow for the Defense*, 418.

28. John Raulston, quoted in ibid.

29. Darrow, *Story of My Life*, 254.

30. Coletta, *Political Puritan*, 262.

31. Darrow, *Story of My Life*, 277.

32. Ibid., 275.

33. Conkin, *When All the Gods Trembled*, 86.

34. Ibid.

35. Ibid., 86.

36. Ibid., 99.

37. Coletta, *Political Puritan*, 240.

38. Long, *Bryan*, 380.

39. Koenig, *Bryan*, 638.

40. "Man vs. Monkey Tilt Has Aspect of Circus."

41. Hermelink, "Darwin and the Bible Abroad," 410.

42. Siegfried, *America Comes of Age*, 58–59; Coletta, *Political Puritan*, 241.

43. Ratcliffe, "America and Fundamentalism," 422.

44. Hermelink, "Darwin and the Bible Abroad," 381.

45. D. W. Brogan, quoted in Bernabo, "Scopes Myth," 161.

46. "English Versifiers Contest on a Scopes Trial Limerick," 1.

47. Bernabo, "Scopes Myth," 162.

48. Davidson, *The New River: Civil War to TVA*, 200.

49. Bernabo, "Scopes Myth," 159–60.

50. De Camp, *Great Monkey Trial*, 106.

51. Ibid.

52. Moran, *The Scopes Trial*, 67.

53. Moran, "The Scopes Trial and Southern Fundamentalism," 118. According to the author, "although school attendance for African American youth was likewise on the rise, only a quarter to a third of American seventeen-year-olds, for example, attended school of any kind."

54. Norris, "Evolution Not a Fact—the Bible a Fact," 323–24.

55. "If Monkeys Could Speak," 12.

56. Du Bois, "Scopes," 218.

57. A survey of Canadian media coverage revealed a similar Canadian exceptionalism; see Betts, "Argument of the Century," iii.

58. Page Smith, *Redeeming the Time*, 862.

59. H. L. Mencken, quoted in Smylie, "William Jennings Bryan and the Cartoonists," 92.

60. Quin Ryan, quoted in Wesolowski, "Before Canon 35," 77.

61. Darrow, *Story of My Life*, 279.

62. "Cranks and Freaks Flock to Dayton," 1.

63. *The Nation*, quoted in Caudill, *Darwinism in the Press*, 105.

64. Julia and Julian Harris, quoted in Lisby and Harris, "Georgia Reporters at the Scopes Trial," 795–96.

65. Krutch, "The Monkey Trial," 84.

66. Krutch, "Tennessee," 87.

67. Krutch, "Darrow vs. Bryan," 136.

68. Clarence Darrow, quoted in ibid.

69. Krutch, "Dayton: Then and Now," 367.

70. Bierstadt, *Curious Trials and Criminal Cases*, 366.

71. Larson, *Trial and Error*, 83.

72. Carpenter, *Revive Us Again*, 3–4.

73. Hofstadter, *Anti-intellectualism in American Life*, 123.

74. Davidson, *The New River: Civil War to TVA*, 204.

75. Ibid.

76. Austin Peay, quoted in Howell, "James I. Vance," 23.

77. Caudill, Larson, and Mayshark, *Scopes Trial*, 20.

Chapter 3

1. Conkin, *When All the Gods Trembled*, xi.

2. Walter Lippmann, quoted in Tompkins, *D-Days at Dayton*, viii.

3. Ginger, *Six Days or Forever*, 223.

4. Long, *Bryan*, 398–99.

5. Quoted in Marsden, *Fundamentalism and American Culture*, 184.

6. Cooke, *Vintage Mencken*, 162.

7. Mencken, "In Memoriam: W. J. B.," 83.

8. Cooke, *Vintage Mencken*, 163.

9. Ibid., 165.

10. Bierstadt, *Curious Trials and Criminal Cases*, 346.

11. Marsden, *Fundamentalism and American Culture*, 184.

12. Tompkins, *D-Days at Dayton*, 139.

13. Sandeen, "Fundamentalism and American Identity," 60.

14. Gatewood, *Preachers, Pedagogues, and Politicians*, 9.

15. Olson, *Legacy of Faith*, 5.

16. Don Wharton, "The Lord's College," *Outlook*, n.d., folder unmarked, WJBCP.

17. "Bryan Memorial Association, Dayton, Tennessee: Campaign for Five Million Dollars," December 1, 1925, WJBCP.

18. W. J. Cash, quoted in Cobb, *Away Down South*, 178.

19. Pledge card, Cordell Hull, n.d., Folder "Very Beginnings of University," WJBCP.

20. "Fund for Bryan Memorial University Grows," March 12, 1928, Folder "Literature, University Beginnings," WJBCP.

21. A. W. Murray to Malcolm Lockhart, July 3, 1926, ibid.

22. Gatewood, "After Scopes: Evolution in the South," 131.

23. George Washburn to Malcolm Lockhart, March 15, 1930, Folder "Literature, University Beginnings," WJBCP.

24. George Washburn to Malcolm Lockhart, March 15, 1930, ibid.

25. Dan Bride to "Colonel," May 18, 1932, WJBCP.

26. P. H. Callahan to Clifton C. Berryman, May 21, 1932, WJBCP.

27. Lehman Johnson to Governor Austin Peay, March 20, 1926, microfilm 24, box 96, APP.

28. Governor Austin Peay to Lehman Johnson, March 27, 1926, ibid.

29. Malcolm Lockhart to staff, March 29, 1928, Folder "Literature, University Beginnings," WJBCP.

30. Mrs. W. H. Jeffries to Malcolm Lockhart, November 18, 1926, ibid.; "World's Christian Fundamental Association Endorses Bryan University," May 9, 1927, WJBCP.

31. "Copy for Shields," n.d., Folder "Literature, University Beginnings," WJBCP.

32. Malcolm Lockhart memo, ibid.

33. J. H. Chappell letter, April 9, 1928, ibid.

34. "The Birth of the Idea," in "Bryan Memorial Association, Dayton, Tennessee: Campaign for Five Million Dollars," December 1, 1925, WJBCP.

35. Ibid.

36. "First Statement of Faith," typescript draft included in University Charter, n.d., WJBCP.

37. "Prospectus, William Jennings Bryan University," n.d., Folder "Bryan College Beginnings—Mementos, Brochures," WJBCP.

38. William Jennings Bryan, "The Modern Arena," in "The Modern America," pamphlet by Bryan Memorial Association, n.d., ibid.

39. Quoted in "Bryan University: Standing for the Old Faith," n.d., ibid.

40. J. H. Hunter, "A University in the Making," in "A University in the Making: . . . A Memorial to the Great Commoner," n.d., ibid.

41. "In Order That You May Know: William Jennings Bryan University," n.d., ibid.

42. "The Difference," in "The Last Battle, Bryan Memorial Association," n.d., ibid.

43. Leo E. Guile to "Friend," January 1, 1931, Folder "History of Bryan College—miscellaneous," WJBCP.

44. "Foreword," typescript, n.d., ibid.

45. "Reasons for Building Bryan College," n.d., ibid.

46. John T. D. Blackburn, "Evolution," 1903, Folder "Literature, University Beginnings," WJBCP.

47. James Jefferson Davis Hall, in *Southern Churchmen*, typescript, n.d., ibid.

48. Ibid.

49. "Purchase 'The Scopes Trial: Inherit the Truth ' DVD," www.bryan.edu/inherit_the_truth.html.

50. "Bryan Institute for Critical Thought & Practice," http://www.bryan.edu/bi.

51. "About Us," Center for Origins Research, www.bryancore.org/about.html.

52. "Origins Studies Minor at Bryan College," Center for Origins Research, http://www.bryancore.org/minor.html.

53. "Bibliography," Center for Origins Research, http://www.bryancore.org/bibliography.html.

54. "Resources," Center for Origins Research, www.bryancore.org/resources.html.

55. "Todd's Blog," http://toddcwood.blogspot.com.

56. "Creationist Scientist Donates Papers to CORE."

57. Caudill, Larson, and Mayshark, *Scopes Trial*, 64.

58. Larson, *Summer for the Gods*, 237.

59. House, *Intelligent Design 101*, 101.

60. "Reading the Polls on Evolution and Creationism," http://www.pewtrusts.org/our_work_report_detail.aspx?id=23428.

61. "Officials Reverse Motion on Banning Gays from Living in Rhea Co," http://www.wate.com/Global/story.asp?S=1720968.

62. "Politicized Science: A Challenge to Evangelical Thinking," http://www.bryan.edu/5031. See related videos on this site as well.

63. Tompkins, *D-Days at Dayton*, 135.

64. George Washburn, quoted in Caudill, Larson, and Mayshark, *Scopes Trial*, 64.

Part II

1. H. L. Mencken, quoted in Roland, "The South of the Agrarians," 37–38.

2. Donald Davidson, "The South and the Nation: A Historical interpretation, No. 2," typescript, n.d., p. 5, box 27, folder 37, DDP. Editing marks reveal that the original quotation described the "eminent attorneys" as "publicity-seeking attorneys."

3. Davidson, *Attack on Leviathan*, 134.

4. Davenport, *Myth of Southern History*, 52.

5. Woodward, "Why the Southern Renaissance," 232.

6. John Crowe Ransom, quoted in Murphy, *Rebuke of History*, 14–15.

7. William Knickerbocker, quoted in Young, *Gentleman in a Dustcoat*, 199.

8. Ransom, *New Criticism*.

9. Eagleton, *Literary Theory*, 44.

Chapter 4

1. Davidson, *Southern Writers*, 34.

2. Ibid., 30.

3. Tate, "A Southern Mode of the Imagination," 12.

4. Donald Davidson, "The South and the Nation: A Historical Interpretation, No. 2," typescript, n.d., p. 7, box 27, folder 37, DDP.

5. Ibid.

6. Bradbury, *The Fugitives*, 12.

7. Donaldson, "The Fugitives Gather," 890.

8. Tate, *Memoirs*, 24.

9. Blotner, *Robert Penn Warren*, 33.

10. Robert Penn Warren, quoted in ibid.

11. John Crowe Ransom, quoted in ibid., 35.

12. Clark, *American Vision of Robert Penn Warren*, 21.

13. Bradbury, *The Fugitives*, 4.

14. Tate, *Memoirs*, 28.

15. Young and Inge, *Donald Davidson*, 36.

16. Ibid., 36–37.

17. Tate, *Memoirs*, 28.

18. Ibid., 29.

19. Young, *Waking Their Neighbors Up*, 1.

20. Hobson, *Serpent in Eden*, 19.

21. Ibid., 20.

22. Mencken, *Thirty-five Years of Newspaper Work*, 151.

23. Mencken, "Sahara of the Bozart."

24. Tate, *Memoirs*, 14.

25. Hobson, *Serpent in Eden*, 184.

26. Bradbury, *The Fugitives*, 7.

27. Hobson, *Serpent in Eden*, 73.

28. Foreword, *The Fugitive: A Journal of Poetry*, 2.

29. Tate, "Last Days of the Charming Lady," 485–86.

30. Cowan, *Fugitive Group*, 34.

31. Bradbury, *The Fugitives*, 13.

32. Weaver, "Agrarianism in Exile," 589. In this seminal article, Weaver argues that this new introspection resulted from the experience of going abroad that many southern men had as a result of their service in World War I. He argues that by the time these soldiers left home, "there had been enough criticism of the ignorant and spiteful sort to make the Southern-born defense minded, as every student of our national psychology knows." Thus, "it was only natural," Weaver contends, "that these voyagers should return home determined to take a fresh look at their inheritance, to strip from it those

accretions which were historical and geographical accidents, and to see whether the remainder deserved a champion." Surely, the war years and the distance from home made many southern defenders reconsider their views, thus explaining the outpouring of southern criticism from local journalists in the 1920s. And although these southern critiques were a part of the Southern Literary Renaissance in its broad and contemporary definition, the Fugitives were traditionally cited as the fathers of the Southern Literary Renaissance. And they do not seem to follow Weaver's model. Their introspection seems to follow the barrage of criticism that characterized the events in Dayton and the general "benighted South" image that proliferated in the 1920s.

33. H. L. Mencken, quoted in Hobson, *Serpent in Eden*, 73. Originally published in "Violets in the Sahara," *Baltimore Evening Sun*, May 15, 1922.

34. Hobson, *Serpent in Eden*, 73.

35. Ibid., 59.

36. Singal, *The War Within*, 199.

37. Quoted in Bradbury, *The Fugitives*, 6.

38. Cowan, "Fugitive Poets in Relation to the South," 5.

39. Hobson, *Serpent in Eden*, 77.

40. H. L. Mencken, quoted in ibid.

41. John Crowe Ransom, quoted in ibid.

42. Hobson, *Serpent in Eden*, 75.

43. Bradbury, *The Fugitives*, 11.

44. Donaldson, "The Fugitives Gather," 898.

45. Ibid.

46. Ransom, "Ego," 4.

47. Jancovich, *Cultural Politics of the New Criticism*, 21.

48. Yeats, "Second Coming," 460.

49. Wood, "On Native Soil," 180.

50. Blotner, *Robert Penn Warren*, 35.

51. Robert Penn Warren, quoted in ibid.

52. Ibid.

53. Ibid., 71.

54. Rubin, "Gathering of the Fugitives," 665.

55. Tate, "The Fugitive," 83.

56. Bradbury, *The Fugitives*, 27. The phrase "White Hope of the South" was originally quoted in Tate, "The Fugitive," 81; and the reference to Tate being the "only critic worth reading in the United States" was made in Winters, "Fugitives," 102.

57. Beck, *Fugitive Legacy*, 5.

58. Allen Tate to Donald Davidson, May 27, 1925, box 13, folder 27, DDP.

59. Shapiro, "The Southern Agrarians," 77.

60. Jancovich, *Cultural Politics of the New Criticism*, 22.

61. John Crowe Ransom to Allen Tate, in Young and Core, *Selected Letters of John Crowe Ransom*, 166.

62. Allen Tate, quoted in Cowan, "Fugitive Poets in Relation to the South," 7.

63. Ibid., 9.

64. Doyle, *Nashville since the 1920s*, 9.

65. Singal, *The War Within*, 200.

66. Ibid., 200–201.

67. Davidson, *Southern Writers*, 35–36.

68. Hobson, *Serpent in Eden*, 82.

69. Ibid., 83. The winners included the *Memphis Commercial Appeal* of Memphis, Tennessee, in 1923 "for its courageous attitude in the publication of cartoons and the handling of news in reference to the operations of the Ku Klux Klan"; the *Charleston News and Courier* of Charleston, South Carolina, in 1925 "for the editorial entitled 'The Plight of the South'"; the *Columbus Ledger-Enquirer* of Columbus, Georgia, in 1926 "for the service which it rendered in its brave and energetic fight against the Ku Klux Klan; against the enactment of a law barring the teaching of evolution; against dishonest and incompetent public officials and for justice to the Negro and against lynching"; Grover Cleveland Hall of the *Montgomery Advertiser* of Montgomery, Alabama, in 1928 "for his editorials against gangsterism, floggings and racial and religious intolerance"; Louis Isaac Jaffe of the *Norfolk Virginian-Pilot* of Norfolk, Virginia, in 1929 "for his editorial entitled 'An Unspeakable Act of Savagery,' which is typical of a series of articles written on the lynching evil and in successful advocacy of legislation to prevent it." See www.pulitzer.org.

70. Davidson, "Artist as Southerner," 782.

71. Arnold, "The Buried Life," 419–21. "The Buried Life" first appeared in 1852.

Chapter 5

1. Havard and Sullivan, *Band of Prophets*, 8.

2. Cowan, "Fugitive Poets in Relation to the South," 8.

3. Quoted in Karanikas, *Tillers of a Myth*, 13.

4. Shapiro, "The Southern Agrarians," 78.

5. John Crowe Ransom, quoted in Singal, *The War Within*, 212.

6. Stewart, *John Crowe Ransom*, 35.

7. Ibid.

8. Richard H. King, *A Southern Renaissance*, 53.

9. Middleton, "Thunder without Light," 385–86.

10. John Crowe Ransom, quoted in Singal, *The War Within*, 212.

11. Ransom, *God without Thunder*, 203.

12. Conkin, *Gone with the Ivy*, 326.

13. Ibid., 327.

14. John Crowe Ransom, quoted in Brown, "A Note on *God without Thunder*," 35–36.

15. Cowan, "Fugitive Poets in Relation to the South," 9.

16. Ransom, "The South—Old or New," 139.

17. Ibid.

18. Ibid., 141.

19. Fain, *The Spyglass: Views and Reviews*, 209.

20. Ransom, "The South Defends Its Heritage," 109.

21. Ibid., 118.

22. Allen Tate, quoted in Young, *Gentleman in a Dustcoat*, 186.

23. Ibid.

24. Tate, "Profession of Letters in the South," 164.

25. Underwood, *Allen Tate*, 121.

26. Arnold, *Social Ideas of Allen Tate*, 41.

27. Brinkmeyer, *Three Catholic Writers*, 15.

28. Allen Tate to Donald Davidson, June 5, 1930, box 13, folder 44, DDP.

29. Allen Tate, quoted in Brinkmeyer, *Three Catholic Writers*, 16.

30. Donaldson, "The Fugitives Gather," 904.

31. Underwood, *Allen Tate*, 129.

32. Donaldson, "The Fugitives Gather," 904.

33. Clark, *American Vision of Robert Penn Warren*, 12.

34. Ibid., 33.

35. Huff, *Allen Tate and the Catholic Revival*, 46.

36. Tate, *Stonewall Jackson: The Good Soldier*, 25; also cited in Meiners, *Last Alternative*, 27.

37. Michael O'Brien, quoted in Singal, *The War Within*, 241.

38. Arnold, *Social Ideas of Allen Tate*, 20.

39. Tate, "Ode to the Confederate Dead," 22–23.

40. Bohner, *Robert Penn Warren*, 20.

41. Bradbury, *The Fugitives*, 92.

42. Clark, *American Vision of Robert Penn Warren*, 35.

43. Edgar, *Southern Renascence Man*, 1.

44. Donald Davidson, quoted in Young, *Waking Their Neighbors Up*, 6.

45. Donald Davidson, "The South and Intellectual Progress," typescript, n.d., p. 12, box 27, folder 35, DDP.

46. Donald Davidson, "The Southerner," typescript, n.d., p. 1, box 27, folder 46, DDP.

47. Donald Davidson, quoted in Huff, "Donald Davidson," 228.

48. Ibid.

49. Donald Davidson, "The South and Intellectual Progress," typescript, n.d., p. 3, box 27, folder 35, DDP.

50. Davidson, "First Fruits of Dayton," 902–3.

51. Winchell, *Where No Flag Flies*, 130.

52. Young and Inge, *Donald Davidson*, 131.

53. Daniel Singal cited this piece, which Davidson actually began writing about two months prior to the Scopes Trial, to downplay the significance of the Dayton affair, arguing that Davidson's frustration preceded the "circus" in Dayton. But much hype and debate preceded the actual days in the courtroom, even beginning with the passage of the Butler Act, and Davidson's piece reflected this burgeoning anxiety.

54. Davidson, "Artist as Southerner," 782–83.

55. Young and Inge, *Donald Davidson*, 123.

56. Davidson, "Stark Young and Others," 34. The book page of the *Tennessean* was originally called "The Spyglass" and contained book reviews, commentary on literary events, and what were often called "Extra Reviews." The name of the book page was changed in 1928 to "The Critic's Almanac."

57. Davidson, "H. L. Mencken," 197.

58. Davidson, "Bower's *The Tragic Era*," 218.

59. Young and Inge, *Donald Davidson*, 14.

60. Warren and Brooks, *Understanding Fiction*, xvi.

61. Winchell, *Where No Flag Flies*, 119.

62. Donald Davidson, "Counterattack, 1930–1940: The South against Leviathan," typescript, n.d., p. 13, box 24, folder 36, DDP. The speech was delivered as the second lecture in the Eugenia Dorothy Blount Lamar Memorial Lectures in November 1957 at Mercer University.

63. Davidson, *Tall Men*, 30.

64. Donaldson, "The Fugitives Gather," 907.

65. Young and Inge, *Donald Davidson*, 92.

66. Singal, *The War Within*, 225.

67. Donald Davidson, quoted in ibid.

68. Young, *Waking Their Neighbors Up*, 9.

69. Fain and Young, *Literary Correspondence*, 229–30. Emphasis in original.

70. Davidson, *Southern Writers*, 57.

71. Ransom, "Reconstructed but Unregenerate," 22.

72. Ibid., 23.

73. Tate, "Remarks on the Southern Religion," 168.

74. Davidson, "A Mirror for Artists," 50.

75. Warren, "The Briar Patch," 251.

76. Ibid., 259.

77. Ibid., 264.

78. Purdy, *Fugitives' Reunion*, 181.

79. Simpson, "Southern Republic of Letters," 71.

80. Karanikas, *Tillers of a Myth*, 64.

81. Gray, *Writing the South*, 145.

82. Dorman, *Revolt of the Provinces*, 19.

83. Ibid., 107.

84. Solomon Fishman, quoted in Karanikas, *Tillers of a Myth*, 7.

85. Ibid., 6.

86. "I'll Take My Stand," *Leaf Chronicle*, Clarksville, Tennessee, November 13, 1930, box 36, folder 9, DDP.

87. "Making of Protest by 12 Southerners of Agrarian Tradition Issued Today: 'I'll Take My Stand,' Published by Harpers, Voices Opposition to Industrialism," *Tennessean*, Nashville, Tennessee, November 12, 1930, clipping in box 36, folder 9, DDP.

88. W. J. M. Jr., "A Militant Indictment of 'Progress,'" *Advertiser*, Montgomery, Alabama, November 23, 1930, clipping in ibid.

89. Young, *Gentleman in a Dustcoat*, 216.

90. Young, "From Fugitives to Agrarians," 422.

91. Harry Hansen, "The First Reader," *Mercury*, New Bedford, Massachusetts, November 13, 1930, clipping in box 36, folder 9, DDP.

92. James L. Finney, "Southern Agrarians Protest Industrialism's Encroachment," *Journal*, Knoxville, Tennessee, November 16, 1930, clipping in box 25, folder 27, DDP.

93. "The Young Confederates," *Chattanooga News*, September 3, 1930, clipping in ibid.

94. John G. Neihardt, "Anatean Voices," in "Of Making Many Books," *Post Dispatch*, St. Louis, Missouri, November 17, 1930, clipping in box 36, folder 9, DDP.

95. *Publisher's Weekly*, November 22, 1930, clipping in ibid.

96. Hazlitt, "So Did King Canute," 48.

97. Ibid.

98. Krock, "Industrialism and the Agrarian Tradition in the South," 3.

99. "Lee, We Are Here!" *Macon Telegraph*, September 24, 1930, clipping in box 36, folder 9, DDP.

100. Ibid.

101. Guy B. Johnson, "The South Faces Itself," 157.

102. Ibid.

103. Barr, "Uncultured South," 192.

104. Shapiro, "The Southern Agrarians," 84.

105. Barr, "Shall Slavery Come South?" 488.

106. Donald Davidson, "Whither Dixie? Mr. Barr and Mr. Ransom in the Great Debate at Richmond," *Chattanooga News*, November 22, 1930, clipping in box 28, folder 31, DDP.

107. John Crowe Ransom, quoted in ibid.

108. Young and Inge, *Donald Davidson*, 135.

109. Donald Davidson, "Whither Dixie? Mr. Barr and Mr. Ransom in the Great Debate at Richmond," *Chattanooga News*, November 22, 1930, clipping in box 28, folder 31, DDP.

110. Tindall, "Significance of Howard W. Odum," 294.

111. Odum, An American Epoch.

112. Howard Odum, quoted in Hobson, *Serpent in Eden*, 68.

113. H. L. Mencken, quoted in ibid., 169.

114. Mencken, "Uprising in the Confederacy," 380.

115. Mencken, "The South Astir," 55.

116. Ibid., 59.

117. Allen Tate to Lambert Davis, quoted in Shapiro, "The Southern Agrarians," 86.

118. Ibid.

119. Ibid.

120. Frank Owsley, quoted in ibid., 87.

121. Owsley, "Pillars of Agrarianism," 529.

122. Donald Davidson, quoted in Winchell, *Where No Flag Flies*, 163.

123. Donald Davidson, quoted in ibid.

124. Young, *Gentleman in a Dustcoat*, 240–42.

125. Blotner, *Robert Penn Warren*, 133.

126. Underwood, *Allen Tate*, 210.

127. Quoted in Young, *Cultivating Cooperation*, 115.

128. Underwood, *Allen Tate*, 251.

129. Donaldson, "The Fugitives Gather," 909.

130. Ransom, "What Does the South Want," 181.

131. Ibid., 178.

132. Davidson, "That This Nation May Endure," 118.

133. Ibid., 134.

134. Gray, *Literature of Memory*, 45.

135. Ibid.

136. Davidson, "I'll Take My Stand: A History," 301–2.

Chapter 6

1. Jancovich, *Cultural Politics of the New Criticism*, 28.

2. Ransom, *World's Body*, x.

3. Arnold, *Culture and Anarchy*.

4. Ibid., 5.

5. Richards, *Practical Criticism*.

6. Eliot, "The Function of Criticism," 13.

7. Erlich, "Russian Formalism," 627–38.

8. Leitch, *American Literary Criticism*, 35.

9. Bradbury, *The Fugitives*, 102.

10. Berman, *From the New Criticism to Deconstruction*, 32.

11. Eliot, *On Poetry and Poets*, 113; also quoted in Shusterman, *T. S. Eliot and the Philosophy of Criticism*, 137.

12. Richard H. King, *A Southern Renaissance*, 213.

13. Davis, "The New Criticism and the Democratic Tradition," 10.

14. Hawkes, *Structuralism and Semiotics*, 157.

15. Culler, *Structuralist Poetics*, 255.

16. Stallman, "The New Critics," 489.

17. Lentricchia, *After the New Criticism*, xiii.

18. Gray, *Southern Aberrations*.

19. Brinkmeyer, "Southern Aberrations," 126.

20. Richard Gray, quoted in ibid.

21. Fekete, *Critical Twilight*, 45.

22. Ibid.

23. Godden, *Fictions of Capital*, 169.

24. Heilman, *Southern Connection*, 254–55.

25. Graff, *Literature against Itself*, 133–34.

26. Kreyling, *Inventing Southern Literature*, 37.

27. Ibid.

28. Norman Podhoretz, quoted in ibid., 44.

29. Ibid.

30. Jancovich, *Cultural Politics of the New Criticism*, ix.

31. Ibid., x.

32. Ibid., 71.

33. Ibid., 12.

34. Singal, *The War Within*, 209.

35. Ibid.

36. Young and Hindle, *Selected Essays of John Crowe Ransom*, 10.

37. Malvasi, *Unregenerate South*, 83.

38. Berman, *From the New Criticism to Deconstruction*, 29.

39. Jancovich, *Cultural Politics of the New Criticism*, 51.

40. Ransom, *New Criticism*, 280.

41. John Crowe Ransom, quoted in Young, *Gentleman in a Dustcoat*, 345.

42. Young and Hindle, *Selected Essays of John Crowe Ransom*, 1.

43. Jancovich, *Cultural Politics of the New Criticism*, 143.

44. Young, *Gentleman in a Dustcoat*, 403.

45. Leitch, *American Literary Criticism*, 29.

46. Jancovich, *Cultural Politics of the New Criticism*, 46.

47. Ransom, *New Criticism*, 295–96.

48. Ibid., 299.

49. Young, *New Criticism and After*, 6–7.

50. Tate, "Miss Emily and the Bibliographer," 153.

51. Warren and Brooks, *Understanding Poetry*, iv.

52. Ibid., ix.

53. Scholes, *Semiotics and Interpretations*, 11.

54. Edgar, *A Southern Renascence Man*, 30.

55. René Wellek, quoted in Leitch, *American Literary Criticism*, 38.

56. Warren and Brooks, *Understanding Poetry*, 360, 362.

57. Ibid., xxi–xxiv.

58. Tate, "Narcissus as Narcissus," 595.

59. Rubin and Jacobs, *Southern Renascence*.

60. Warren, "Pure and Impure Poetry," 3.

61. Warren, *Who Speaks for the Negro*.

62. "Robert Penn Warren, Poet and Author, Dies," 11.

63. Donald Davidson, quoted in Donaldson, "The Fugitives Gather," 911.

64. Winchell, *Where No Flag Flies*, 290.

65. Bartley, *Rise of Massive Resistance*, 99–100.

66. McMillen, *Citizens' Council*, 110.

67. Warren, *Legacy of the Civil War*, 36–37.

68. Ibid., 56, 58–59.

Part III

1. Woodward, *Strange Career of Jim Crow*, 132.

2. Ibid., 132–33.

3. Cobb, *Redefining Southern Culture*, 49.

4. Ashmore, *An Epitaph for Dixie*, 29.

5. Klarman, "How Brown Changed Race Relations," 82.

6. Ibid.

Chapter 7

1. Hodding Carter Jr., *Southern Legacy*, 120.

2. Ashmore, *An Epitaph for Dixie*, 83.

3. *Roanoke World News*, quoted in Ely, *Crisis of Conservative Virginia*, 4.

4. Ibid.

5. J. Lindsay Almond Jr., quoted in Friedman, *Argument*, 99.

6. Thomas B. Stanley, quoted in "The Gravest Crisis," http://www.time.com/time/magazine/article/0,9171,863861,00.html.

7. Fishwick, *Virginia*, 225.

8. Bob Smith, *They Closed Their Schools*, 84.

9. Ibid.

10. Peters, *Southern Temper*, 61.

11. James J. Kilpatrick, quoted in Egerton, *Speak Now against the Day*, 610.

12. Savage, *Seeds of Time*, 259–60.

13. Ibid., 264.

14. Ibid., 262–63.

15. Maddox, *Free School Idea in Virginia*, 188–89.

16. Ibid., 192.

17. Aubrey Williams, quoted in Klibaner, *Conscience of a Troubled South*, 47.

18. Southern Conference Education Fund, quoted in Linda Reed, *Simple Decency and Common Sense*, 154.

19. Aubrey Williams, quoted in Klibaner, *Conscience of a Troubled South*, 47.

20. Linda Reed, *Simple Decency and Common Sense*, 148–49.

21. Egerton, *Speak Now against the Day*, 599.

22. J. Lindsay Almond Jr., quoted in ibid., 600.

23. Ibid.

24. Ibid.

25. Ibid., 603.

26. Ibid., 605.

27. Ibid., 588–89.

28. Thomas B. Stanley, quoted in Muse, *Virginia's Massive Resistance*, 7.

29. Quoted in ibid.

30. Gates, *Making of Massive Resistance*, 34.

31. Ibid.

32. *Nelson County Times*, quoted in Ely, *Crisis of Conservative Virginia*, 36.

33. Quoted in Gates, *Making of Massive Resistance*, 36.

34. Boyle, *Desegregated Heart*, 194.

35. *Brown et al. v. Board of Education et al.*, 349 U.S. 294 (Implementation Decision, May 31, 1955).

36. *Davis et al. v. County School Board of Prince Edward County et al.*, 103 F. Supp. 337, 1 Race Rel. L. Rep. 82.

37. Appendix I, Garland Gray to Thomas B. Stanley, "Public Education, Report of the Commission to the Governor of Virginia," Senate Document No. 1, Accession #37566, box 5, folder 6, p. 14, RVHD.

38. *Norfolk Virginian-Pilot*, quoted in Gates, *The Making of Massive Resistance*, 45.

39. Gates, *The Making of Massive Resistance*, 45.

40. "Public Education, Report of the Commission to the Governor of Virginia," Accession #37566, box 5, folder 6, p. 6, RVHD.

41. Ibid.

42. Ibid., 7–8.

43. Ely, *Crisis of Conservative Virginia*, 30.

44. Bob Smith, *They Closed Their Schools*, 100.

45. Robert B. Crawford, quoted in ibid.

46. Gates, *The Making of Massive Resistance*, 36.

47. Quoted in ibid., 161.

48. Bob Smith, *They Closed Their Schools*, 98.

49. Robert B. Crawford, quoted in Hanson, "No Surrender in Farmville, Virginia," 15.

50. Bob Smith, *They Closed Their Schools*, 98.

51. McMillen, *Citizens' Council*, 106.

52. Ibid., 107.

53. Bob Smith, *They Closed Their Schools*, 106.

54. Vander Zanden, "The Klan Revival," 460.

55. Ibid., 462.

56. Alfred P. Goddin to FitzGerald Bemiss, January 23, 1956, MssiB4252aFA2, box 1, "General Assembly, 1955–extra session, 1959 (*Harrison v. Day*)," FBC.

57. Peltason, *Fifty-eight Lonely Men*, 214.

58. Bob Smith, *They Closed Their Schools*, 104.

59. Ibid., 142.

Chapter 8

1. Hodding Carter Jr., *Southern Legacy*, 132.

2. Ibid., 133.

3. Ibid., 134. Emphasis in original.

4. Savage, *Seeds of Time*, 289.

5. James J. Kilpatrick to J. Lindsay Almond Jr., April 9, 1957, collection 6626b, box 7, Folder "Lindsay J. Almond, Jr. [sic]," JJKP.

6. Waring, "Southern Case against Desegregation," 39.

7. Quoted in Muse, *Ten Years of Prelude*, 18.

8. Quoted in ibid., 18–19.

9. Robert Jackson, quoted in Patterson, *Brown v. Board of Education*, 70.

10. *Atlanta Daily World*, quoted in Muse, *Ten Years of Prelude*, 19.

11. Charles Johnson, quoted in Patterson, *Brown v. Board of Education*, 71.

12. McMillen, *Citizens' Council*, 208.

13. Patterson, *Brown v. Board of Education*, 71.

14. Quoted in Muse, *Ten Years of Prelude*, 16–17.

15. Dudziak, *Cold War Civil Rights*, 34.

16. Ibid., 39–40.

17. Ibid., 35.

18. United Nations Human Rights Commission, quoted in ibid., 43.

19. Dean Rusk, quoted in ibid.

20. NAACP, quoted in ibid., 44.

21. Ibid.

22. Cobb, "Real Story of the White Citizens' Councils."

23. Wakefield, "Respectable Racism," 222.

24. James O. Eastland, quoted in ibid.

25. Patterson, *Brown v. Board of Education*, 87.

26. Tom Brady, quoted in Cook, *The Segregationists*, 19.

27. Richardson, "Charge Two with Lynch Death of 14-Year-Old Girl," 211.

28. Ibid., 212.

29. Whitfield, *A Death in the Delta*, 35.

30. Ibid., 33.

31. Ibid., 34, 36.

32. Kempton, "He Went All the Way," 214.

33. Ibid., 216.

34. Wakefield, "Justice in Summer," 217.

35. Ibid., 221.

36. Huie, "Shocking Story of Approved Killing," 232.

37. Stone, *The Best of I. F. Stone*, 169–70.

38. Torres, *Black, White, and in Color*, 26.

39. Ibid., 27.

40. Ibid.

41. Chappell, *Inside Agitators*, 54–55.

42. Dabbs, *Who Speaks for the South*, 96–97.

43. Martin Luther King Jr., "MIA Mass Meeting at Holt Street Baptist Church," http://mlk-kpp01.stanford.edu/index.php/encyclopedia/documentsentry/mia_mass_meeting_at_holt_street_baptist_church.

44. Francis McLeod, quoted in Chappell, *Inside Agitators*, 65.

45. Mrs. E. R. J., quoted in ibid., 66.

46. Glenn Smiley, quoted in ibid., 60.

47. Dabbs, *Who Speaks for the South*, 102–3.

48. Chappell, *Inside Agitators*, 70.

49. Azbell, "At Holt Street Baptist Church," 231.

50. Waring, "Unite to Restore the Republic."

51. Waring, "The South Has Lost Its Voice."

52. Waring, "Carpetbagger Press Not Wanted."

53. Ward, *Radio and the Struggle for Civil Rights*, 5.

54. Julian Bond, quoted in ibid.

55. Ibid., 43.

56. Waring, "Do-Gooders Stirring Bloodshed."

57. Ibid.

58. Debnam, *Then My Old Kentucky Home Good Night*, 6.

59. Dunford, *Richmond Times-Dispatch*, 357.

60. Thomas R. Waring Jr. to James J. Kilpatrick, July 27, 1955, collection 6626b, box 13, Folder "Hamilton, Charles," JJKP.

61. Louis D. Rubin Jr. to James J. Kilpatrick, August 6, 1952, collection 6626b, box 18, Folder "Louis D. Rubin, Jr.," JJKP.

62. Ibid.

63. Louis D. Rubin Jr. to James J. Kilpatrick, n.d., ibid.

64. James J. Kilpatrick, no title, n.d., p. 2, collection 6626C, box 1, Folder "Speeches, University of Richmond on Integration, 1955," JJKP.

Chapter 9

1. James J. Kilpatrick to Harry F. Byrd, May 20, 1954, collection 6626b, box 7, Folder "Harry Byrd, Jr.," JJKP.

2. Ibid.

3. James J. Kilpatrick, quoted in Muse, *Ten Years of Prelude*, 29. Emphasis in original.

4. Faulkner, "A Letter to the North," 52.

5. Ibid., 51.

6. Thorndike, "Kilpatrick and the Campaign against *Brown*," 61.

7. James J. Kilpatrick to Harry F. Byrd, December 28, 1955, in collection 6626b, box 7, Folder "Harry Byrd, Jr.," JJKP.

8. Thorndike, "Kilpatrick and the Campaign against *Brown*," 59.

9. Brant, "'Interposition' Really Spells Nullification."

10. Dunford, *Richmond Times-Dispatch*, 315–19.

11. Ely, *Crisis of Conservative Virginia*, 14.

12. Ibid.

13. Wilhoit, *Politics of Massive Resistance*, 93.

14. Ely, *Crisis of Conservative Virginia*, 15.

15. Harry F. Byrd to James J. Kilpatrick, December 2, 1955, collection 6626b, box 7, Folder "Harry Byrd, Sr.," JJKP.

16. J. Lindsay Almond Jr. to James J. Kilpatrick, November 14, 1957, collection 6626b, box 7, Folder "Lindsay J. Almond, Jr. [*sic*]," JJKP.

17. James J. Kilpatrick, no title, n.d., p. 30, collection 6626C, box 1, Folder "Speeches, University of Richmond on Integration, 1955," JJKP.

18. Kilpatrick, *Southern Case for School Segregation*, 7.

19. Ibid., 8.

20. James J. Kilpatrick, quoted in Lewis, *The White South and the Red Menace*, 1.

21. Ibid.

22. James O. Eastland, "The Supreme Court's 'Modern Scientific Authorities' in the Segregation Cases," clipping in collection 6626C, box 8, Folder "Interposition Action in Other States," JJKP.

23. Ibid., 4.

24. Ibid., 8.

25. Ibid., 11.

26. Dr. L. Nelson Bell, "Christian Race Relations Must Be Natural Not Forced," *Southern Presbyterian Journal*, August 17, 1955, 6, clipping in collection 6626b, box 61, Folder "Right of Interposition," JJKP.

27. Gates, *The Making of Massive Resistance*, 104.

28. William Old, quoted in ibid.

29. James J. Kilpatrick to James O. Eastland, December 22, 1955, p. 1, collection 6626C, box 8, Folder "Constitution as Compact, II-A," JJKP.

30. Ibid., 3.

31. Kilpatrick, *Interposition*, 57–58. Kilpatrick's editorials were collected into a small book in order to be distributed more easily.

32. James J. Kilpatrick to James O. Eastland, December 22, 1955, p. 7, collection 6626C, box 8, Folder "Constitution as Compact, II-A," JJKP.

33. Kilpatrick, "Transcendent Issue." The quotation from the Constitution of Virginia, section 15, was included as an epigraph to the article.

34. Ibid.

35. Kilpatrick, "Kentucky-Virginia Resolutions."

36. Ibid.

37. Ibid.

38. Kilpatrick, "Right of Interposition."

39. Kilpatrick, "What Is This Right?"

40. Kilpatrick, "'Interposition' Is Basic Right."

41. Kilpatrick, "New England Proclaimed the Right."

42. Kilpatrick, "Iowa Successfully Challenged."

43. Kilpatrick, "Wisconsin Proclaimed the Right."

44. Kilpatrick, "Interposition, Now!"

45. 1829 General Assembly of Virginia, quoted in ibid.

46. Ibid.

47. James J. Kilpatrick, no title, n.d., p. 18, collection 6626C, box 8, Folder "Interposition, November 1955," JJKP.

48. James J. Kilpatrick, no title, n.d., p. 17, ibid.

49. Harry F. Byrd to James J. Kilpatrick, December 3, 1955, collection 6626b, box 7, Folder "Harry Byrd, Sr.," JJKP.

50. James J. Kilpatrick to Harry F. Byrd, December 19, 1955, collection 6626b, box 61, Folder "Right of Interposition," JJKP.

51. James J. Kilpatrick to Harry F. Byrd, December 28, 1955, collection 6626b, box 7, Folder "Harry Byrd, Sr.," JJKP.

52. FitzGerald Bemiss to Prescott S. Bush, December 21, 1955, collection 6626b, box 61, Folder "Right of Interposition," JJKP.

53. Kilpatrick, "Interposition: Yesterday and Today."

54. Thorndike, "Kilpatrick and the Campaign against *Brown*," 62.

55. Robert B. Patterson to James J. Kilpatrick, December 6, 1955, collection 6626b, box 61, Folder "Right of Interposition," JJKP.

56. James J. Kilpatrick to Robert B. Patterson, December 13, 1955, ibid.

57. James J. Kilpatrick to Robert B. Patterson, December 14, 1955, ibid.

58. James J. Kilpatrick to Thomas R. Waring Jr., December 9, 1955, ibid.

59. James J. Kilpatrick to Morris Cunningham, December 13, 1955, ibid.

60. James J. Kilpatrick to Richard D. Morphew, December 28, 1955, ibid.

61. Luther H. Hodges to James J. Kilpatrick, December 9, 1955, ibid.

62. James J. Kilpatrick to Allan Shivers, January 3, 1956, ibid.

63. Tom P. Brady to James J. Kilpatrick, January 10, 1956, collection 6626c, box 8, Folder "Interposition Action in Other States," JJKP.

64. Waring, "South's Appeal to Sister States."

65. Ely, *Crisis of Conservative Virginia*, 38.

66. "Vote January 9 against the Convention," n.d., collection 6626c, box 8, Folder "Gray Commission, Opposition," JJKP.

67. "Vote No Next Monday January 9th," n.d., ibid.

68. "A Plan toward Referendum Vote, January 9," n.d., MssiB4252aFA2, box 1, "General Assembly, 1955–extra session, 1959 (Harrison v. Day)," FBC.

69. Wilkinson, *Harry Byrd*, 127.

70. Muse, *Virginia's Massive Resistance*, 22.

71. Muse, *Ten Years of Prelude*, 66.

72. Ibid., 88.

73. Egerton, *Speak Now against the Day*, 623.

74. Patterson, *Brown v. Board of Education*, 98.

75. "The Southern Manifesto," 221.

76. Wilhoit, *Politics of Massive Resistance*, 53.

77. Harry F. Byrd, quoted in Muse, *Virginia's Massive Resistance*, 29.

78. Ibid., 31.

79. Ibid.

80. Ibid., 29.

81. FitzGerald Bemiss, no title, n.d., MssiB4252aFA2, box 1, "General Assembly, 1955–extra session, 1959 (Harrison v. Day)," FBC.

82. Ibid.

83. Muse, *Ten Years of Prelude*, 150.

84. J. Lindsay Almond Jr., quoted in ibid., 150.

85. J. Lindsay Almond Jr., quoted in Ely, *Crisis of Conservative Virginia*, 70.

86. Ibid., 71.

87. Wilkinson, *Harry Byrd*, 138–39.

88. Ibid., 145.

89. *Harrison v. Day*, 200 Va. 439 (1959).

90. Wilkinson, *Harry Byrd*, 146.

91. John W. Eggleston, quoted in ibid.

92. Almond, Inaugural Speech. The full text of Governor's Almond's inaugural speech was carried in the *News Leader*.

93. James J. Kilpatrick, quoted in Thorndike, "Kilpatrick and the Campaign against *Brown*," 70.

94. James J. Kilpatrick, quoted in ibid., 66.

95. Bob Smith, *They Closed Their Schools*, 87.

96. Ely, *Crisis of Conservative Virginia*, 99.

97. James J. Kilpatrick, quoted in ibid.

98. Thorndike, "Kilpatrick and the Campaign against *Brown*," 61.

Epilogue

1. Debnam, *Then My Old Kentucky Home Good Night*, 2.

2. Ibid.

3. Griffin, "Why Was the South a Problem to America," 16–17.

4. "Reasons for Building Bryan College," n.d., Folder "History of Bryan College—miscellaneous," WJBCP.

5. Waring, "Southern Case against Desegregation," 39.

6. Edsall and Edsall, *Chain Reaction*, 45.

7. Ibid., 7.

8. Ibid., 1.

9. Aistrup, *Southern Strategy Revisited*, 20.

10. Mason, *Richard Nixon*, 5.

11. Ibid.

12. Goldwater, *Conscience of a Conservative*.

13. Mason, *Richard Nixon*, 9.

14. Goldwater, quoted in Aistrup, *Southern Strategy Revisited*, 25.

15. Brennan, *Turning Right in the Sixties*, 125.

16. Dan T. Carter, *From George Wallace to Newt Gingrich*, xiii.

17. George H. W. Bush, quoted in ibid.

18. Skorownek, *The Politics Presidents Make*.

19. George Wallace, quoted in Dan T. Carter, *From George Wallace to Newt Gingrich*, 1.

20. George Wallace, quoted in ibid., 3.

21. George Wallace, quoted in ibid.

22. George Wallace, quoted in ibid., 4.

23. Greenberg, *Two Americas*, 46.

24. George Wallace, quoted in Fayer, Mccabe, and Stekler, *Settin' the Woods on Fire*.

25. George Wallace, quoted in Dan T. Carter, *From George Wallace to Newt Gingrich*, 18.

26. George Wallace, quoted in ibid., 40.

27. Ibid., 17.

28. Ibid.

29. Ibid., 12.

30. Mason, *Richard Nixon*, 2.

31. Edsall and Edsall, *Chain Reaction*, 77.

32. Black and Black, *Vital South*, 7–8.

33. Richard Nixon, quoted in Edsall and Edsall, *Chain Reaction*, 75.

34. Egerton, *Americanization of Dixie*, 137.

35. George McGovern, quoted in Aistrup, *Southern Strategy Revisited*, 5.

36. Brennan, *Turning Right in the Sixties*, 134.

37. Phillips, *Emerging Republican Majority*.

38. Fayer, Mccabe, and Stekler, *Settin' the Woods on Fire*. Full transcript available at http://www.pbs.org/wgbh/amex/wallace/filmmore/transcript/transcript1.html.

39. Lassiter, *Silent Majority*.

40. Aistrup, *Southern Strategy Revisited*, 11.

41. Dochuk, "Evangelicalism Becomes Southern," 314.

42. Greenberg, *Two Americas*, 58.

43. Ronald Reagan, quoted in ibid.

44. Ibid., 57.

45. Numbers, *The Creationists*, 243–44.

46. Mason, *Richard Nixon*, 20.

47. Dan T. Carter, *From George Wallace to Newt Gingrich*, 15.
48. Fish, *There's No Such Thing as Free Speech*.
49. Egerton, *Americanization of Dixie*; Applebome, *Dixie Rising*.

BIBLIOGRAPHY

Archives

Austin Peay Papers (Governor). Tennessee State Library and Archives, Nashville, Tennessee.

Donald Davidson Papers. Jean and Alexander Heard Library Special Collections, Vanderbilt University, Nashville, Tennessee.

FitzGerald Bemiss Collection. Virginia Historical Collection, Richmond, Virginia.

James Jackson Kilpatrick Papers. Albert and Shirley Small Special Collections, Mary and David Harrison Institute for American History, Literature, and Culture, University of Virginia, Charlottesville, Virginia.

Records of the Virginia House of Delegates, Office of the Clerk, 1956 Constitutional Convention. State Library and Archives, Library of Virginia, Richmond, Virginia.

William Jennings Bryan College Papers. Office of Richard M. Cornelius, Scopes Archivist and Professor Emeritus of English, William Jennings Bryan College, Dayton, Tennessee. This unarchived material was accessed and copied with the permission of Professor Richard M. Cornelius in January 2006. Author and publisher have retained copies.

Additional Sources

"About Us." Center for Origins Research. www.bryancore.org/about.html. Accessed August 10, 2012.

Adler, Alfred. *Superiority and Social Interest: A Collection of Later Writings.* New York: Viking, 1964.

Agar, Herbert, and Allen Tate, eds. *Who Owns America? A New Declaration of Independence.* Boston: Houghton Mifflin, 1936.

Aistrup, Joseph A. *The Southern Strategy Revisited: Republican Top-Down Advancement in the South.* Lexington: University Press of Kentucky, 1996.

Allen, Leslie H., ed. *Bryan and Darrow at Dayton: The Record and Documents of the "Bible-Evolution Trial."* New York: Arthur Lee, 1925.

Almond, J. Lindsay, Jr. Inaugural Speech. Reprinted in *Richmond News Leader,* January 21, 1959.

Althusser, Louis, and Etienne Balibar. *Reading Capital.* Translated by Ben Brewster. London: Verso, 1979.

Anderson, Carol. *Eyes Off the Prize: The United Nations and the African American Struggle for Human Rights, 1944–1955.* Cambridge: Cambridge University Press, 2003.

Applebome, Peter. *Dixie Rising: How the South Is Shaping American Values, Politics, and Culture.* San Diego: Harcourt, Brace & Company, 1996.

Arnold, Matthew. "The Buried Life." In *Victorian Poetry*, edited by E. K. Brown and J. O. Bailey. New York: Ronald Press, 1962.

Arnold, Willard Burdett. *Culture and Anarchy*. 1869. Reprint, New Haven, Conn.: Yale University Press, 1994.

———. *The Social Ideas of Allen Tate*. Boston: Bruce Humphries, 1955.

Ashby, Le Roy. *William Jennings Bryan: Champion of Democracy*. New York: Macmillan, 1987.

Ashmore, Harry S. *An Epitaph for Dixie*. New York: W. W. Norton, 1958.

———. *The Negro and the Schools*. Chapel Hill: University of North Carolina Press, 1954.

Azbell, Joe. "At Holt Street Baptist Church." In *Reporting Civil Rights: Part One, American Journalism*, compiled by Clayborne Carson et al. New York: Library of America, 2003. Originally published in *Montgomery Advertiser*, December 7, 1955.

Bailey, Kenneth K. "The Enactment of Tennessee's Anti-Evolution Law." *Journal of Southern History* 16, no. 4 (November 1950): 472–90.

———. *Southern White Protestantism in the Twentieth Century*. New York: Harper & Row, 1964.

Barr, Stringfellow. "Shall Slavery Come South?" *Virginia Quarterly Review* 6, no. 4 (October 1930): 481–94.

———. "The Uncultured South." *Virginia Quarterly Review* 5, no. 2 (April 1929): 192–200.

Bartley, Numan. *The Rise of Massive Resistance: Race and Politics in the South during the 1950s*. 1969. Reprint, Baton Rouge: Louisiana State University Press, 1999.

Beck, Charlotte. *The Fugitive Legacy: A Critical History*. Baton Rouge: Louisiana State University Press, 2001.

Berman, Art. *From the New Criticism to Deconstruction: The Reception of Structuralism and Post-Structuralism*. Urbana-Champaign: University of Illinois Press, 1988.

Bernabo, Lawrence Mark. "The Scopes Myth: The Scopes Trial in Rhetorical Perspective." Ph.D. diss., University of Iowa, 1990.

Betts, Edward G. "The Argument of the Century: The Ontario Press Coverage of the Scopes Trial and the Death of William Jennings Bryan." Master's thesis, Queen's University, Kingston, Canada, 1992.

"Bibliography." Center for Origins Research. http://www.bryancore.org/bibliography.html. Accessed August 10, 2012.

Bierstadt, Edward Hale. *Curious Trials and Criminal Cases: From Socrates to Scopes*. New York: Coward-McCann, 1928.

Black, Earl, and Merle Black. *The Vital South: How Presidents Are Elected*. Cambridge, Mass.: Harvard University Press, 1992.

Blotner, Joseph. *Robert Penn Warren: A Biography*. New York: Random House, 1997.

Bohner, Charles. *Robert Penn Warren*. Rev. ed. Boston: Twayne, 1981.

Boyle, Sarah Patton. *The Desegregated Heart: A Virginian's Stand in Time and Transition*. New York: Morrow, 1962.

Brachfield, Oliver. *Inferiority Feelings in the Individual and the Group*. 2nd ed. Westport, Conn.: Greenwood, 1972.

Bradbury, John M. *The Fugitives: A Critical Account*. Chapel Hill: University of North Carolina Press, 1958.

Brady, Tom P. *Black Monday: Segregation or Amalgamation . . . America Has Its Choice*. Association of Citizens' Councils, 1955.

Brant, Irving. "'Interposition' Really Spells Nullification." *Washington Post*, January 22, 1956, E3.

Brennan, Mary C. *Turning Right in the Sixties: The Conservative Capture of the GOP*. Chapel Hill: University of North Carolina Press, 1995.

Brinkmeyer, Robert H., Jr. "Southern Aberrations: Writers of the American South and the Problems of Regionalism." *Southern Literary Journal* 34 (Fall 2001): 124–36.

———. *Three Catholic Writers of the Modern South*. Jackson: University Press of Mississippi, 1985.

Brown, Ashley. "A Note on *God without Thunder*." *Shenandoah* 6 (Summer 1955): 34–37.

Brown et al. v. Board of Education et al. 349 U.S. 294. Implementation Decision, May 31, 1955.

"*Brown v. Board of Education*: Virginia Responds." An Exhibition at the Library of Virginia. http://www.lva.lib.va.us/whoweare/exhibits/brown/resistance.htm. Accessed September 17, 2013.

Bryan, William Jennings. "A Very Present Help in Trouble." *Commoner* (November 1922): 8–9.

"Bryan Institute for Critical Thought & Practice." http://www.bryan.edu/bi. Accessed August 10, 2012.

"Bryan Says North Would Act as South on Negro Question." *New York Times*, March 18, 1923, 21. http://o-search.proquest.com.library.uark.edu/docview/103598501/fulltextPDF/13D12328D8A785E41AD/1?accountid=8361. Accessed March 12, 2013.

Burnham, Walter Dean. *Critical Elections and the Mainsprings of American Politics*. New York: W. W. Norton, 1970.

Calhoun, John C. "Speech on the Reception of Abolition Petitions." In *Slavery Defended: The Views of the Old South*, edited by Eric McKitrick. Englewood Cliffs, N.J.: Prentice-Hall, 1963.

Carpenter, Joel A. *Revive Us Again: The Reawakening of American Fundamentalism*. New York: Oxford University Press, 1999.

Carson, Clayborne, and Peter Holloran, eds. *A Knock at Midnight: Inspiration from the Great Sermons of Reverend Martin Luther King, Jr.* New York: Warner Books, 1998.

Carter, Dan T. *From George Wallace to Newt Gingrich: Race in the Conservative Counterrevolution, 1963–1994*. Baton Rouge: Louisiana State University Press, 1996.

Carter, Hodding, Jr. *Southern Legacy*. Baton Rouge: Louisiana State University Press, 1950.

Cash, W. J. *The Mind of the South*. New York: Alfred A. Knopf, 1941.

Caudill, Edward. *Darwinism in the Press: The Evolution of an Idea*. Knoxville: University of Tennessee Press, 1997.

Caudill, Edward, Edward Larson, and Jesse Fox Mayshark. *The Scopes Trial: A Photographic History*. Knoxville: University of Tennessee Press, 2000.

Chappell, David. *Inside Agitators: White Southerners in the Civil Rights Movement*. Baltimore: Johns Hopkins University Press, 1994.

Clark, William Bedford. *The American Vision of Robert Penn Warren*. Lexington: University Press of Kentucky, 1991.

Coate, Lowell Harris. "Evolution Disproved." In *The Dawn of Humanity: The Menace of Darwinism*, edited by William Jennings Bryan. Chicago: Altruist Foundation, 1925.

Cobb, James C. *Away Down South: A History of Southern Identity.* New York: Oxford University Press, 2005.

———. "The Real Story of the White Citizens' Councils." History News Network. http://hnn.us/articles/134814.html. Accessed June 12, 2012.

———. *Redefining Southern Culture: Mind and Identity in the Modern South.* Athens: University of Georgia Press, 1999.

Cochran, Augustus B., III. *Democracy Heading South: National Politics in the Shadow of Dixie.* Lawrence: University Press of Kansas, 2001.

Coletta, Paolo E. *Political Puritan, 1915–1925,* vol. 3 of *William Jennings Bryan.* Lincoln: University of Nebraska Press, 1969.

Conkin, Paul K. *Gone with the Ivy: A Biography of Vanderbilt University.* Knoxville: University of Tennessee Press, 1985.

———. *When All the Gods Trembled: Darwinism, Scopes, and American Intellectuals.* Lanham, Md.: Rowman & Littlefield, 1998.

Connelly, Thomas L. "The Vanderbilt Agrarians: Time and Place in Southern Tradition." *Tennessee Historical Quarterly* 22 (March 1963): 22–37.

Connelly, Thomas L., and Barbara L. Bellows. *God and General Longstreet: The Lost Cause and the Southern Mind.* Baton Rouge: Louisiana State University Press, 1982.

Cook, James Graham. *The Segregationists.* New York: Appleton-Century-Crofts, 1962.

Cooke, Alistair, ed. *The Vintage Mencken.* New York: Vintage Books, 1955.

Cooper, William J., and Thomas E. Terrill. *The American South: A History.* Vol. 2. 4th ed. Lanham, Md.: Rowman & Littlefield, 2009.

Cowan, Louise. *The Fugitive Group: A Literary History.* Baton Rouge: Louisiana State University Press, 1959.

———. "The Fugitive Poets in Relation to the South." *Shenandoah* 6 (Summer 1955): 3–10.

"Cranks and Freaks Flock to Dayton." *New York Times,* July 11, 1925, 1–2. http://0-search .proquest.com.library.uark.edu/docview/103598501/fulltextPDF/13D12317CB428954 C75/1?accountid=8361. Accessed March 12, 2013.

"Creationist Scientist Donates Papers to CORE." http://www.bryan.edu/5256.html. Accessed September 27, 2011.

Crespino, Joseph. *In Search of Another Country: Mississippi and the Conservative Counterrevolution.* Princeton, N.J.: Princeton University Press, 2007.

Culler, Jonathan. *Structuralist Poetics.* London: Routledge and Kegan Paul, 1975.

Dabbs, James McBride. *Who Speaks for the South?* New York: Funk & Wagnalls, 1964.

Darrow, Clarence. "Darrow Asks W. J. Bryan to Answer These." *Chicago Tribune,* July 4, 1923, 1, 12. http://pqasb.pqarchiver.com/chicagotribune. Accessed September 13, 2013.

———. *The Story of My Life.* New York: Charles Scribner's, 1932.

Davenport, F. Garvin, Jr. *The Myth of Southern History: Historical Consciousness in Twentieth-Century Southern Literature.* Nashville: Vanderbilt University Press, 1970.

Davidson, Donald. "The Artist as Southerner." *Saturday Review of Literature,* May 15, 1926, 781–83.

———. *The Attack on Leviathan: Regionalism and Nationalism in the United States.* Chapel Hill: University of North Carolina Press, 1938.

———. "Bower's *The Tragic Era*." In *The Spyglass: Views and Reviews, 1924–1930*, edited by John Tyree Fain. Nashville: Vanderbilt University Press, 1963. Originally published in *Tennessean*, September 15, 1929.

———. "Geography of the Brain." In *The Tall Men*. Boston: Houghton Mifflin, 1927.

———. "H. L. Mencken." In *The Spyglass: Views and Reviews, 1924–1930*, edited by John Tyree Fain. Nashville: Vanderbilt University Press, 1963. Originally published in *Tennessean*, December 12, 1926.

———. "*I'll Take My Stand*: A History." *American Review* 5 (Summer 1935): 301–21.

———. "A Mirror for Artists." In *I'll Take My Stand: The South and the Agrarian Tradition*, edited by Twelve Southerners. 1930. Reprint, Baton Rouge: Louisiana State University Press, 1977.

———. *The Tennessee: Volume II: The New River: Civil War to TVA*. New York: Rinehart, 1946.

———. *Southern Writers in the Modern World*. Athens: University of Georgia Press, 1958.

———. "Stark Young and Others." In *The Spyglass: Views and Reviews, 1924–1930*, edited by John Tyree Fain. Nashville: Vanderbilt University Press, 1963. Originally published in *Critic's Almanac*, October 6, 1929.

———. "That This Nation May Endure: The Need for Political Regionalism." In *Who Owns America? A New Declaration of Independence*, edited by Herbert Agar and Allen Tate. Boston: Houghton Mifflin, 1936.

Davis, Robert Gorham. "The New Criticism and the Democratic Tradition." *American Scholar* 19 (Winter 1949–50): 9–19.

Davis et al. v. County School Board of Prince Edward County et al. 103 F. Supp. 337, 1 Race Rel. L. Rep. 82.

"Dayton: Good Advertising for the South: *The Manufacturers' Record*." In *Controversy in the Twenties: Fundamentalism, Modernism, and Evolution*, edited by Willard B. Gatewood Jr. Nashville: Vanderbilt University Press, 1969.

Debnam, W. E. B. *Then My Old Kentucky Home Good Night!* Raleigh, N.C.: Graphic Press, 1955.

———. *Weep No More, My Lady: A Southerner Answers Mrs. Roosevelt's Report on the "Poor and Unhappy South."* Raleigh, N.C.: Graphic Press, 1950.

de Camp, L. Sprague. *The Great Monkey Trial*. Garden City, N.J.: Doubleday, 1968.

Degler, Carl N. *Place over Time: The Continuity of Southern Distinctiveness*. Baton Rouge: Louisiana State University Press, 1977.

Dewey, John. "The American Intellectual Frontier." *New Republic*, May 10, 1922, 303–5.

Dixon, Amzi Clarence. "The Root of Modern Evils." In *Controversy in the Twenties: Fundamentalism, Modernism, and Evolution*, edited by Willard B. Gatewood Jr. Nashville: Vanderbilt University Press, 1969.

Dochuk, Darren. "Evangelicalism Becomes Southern, Politics Becomes Evangelical: From FDR to Ronald Reagan." In *Religion and American Politics: From the Colonial Period to the Present*, edited by Mark A. Noll and Luke E. Harlow. 2nd ed. New York: Oxford University Press, 2007.

Donaldson, Scott. "The Fugitives Gather." *Southern Review* 38, no. 4 (Autumn 2002): 889–913.

Dorman, Robert L. *The Revolt of the Provinces: The Regionalist Movement in America, 1920–1945*. Chapel Hill: University of North Carolina Press, 1993.

Doyle, Don H. *Nashville since the 1920s.* Knoxville: University of Tennessee Press, 1985.

Du Bois, W. E. B. *Black Reconstruction in America, 1860–1880.* 1935. Reprint, New York: Free Press, 1962.

———. "Scopes." *Crisis* 30 (September 1925): 218.

Duck, Leigh Anne. *The Nation's Region: Southern Modernism, Segregation, and U.S. Nationalism.* Athens: University of Georgia Press, 2006.

Dudziak, Mary L. *Cold War Civil Rights: Race and the Image of American Democracy.* Princeton, N.J.: Princeton University Press, 2000.

Dunford, Earle. *Richmond Times-Dispatch: The Story of a Newspaper.* Richmond: Cadmus, 1995.

Eagleton, Terry. *Literary Theory: An Introduction.* Oxford, U.K.: Blackwell, 1983.

Edgar, Walter B., ed. *A Southern Renascence Man: Views of Robert Penn Warren.* Baton Rouge: Louisiana State University Press, 1984.

Edsall, Thomas Byrne, and Mary D. Edsall. *Chain Reaction: The Impact of Race, Rights, and Taxes on American Politics.* New York: W. W. Norton, 1991.

Egerton, John. *The Americanization of Dixie: The Southernization of America.* New York: Harper's Magazine Press, 1974.

———. *Speak Now against the Day: The Generation before the Civil Rights Movement in the South.* Chapel Hill: University of North Carolina Press, 1994.

Eliot, T. S. "The Function of Criticism." In *Selected Essays.* 1932. Reprint, New York: Harcourt, Brace & World, 1964.

———. *On Poetry and Poets.* London: Faber, 1957.

Ely, James W. *The Crisis of Conservative Virginia: The Byrd Organization and the Politics of Massive Resistance.* Knoxville: University of Tennessee Press, 1976.

"English Versifiers Contest on a Scopes Trial Limerick." *New York Times,* July 26, 1925, 1. http://o-search.proquest.com.library.uark.edu/docview/103598501/fulltextPDF/13D1 22A8145368A3D3B/1?accountid=8361. Accessed March 12, 2013.

Erlich, Victor. "Russian Formalism." *Journal of the History of Ideas* 34, no. 4 (1973): 627–38.

"Europe Is Amazed by the Scopes Case." *New York Times,* July 11, 1925, 1–2.

Fain, John Tyree, ed. *The Spyglass: Views and Reviews, 1924–1930.* Nashville: Vanderbilt University Press, 1963.

Fain, John Tyree, and Thomas Daniel Young, eds. *The Literary Correspondence of Donald Davidson and Allen Tate.* Athens: University of Georgia Press, 1974.

Fanon, Frantz. *Black Skin, White Masks.* Translated by Charles Lam Markmann. New York: Grove, 1967.

Faulkner, William. *Absalom, Absalom!* New York: Vintage International, 1991.

———. "A Letter to the North." *Life,* March 5, 1956, 51–52.

Fayer, Steve, Daniel Mccabe, and Paul Stekler. *Settin' the Woods on Fire.* Big House Productions and Midnight Films, 2000.

Fecher, Charles A. *Mencken: A Study of His Thought.* New York: Alfred A. Knopf, 1978.

Fekete, John. *The Critical Twilight: Explanations in the Ideology of Anglo-American Literary Theory from Eliot to McLuhan.* London: Routledge, 1978.

Fish, Stanley. *There's No Such Thing as Free Speech: And It's a Good Thing, Too.* New York: Oxford University Press, 1994.

Fishwick, Marshall William. *Virginia: A New Look at an Old Dominion.* New York: Harper & Row, 1959.

Fitzhugh, George. "Sociology for the South." In *Antebellum: Writing of George Fitzhugh and Hinton Rowan Helper on Slavery*, edited by Harvey Wish. New York: Capricorn Books, 1960.

Frank, Andrew K. *The Routledge Historical Atlas of the American South*. New York: Routledge, 1999.

Freud, Sigmund. *The Interpretation of Dreams*. 3rd ed. Translated by A. A. Brill. New York: Macmillan, 1927.

Friedman, Leon, ed. *Argument: The Oral Argument before the Supreme Court in Brown v. Board of Education of Topeka, 1952–1953*. New York: Chelsea, 1969.

Friend, Craig Thompson, ed. *Southern Manhood: Perspectives on Manhood in the South since Reconstruction*. Athens: University of Georgia Press, 2009.

Friend, Craig Thompson, and Lorri Glover, eds. *Southern Manhood: Perspectives on Masculinity in the Old South*. Athens: University of Georgia Press, 2004.

The Fugitive: A Journal of Poetry, vols. 1–4, 1922–1925. New York: Johnson Reprint Corporation, 1966.

Gates, Robbins L. *The Making of Massive Resistance: Virginia's Politics of Public School Desegregation, 1954–1956*. Chapel Hill: University of North Carolina Press, 1962.

Gatewood, Willard B., Jr. "After Scopes: Evolution in the South." In *The South Is Another Land: Essays on the Twentieth-Century South*, edited by Bruce Clayton and John A. Salmond. Westport, Conn.: Greenwood Press, 1987.

———. *Preachers, Pedagogues, and Politicians: The Evolution Crisis in North Carolina, 1920–1927*. Chapel Hill: University of North Carolina Press, 1966.

———, ed. *Controversy in the Twenties: Fundamentalism, Modernism, and Evolution*. Nashville: Vanderbilt University Press, 1969.

Ginger, Ray. *Six Days or Forever? Tennessee vs. John Thomas Scopes*. Boston: Beacon, 1959.

———, ed. *William Jennings Bryan: Selections*. Indianapolis: Bobbs-Merrill, 1967.

Glad, Paul W. *McKinley, Bryan, and the People*. Philadelphia: J. B. Lippincott, 1964.

Godden, Richard. *Fictions of Capital: The American Novel from James to Mailer*. Cambridge: Cambridge University Press, 1990.

Goldfield, David. *Black, White, and Southern: Race Relations and Southern Culture, 1940 to the Present*. Baton Rouge: Louisiana State University Press, 1990.

Goldwater, Barry. *The Conscience of a Conservative*. New York: Hillman Books, 1960.

Graff, Gerald. *Literature against Itself: Literary Ideas in Modern Society*. Chicago: University of Chicago Press, 1979.

Grantham, Dewey W. *The South in Modern America: A Region at Odds*. New York: Harper Collins, 1994.

Graves, John Temple. *The Fighting South*. New York: G. P. Putnam's Sons, 1943.

"The Gravest Crisis." *Time*, September 22, 1958. http://www.time.com/time/magazine/article/0,9171,863861,00.html. Accessed March 12, 2013.

Gray, Richard. *The Literature of Memory: Modern Writers of the American South*. Baltimore: Johns Hopkins University Press, 1977.

———. *Southern Aberrations: Writers of the American South and the Problems of Regionalism*. Baton Rouge: Louisiana State University Press, 2000.

———. *Writing the South: Ideas of an American Region*. Cambridge: Cambridge University Press, 1986.

Green, Fletcher M. "Resurgent Southern Sectionalism, 1933–1955." *North Carolina Historical Review* 33 (April 1956): 222–40.

Greenberg, Stanley B. *The Two Americas: Our Current Political Deadlock and How to Break It.* New York: Thomas Dunne Books/St. Martin Griffin, 2005.

Grey, Loren. *Alfred Adler, the Forgotten Prophet: A Vision for the 21st Century.* Westport, Conn.: Praeger, 1998.

Griffin, Larry J. "Why Was the South a Problem to America." In *The South as an American Problem,* edited by Larry J. Griffin and Don H. Doyle. Athens: University of Georgia Press, 1995.

Guindon, Mary G., Alan G. Green, and Fred J. Hanna. "Intolerance and Psychopathology: Toward a General Diagnosis for Racism, Sexism, and Homophobia." *American Journal of Orthopsychiatry* 73, no. 4 (2003): 167–76.

H. J. Shelton to Jason Blakenship. April 20, 1990. Personal unarchived correspondence.

Hackney, Sheldon. "Southern Violence." *American Historical Review* 74, no. 3 (February 1969): 906–25.

Hanson, Haldore. "No Surrender in Farmville, Virginia." *New Republic,* October 10, 1955, 11–15.

Harrison v. Day. 200 Va. 439 (1959). http://www.leagle.com/xmlResult.aspx?xmldoc=1959 742106SE2d636_1726.xml&docbase=CSLWAR1–1950–1985. Accessed March 12, 2013.

Havard, William C., and Walter Sullivan, eds. *A Band of Prophets: The Vanderbilt Agrarians after Fifty Years.* Baton Rouge: Louisiana State University Press, 1982.

Hawkes, Terence. *Structuralism and Semiotics.* London: Methuen, 1977.

Hazlitt, Henry. "So Did King Canute." *Nation,* January 14, 1931, 48–49.

Heilman, Robert B. *The Southern Connection.* Baton Rouge: Louisiana State University Press, 1991.

Hermelink, Heinrich. "Darwin and the Bible Abroad." In *Controversy in the Twenties: Fundamentalism, Modernism, and Evolution,* edited by Willard B. Gatewood Jr. Nashville: Vanderbilt University Press, 1969. Originally published in *Living Age* 336 (August 1925): 393–95.

Hibben, Paxton. *The Peerless Leader: William Jennings Bryan.* New York: Farrar and Rinehart, 1929.

Higdon, Hal. *Leopold and Loeb: The Crime of the Century.* Urbana-Champaign: University of Illinois Press, 1999.

Hobson, Fred C., Jr. *Serpent in Eden: H. L. Mencken and the South.* Chapel Hill: University of North Carolina Press, 1974.

———. *Tell about the South: The Southern Rage to Explain.* Baton Rouge: Louisiana State University Press, 1983.

Hofstadter, Richard. *Anti-intellectualism in American Life.* New York: Alfred A. Knopf, 1970.

House, Wayne H. *Intelligent Design 101: Leading Experts Explain the Key Issues.* Grand Rapids, Mich.: Kregel Publications, 2008.

Howell, Sarah M. "James I. Vance, Transformations in Religion and Society: 1922–1932." *Tennessee Historical Quarterly* 49, no. 1 (Spring 1990): 18–27.

Huff, Peter. *Allen Tate and the Catholic Revival: Trace of the Fugitive Gods.* New York: Paulist Press, 1996.

Huie, William Bradford. "The Shocking Story of Approved Killing in Mississippi." In
  Reporting Civil Rights: Part One, American Journalism, compiled by Clayborne Carson et
  al. New York: Library of America, 2003. Originally published in *Look*, January 14,
  1956.
Israel, Charles A. *Before Scopes: Evangelicalism, Education, and Evolution in Tennessee,*
  1870–1925. Athens: University of Georgia Press, 2004.
Jancovich, Mark. *The Cultural Politics of the New Criticism.* Cambridge: Cambridge
  University Press, 1993.
Johnson, Gerald W. "Critical Attitudes North and South." *Journal of Social Forces* 2, no. 4
  (May 1924): 575–79.
Johnson, Guy B. "Freedom, Equality, and Segregation." In *Integration vs. Segregation:*
  The Crisis in Our Schools as Viewed by 17 Outstanding Commentators, edited by Hubert H.
  Humphrey. New York: Crowell, 1964.
———. "The South Faces Itself." *Virginia Quarterly Review* 7 (January 1931): 152–57.
Josephson, Matthew. "The Bryan Campaign." In *William Jennings Bryan and the Campaign*
  of 1896, edited by George F. Whicher. Problems in American Civilization. Boston:
  D. C. Heath, 1953.
Karanikas, Alexander. *Tillers of a Myth: Southern Agrarians as Social and Literary Critics.*
  Madison: University of Wisconsin Press, 1966.
Kazin, Michael. *A Godly Hero: The Life of William Jennings Bryan.* New York: Alfred A.
  Knopf, 2006.
———. *The Populist Persuasion: An American History.* New York: Basic Books, 1995.
Kemper, Steve. "Evolution on Trial." *Smithsonian* 36, no. 1 (April 2005): 52–61.
Kempton, Murray. "He Went All the Way." In *Reporting Civil Rights: Part One, American*
  Journalism, compiled by Clayborne Carson et al. New York: Library of America, 2003.
Key, V. O., Jr. *Southern Politics in State and Nation.* New York: Alfred A. Knopf, 1949.
Killian, Lewis M. *White Southerners.* Rev. ed. Amherst: University of Massachusetts
  Press, 1985.
Kilpatrick, James J. *Interposition: Editorials and Editorial Page Presentations.* Richmond:
  Richmond News Leader, 1955–56.
———. "'Interposition' Is Basic Right of Sovereign States, John Calhoun Believed."
  Richmond News Leader, November 23, 1955, editorial page.
———. "Interposition, Now!" *Richmond News Leader*, November 30, 1955, editorial page.
———. "Iowa Successfully Challenged." *Richmond News Leader*, November 28, 1955,
  editorial page.
———. "Kentucky-Virginia Resolutions." *Richmond News Leader*, November 21, 1955,
  editorial page.
———. "New England Proclaimed the Right." *Richmond News Leader*, November 28,
  1955, editorial page.
———. "The Right of Interposition." *Richmond News Leader*, November 22, 1955,
  editorial page.
———. *The Southern Case for School Segregation.* Richmond: Crowell-Collier, 1962.
———. "The Transcendent Issue." *Richmond News Leader*, November 21, 1955, editorial
  page.
———. "What Is This Right?" *Richmond News Leader*, November 22, 1955, editorial page.

———. "Wisconsin Proclaimed the Right." *Richmond News Leader*, November 28, 1955, editorial page.

Kimmel, Michael S. *Manhood in America: A Cultural History*. New York: Free Press, 1996.

King, Martin Luther, Jr. "MIA Mass Meeting at Holt Street Baptist Church" (December 5, 1955). In *Volume 3: Birth of a New Age, December 1955–December 1956*. http://mlk-kpp01 .stanford.edu/index.php/encyclopedia/documentsentry/mia_mass_meeting_at_ holt_street_baptist_church. Accessed August 11, 2012.

King, Richard H. *A Southern Renaissance: The Cultural Awakening of the American South, 1930–1955*. New York: Oxford University Press, 1980.

Kirby, Jack Temple. *Media-Made Dixie: The South in the American Imagination*. Baton Rouge: Louisiana State University Press, 1978.

Klarman, Michael J. "How Brown Changed Race Relations: The Backlash Thesis." *Journal of American History* 81 (June 1994): 81–118.

Klibaner, Irwin. *Conscience of a Troubled South: The Southern Conference Education Fund, 1946–1966*. Brooklyn, N.Y.: Carlson, 1989.

Koenig, Louis W. *Bryan: A Political Biography of William Jennings Bryan*. New York: G. P. Putnam's Sons, 1971.

Kreyling, Michael. *Inventing Southern Literature*. Jackson: University Press of Mississippi, 1998.

Krock, Arthur. "Industrialism and the Agrarian Tradition in the South." *New York Times Book Review*, January 4, 1931, 3.

Krutch, Joseph Wood. "Darrow vs. Bryan." *Nation*, July 29, 1925, 136.

———. "Dayton: Then and Now." In *Controversy in the Twenties: Fundamentalism, Modernism, and Evolution*, edited by Willard B. Gatewood Jr. Nashville: Vanderbilt University Press, 1969

———. "The Monkey Trial." *Commentary* 43, no. 5 (May 1967): 83–84.

———. "Tennessee: Where Cowards Rule." *Nation*, July 15, 1925, 87–88.

Kurczewska, Joanna. "What Is Likely to Happen to Polish Collective Consciousness after Accession to the European Union?" *Polish Sociological Review* 141 (2003): 83–92.

Larson, Edward J. "The Scopes Trial in History and Legend." In *When Science and Christianity Meet*, edited by David C. Lindberg and Ronald L. Numbers. Chicago: University of Chicago Press, 2003.

———. *Summer for the Gods: The Scopes Trial and America's Continuing Debate over Science and Religion*. New York: Basic Books, 1997.

———. *Trial and Error: The American Controversy over Creation and Evolution*. New York: Oxford University Press, 1985.

Lasch, Christopher. *The Culture of Narcissism: American Life in an Age of Diminishing Expectations*. New York: W. W. Norton, 1978.

Lassiter, Matthew D. *The Silent Majority: Suburban Politics in the Sunbelt South*. Princeton, N.J.: Princeton University Press, 2006.

Leggett, Carroll. "Between You and Me: Sold to American." *Metro Magazine: Raleigh, Research Triangle, Eastern North Carolina* 3, no. 8. http://www.metronc.com/ article/?id=271. Accessed August 12, 2012.

Leitch, Vincent B. *American Literary Criticism: From the Thirties to the Eighties*. New York: Columbia University Press, 1988.

Lentricchia, Frank. *After the New Criticism*. London: Methuen, 1983.

Levine, Lawrence W. *Defender of the Faith: William Jennings Bryan, the Last Decade, 1915–1925*. New York: Oxford University Press, 1968.

Lewis, George. *The White South and the Red Menace: Segregationists, Anticommunism, and Massive Resistance, 1945–1965*. Gainesville: University Press of Florida, 2004.

Link, Arthur S. *The Road to the White House*. Princeton, N.J.: Princeton University Press, 1947.

Lippmann, Walter. *American Inquisitors: A Commentary on Dayton and Chicago*. New York: Macmillan, 1928.

Lisby, Gregory C., and Linda L. Harris. "Georgia Reporters at the Scopes Trial: A Comparison of Newspaper Coverage." *Georgia Historical Quarterly* 75, no. 4 (Winter 1991): 784–803.

Long, J. C. *Bryan: The Great Commoner*. New York: D. Appleton, 1928.

Lundin, Robert W. *Alfred Adler's Basic Concepts and Implications*. Muncie, Ind.: Accelerated Development, 1989.

"Lynchings: By Year and Race." Compiled by the Tuskegee Institute. www.law.umkc .edu/faculty/projects/ftrials/shipp/lynchingyear.html. Accessed May 10, 2012.

Maddox, William Arthur. *The Free School Idea in Virginia before the Civil War: A Phase of Political and Social Evolution*. New York: Teachers College, Columbia University, 1918.

Malvasi, Mark G. *The Unregenerate South: The Agrarian Thought of John Crowe Ransom, Allen Tate, and Donald Davidson*. Baton Rouge: Louisiana State University Press, 1997.

"Man vs. Monkey Tilt Has Aspect of Circus." *Los Angeles Daily Times*, July 5, 1925, metropolitan features.

Marsden, George M. *Fundamentalism and American Culture: The Shaping of Twentieth-Century Evangelicalism, 1870–1925*. New York: Oxford University Press, 1980.

Martin, T. T. *Hell and the High Schools: Christ or Evolution—Which?* Kansas City, Mo.: Western Baptist Publishing, 1923.

Mason, Richard. *Richard Nixon and the Quest for a New Majority*. Chapel Hill: University of North Carolina Press, 2004.

McMillen, Neil R. *The Citizens' Council: Organized Resistance to the Second Reconstruction, 1954–1964*. 2nd ed. Urbana-Champaign: University of Illinois Press, 1994.

Meiners, R. K. *The Last Alternative: A Study of the Works of Allen Tate*. Denver, Colo.: Swallow, 1965.

Mencken, H. L. *George Bernard Shaw: His Plays*. Boston: John W. Luce, 1905.

———. *The Gist of Nietzsche*. Boston: John W. Luce, 1910.

———. "Invitation to the Dance." In *Prejudices: Sixth Series*. New York: Alfred A. Knopf, 1927.

———. "In Memoriam: W. J. B." In *William Jennings Bryan and the Campaign of 1896*, edited by George F. Whicher. Problems in American Civilization. Boston: D. C. Heath, 1953.

———. "The Sahara of the Bozart." In *Mencken, Prejudices: First, Second, and Third Series*, edited by Marion Elizabeth Rodgers. New York: Library of America, 2010. Originally published in *New York Evening Mail*, November 13, 1917.

———. "The South Astir." *Virginia Quarterly Review* 11 (January 1935): 47–60.

———. *Thirty-five Years of Newspaper Work: A Memoir*. Baltimore: Johns Hopkins University Press, 1994.

———. "Uprising in the Confederacy." *American Mercury* 22 (March 1931): 379–81.

Middleton, John S. "Thunder without Light." Review of *God without Thunder*, by John Crowe Ransom. *Commonweal* 13 (February 4, 1931): 385–86.

Modisett, Franklin, ed. *The Credo of the Commoner: William Jennings Bryan*. Los Angeles: Occidental College, 1968.

Moran, Jeffrey. "Reading Race into the Scopes Trial: African American Elites, Science, and Fundamentalism." *Journal of American History* 90, no. 3 (December 2003): 891–911.

———. *The Scopes Trial: A Brief History with Documents*. Boston: Bedford/St. Martin's, 2002.

———. "The Scopes Trial and Southern Fundamentalism in Black and White: Race, Region, and Religion." *Journal of Southern History* 70, no. 1 (February 2004): 95–120.

Morrison, Toni. *Playing in the Dark: Whiteness and the Literary Imagination*. Cambridge, Mass.: Harvard University Press, 1992.

Mosak, Harold H., ed. *Alfred Adler: His Influence on Psychology Today*. Park Ridge, N.J.: Noyes Press, 1973.

Murphy, Paul V. *The Rebuke of History: The Southern Agrarians and American Conservative Thought*. Chapel Hill: University of North Carolina Press, 2001.

Muse, Benjamin. *Ten Years of Prelude: The Story of Integration since the Supreme Court's 1954 Decision*. New York: Viking, 1964.

———. *Virginia's Massive Resistance*. Bloomington: University of Indiana Press, 1961.

Nakayama, Thomas K., and Judith N. Martin, eds. *Whiteness: The Communication of Social Identity*. Thousand Oaks, Calif.: Sage, 1999.

Narain, Dhirendra. "Indian National Character in the Twentieth Century." *Annals of the American Academy of Political and Social Science* 370 (1967): 124–32.

Nietzsche, Friedrich Wilhelm. *The Portable Nietzsche*. New York: Viking, 1954.

Norris, John W. "Evolution Not a Fact—the Bible a Fact." *A.M.E. Church Review* (October 1925): 331–32.

Numbers, Ronald L. *The Creationists*. New York: Alfred A. Knopf, 1992.

Odum, Howard W. *An American Epoch: Southern Portraiture in the National Picture*. New York: Henry Holt, 1930.

———. *Southern Regions of the United States*. Chapel Hill: University of North Carolina Press, 1936.

Official Report of the Proceedings of the Democratic National Convention (1924). Indianapolis: Bookwalter-Ball-Greathouse, 1924.

"Officials Reverse Motion on Banning Gays from Living in Rhea Co." Wate.com, Knoxville, Tenn., March 18, 2004. www.wate.com/Global/story.asp?s=17209068&clienttype=printable. Accessed July 15, 2009.

Olson, LaDonna Robinson. *Legacy of Faith: The Story of Bryan College*. Hayesville, N.C.: Schoettle, 1995.

Orgler, Hertha. *Alfred Adler, the Man and His Work: Triumph over the Inferiority Complex*. London: C. W. Daniel, 1939.

"Origins Studies Minor at Bryan College." Center for Origins Research. http://www
.bryancore.org/minor.html. Accessed August 10, 2012.

Owen, Russell. "Dayton's Remote Mountaineers Fear Science." *New York Times*, July 19,
1925, 23.

Owsley, Frank L. "The Pillars of Agrarianism." *American Review* 4 (March 1935): 529–47.

Patterson, James T. *Brown v. Board of Education: A Civil Rights Milestone and Its Troubled
Legacy*. New York: Oxford University Press, 2001.

Peltason, J. W. *Fifty-eight Lonely Men: Southern Federal Judges and School Desegregation*. New
York: Harcourt, Brace & World, 1962.

Peters, William. *The Southern Temper*. Garden City, N.Y.: Doubleday, 1959.

Phillips, Kevin P. *The Emerging Republican Majority*. New York: Arlington House, 1969.

"Politicized Science: A Challenge to Evangelical Thinking." Bryan Center. www.bryan
.edu/5085.html. Accessed September 10, 2009.

Porter, Kirk Harold, and Donald Bruce Johnson. *National Party Platforms, 1840–1972*. 5th
rev. ed. Urbana-Champaign: University of Illinois Press, 1973.

Powers, Robert L. "Myth and Memory." In *Alfred Adler: His Influence on Psychology Today*,
edited by Harold Mosak. Park Ridge, N.J.: Noyes Press, 1973.

"Purchase 'The Scopes Trial: Inherit the Truth' DVD." www.bryan.edu/inherit_the_
truth.html. Accessed August 10, 2012.

Purdy, Rob Roy, ed. *Fugitives' Reunion: Conversations at Vanderbilt, May 3–5, 1956*. Nashville:
Vanderbilt University Press, 1959.

Ransom, John Crowe. "Ego." In *The Fugitive: A Journal of Poetry, Volumes 1–4, 1922–1925*.
New York: Johnson Reprint Corporation, 1966.

———. *God without Thunder: An Unorthodox Defense of Orthodoxy*. New York: Harcourt,
Brace, 1930.

———. *The New Criticism*. 1941. Reprint, Westport, Conn.: Greenwood Press, 1979.

———. "Reconstructed but Unregenerate." In *I'll Take My Stand: The South and the
Agrarian Tradition*, edited by Twelve Southerners. 1930. Reprint, Baton Rouge:
Louisiana State University Press, 1977.

———. "The South Defends Its Heritage." *Harper's*, June 1929, 108–18.

———. "The South—Old or New?" *Sewanee Review* 36 (April 1928): 139–47.

———. "What Does the South Want?" In *Who Owns America? A New Declaration of
Independence*, edited by Herbert Agar and Allen Tate. Boston: Houghton Mifflin,
1936.

———. *The World's Body*. New York: Scribner's, 1938.

Ratcliffe, S. K. "America and Fundamentalism." In *Controversy in the Twenties:
Fundamentalism, Modernism, and Evolution*, edited by Willard B. Gatewood Jr. Nashville:
Vanderbilt University Press, 1969. Originally published in *Contemporary Review* 128
(September 1925): 288–95.

Rattner, Josef. *Alfred Adler*. Translated by Harry Zohn. New York: Frederick Ungar, 1983.

"Reading the Polls on Evolution and Creationism." Pew Research Poll Watch,
September 28, 2005. http://people-press.org/commentary/?analysisid=118. Accessed
August 15, 2009.

Reed, John Shelton. *The Enduring South: Subcultural Persistence in Mass Society*. Chapel Hill:
University of North Carolina Press, 1972.

Reed, Linda. *Simple Decency and Common Sense: The Southern Conference Movement, 1938–1963*. Bloomington: University of Indiana Press, 1991.

Reid, Ronald F. *Three Centuries of American Rhetorical Discourse*. Prospect Heights, Ill.: Waveland Press, 1988.

"Resources." Center for Origins Research. www.bryancore.org/resources.html. Accessed August 10, 2012.

Richards, I. A. *The Philosophy of Rhetoric*. New York: Oxford University Press, 1936.

———. *Practical Criticism: A Study of Literary Judgment*. New York: Harcourt, Brace, 1929.

Richardson, Marty. "Charge Two with Lynch Death of 14-Year-Old." In *Reporting Civil Rights: Part One, American Journalism*, compiled by Clayborne Carson et al. New York: Library of America, 2003. Originally published in *Cleveland Call and Post*, September 10, 1955.

"Robert Penn Warren, Poet and Author, Dies." *New York Times*, September 16, 1989, 1, 11. http://www.nytimes.com/1989/09/16/obituaries/robert-penn-warren-poet-and-author-dies.html. Accessed March 12, 2013.

Roediger, David R. *The Wages of Whiteness: Race and the Making of the American Working Class*. New York: Verso, 1991.

Roland, Charles P. "The South of the Agrarians." In *A Band of Prophets: The Vanderbilt Agrarians after Fifty Years*, edited by William C. Havard and Walter Sullivan. Baton Rouge: Louisiana State University Press, 1982.

Roosevelt, Eleanor. "My Day" (February 4, 1950). www.gwu.edu/~erpapers/myday/displaydoc.cfm?_y=1950&_f=md001507. Accessed July 16, 2009.

Rosser, Charles McDaniel. *The Crusading Commoner: A Close-up of William Jennings Bryan and His Times*. Dallas: Mathis, Van Nort, 1937.

Rubin, Louis D., Jr. "The Gathering of the Fugitives: A Recollection." *Southern Review* 30 (Autumn 1994): 658–73.

Rubin, Louis D., Jr., and Robert D. Jacobs. *Southern Renascence: The Literature of the Modern South*. Baltimore: Johns Hopkins University Press, 1953.

Ruffin, Edmund. "The Political Economy of Slavery." In *Slavery Defended: The Views of the Old South*, edited by Eric McKitrick. Englewood Cliffs, N.J.: Prentice-Hall, 1963.

Russell, C. Allyn. "William Jennings Bryan: Statesman-Fundamentalist." *Journal of Presbyterian History* 53, no. 2 (Summer 1975): 93–119.

Sandeen, Ernest R. "Fundamentalism and American Identity." *Annals of the American Academy of Political and Social Science* 387 (January 1970): 56–65.

Savage, Henry, Jr. *Seeds of Time: The Background of Southern Thinking*. New York: Henry Holt, 1959.

Scholes, Robert. *Semiotics and Interpretations*. New Haven, Conn.: Yale University Press, 1982.

Shapiro, Edward S. "The Southern Agrarians, H. L. Mencken, and the Quest for Southern Identity." *American Studies* 13, no. 2 (1972): 75–92.

Shusterman, Richard. *T. S. Eliot and the Philosophy of Criticism*. New York: Columbia University Press, 1988.

Siegfried, André. *America Comes of Age: A French Analysis*. New York: Harcourt, Brace, 1927.

Silber, Nina. *The Romance of Reunion: Northerners and the South, 1865–1900*. Chapel Hill: University of North Carolina Press, 1993.

Simkins, Francis Butler. *Pitchfork Ben Tillman: South Carolinian*. Baton Rouge: Louisiana State University Press, 1944.

Simpson, Lewis. "The Southern Republic of Letters and *I'll Take My Stand*." In *A Band of Prophets: The Vanderbilt Agrarians after Fifty Years*, edited by William C. Havard and Walter Sullivan. Baton Rouge: Louisiana State University Press, 1982.

Singal, Daniel Joseph. *The War Within: From Victorian to Modernist Thought in the South, 1919–1945*. Chapel Hill: University of North Carolina Press, 1982.

Skowronek, Stephen. *The Politics Presidents Make: Leadership from John Adams to Bill Clinton*. Cambridge, Mass.: Belknap Press, 1993.

Smith, Bob. *They Closed Their Schools: Prince Edward County, Virginia, 1951–1964*. Chapel Hill: University of North Carolina Press, 1965.

Smith, Page. *Redeeming the Time: A People's History of the 1920s and the New Deal*. New York: McGraw-Hill, 1987.

Smith, Willard H. *The Social and Religious Thought of William Jennings Bryan*. Lawrence, Kans.: Coronado Press, 1975.

Smout, Kary D. *The Creation/Evolution Controversy: A Battle for Cultural Power*. Westport, Conn.: Praeger, 1998.

Smylie, James H. "William Jennings Bryan and the Cartoonists: A Political Lampoon, 1896–1925." *Journal of Presbyterian History* 53, no. 2 (Summer 1975): 83–92.

Sokol, Jason. *There Goes My Everything: White Southerners in the Age of Civil Rights, 1945–1975*. New York: Alfred A. Knopf, 2006.

"The Southern Manifesto." In *Brown v. Board of Education of Topeka: A Brief History with Documents*, edited by Waldo E. Martin. Boston: Bedford/St. Martin's, 1998.

Sperber, Manes. *Masks of Loneliness: Alfred Adler in Perspective*. Translated by Krishna Winston. New York: Macmillan, 1974.

Stallman, R. W. "The New Critics." In *Critiques and Essays in Criticism, 1920–1948*, edited by R. W. Stallman. New York: Ronald Press, 1949.

Stanley, Thomas B. Response to the United States Supreme Court decision in *Brown v. Board of Education*. WRVA Radio, May 14, 1954.

Stepansky, Paul E. *In Freud's Shadow: Adler in Context*. Hillsdale, N.J.: Analytic Press, 1983.

Stewart, John L. *John Crowe Ransom*. Pamphlets on American Letters. Minneapolis: University of Minnesota Press, 1962.

Stone, I. F. "The Murder of Emmett Till." In *The Best of I. F. Stone*, edited by Karl Weber. New York: Public Affairs, 2007. Originally published in *Weekly*, October 3, 1955.

Stone, Irving. *Clarence Darrow for the Defense*. Garden City, N.Y.: Doubleday, 1941.

Supriya, K. E. "White Difference: Cultural Constructions and White Identity." In *Whiteness: The Communication of Social Identity*, edited by Thomas K. Nakayama and Judith N. Martin. Thousand Oaks, Calif.: Sage, 1999.

Tate, Allen. "The Fugitive, 1922–1925: A Personal Recollection Twenty Years After." *Princeton University Library Chronicle* 3, no. 3 (1942): 75–84.

———. "Last Days of the Charming Lady." *Nation*, October 28, 1925, 485–86.

———. *Memoirs and Opinions, 1926–1974*. Chicago: Swallow Press, 1975.

———. "Miss Emily and the Bibliographer." (1940). In *Essays of Four Decades*. Chicago: Swallow Press, 1968.

———. "Narcissus as Narcissus" (1938). In *Essays of Four Decades*. Chicago: Swallow Press, 1968.

———. "Ode to the Confederate Dead." In *Selected Poems*. New York: Charles Scribner's Sons, 1937.

———. "The Profession of Letters in the South." *Virginia Quarterly Review* 11 (April 1935): 161–76.

———. "Remarks on the Southern Religion." In *I'll Take My Stand: The South and the Agrarian Tradition*, edited by Twelve Southerners. 1930. Reprint, Baton Rouge: Louisiana State University Press, 1977.

———. "A Southern Mode of the Imagination: Circa 1918 to the Present." *Carleton Miscellany* 1 (Winter 1960): 9–23.

———. *Stonewall Jackson: The Good Soldier*. New York: Minton Balch, 1928.

Taylor, William R. *Cavalier and Yankee: The Old South and American National Character*. New York: George Braziller, 1961.

Teachout, Terry. *The Skeptic: A Life of H. L. Mencken*. New York: Harper Collins, 2002.

"Tennessee vs. Civilization." *New Republic*, July 22, 1925, 220–22.

"They Sang 'Dixie's Land': The New York Southern Society's Dinner." *New York Times*, February 23, 1893, 3. http://query.nytimes.com/mem/archive-free/pdf?res=950DEFD C1F3FEF33A25750C2A9649C94629ED7CF. Accessed March 12, 2013.

Thorndike, Joseph J. "Kilpatrick and the Campaign against *Brown*." In *The Moderates' Dilemma: Massive Resistance to School Desegregation in Virginia*, edited by Matthew D. Lassiter and Andrew B. Lewis. Charlottesville: University Press of Virginia, 1998.

Tierney, Kevin. *Darrow: A Biography*. New York: Crowell, 1979.

Tindall, George B. "The Benighted South: Origins of a Modern Image." *Virginia Quarterly Review* 40, no. 2 (Spring 1964): 281–94.

———. *The Emergence of the New South, 1913–1945*. Baton Rouge: Louisiana State University Press, 1967.

———. *The Ethnic Southerners*. Baton Rouge: Louisiana State University Press, 1976.

———. "The Significance of Howard W. Odum to Southern History: A Preliminary Estimate." *Journal of Southern History* 24, no. 3 (August 1958): 285–307.

"Todd's Blog." http://toddcwood.blogspot.com. Accessed September 27, 2011.

Tompkins, Jerry D. *D-Days at Dayton: Reflections on the Scopes Trial*. Baton Rouge: Louisiana State University Press, 1965.

Torres, Sasha. *Black, White, and in Color: Television and Black Civil Rights*. Princeton, N.J.: Princeton University Press, 2003.

Twelve Southerners. *I'll Take My Stand: The South and the Agrarian Tradition*. 1930. Reprint, Baton Rouge: Louisiana State University Press, 1977.

Underwood, Thomas A. *Allen Tate: Orphan of the South*. Princeton, N.J.: Princeton University Press, 2000.

Valpy, Michael. "God Is Big These Days." Interview with Karen Armstrong. *Shambhala Sun* 13, no. 3 (January 2005). http://www.shambhalasun.com/index .php?option=com_content&task=view&id=1415. Accessed March 13, 2013.

Vander Zanden, James W. "The Klan Revival." *American Journal of Sociology* 65 (March 1960): 456–62.

"Virginius Dabney, Pulitzer Winner, Dies: As Historian, Author, Richmond Editor, He Challenged Views on Race and History." *Virginian-Pilot*, December 29, 1995, A9.

Wakefield, Dan. "Justice in Summer: An Hour and Seven Minutes." In *Reporting Civil Rights: Part One, American Journalism*, compiled by Clayborne Carson et al. New York: Library of America, 2003. Originally published in *Nation*, October 1, 1955.

———. "Respectable Racism." In *Reporting Civil Rights: Part One, American Journalism*, compiled by Clayborne Carson et al. New York: Library of America, 2003. Originally published in *Nation*, October 22, 1955.

Wang, Yan. "Value Changes in an Era of Social Transformations: College-Educated Chinese Youth." *Educational Studies* 31, no. 2 (2006): 233–40.

Ward, Brian. *Radio and the Struggle for Civil Rights in the South*. New Perspectives on the History of the South. Gainesville: University Press of Florida, 2004.

Waring, Thomas R., Jr. "Carpetbagger Press Not Wanted." In *We Take Our Stand*. Charleston, N.C.: Evening Post Co., 1956.

———. "Do-Gooders Stirring Bloodshed." In *We Take Our Stand*. Charleston, N.C.: Evening Post Co., 1956.

———. "The Southern Case against Desegregation." *Harper's*, January 1956, 39–45.

———. "The South Has Lost Its Voice." In *We Take Our Stand*. Charleston, N.C.: Evening Post Co., 1956.

———. "South's Appeal to Sister States." In *We Take Our Stand*. Charleston, N.C.: Evening Post Co., 1956.

———. "Unite to Restore the Republic." In *We Take Our Stand*. Charleston, N.C.: Evening Post Co., 1956.

Warren, Robert Penn. "The Briar Patch." In *I'll Take My Stand: The South and the Agrarian Tradition*, edited by Twelve Southerners. 1930. Reprint, Baton Rouge: Louisiana State University Press, 1977.

———. *The Legacy of the Civil War: Meditations on the Centennial*. New York: Random House, 1961.

———. "Pure and Impure Poetry" (1943). In *New and Selected Essays*. New York: Random House, 1989.

———. *Who Speaks for the Negro?* New York: Random House, 1965.

Warren, Robert Penn, and Cleanth Brooks. *Understanding Fiction*. New York: F. S. Crofts, 1943.

———. *Understanding Poetry*. New York: Henry Holt, 1938.

Watts, Trent, ed. *White Masculinity in the Recent South*. Baton Rouge: Louisiana State University Press, 2008.

Way, Lewis. "The Psychology of Prejudice." In *Alfred Adler: His Influence on Psychology Today*, edited by Harold H. Mosak. Park Ridge, N.J.: Noyes Press, 1973.

Weaver, Richard. "Agrarianism in Exile." *Sewanee Review* 58 (Autumn 1950): 586–606.

Wesolowski, James Walter. "Before Canon 35: WGN Broadcasts the Monkey Trial." *Journalism History* 2, no. 3 (1975): 76–79, 86–87.

We Take Our Stand: A Southern Newspaper Speaks. Charleston, N.C.: Evening Post Co., 1956.

Whitehead, Antony. "Man to Man Violence: How Masculinity May Work as a Dynamic Risk Factor." *Howard Journal* 44, no. 4 (September 2005): 411–22.

Wilhoit, Francis M. *The Politics of Massive Resistance*. New York: George Braziller, 1973.

Wilkinson, J. Harvie, III. *Harry Byrd and the Changing Face of Virginia Politics, 1945–1966*. Charlottesville: University Press of Virginia, 1968.

Wilson, Charles Reagan. *Baptized in Blood: The Religion of the Lost Cause, 1865–1920.* Athens: University of Georgia Press, 1980.

Winchell, Mark Roydon. *Where No Flag Flies: Donald Davidson and the Southern Resistance.* Columbia: University of Missouri Press, 2000.

Winters, Yvor. "Fugitives." *Poetry* 32, no. 2 (1928): 102–7.

Wood, Edwin Thomas. "On Native Soil: A Talk with Robert Penn Warren." *Mississippi Quarterly* 37 (Spring 1984): 179–86.

Woodcock, O. H. Foreword to *Alfred Adler, the Man and His Work: Triumph over the Inferiority Complex,* by Hertha Orgler. London: C. W. Daniel, 1939.

Woodward, C. Vann. *The Burden of Southern History.* Rev. ed. Baton Rouge: Louisiana State University Press, 1968.

———. *The Strange Career of Jim Crow.* 2nd rev. ed. New York: Oxford University Press, 1966.

———. "Why the Southern Renaissance?" *Virginia Quarterly Review* 51, no. 2 (Spring 1975): 222–39.

Yeats, William Butler. "The Second Coming." *Dial* 69, no. 5 (November 1920): 460.

Young, Raymond A. *Cultivating Cooperation: A History of the Missouri Farmer's Association.* Columbia: University of Missouri Press, 1995.

Young, Thomas Daniel. "From Fugitives to Agrarians." *Mississippi Quarterly* 33 (Fall 1980): 420–24.

———. *Gentleman in a Dustcoat: A Biography of John Crowe Ransom.* Baton Rouge: Louisiana State University Press, 1976.

———. *Waking Their Neighbors Up: The Nashville Agrarians Rediscovered.* Athens: University of Georgia Press, 1982.

———, ed. *John Crowe Ransom: Critical Essays and a Bibliography.* Baton Rouge: Louisiana State University Press, 1968.

———, ed. *The New Criticism and After.* Charlottesville: University Press of Virginia, 1976.

Young, Thomas Daniel, and M. Thomas Inge. *Donald Davidson.* New York: Twayne, 1971.

Young, Thomas Daniel, and George Core, eds. *Selected Letters of John Crowe Ransom.* Baton Rouge: Louisiana State University Press, 1984.

Young, Thomas Daniel, and John J. Hindle, eds. *Selected Essays of John Crowe Ransom.* Baton Rouge: Louisiana State University Press, 1984.

INDEX

77; as presidential candidate, 32–35, 62; "Cross of Gold" speech, 33; on race relations, 37–41, 42, 64; on evolution, 41, 42, 43, 44, 45, 48, 56, 57, 58, 63, 75, 77, 80, 254 (n. 74); "The Bible and Its Enemies" speech, 42; "The Menace of Darwinism" speech, 42; Weekly Bible Talks, 44–45; rural appeal of, 45, 49; on Nietzsche, 51; "Is the Bible True?" address, 54; and sectional conflict, 58; eulogies for, 71–73; legacy of, 73, 77–78; sculpture of, 78; "The Modern Arena," 80; and Ransom, 110; and Davidson, 119, 120; Agrarians compared to, 133; Wallace compared to, 242; Reagan compared to, 245; "The Prince of Peace" lecture, 254 (n. 74). See also William Jennings Bryan College

Bryant, Roy, 198, 199, 200

Burnham, Walter Dean, 252 (n. 9)

Bush, George H. W., 225, 239–40

Bush, George W., 225, 246

Bush, Prescott S., 225

Butler, John Washington, 54

Butler Act, 27, 54–55, 57, 58, 59, 61, 63, 64, 84, 102, 104

Byrd, Harry F.: and Massive Resistance, 168, 189; and Kilpatrick, 170, 212, 215–16, 224–25, 226, 227; and local control, 188; and Brown v. Board of Education, 190, 229; and Gray Commission, 214; Southern Manifesto, 228–29; and Almond, 232

Byrd, Howard G., 58

Byrnes, James F., 174

Byron, George, Lord, 161

Cabell, James Branch, 95, 122

Calhoun, John C., 13, 129, 219, 220, 222, 231

Callahan, P. H., 78

Canonicity, 247

Capitalism: and Populist movement, 15; and Agrarians, 88, 111, 131; development of, 99; and Davidson, 127; and Tate, 141, 158

Capital punishment, 47

Carlyle, Thomas, 82

Carmichael, Stokely, 163

Carpenter, Joel, 68

Carswell, Harrold, 243

Carter, Dan, 239, 242

Carter, Hodding, Jr., 172–73, 191–92

Carter, Roy, Jr., 209

Cash, W. J., 2, 3, 11, 20, 27, 44, 76, 168

Catholicism, 36, 37, 116, 187

CELD, 83

Center for Origins Research (CORE), 83

Center for Worldview Studies (CWS), 83

Chappell, David, 203

Chappell, J. H., 79

Chase, Salmon P., 207

Chaucer, Geoffrey, 100

Christianity, and modernism, 99. See also Catholicism; Evangelical Christianity; Fundamentalism; Protestantism

Citizens' Council of America, 196

Civil Rights Act of 1964, 231, 237, 239–40, 246

Civil rights movement: and southern inferiority, 3, 167, 173; southern white resistance to, 22, 24–25, 169–70, 225; and Davidson, 118, 142; Robert Penn Warren on, 162; and public criticism, 169, 182, 192–93, 203; and mass media, 170, 188, 201–9, 211; and Montgomery Bus Boycott, 201–4; and Democratic Party, 237, 244; and Republican Party, 239, 242

Civil War: and southern whiteness, 13; revised narrative of, 14; and myth of difference, 20; legacy of, 21; and southern masculinity, 23; Davidson on, 91, 122; Mencken on, 94; Ransom on, 112; Tate on, 114–16, 141; Robert Penn Warren on, 164–65; and Gray Commission, 183; and Virginia Defenders of State Sovereignty and Liberty, 187–88. See also Sectional conflict; Sectional reconciliation

Clark, Tom, 196

associated with, 47; Nietzsche's philosophy synonymous with, 48; and Scopes Evolution Trial, 53, 99; and anti-evolution movement, 55, 56, 68; and William Jennings Bryan College, 80–81, 85; and Fugitives, 87, 98, 99–102, 106, 108, 118, 124; and New Criticism, 89; and Ransom, 133; and Agrarians, 145

Monroe, Harriet, 97

Monroe, James, 193

Montgomery Bus Boycott, 169, 188, 191, 201–4, 209, 224, 228

Moore, Merrill, 92

Morality: moral superiority, 13, 20; and William Jennings Bryan, 15, 45; and biblical justification of slavery, 20; and Victorian values, 43, 50, 99, 106; and fundamentalism, 70–71; and Tate, 113; and Fugitives, 117; and Davidson, 119, 120, 124; and Ransom, 157

Moran, Jeffrey, 44, 53, 254 (n. 48), 256 (n. 53)

Morphew, Richard D., 226

Morris, Henry M., 83–84

Morrison, Toni, 22

Moses, Montrose J., 94

Moton, Robert R., 177

Murphy, Reg, 243

Murray, A. W., 77

Murrow, Edward R., 231

Muse, Benjamin, 229–30

Mussolini, Benito, 140

Myrdal, Gunnar, 163, 172, 183, 190, 217

Nakayama, Thomas K., 22

Narain, Dhirendra, 250 (n. 27)

National Association for the Advancement of Colored People (NAACP): and school desegregation, 5, 171, 229; and lynchings, 17; and Scopes Evolution Trial, 64; and educational equality, 177, 178, 181, 194; and mass media, 192, 206, 212; "Appeal to the World," 195–96; and Till murder, 200; and Montgomery Bus Boycott, 201–2; and Kilpatrick, 224, 227, 233; Communists associated with, 239

National Association of Evangelicals, 245

National identity: relationship of regional identity to, 18–19, 23, 87, 90, 111, 112, 130, 142–43; destabilization after World War I, 42–43; and Agrarians, 107

Nationalism, 4, 10, 167

National Presbyterian General Assembly, 40–41

Native Americans, 129

Nazi Germany, 48, 167

Neihardt, John G., 132

New Criticism: and Agrarians, 5, 25, 89, 146, 148, 149–52, 153, 154, 155, 156, 157, 162, 165, 220, 236, 247; and Fugitives, 5, 101, 152, 155, 156, 165; as collective response to public criticism, 18, 152–53; and overdetermination, 23; aesthetics of, 25, 89, 144–46, 151, 153, 154, 155, 160, 162, 220, 247; and Ransom, 88–89, 144–46, 147, 149, 150, 151–59, 161, 162, 164; and language of text, 145, 147, 148, 150, 151, 153, 156–57, 159, 160, 165, 171; and recognition, 146, 152, 165; defining of, 146–48; trends against, 148; dogmatic nature of, 148–49; and southern white identity, 149, 153, 154, 159, 162–63, 165; politics of, 151, 152–60; and southern inferiority, 152, 153, 159, 165; and public criticism, 152–53, 156–57, 165; self-promotional aspect of, 161–62

New Deal, 136, 140

New Historicism, 147

New Orleans World's Fair (1884), 14

New South: as regional mythology, 3; and sectional reconciliation, 14; and industrialism, 15, 111; and Agrarians, 88, 142, 236; as intellectual vacuum, 95–96; and progress, 106; Ransom on, 111; Davidson on, 120, 123, 124, 142; Barr on, 134–35

identity, 18–20, 91; and Agrarians, 20, 88–89, 107, 128, 134, 139, 146, 152; and communication, 22; and Populist movement, 34; and William Jennings Bryan, 38, 41; and Scopes Evolution Trial, 54, 80, 102–4, 107, 109, 155; and Fugitives, 88, 90, 91, 106, 114; and southern white identity, 89, 170; and Davidson, 123; and New Criticism, 152–53, 156–57, 165; and Robert Penn Warren, 164–65; and civil rights movement, 169, 182, 192–93, 203; and Virginia Defenders of State Sovereignty and Liberty, 188; and Till murder, 209

Public housing, 237, 238

Pulitzer Prize, 105, 164, 261 (n. 69)

Pullman Strike of 1894, 47

Quietism, 157

Race relations: William Jennings Bryan on, 37–41, 42, 64; and evolution, 44, 254 (n. 48); Mencken on, 50; and Jim Crow laws, 55; Robert Penn Warren on, 127–28, 129, 162–63; and New Criticism, 151; and United Nations, 167, 195–96; and public criticism, 188, 231; and moderates, 191–92; and mass media, 194–95, 205; Faulkner on, 212. See also Civil rights movement

Race theories, 15, 44

Racial hierarchy: and southern white identity, 13, 14, 15, 17, 19, 20, 22–25, 63, 163; northern tolerance of, 15–16; as evidence for evolution, 63; Robert Penn Warren on, 128; and self-preservation, 184; and Crawford, 185

Racism: Marxist explanation of, 22; continuity of, 24; and southern inferiority, 26; Mencken on, 52; and regional identity, 91; psychology of, 168; and Interposition, 171

Rackham, E. J., 62

Radical Republicans, 38, 122

Randolph, A. Phillip, 233

Ransom, John Crowe: and Fugitives, 5, 87, 88, 91–92, 93, 97, 98–99, 101, 109; and New Criticism, 88–89, 144–46, 147, 149, 150, 151–59, 161, 162, 164; and Scopes Evolution Trial, 90; and southern inferiority, 91, 110–11, 113, 114, 126; *Poems about God*, 92; and Mencken, 97; and Eliot, 100, 101; *Chills and Fever*, 101; and Tate, 103, 110, 111, 113, 140, 156, 159; and Agrarians, 107, 108, 136, 138, 139–40, 141, 142, 145, 151, 154; and fundamentalism, 108, 109–13, 119; *God without Thunder*, 109, 110–12, 115, 121, 131, 155; "The South Defends Its Heritage," 112; and southern white identity, 113, 124, 155; on southern culture, 114, 116, 118, 126–27; and modernism, 133; and Barr, 134, 135, 136; "What Does the South Want?," 141; *The World's Body*, 145, 154–55; *The New Criticism*, 145, 156; and Vanderbilt University, 159, 175; and Kershaw, 163

Rappelyea, George, 57

Ratcliffe, S. K., 61–62

Rationalism, 42, 48, 110, 111

Raulston, John, 58–59

Reader-Response criticism, 147

Reagan, Ronald, 245

Reconstruction, 11, 12, 14, 18, 33, 36, 40, 122, 142

Reed, John Shelton, 11–12, 25

Regional identity: relationship of national identity to, 18–19, 23, 87, 90, 111, 112, 130, 142–43; and public criticism, 18–20, 91; and myth of difference, 20; and Scopes Evolution Trial, 31–32; and Fugitives, 87, 118; and Agrarians, 108, 129–30, 142

Regionalism: and fundamentalism, 74; and modernism, 100; and Fugitives, 107; and Mencken, 137, 138; and New Criticism, 151

Religion: and southern whiteness, 4, 22; and inferiority complex, 8, 11; and regional identity, 18, 19; and Scopes

Evolution Trial, 25, 94; and science, 29, 30, 41, 53, 55, 56, 59, 71, 84, 91, 109, 111; and William Jennings Bryan, 40–41, 45; and World War I, 43; and Mencken, 51–52, 94; role in public life, 84; and Fugitives, 88; civil, 116, 156; and Tate, 127; and New Criticism, 146; and race relations, 218. *See also* Catholicism; Christianity; Fundamentalism; Protestantism

Republican Party: and slavery, 14; and Populist movement, 15; Southern Strategy, 26, 238–40, 242–45; William Jennings Bryan on, 37, 38, 39; strategies for, 237, 238, 246–47

Reviewer, 93, 97

Richards, I. A., 23, 146, 156

Richardson, Marty, 198

Riding, Laura Gottschalk, 92

Riley, William Bell, 42, 54

Robert R. Moton High School (Farmville, Va.), 177–78

Robertson, Pat, 245

Robeson, Paul, 218

Robinson, F. E., 75

Robinson, Jo Ann, 202

Robinson, Spotswood, 177

Rockefeller, John D., 129

Roediger, David, 22

Roe v. Wade (1973), 245

Roosevelt, Eleanor, 1–4, 18, 19, 187, 207

Roosevelt, Franklin Delano, 76, 140

Roosevelt, Theodore, 37–38, 78

Rubin, Louis D., Jr., 100, 162, 208–9

Rudd, Judson A., 84

Ruffin, Edmund, 20

Rural areas: fundamentalism associated with, in South, 28–29, 51, 68, 94; appeal of William Jennings Bryan in, 45, 49, 77; and evangelical Christians, 49; conflict with urban areas, 50, 91, 102, 107; and evolution, 55; and mass media, 66; and New Criticism, 89; and Ransom, 111; population of, 175; and school integration crisis, 183

Rusk, Dean, 195

Russian Formalists, 146

Ryan, Quin, 66

Sandeen, Eric, 75

Sanders, Roger, 83

Santorum, Rick, 246

Savage, Henry, 192

School integration crisis: and Gray Commission on Public Education, 5, 168–69, 170, 179–85, 188, 189, 214, 220–21, 224, 227–29; and home rule of public education, 57; and Almond, 168, 173, 178, 230–32; and Virginia, 169, 173, 174, 177, 179–85; and Interposition, 171, 231; and Stanley, 173, 174, 179, 180, 181, 182, 185, 196, 229–30; and Kilpatrick, 212, 235. See also *Brown v. Board of Education*

School of Individual Psychology, 7

Science: and southern whiteness, 22, 41, 72; and religion, 29, 30, 41, 53, 55, 56, 59, 71, 84, 91, 109, 111; skepticism of, 42; and psychology, 43, 99; and fundamentalism, 74, 80, 235; and modernism, 99; Ransom on, 109–13, 147, 155, 156, 158; and Vanderbilt University, 119; and New Criticism, 146, 147, 150, 155; and *Brown v. Board of Education*, 217–18; and Republican Party, 238

Scientific management, 99

Scopes, John, 27, 29, 57, 60, 69, 81, 105

Scopes Evolution Trial: impact of, 4–5, 27, 70, 107; and fundamentalism, 5, 27, 28, 29–30, 52, 59, 71, 72, 79, 80, 82–85, 109, 110; Mencken's coverage of, 17, 18, 28, 43, 50, 87, 102, 245; and civil liberties, 25; and mass media, 28, 29, 53, 54, 60, 61–62, 65–68, 71, 75, 79, 87, 102, 104, 110, 121, 200, 256 (n. 57); and sectional conflict, 30, 53–54, 57–58, 69; and regional identity, 31–32; and "moral blindness" of South, 35; Darrow's cross-examination of Bryan at, 46; and William Jennings Bryan on Nietzsche,

11–12; and perception of exclusion, 19; and siege mentality, 21–22; and reactionary fundamentalism, 26, 69, 71, 74–75, 79, 85; growing sense of, 42; and Scopes Evolution Trial, 60–69, 103, 111; Davidson on, 91, 118, 121, 122, 126, 164; masking of, 108; and Agrarians, 128, 130, 142; and southern whiteness, 192, 233; and Republican Party, 238, 239

Southern Literary Renaissance, 260 (n. 32)

Southern literature: and sympathy to Confederacy, 56; Mencken on, 90, 93–97, 103; canon of, 161, 162. *See also* Fugitives

Southern masculinity, and southern whiteness, 23–24

Southern Regional Council (SRC), 178

Southern Review, 92

Southern romanticism, 87

Southern white identity: and southern inferiority, 4, 11, 108; and moderates, 5, 13, 168–71, 172, 174, 176, 180–81, 184–85, 188, 191–92, 196, 199, 200, 203–4, 207, 209–10, 212–14, 216, 224, 225, 227, 231, 232, 238–39; homogeneity of, 6; evolution of, 7; and northern migration, 11; self-representation of, 13; and crisis psychology, 14; and Woodrow Wilson, 16; and national identity, 19; and collective sense of persecution, 20–21; and sectional conflict, 57–58; and William Jennings Bryan, 73; and public criticism, 89, 170; and Fugitives, 90, 103, 104, 105, 106, 118, 124, 159; and modernism, 99; and Scopes Evolution Trial, 107; and Agrarians, 108, 142–43; and Ransom, 113, 124, 155; complexity of, 210; and "us versus them" political culture, 240; and Wallace, 241

Southern whiteness: complexity of, 4, 24; and patriotism, 6; and negative identity construction, 12–13, 29, 30, 34, 68, 91, 112, 188, 235, 245; overdetermination of, 22–25, 237, 248; conflict with nonsouthern whiteness, 23; political identity of, 35; expanding territory of, 36; and resistance to northern values, 54; and Agrarians, 111, 142; and exceptionalism, 112; social construction of, 184; and southern inferiority, 192, 233; persistence of, 237

Southern whites: and Darrow, 28, 31, 47, 50; and William Jennings Bryan, 31, 32, 35, 38, 39, 41, 42, 50, 71; and Jim Crow laws, 36; political rhetoric of, 39; and self-preservation, 39; and evolution, 44; and Scopes Evolution Trial, 52, 60, 71; and Massive Resistance, 199; and Till murder, 200; and Republican Party, 238–40, 242–43; and Wallace, 241–42

Soviet Union, 195

Stanley, Thomas B.: and balance between national and local desires, 169, 172; and Kilpatrick, 170, 224, 227; and school integration crisis, 173, 174, 179, 180, 181, 182, 185, 196, 229–30

Stanton, John Roach, 42, 76

Starr, Alfred, 92

States' rights: and William Jennings Bryan, 15, 32; and southern whiteness, 26, 30; and Scopes Evolution Trial, 53–54; and Davidson, 142, 163; and Kilpatrick, 170–71, 172, 209, 232; and Virginia Defenders of State Sovereignty and Liberty, 187; and mass media, 205

State Teachers' Association, 56

Stekler, Paul, 244

Steunenberg, Frank, 47

Stevenson, Alec Brock, 92, 93

Stewart, John L., 109–10

Stone, I. F., 200–201

Stowe, Harriet Beecher, 136

Straton, John Roach, 133

Stribling, T. S., 97, 122–23

Structuralism, 148

Vanderbilt University, 87, 92–93, 95, 98, 119, 159, 175

Vander Zander, James W., 187

Villard, Oswald Garrison, 105

Violence: and inferiority complex, 10, 11; racial, 16–17, 21, 35; and Ku Klux Klan, 112, 202, 203; Virginia Defenders of State Sovereignty and Liberty's condemning, 186; and Till murder, 188, 191, 200

Virginia: and Massive Resistance, 5, 168, 170, 173, 174, 179, 182, 217, 228–33; and school integration crisis, 169, 173, 174, 177, 179–85; idealization of, 173; history of education in, 175–76; and southern white identity, 183–84; and local control option, 184–85, 188, 229; Proposition 141, 185; and Interposition, 216–17, 219–25, 227, 233. *See also* Gray Commission on Public Education

Virginia Council on Human Relations, 227

Virginia Defenders of State Sovereignty and Liberty, 164, 174, 185–88, 196, 203, 211, 247

Virginia Resolution of 1798, 213, 219, 221

Virginia Society for the Preservation of Public Schools, 227, 228

Virtual despair, 71

Voting restrictions, 39, 44

Wakefield, Dan, 196, 200

Wall, J. Barrye, 185, 187, 215

Wallace, George, 238, 240–42, 244, 246

Wang, Yan, 250 (n. 27)

Ward, Brian, 206

Waring, Thomas R., Jr., 190, 192, 205, 206–8, 226, 229, 236

War of 1812, 222–23

Warren, Earl, 168, 194, 218

Warren, Robert Penn "Red": and Fugitives, 5, 87, 92, 97, 101, 102, 164; on psychological consequences of defeat in Civil War, 21; and South's "Great

Alibi," 21, 165; *Understanding Fiction*, 89, 92, 145, 160; *Understanding Poetry*, 89, 92, 145, 160, 161; and New Criticism, 89, 144–45, 149, 151–52, 153, 158, 159, 160–63, 164; and southern inferiority, 91, 113, 118, 126, 164; and Eliot, 99–100; and Agrarians, 107, 108, 138, 139, 140, 141, 142, 151, 159, 164; *John Brown*, 117, 118; and influence of history, 118; and southern white identity, 118, 121, 124; on industrialism, 127–28; on race relations, 127–28, 129, 162–63; and Ransom, 137; *Who Speaks for the Negro?*, 163; and public criticism, 164–65

Washburn, George, 77, 85

Washington, Booker T., 37–38, 127, 177

Watson, John, 43

Watson, Tom, 34

Watts, Trent, 23–24

Way, Lewis, 9, 25

Weaver, Richard, 259–60 (n. 32)

Welfare, 237

Wellek, René, 161

Wesselenyi, Baron de, 10

Western Union, 27

Weston, Jessie, 100

Wharton, Don, 76

White, Walter, 75, 85, 206

White Citizens' Councils, 164, 174, 186, 196, 202, 203, 204, 225

Whitehead, Anthony, 10

Whitehead, Robert, 215

Whiteness: and identity construction, 13, 22; as norm, 22. *See also* Southern whiteness

White religious identity, 85

White superiority, 2, 73

White supremacy: preservation of, 3; and southern masculinity, 24; and Ku Klux Klan, 36; and William Jennings Bryan, 39, 40, 64; and evolutionary theory, 44; and vigilantism, 47; and Davidson, 163; and education, 176; justifications for, 184; and Till murder, 191, 197, 200; and Montgomery Bus Boycott, 204